THE ANTHROPOSOPHIC APPROACH TO MEDICINE

VOLUME III

Established by

FRIEDRICH HUSEMANN

Newly edited and revised by

OTTO WOLFF

With contributions by
Georg Graflin, Ilse Knauer, Alexandre Leroi, Rita Leroi,
Wilhelm zur Linden, Kurt Magerstadt, Erich Joseph Thiel,
Rudolf Treichler, and Otto Wolff

Translated by Peter Luborsky and Brian Kelly.
Translations Revised by Brian Kelly and Gerald Karnow
with additional translations by Maria St. Goar.

MERCURY PRESS
Chestnut Ridge, NY

This volume is a revised edition of *The Anthroposophical Approach to Medicine,* Volume III, published by Anthroposophic Press, 1989. With the exception of the chapter on gynecology and obstetrics, it is a translation of the second half of the fourth, revised, edition of *Das Bild des Menschen als Grundlage der Heilkunst,* Band III, published by Verlag Freies Geistesleben, Stuttgart, 1993. It is published with permission of the German publisher. The chapter "Gynecology and Obstetrics" was written specifically for the American edition. It was translated by Brian Kelly and is published with permission of the authors.

Second printing 2017

Published by Mercury Press
The Fellowship Community
241 Hungry Hollow Road
Chestnut Ridge, NY 10977

Library of Congress Control Number: 03106726

ISBN 978-0-929979-84-7

Printed in the United States of America

THE ANTHROPOSOPHIC APPROACH TO MEDICINE

Volume III

CONTENTS

FOREWORD

This book is the third in a planned four-volume series. Readers unfamiliar with the two preceding volumes may appreciate a description of their contents. Volume I explains the anthroposophical conception of human physiology and development, of basic disease types, and of biochemistry and pharmacology. The first half of Volume II deals with the fundamentals of therapy, and includes discussions of specific mineral, metallic, and animal remedies. The second half of Volume II contains an in-depth discussion of each of the four basic organ systems, the hepatobiliary, renal, cardiovascular, and pulmonary. Finally, this volume presents the contributions of anthroposophical medicine to various medical specialties. Even though it presupposes the more fundamental material contained in the earlier volumes, it has been translated and edited in such a way as to allow it, as far as possible, to stand on its own. Readers are counselled to refer to the earlier volumes if questions or doubts arise that cannot be resolved by this volume alone.

It is especially important for those unfamiliar with the anthroposophical approach to realize that this book, far from being an exhaustive treatment of the specialties discussed in it, presupposes and builds upon a basic knowledge of the relevant physiologies and pathologies. Its main purpose is to suggest new ways of conceptualizing and treating familiar diseases.

One source of possible misunderstandings should be anticipated here. Rudolf Steiner, the founder of anthroposophy, not only created the theoretical basis for a new art of healing, he also suggested several new remedies and techniques of preparation. The remedies derive almost entirely from natural substances—mineral, plant, and animal. The main procedure for their preparation is potentization, a series of progressive admixtures of a diluting medium that often leaves only an infinitesimal and sometimes nonexistent amount of the original substance in the remedy (see volume I, p. 302f.). Thus the reader must not be shocked to see frequent references to mercury and belladonna as remedies, since it is almost always the potentized form and not the original substance that is being referred to. The reader will also find frequent references to two pharmaceutical firms that employ the methods of preparation recommended by Steiner. The names of these firms are Weleda and Wala. The remedy lists published by these firms, especially that of Weleda, can be helpful in deciphering the names of anthroposophical remedies, most of which are in Latin and therefore occasionally hard to understand. The addresses of both firms are given in the list of indications at the end of this book.

Some of the plants and mineral remedies mentioned in this book have common names that are accepted words in English, such as arnica and pyrite. In this translation, those words have been left in lowercase, except when specific potencies or forms are being referred to (e.g., Belladonna D6). All other remedy names, such as Apis and Formica, have been capitalized throughout.

Brian Kelly

About the Reference Notes

In references to periodicals, the number preceding the year is the volume number; the one following it is the issue number. The year is in parentheses. If no year is given, volume and issue numbers are separated by a slash. Occasionally no volume number could be given, and sometimes the abbreviated name of a month is provided instead of an issue number.

Some books by Rudolf Steiner have yet to be published in English. GA# (Gesamtausgabe, or collected works) appear after works by Dr. Steiner. They are published by Rudolf Steiner Verlag in Dornach, Switzerland. Typescripts of English translations of some unpublished lectures are available as indicated from Rudolf Steiner Library, R.D. 2, Box 215, Ghent, NY 12075, (telephone, 518-672-7690).

Abbreviations for periodicals:

BEH = Beiträge zu einer Erweiterung der Heilkunst
DMW= Deutsche Medizinische Wochenschrift
MMW= Münchener Medizinische Wochenschrift

Abbreviations for book titles:

FT = Rudolf Steiner & Ita Wegman, Fundamentals of Therapy: An Extension of the Art of Healing through Spiritual Knowledge, (GA 27) (Spring Valley, NY: Mercury Press, 1999).

SM = Rudolf Steiner, Introducing Anthroposophical Medicine (GA 312) (Hudson, NY: Anthroposophic Press, 1999; previously published as Spiritual Science and Medicine

GG = Rudolf Steiner, Anthroposophical Spiritual Science and Medical Therapy (GA 313) (Spring Valley, NY: Mercury Press, 1991).

CE = Rudolf Steiner, Curative Education (GA 317) (London: Rudolf Steiner Press, 1972).

I

Infectious Diseases

OTTO WOLFF

The Concept of Infection

SCARCELY ANY AREA OF MEDICINE has undergone such a radical transformation since the early part of this century as has the treatment of infectious diseases, a fact due largely to the development of modern antibiotics. The use of antibiotics is based on the theory that disease is caused by invading microorganisms that are therefore called "pathogens." Robert Koch and Louis Pasteur, who developed this theory as a result of their discovery of bacteria, did not mean thereby to reduce the problem of disease to a relation of simple causation. Nevertheless, subsequent medical practice has taken this as a working assumption. It is interesting to note, however, that the bacterial theory of disease was at first strongly resisted despite its successful applications. Ignaz Semmelweiss's battle for the introduction of antisepsis to control puerperal fever is the classic example of this.

Until the decisive work of Koch and Pasteur, the dominant teaching on the origin of epidemics was that of Sydenham. Sydenham attributed epidemics to certain temporal, climatic, and telluric influences, which together made up what he called the "epidemic constitution." This theory was elaborated and strengthened by Pettenkofer, one of the most universal geniuses of his time, who saw epidemics as natural occurrences resulting from a combination of telluric and metereological factors. His suggestions for reducing epidemics therefore focused on improving the quality of the human environment rather than on the elimination of bacteria. It was Pettenkofer who started the practice of assuring sanitary water sources and of purifying sewage, which reduced the incidence of such epidemics as cholera.

Claude Bernard said: "Tout est le terrain, rien le microbe." (Another version has it: "Le terrain est tout et le germe n'est rien"). Later, the cell pathologist Virchow opposed the shift in attention toward bacteria, holding that "knowledge of the bacillus, necessary as it is for a full understanding of the origination of the disease process, still by no means explains the process itself, nor renders a distinct investigation of it superfluous."[1] Virchow also concluded that epidemics indicated "an endemicity of the causes of disease that merely masquerades ... as transmission from person to person."[2] Infection in the sense of communication from person to person is a problem to which we shall return below.

Still earlier times explained disease in terms of "miasm" and "contagium," concepts that by their very nature were not sharply defined but nonetheless anticipated a more sophisticated view. Miasm referred to environmental influences such as climate, while contagium designated what today we would refer to as infectious material.

The anatomist Jakob Henle wrote in his basic treatise that the cause of epidemics is not atmospheric or chemical, but a parasitic "contagium vivum," and thus anticipated the assumptions of modern bacteriology three and a half decades before Koch.[3] "Investigation of the cause of miasmatic-contagious diseases must begin with the contagium." Henle raised the question "of what nature the as yet unseen body of this parasite must be, whose life manifests itself so clearly and with such devastating effect." Fracastorius postulated the principle of contagium and of invisible microorganisms approximately one hundred years before the invention of the microscope.

After Koch's fundamental studies on the biology of anthrax (1876), the contagium was considered verified and bacteria became the main object of research. Natural science was in its infancy and therefore tended to oversimplify; disease could only have one cause, not several. Likewise, it was natural for science at this stage to concentrate on discrete, observable phenomena, such as bacteria and viruses. Of course

1. R. Virchow, "Der Kampf der Zellen und Bakterien," Arch. Path. Anat. Phys. Klin. Med. 101/1 (10th series).
2. Quote in F. Wolter, Vergleichende Epidemiologie (1940), vol. 29 of the series Medizinische Praxis.
3. J. Henle, Von den Miasmen und Contagien und von den miasmatisch-contagiösen Krankheiten (1840).

there were always those who realized that disposition and constitution are at least as important in the genesis of infectious disease as are bacteria. Clinicians in particular held this view, among them such figures as Rosenbach, Gottstein, Martius, and Hueppe. Virchow too could never wholly accept the new view of the role of bacteria.1 He argued vehemently that microorganisms seek out the environment which is natural to them, unhealthy tissue, but that they are no more the cause of illness than mosquitoes are the cause of stagnant water, although they seek it out and need it in order to reproduce.

Only in the 1950s, when the influence of weather on disease began to be considered, did the focus of research broaden at all beyond bacteria. Nevertheless, inner events are still given short shrift compared to external factors, though both are of equal importance.

The classic technique of infecting an organism by injection or by other means in order to produce disease met with criticism from the very beginning. The direct administration of infectious material represents a circumvention of natural barriers, in effect a "deception" of the organism. This is precisely not how infectious diseases arise (apart from such diseases as inoculation hepatitis, AIDS transmission through blood transfusions and infected needles, etc.), and the results of such unnatural experiments have little significance for how diseases or epidemics develop in nature. As early as 1903, Rosenbach clearly distinguished between illnesses of injection and illnesses of infection. He emphasized the importance of disposition, writing:

> In my estimation, bacteriology has solved none of the riddles it pretended to wish to solve. Instead, it has only made more obvious the difficulty and multiplicity of problems that cannot be definitively solved from within the narrow confines of the laboratory.[4]

Pettenkofer sought to decide the smoldering dispute between himself and Koch with an experiment that has become famous: On October 7, 1892, before witnesses the 74-year-old scientist drank a suspension of Vibrio cholerae that Koch had sent him, but did not fall ill. Pettenkofer thus demonstrated that the so-called pathogenic bacteria are not solely nor even primarily responsible for infectious disease. This experiment

4. O. Rosenbach, Arzt contra Bakteriologie (Berlin/Vienna: 1903). See also W. Guttman, Ausgewählte Abhandlungen von O. Rosenbach (Leipzig: 1903).

was repeated ten days later by Pettenkofer's pupil Emmerich. He too was unaffected, even in his mood or ability to work, and apart from a transitory case of diarrhea manifested no pathological symptoms.[5]

A similar case is recounted by Letterer. A young colleague apparently injected himself intravenously with a virulent culture of tubercle bacilli in order to kill himself, but to his own amazement did not even get sick.[6]

As "proof" of the primary role played by bacteria, the argument has been adduced that it is possible to infect any human being, even the most resistant, with a suitably high concentration of pathogenic microorganisms. This argument, however, is based on a fundamental confusion: it is only through an arbitrary experimental measure, namely, the introduction of a "suitably high concentration" of pathogens, that physiological defenses are circumvented or overwhelmed. Of course, some illnesses do arise in this way, for example, through careless handling of infectious material in the laboratory or during operations. Yet even in infectious disease wards, this mode of pathogenesis is only secondary, as is shown again and again by the fact that even there only some of those actually exposed become ill. Experiments of this kind, though they show something about the mechanism of disease, do not say anything about its cause.

Tests on volunteers revealed that 108 to 1011 cholera organisms must be introduced before a person will actually fall ill with the disease. When stomach acids are neutralized, the critical dose is reduced to 104-108 bacteria.[7] Infection alone is thus by no means the decisive factor; even in a susceptible organism it does not cause illness. The probability that illness will develop is expressed in a microorganism's "manifestation index." The latter shows, for example, that measles virus will produce measles in 95–98 out of 100 receptive individuals, while for scarlet fever the figure is 8–10 and for polio 1 at the most.[8] In polio, therefore, actual infection plays scarcely any role. A much larger role is played by a person's nonspecific resistance, i.e., his health, constitution, and disposition.

5. K. Kisskalt, "Max von Pettenkofer" in Grosse Naturforscher, vol. 4 (Stuttgart: 1948).
6. Letterer, Die Medizinische (1953) 1.
7. Hornick, Wenzel, et. al., Bulletin of the New York Academy of Medicine 47 (1971): 1181.
8. G. Joppich, Lehrbuch der Kinderheilkunde (Stuttgart: 1975)

It is hard to believe in the face of facts such as these that medicine could have continued for so long to reduce the phenomenon of illness to simple "causation" by exogenous agents. Höring explains this as follows:

> The extension of a strictly physicalistic and causal approach to the infectious diseases, a product of the materialistic world view, was unconsciously favored by the more ancient and primitive view that demons cause disease. The fear of bacilli that befell the public and in part still dominates it even today can only be explained by the belief that the bacillus is the evil demon in person, disease objectified, and that one need only avoid this demon to remain healthy. The equation of agent and illness led to the erroneous view that mastery of the agent was also mastery of the disease.[9]

At any rate it is clear that the physicalistic conception shifted the entire problem of disease to the outside and thereby reduced the human being to an object of only secondary importance. In a certain way this notion relieved us of an unconscious psychological burden, objectifying the "guilty" party—i.e. the cause of disease-related suffering—in the form of bacteria. However, it also destroyed any possible personal meaning the disease might have: the abstract concept of blind chance in the form of infection completely replaced the subjective sense of destiny. The reason why pathogens "attack" a particular organism seemed beyond comprehension; thus the ground was laid for a far-reaching but essentially unnecessary agnosticism.

Although not every researcher in bacteriology has espoused such a narrow view, it is in that form that it has become common property. Emphasis on the pathogenic agent naturally deflected attention from the organism. As a result, all sense for the peculiarity of each disease was lost. For example, the age-dependence and the many common features of the childhood diseases became unimportant as soon as they were seen as cyclical infectious illnesses. This has practical consequences. Antibiotic therapy, since it is concerned only with the sensitivity of the pathogen, disregards the significance of the locus of infection. The affected organ is obviously the weak link in the body's resistance, and if this is not taken into account, the underlying functional disorder remains

9. F. Höring, Klinische Infektionslehre, 3rd ed. (Berlin: 1962).

untreated. The stage is thus set for recurrent, chronic inflammations or for more severe illnesses of the affected functional system.

The individual character of infectious diseases, each having its characteristic course, was brought out by the studies of Höring[10] on the cyclical infectious illnesses. These include not only the childhood diseases also lobar pneumonia. Once the infection has been triggered by agents, it "takes a course independent of the species and nature of the agent, following only the organism's inner laws."

Since bacterial agents have only an eliciting character, and infection only makes manifest what was prefigured in the organism, it would be more accurate to call infectious diseases information diseases": they inform" the organism, setting a process in motion that compensates for an internal disorder, deficiency or defect. In this sense, infection is a means to an end.

Bacteria

Experimental studies alone, though they cast light on the relationship between bacteria and the human being, can never completely explain it.[11] That this is an epistemological problem was first convincingly demonstrated by Hueppe, who showed that the concepts of cause and effect and of survival of the fittest are not applicable to this relationship.[12] A more appropriate model is that of an explosion, whose real cause is not the spark that sets it off, but rather the potential energy of the explosive. In this analogy, the spark corresponds to the bacteria that initiate a disease process. "The sufficient cause for fermentation and illness lies exclusively in the structure and disposition of the infected host, in the constitution of the body susceptible to fermentation. Nothing that is not predisposed here can ever enter into manifestation." Bacteria "can only elicit what is prefigured in the body's constitution."[13]

10. F. Höring, Klinische Infektionslehre, 3rd ed. (Berlin: 1962).
11. See also G. Schmidt, Wandlungen in der Anschauung über die Bedeutung der Mikroorganismen," Anthrop. Med. Jahrbuch, vol. 3 (Dornach: 1952).
12. F. Hueppe, in Verhandlungen der Gesellschaft der Naturforscher und Ärzte 65 (1893) and in Handbuch der Hygiene (1899). See also G. Schmidt, "Wandlungen in der Anschauung über die Bedeutung der Mikroorganismen," Anthroposophisch-Medizinisches Jahrbuch, vol. 3 (Dornach: 1952).
13. F. Höring, Klinische Infektionslehre, 3rd ed. (Berlin: 1962).

Disease can therefore not be explained solely by the concept of bacteria as initiators. Predisposition and constitution are at least equally important as pathogenic factors, as research has been increasingly forced to recognize. (Cf. Vol. II, p. 6ff). Furthermore, the critical role played in certain diseases by such external factors as weather, climate, time, and location was demonstrated by as early a figure as Pettenkofer. Much later, de Rudder summarized the observed connections between disease incidence and meteorological conditions.[14]

The critical effect of a culture medium on the growth of bacteria is known to every bacteriologist. Nevertheless, due to its concentration on the bacteria themselves, research has paid relatively little attention to the significance of the living organism as a culture medium. In what follows, we cite several experiments that could lead to a new way of understanding infection.

When a mycelium is grown in a culture medium, "the filaments display a chaotic, criss-cross pattern of growth." However, when the same mycelium is grown on the inside of the skin of a freshly killed frog, the filaments correlate and align in strikingly regular patterns. "The units of growth seem to have become conscious of one another."[15] Furthermore, when filaments are grown in blood serum, they assume forms similar to blood cells, even when the serum is pure, i.e. free of cells. It would thus seem that fresh living substances exert a forming influence on microorganisms, imposing the laws of the host organism upon them. Blood, for example, must be imbued with a formative principle that not only limits the random growth of fungi but also forms them according to its own laws. Meinecke concludes from this that "foreign elements are subordinated to the host organism's structural plan."

These experiments call to mind the copper chloride crystallization method described in volume I, chapter 13. Erratically crystallizing salt needles, when subjected to the superordinate formative force of a living source, arrange themselves in a way uniquely correlated with that source.

Thus "pathogenic agents" do not determine the disease. Rather, the organism "produces" disease by making use of the microorganisms, specifically choosing among them according to the organ and nature of the

14. See B. de Rudder, Grundriss der Meteorobiologie des Menschen (Berlin: 1952).
15. Meinecke, Med. Klinik 45 (1950): 803, 1626; Med. Klinik 47 (1952): 44.

disorder. The universality and ubiquity of microorganisms certainly offers ample "selection" from which to choose. The clear affinity of bacteria for the metabolic organs and of viruses for nerve tissue is discussed below. "The remarkable fact that the human being reacts identically, although different microorganisms are involved, can only be meaningfully interpreted as an indication that he "makes" his illness himself and "uses" microorganisms as initiators. In this sense the human being is the "producer" of his own pathogenic materials and master of his susceptibility and immunity.[16]

Living tissue thus seems to contain an inherent law that governs even invading microorganisms. Body fluids also give evidence of such a law, as witnessed by the inhibition of diphtheria bacilli by healthy saliva, an inhibition that ceases just prior to contraction of the illness. One milliliter of blood from a healthy human being kills more than ten million influenza agents in vitro. Human albumin destroys certain staphylococci at body temperature in one and a half hours, and is thus a stronger bacteriostatic than penicillin.[17]

Bacteria thus do not reproduce at will in a healthy body. Moreover, even outside of the organism bacteria are never as autonomous as was once believed. For example, soil bacteria grow more rapidly and produce more nitrogen when atmospheric pressure is rising. Even the precipitation of salts (potassium phosphate) and the aging of colloids depends on weather and radiation. Interestingly, the same results are obtained with bacteria grown and transplanted in hermetically sealed containers, suggesting that bacteria are subject to influences not transmitted materially.[18]

We are dealing here with direct meteorological influences, which, whether they act by material means or by "radiation," are a demonstrated fact. Such things can be understood only when the earth and its living creatures are seen as a living whole rather than as completely disconnected.[19] We must therefore conclude that the reproductive potential of bacteria is realized only when it is not limited by some higher principle.

---

16. Brettschneider, Tycho Brahe Jahrbuch (Stuttgart: 1984), pp. 119 and 126
17. Dold, MMW 96 (1954):1083, 1118.
18. Bortels, Die Naturwissenschaften 38 (1951):165.
19. G. Wachsmuth, Die Entwicklung der Erde (Dornach: 1950). W. Cloos, The Living Earth (London: Lanthorn Press, 1977).

Within the living organism, this higher principle is the etheric body, which receives guiding impulses from the astral body and the ego organization. As long as an organism's vital processes are well ordered and integrated into the etheric body, bacteria cannot grow or multiply uninhibitedly, since they find no suitable medium.

The integrity of the vital processes is affected by emotional and spiritual as well as by physical factors. Anxiety and fear, for example, exercise a negative influence on the physical organism.

> When one goes to sleep harboring fearful thoughts and thus takes them into the night, unconscious after-images of them rise up in the soul; this is a good way to nurture bacilli. If one can lessen this fear even a little—through active love, for example, so that in caring for the ill one forgets one's own worries of infection—one also lessens the forces that nurture the bacilli.[20]

Infection as an Ecological Problem

For a long time medical research, due to the emphasis it placed upon bacteria, paid little attention to external influences and to the significance of the human being as a "culture medium." In reality all three factors interact; the human being is unthinkable without an environment, and colonizing bacteria react to the state of their host. The preponderance of one factor over another is always a special case and hence of limited theoretical significance. The relationship of human being to germ is now conceived of as a kind of host-parasite relationship, in which the host determines the conditions under which the parasite will live.

A special case of this is our relationship with microorganisms that live on or in our bodies more or less permanently. The human skin harbors germs that depend greatly on external conditions, and the mucous membranes of the mouth, nose, rectum, and vagina constitute an ideal medium for bacteria known as saprophytes. How well these bacteria fare depends on the condition of the mucous membrane, which in turn depends on internal conditions. Thus the bacterial population of a membrane has diagnostic value. Bacteria both indicate and influence

20. R. Steiner, Wie erwirbt man sich Verständnis für die geistige Welt? (GA 154), lecture of May 5, 1914; see also BEH 34 (1981):29.

the state of health. Their relationship with the human being is reciprocal.

In the mucous membranes, the external world is to a certain extent internalized. This invasion must be limited, however, since the internal organs cannot tolerate foreign life. The human self is threatened unless such life is continually overcome. For this reason bacterial populations decrease toward the interior.

At its boundaries, the organism thus communicates in a special way with the surrounding world. Living substance on the verge of excretion or of death becomes the growth medium for germs that break down organic substance by putrefaction (coliform bacteria in the intestine) or by glycolysis (Doederleins's bacilli in the vagina). These catabolic processes are typical of the external world and must not be allowed to occur within the organism, i.e., in the intermediate metabolism.

Decomposition liberates forces that the human being requires in other areas; the intensely proliferating life within the intestine is continuously limited and broken down in order to make its forces available in a different form for consciousness.[21] A form of life that is neither entirely internal nor entirely external (the intestinal bacteria) continuously enables us to convert forces of the external world into forces of consciousness. Through the food we eat and the way we digest it we determine the culture medium of our intestinal flora and thus indirectly the kind of forces that are available to us.

For bacteria, if the culture medium changes, so does the population. Bacteria that have a preference for the new condition will propagate; frequently, pathogenic bacteria will replace the normal, harmless parasites. "Pathogenic" of course implies that these agents produce the disease, but as we saw above, this is true only in a limited sense or in exceptional situations. It also implies a moral judgment, which has of course no place in a description of natural processes.

Plant ecology offers an analogous situation. When soil conditions are altered by human activity (e.g., monoculture, imbalanced fertilization, overacidity), certain "weeds" begin to proliferate. Such plants, although unwelcome to humans, eliminate imbalances in the soil and thus help heal the earth as a whole. Soil can be protected from such imbalances by

---

21. R. Steiner, SM, lecture 4.

appropriate rotation of crops. The appearance of "undesirable" plants or the failure of cultivated plants to thrive is also a sign of a deeper disturbance, which in this case lies in the soil. It is known that certain plants have diagnostic value for the condition of the soil in which they grow.

It is an instructive though little heeded fact that many physiological symbionts have close relatives that are "pathogenic," see Table 1.[22]

Whether these related bacteria can be converted into one another is beyond the scope of the present discussion. However, certain studies suggest that our notions of the nature of bacteria may have to be revised.[23] Specifically, Schanderl demonstrated that under the right conditions, sterile tissue samples metamorphose into bacteria cultures in several days, and that depending on treatment, algae cells can decompose into either bacteria or yeasts. These results, of course, do not square with current conceptions of heredity and mutation, which thus stand in the way of unbiased investigation. However, heredity, the reality of which is indisputable, is not a merely random "jumbling," but rather an instrument of higher spiritual forces, whose existence must be recognized if heredity is to be understood as anything other than random play and coincidence.

Infectious material	Related normal symbiont
hem. staphylococci	epidermal staphylococci
hem. streptococci pneumococci	mucosal streptococci
meningococci gonococci	micrococci of the upper respiratory passages
pertussis bacilli	hemophilus bacilli (mucosal saprophytes)

Table 1: Physiological and pathogenic symbionts

22. F. Höring, Klinische Infektionslehre, 3rd ed. (Berlin: 1962).
23. Schanderl, Zeitschrift für angewandte Ökologie (1970)7; Berichte der Deutschen Botanischen Gesellschaft (1933):79; Botanische Bakteriologie auf neuer Grundlage (Stuttgart: 1974). Santo and Rusch in Wiener medizinische Wochenschrift (1951):706, 725.

Infectious material	Related normal symbiont
diptheria bacilli	pseudodiphtheria bacilli
dysentery bacteria typhoid bacteria parathyphoid bacteria	coliform bacteria
cholera bacilli	vibrio metschnikovii and other Vibrio species

Table 1: Physiological and pathogenic symbionts

For the issue at hand, the manner in which a new population arises is secondary. The great, many-sided potential of bacteria includes their ability to adapt to new conditions. (One need only recall how "mutation-happy" coliform bacteria are.)

It is characteristic of both bacteria and viruses—in fact of all microorganisms—that they are less fixed in their development than the higher organisms. The resulting adaptability became evident on a grand scale when the attempt was made to eradicate "pathogenic" insects using DDT: In a very short time resistant insects had developed, even ones dependent on DDT for their life. How much greater the adaptability of microorganisms must be to vaccines or medicines aimed at them. The development of bacterial resistance to antibiotics was the inevitable consequence of a therapeutic concept aimed solely at fighting bacteria without considering the culture medium—the organism—and alterations in it. Curiously, the obvious limits of this therapeutic approach did not lead to a quest for new approaches, but to the development of "new" antibiotics. This leaves the foundation for illness essentially unchanged, however; hence the symbionts become "pathogenic" or new diseases actually arise.

It should be obvious that the "battle" cannot be won—and this holds true across the board, even to the issues of AIDS. The fundamental error starts with the fact that we are not dealing with a "battle" at all, but with a disturbed relationship between man and nature: specifically, an imbalance on the part of the human being, which always—usually after a long time—leads to illness.

The important point is that the development of pathogenicity, like growth, depends on the host as well as the microorganism. The dysentery amoeba Entamoeba histolytica, for example, is

> a normal symbiont of the bowel lumen, where it thrives as a vegetative "minuta" form, replicating or—as spores—forming cysts for excretion in the stool. Only when the intestinal mucosae, sensitized by unspecific damages, allow it to manifest its latent "aggressivity" does it penetrate into them, assuming its vegetative "magna" form, exercising a histolytic influence and phagocytizing erythrocytes. This magna form, though still capable of replication, never forms cysts. Hence here not only the host, but also the endobiont is "ill." This example is additional proof that the metaphor of a "battle" between host and pathogen is mistaken ... here we see how the pathogen and the host undergo parallel changes, even though this is only a local (not cyclical) infection. In the transition from superficial symbiosis to tissue parasitism, the endobiont undergoes a morphological transformation.[24]

In this connection it is highly instructive to recall Loesch's suggestion, made in 1875, that amoebae do not cause ulcers but rather only prevent the healing of those already present.[25] This insight can be usefully applied today to the occurrence of heliobacter in gastric and duodenal ulcers.

That there are no definite boundaries between symbionts and pathogenic bacteria, but rather only transitional stages, is shown by the following examples mentioned by Höring:

> In the course of pneumonia, Pneumococcus gradually ceases its initially marked capsule formation (mucus formation) and loses its ability to destroy blood material; it thus begins more and more to resemble the ordinary viridans strain of oral streptococci, a normal symbiont that dominates the salivary flora in the recovery phase of pneumococcal pheumonia, usually as early as the fourth or fifth day of illness. Typhoid bacteria frequently become more mucilaginous toward the end of the illness and show other arguably regressive signs. In the recovery phase of diphtheria, diphtheria bacilli begin to resemble pseudodiphtheria bacilli and eventually disappear completely. These few examples may suffice to show that numerous morphological and antigenic changes occur in bacteria, changes that

24. F. Höring, Klinische Infektionslehre, 3rd ed. (Berlin: 1962).
25. Lösch, Arch. Path. Anat. 65 (1875):196.

> can be seen as adaptations to endobiosis in the host, and which one might call disease symptoms of the germ. The fact that these changes are genuine "metamorphoses" and not a simple replacement by other germs, as was usually assumed, becomes understandable when one reflects that a bacterial flora is not just a sum of individual germs, but a genetic unit governed by interactions.[26]

The pervasive practice of disinfection, extending from daily hygiene to antibiotic treatment of fresh fish, is a consequence of fear. Necessary as these measures are before operations, etc., they are senseless in daily life because they damage the physiologic saprophytes in the mouth, intestines and vagina as much or more than they do the pathogenic germs. Although it is well known that these "house-mates" perform vital biological tasks (e.g. vitamin B synthesis, inhibition of pathogenic germs, etc.), much less attention has been given to their significance than to that of their pathogenic cousins. Mommsen called them "salutogens"—agents of health—for this reason. In therapy, it is also possible to influence the given flora with correspondingly "strong" strains—a practice developed by Nißle—though of course their success will be influenced by the patient's nutrition and life-style.

Further, the well-known fact may be recalled that tubercle bacilli can survive in a "dormant state" in a latent focus, becoming "active" only when the host is weakened. This bacteria-centered vocabulary diverts attention from the organism, which permits the "activity" in the first place. The phenomenon of the clinically healthy chronic bacteria carrier (especially in diphtheria and typhoid) also shows the relativity of the concept "pathogenic." The same is true of viruses:

> Infected persons who have never experienced the symptoms associated with a certain virus can harbor the fully developed virus in their organs or organ cells even after many years of health.... An acute case of rabies can be provoked in some people who were bitten by a rabid dog many years before but did not fall ill.[27]

The "pathogenization" of microorganisms depends on the host, not on genetic alterations in the pathogen, which are always an effect rather

26. F. Höring, Klinische Infektionslehre, 3rd ed. (Berlin: 1962).
27. R. Bieling and O. Gsell, Die Viruskrankheiten des Menschen (Leipzig: 1962), p. 42.

than a cause. Susceptibility is necessary for an illness to develop. This is far more significant than the defense, which usually captures the attention of investigators. This distinction was emphasized by Höring. What is crucial is not the mere invasion by a "pathogen," but whether or not it gains a foothold in the host organism and proliferates, which is what susceptibility allows to happen. Letterer therefore differentiates between infection and infectious disease. "Infection need not lead to infectious disease. The presence of infectious material is a matter of the tissue; infectious disease is a matter of the organism."[28]

Susceptibility depends on both constitution and disposition. Constitution is the individual, familial, or racial condition of greater or lesser receptivity; disposition is a temporal variation of the constitution. For example, a person may possess, by constitution or by mode of life, a weakened or sensitive nervous system, but only when his disposition is altered—by chilling, overexertion, or hyperglycemia, for example—does the nervous system become receptive to viruses, as the case of polio amply demonstrated (see chapter 3, Poliomyelitis).

Meteorological influences affect not only bacteria but also human predispositions to illness. This phenomenon is well known but as yet little heeded or understood. Variations in air pressure express the astral activity of the earth's air organism, which in turn responds to cosmic and planetary influences. (Cf. Ger. Vol I, pp. 82f.) The latter also interact with the watery-etheric processes of life to produce observable and highly specific effects on all living organisms, especially plants. A number of experiments have demonstrated the connection between the planets and particular plant families. Research has also been done on the influence of the constellations on the distribution of growth in the plant between root, leaf, stem, and blossom. This knowledge has also been applied in practice.[29]

The effects of weather on human beings and animals have now been documented by numerous studies.[30] Familiarity with meteorological influences can lead to a recognition of the cosmic influences active within them. As early at 1920, R. Steiner indicated that epidemic infectious diseases respond to planetary influences: a modification of the (spiritual) activity of the sun by the outer planets Mars, Jupiter, and Sat-

28. Letterer, Die Medizinische (1953) 1.

urn alters the rhythmic activity between chest and head in especially disposed persons in such a way that susceptibility to the flu results.[31] These influences have scarcely begun to be researched.

The Question of Communicability

Communicability requires a "contagium" that can be transmitted. Transmission and contagium are today usually equated with infection. As a phenomenon, however, transmission is by no means limited to the infectious diseases: it can be observed on the mental and emotional planes as well. For example, an idea appears, spreads, and is enthusiastically received by almost everyone. Such an idea can be "in the air" and be grasped simultaneously by several different individuals, as the history of inventions and of scientific theory amply illustrates. Rapid dissemination, however, requires the appropriate receptivity. All that is then required is a "spark" to ignite the process.

The same phenomenon can be observed on an emotional level. We know that both yawning and laughter are "contagious." The precondition for this once again is a receptive atmosphere within a society. Given that receptivity, a small, completely subliminal stimulus is enough to set off a burst of laughter, a storm of enthusiasm, or some other reaction which then appears "endemically." These are in reality more than just "reactions," since the stimulus alone is too weak to account for them.

This is true of practically all emotions. Enthusiasm can be just as infectious as cynicism, a point that Rudolf Steiner made repeatedly in reference to education, but that is little heeded today. Hypnotic sugges-

29. A detailed discussion may be found in E. M. Kranich, Planetary Influences upon Plants: A Cosmological Botany (Wyoming, R.I.: Bio-Dynamic Literature, 1984). See also M. Thun and H. Heinze, Anbauversuche über Zusammenhänge zwischen Mondstellungen im Tierkreis und Kulturpflanzen, Band I und II (Darmstadt: 1973); R. Rissmann, Evolution der Pflanze (Stuttgart: 1969); A. Fyfe, Moon and Plant: Capillary Dynamic Studies, 2nd. ed. (Arlesheim, Switzerland: Society for Cancer Research, 1975); The Signature of the Planet Mercury in Plants: Capillary Dynamic Studies (Arlesheim: Switzerland: Society for Cancer Research, 1973); The Signature of the Planet Venus in Plants (Arlesheim, Society for Cancer Research, 1978); The Signature of the Planet Uranus in Plants (Arlesheim: Society for Cancer Research, 1984); W. Schüpbach, Pflanzengeometrie (Bern: 1944).

30. See H. Heinemann and B. Pflug, eds., "Rhythmusprobleme in der Psychiatrie," Aktuelle Psychiatrie (Stuttgart: Fischer, 1978); G. Hildebrandt, ed., Biologische Rhythmen und Arbeit (Heidelberg/Vienna/New York/London, 1974).

31. Steiner, SM, lecture 13.

tion is also an infection—a conscious, intentional one—of one person's mind by the will of another. Because it is intentional, it is more truly an infection than is the invasion of the body by bacteria or viruses, which have no such intentions. Advertising, to the extent that it involves suggestion, i.e. the conscious circumvention of critical thinking, is thus also a kind of infection.

Fashion is another typical example of this phenomenon. A "creation" will be generally accepted and become "epidemic" only when it encounters a (usually unconscious) tendency, the "tide of the times." Extremes are often preferred, as befits the astral nature of the emotional plane. The art of the successful fashion designer consists in apprehending the current tendency in such a way that his idea "catches on."

Such phenomena are not merely analogous to one another; they are the very same process manifesting on the physical, emotional, and spiritual levels. Thus they express the intrinsic multidimensionality of human development. The same process can appear on various levels or move from one level to another. In human development, processes that are at first exclusively organic processes are later transformed into consciousness and thought. This appears as the partial liberation of the etheric body, the astral body, and the ego in the first three seven-year stages (see German vol. I, pp. 82ff).[32] The transformation can, however, proceed in the opposite direction: emotional and mental processes can be "repressed," i.e. fall back onto the organic level, causing such phenomena as ulcers. Similarly, fear increases susceptibility to infectious disease, while fearlessness lowers it. This interplay between levels must be recognized by anyone wishing to grasp the meaning of the infectious disease process.

The connection of infectious diseases with emotional and mental states is now thoroughly recognized; however, these connections can only be understood in the light of the metamorphosis of growth forces into forces of consciousness and vice versa.[33]

---

32. The first volume of the German edition remains as yet untranslated (2002). Vol. 1 of the English edition is actually a translation of the first book of volume II of the German edition; volume II is a translation of the second book of the German volume II; volume III is a translation of the German volume III. All references are to these English translations unless expressly noted as "German volume I" (Editor's note).

33. H. Hübschmann, "Psyche und Tuberkulose," Beiträge zur allgemeinen Medizin (1952). V. von Weizsäcker, Studien zur Pathogenese, series for DMW 2.

It would be a mistake to see constitution and disposition as the sole factors determining receptivity and hence the occurrence of infection. Like bacteria, human beings are affected by cosmic influences, especially in the realm of disease (e.g. sensitivity to weather). As we develop toward freedom, we are gradually liberated from such cosmic influences, which helps explain, for example, why the lower animals are more dependent on lunar rhythms than the human being is.

A prominent feature of almost all infectious diseases is their periodicity. A case in point is diphtheria. Currently this disease has almost totally regressed, and runs an altogether harmless course when it does appear. Its rate of incidence varies not only over decades, but also within a single year: formerly it increased in late autumn and reached a maximum in winter. A table drawn from U.S. data (see Fig. 1) shows that waves of scarlet fever followed upon those of diphtheria. Superimposed on the annual variation is a longer-term variation, presently at a low.

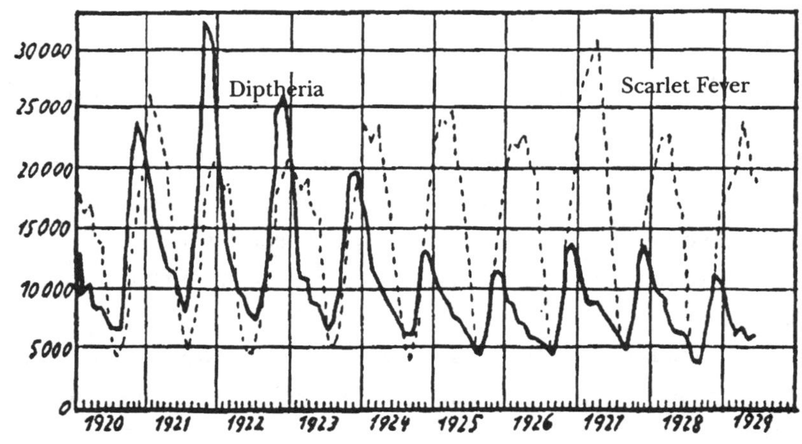

Figure 1. Number of cases of diptheria and scarlet fever reported monthly in the U.S. between 1920 and 1929 (Monthly Reports of the Section for Hygiene of the League of Nations, No. 127, as quoted by de Rudder, Meteorobiologie, p. 105).

In recent times, scarlet fever has also decreased in virulence, though this need not remain so. The same can be said about measles, whooping cough, pneumonia, and tuberculosis, to which we shall return later.

Rabies displays a three-year rhythm in addition to an annual one, while hoof and mouth disease, plague, diphtheria, meningitis, influenza, and smallpox show anywhere from a seven- to ten-year rhythm.[34]

Finally, there are indications that for centuries cholera was endemic in India, but that it did not begin to spread as an epidemic until 1817. By 1892, once the subsequent pandemics had taken their toll of millions, cholera became non-migratory once more.[35]

This is without doubt a problem of many levels. Statistical connections do not in themselves indicate anything about causal relationships, but by now a meteorological or cosmic component has been proven with certainty for a number of diseases, after decades of neglect of such influences. Connections between sunspots and diphtheria were discovered as early at 1939.[36] Weather has been demonstrated to affect the incidence of eclampsia, thrombosis, postoperative lung complications, death—particularly suicide—acute glaucoma, angina, diphtheria, and stroke. Other connections are possible but not yet definite.[37] We should point out once more that a further step in research remains to be taken—that of revealing the cosmic factors underlying the weather, so that we can know which one stands behind a particular meteorological or disease-triggering influence.

Of course, we are never confronted with a disease in the abstract, but rather only by sick people. However, the expression genius epidemicus, used in earlier times, was not meant as an abstraction; it referred to the underlying motive principle of an illness, which in earlier times was experienced as a reality. Each disease has its own character in this regard. With the rise of empiricism, all things not perceptible to the senses were declared unreal or at least not open to scientific investigation. To the extent that nebulous talk about "essences" and "spirit" helps no one, this was healthy; however, it should not blind us to the very real

34. A. Mayr, Naturwissenschaftliche Rundschau 27 (1974): 94. See also de Rudder, "Über das Kommen und Gehen von Seuchen," Jahrbuch der Akademie der Wissenchaften und Literatur (1958):269.

35. Ibid.

36. F. Belak, Monatsschr. Kinderklinik 77 (1939):190.

37. See H. Heinemann and B. Pflug, eds., "Rhythmusprobleme in der Psychiatrie," Aktuelle Psychiatrie (Stuttgart: Fischer, 1978); G. Hildebrandt, ed., Biologische Rhythmen und Arbeit (Heidelberg/Vienna/New York/London, 1974).

effects of spiritual entities and forces, which we intend to illustrate in the following.

Before we attempt to understand the nature of individual diseases, we should note a general phenomenon, namely, that the incidence of infectious diseases is declining.

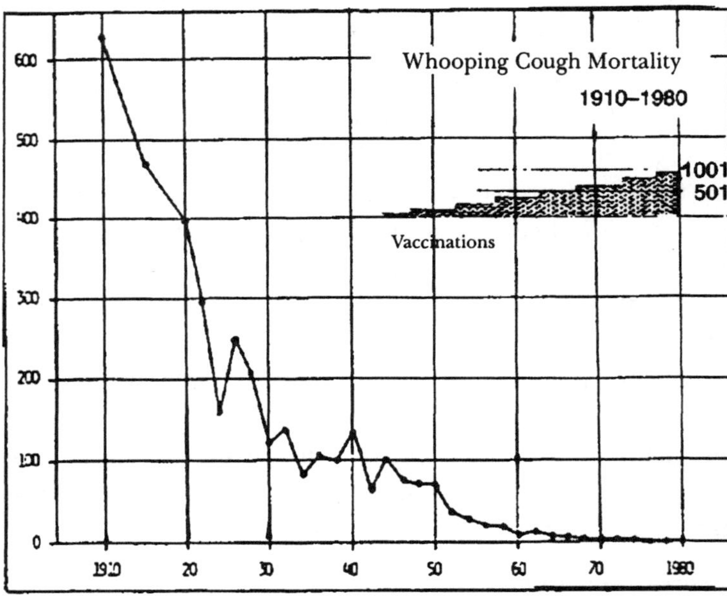

Fig. 2: Whooping cough mortality in Switzerland, 1910-80. Taken from Tönz, O. Keuchhustenimpfung. Therapeut. Umschau 40, S. 203 (1983)

The great contagions of the Middle Ages no longer terrify; nor do such still-occurring diseases as tuberculosis, typhoid, and pneumonia. The general opinion is that modern medicine, with its antibiotics and vaccinations, is responsible for this regression. Whether this is true is open to debate, since a statistical correlation need not indicate a causal relationship, despite our tendency to assume one. Supporting the opposite view is the fact that the great scourges of the Middle Ages subsided without any of the measures approved by contemporary science as effective. Similarly, tuberculosis and pneumonia were on the decline long before the introduction of hygienic measures, as Figures 1 and 2 of the chapter on the lung in Volume II clearly show (pp. 421, 430). Whooping cough was also losing its character as a dangerous disease by the turn of the century—long before vaccination began (Figure 2). The curve drops so uniformly that it most likely would have proceeded the same way without vaccination. The case for this is even clearer for measles (Fig. 5). Scarlet fever became innocuous long before the era of penicillin, and diphtheria was also definitely regressing two to three years before the serum came into use (Fig. 3).

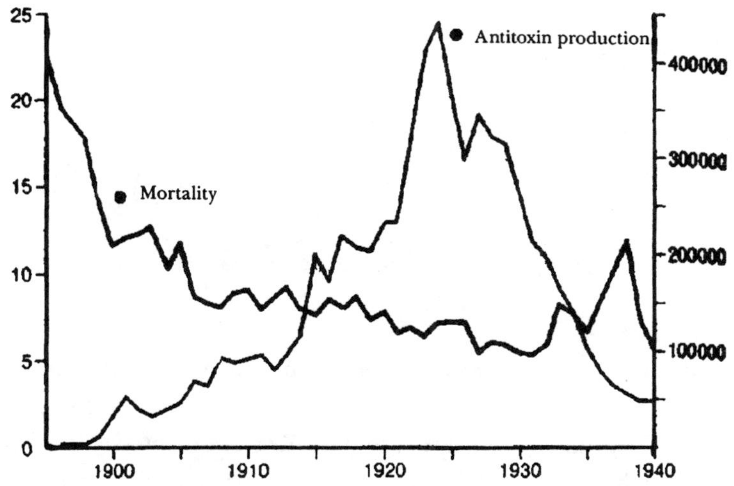

Fig. 3: Changes in the lethality of diptheria in the state of Massachusetts (in percentage of lethal cases) in relation to the production of diptheria antitoxin (number of single doses administered yearly). (From Bingel, DMW 74 (1949). S. 101.)

These are just a few examples of the worldwide regression of bacterial diseases that has been going on for many decades. A drop in the mortality rate was observed in the U.S. beginning around the turn of the century, before chemotherapeutic or prophylactic measures had been introduced.[38]

Figure 4. Number of diptheria cases. Source: Federal Office of Statistics, Wiesbaden Group VII D. From Buchwald, Gesundheitsberater, 8/1988, p. 12.

38. J. and S. McKinlay, "The Questionable Contribution of Medical Measures to the Decline of Mortality in the U.S. in the Twentieth Century," Milbank Memorial Fund Quarterly: Health and Society (1977):425.

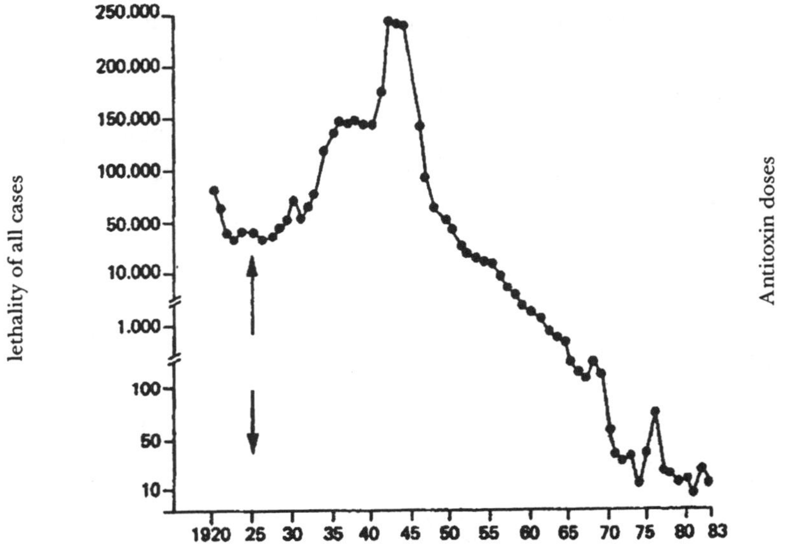

Two examples may be adduced here to clarify the difficulties that arise in judging therapeutic measures. The positive effect of the diphtheria serum on "regular" diphtheria is generally not doubted. Nevertheless this therapy, which rests on Behring's discovery and the antigen-antibody reaction, is anything but well-founded and foolproof. In particular, the malignant cases that are responsible for the high mortality rates of diphtheria respond scarcely or not at all to the serum.In the numerous malignant, so-called toxic cases that are responsible for the high diphtheria mortality, the diphtheria antitoxin has proven powerless, both in high dosages and in combination with streptococcus serum, etc. Only on the first and second day of illness can it have any effect, and even then only a modest one.[39]

From the point of view of medical history, it is interesting to note that no practical success of serum therapy on human beings was ever observed, and this was admitted as early as 1904: "There has been a general theoretical faith in the possibility of great, grand-scale therapeutic successes. But when in practice failure mounted upon failure, the blame was placed not on the prevailing theory but on technical difficulties, and

39. Paschlau, MMW (1936):200.

numerous researchers devoted all their time and energy to the success of serum therapy... in clinical circles as well, the sera were looked on as the salvation of suffering humanity; and as happens so often, people all too easily saw what they wished to see."[40]

Fig. 5: Measles mortality rate for children under 15 in England and Wales. Source: Thomas McKeown, Die Bedeutung der Medizin, Frankfurt 1979.

The testimony of other authors supports this claim. Zischinsky investigated almost eight thousand cases and concluded that the diphtheria serum was completely ineffective in toxic cases, even if administered immediately.[41] We know today that for the antitoxin to be effective, it must be given very early on—within ninety minutes of toxin administration in the animal test—which of course makes it practically useless. Particularly instructive are the voluminous statistical investigations conducted by Bingel of various epidemics, the earliest being in 1918. In comparative studies of treatment with ordinary horse serum ("empty" serum without diphtheria antibodies) and antitoxin serum, no differ-

40. Wolff, A. Centralblatt f. Bakt. etc. 1904 original. Vol. XXXVII, no. 5, p. 703.
41. Zischinsky, Abh. Kinderheilkunde (1934) 36.

ence was found within any one epidemic; comparison of different epidemics, however, did reveal differences in effectiveness.

> This shows again how wrong it is ... to study infectious diseases, particularly diphtheria, by comparing different years with one another and on this basis to draw conclusions concerning the efficacy of the therapy applied. Variations in morbidity, lethality and complications—in short, in the very character of diphtheria—are quite wide; this must be emphasized again and again. [Bingel concludes] The study of 2,919 cases has convinced me and my assistants that the antitoxin is not the effective healing principle in seral treatment of human diphtheria. By contrast, horse serum nonspecifically stimulates the forces of resistance.[42]

Later researchers have come to very much the same conclusions. Most researchers, however, have been reluctant to repeat such studies, no doubt because they are unwilling to abandon a supposedly "proven" remedy. Although Bingel's studies could not be refuted by other investigations, they were nonetheless quite generally rejected as not fitting the prevailing theory. This is a good example of the difficulty of overcoming established convictions, or at least of gaining tolerance for another view.

In evaluating Figure 3, it must be kept in mind that at the same time as antitoxin therapy was introduced, many healthy inspectors were sent out to educate the public in hygiene (isolating the ill, protecting from infection, etc.).[43] As the author concludes, "these figures do not give the impression that antitoxin treatment made a great deal of difference." As we mentioned earlier, improvements in hygiene such as those introduced by Pettenkofer were the critical factor in the regression of the great epidemics. (See The Concept of Infection.) The temporal rhythm in the occurrence of diphtheria has been mentioned. It has a particular character of its own, which seems to be operational in the peaks (1943-45 and 1976) (fig. 4). It must also be recalled that times of war are favorable to infectious diseases. Furthermore, an isolated section of the graph in Fig. 4 for the years 1925 to 1945 could equally well be presented as evidence for the serum's harmful effects, just as Fig. 3 can be misinterpreted as demonstrating its success.

42. Bingel, DMW 74 (1949):101.

43. Cairns, J., "Geschichtliche Entwicklung der Mortalität." Mannheimer Forum 85/86, p. 82.

These examples reveal the difficulty of drawing correct conclusions from a given phenomenon, and particularly the danger of reducing the conclusions to a single parameter—the effect of the serum or vaccination in this case.

The fundamental phenomenon is that bacterial illnesses have been receding across the globe for many decades. In the United States, as well, a drop in the mortality rate has been observed since about the turn of the century, i.e. before the introduction of chemotherapeutic or prophylactic measures.[44]

Unprejudiced evaluation of the effectiveness of antibiotics has also been rare. High rates of cure are claimed and then compared in some cases with earlier data. This is of course methodologically inadmissible; success can be proven only in contrast with a comparable untreated group, which, due to the changes in diseases over time, would have to be contemporary.

> It can be said honestly that the percentage healed by penicillin is zero, since penicillin does not "heal" at all. It can only favor and sometimes accelerate healing. Above all, it is able to prevent complications and thus without doubt lower the lethality, which in unfavorable circumstances formerly stood at ten to twenty percent, though even today it is not zero. The ninety percent recovery rate frequently cited in publications on antibiotic trials is a product of the false, linear-causal thinking that dominates our time.[45]

The examples given here by no means prove these therapeutic measures ineffective. It would be senseless to doubt the efficacy of antibiotics. In individual cases and with appropriate indications they can be highly effective. The problem is rather generalization from individual cases to the course of entire epidemics.[46] Neither should the influence of modern hygienic measures upon the spread of epidemics and infec-

44. McKinlay, J. and S., "The Questionable Contribution of Medical Measures to the Decline of Mortality in the U.S. in the Twentieth Century." Milbank Memorial Fund Quarterly: Health and Society (1977: 425).

45. Hõring, Therapiewoche (1965):1185.

46. To avoid misunderstandings, it should be emphasized that the outcome of a single case can be highly significant and that the lessons gained from it can certainly be applied to other cases. Mass outbreaks of diseases are the result of the interaction between individual factors and the evolutionary phenomena we have discussed. The overall regression of diseases cannot be understood without considering this interaction.

tions be underestimated. Cholera regressed in Europe mainly because of the improvements in drinking water and sewage disposal introduced by Pettenkofer. Despite these successes, however, the approaches of research and concepts of therapy continue to focus almost entirely on pathogens.

Even without hygienic measures, however, contagious diseases would have declined in accordance with their own inherent laws. They are no longer "appropriate" for our times; they belong to another state of humanity. Here we find a situation similar to that described by Charles Elton, the founder of modern ecological research, who discovered that diseases appear only after populations have already begun to decline.[47] Diseases are therefore not primary agents of evolution, but rather only indicators of a developmentally changed situation which they help to intensify or "complete." The same is doubtlessly true of such evolutionary phenomena as the disappearance of the dinosaurs, which occurred in response to a change in the underlying archetypes of animal life.

Contemporary thought about evolutionary phenomena is usually dominated by Darwinist logic: it considers only external influences (such as change of climate) and "genetically determined factors" and is a form of causal-analytic thinking. However, human and earthly development are influenced by spiritual powers higher than human beings. "Divine guidance" was treated as an obvious fact in earlier times until the dawn of the natural scientific era, when human consciousness began to turn exclusively toward the outer world. At that time divine influences were declared superfluous and chance was set in their place; thus the narrow world view that determines our modern way of thinking was created. A more accurate understanding of ourselves and of the world requires acceptance of spiritual influences and willingness to research them in the exact manner inaugurated by Rudolf Steiner.

All of these influences play a part in the regression of bacterial infections. The latter is not an isolated phenomenon, but must in turn be seen in connection with the increase in viral illnesses. The exact connection becomes clear only when one considers the fundamental nature of bacteria and viruses.

47. Charles Elton, Voles, Mice and Lemmings (Oxford: Clarendon Press, 1942).

Viruses[48]

It has been shown that pathogens need a satisfactory growth medium, and that the growth medium can sometimes cast light on the nature of the pathogen. Viruses have a pronounced relationship to the upper part of the human organism, especially to the nervous system. This is most obvious in the case of the neurotropic viruses, which include encephalitis, poliomyelitis, and rabies. Influenza and viral pneumonia are also clearly related to the upper organization: the lungs and upper respiratory tract are much more subject to the formative, catabolic tendencies of the nervous system than are the organs beneath the diaphragm.

A striking trait of many viral diseases is their manifestation on the skin (measles, German measles, herpes, smallpox, chicken pox, pemphigus, etc.). As an organ, the skin is closely related to the nervous system both morphogenetically and functionally, and hence also to the astral formative tendency that issues from the nervous system. The exanthem characteristic of many viral diseases is an attempt by the organism to expel and overcome pathogenic processes and thus to relive the nervous system of them.

The difference between bacteria and viruses becomes especially clear in the parts of the head that each infects. Bacteria infect the meninges, which play a role in the nutrition and metabolism of the nervous system (meningococci, pneumococci). The neural substance proper, however, is attacked by viruses, as in encephalitis, which can be regarded as a typical viral disease.

System	Infectious Agent	Typical, extreme disease
nervous	viruses	encephalitis
blood and metabolic	bacteria	sepsis

The relation of viruses to the nervous system is always present, even if in some diseases it is overlaid by reactions of an inflammatory nature.

48. See W. zur Linden, BEH (1955):165 (1960):14; and M. Jaschke, BEH (1978):189.

Thus one can speak of a neurotropism of viruses. The fact that viruses can be cultured on renal tissue follows from the nature of the kidney, the metabolic organ that is permeated more intensely than any other by impulses from the nervous system. By contrast, bacteria are clearly connected with metabolic processes and with the blood, where they flourish particularly well and where they can also be cultured. Pus production, which starts from the blood, also indicates this connection. Any overabundance of etheric formative forces that results in chaotic metabolic activity sets the stage for bacterial proliferation; a typical example of a locally limited process of this kind is abscess formation in diabetes. Another factor that can favor bacterial growth is a disturbance in an organ that is already constitutionally or dispositionally weakened (pneumonia, pyelonephritis, etc.). When this weakness affects not just a limited area, but the entire organism, the result is the stereotypical bacterial disease, sepsis. Sepsis can never be evoked by viruses, because viruses have no relation to the blood; it is not receptive to them. Bacteria, by contrast, may be described as hemotropic. The polarity between the nervous system and the blood is mirrored in the antagonism between viruses and bacteria.

The primal polarity of nerve and blood, the principle upon which the threefold organization of the human being rests, is also found in the smallest unit, the cell. The nucleus and protoplasm of the cell, though they are parts of the same whole, have different functions. As is known, the nucleus consists of large part of DNA and RNA. Through them, "information" (formative principles) is transmitted, while the protein of the protoplasm is the foundation of life.

Viruses are composed mainly of nucleic acids. They exhibit almost none of the typical signs of life. By contract, bacteria possess extremely varied proteins and a practically inexhaustible vitality, but no nucleus. Viruses thus have a clear relation to the nucleus, and bacteria to the cell body.

Viruses and bacteria represent impulses that have a common origin but have taken different developmental paths.

This polarity of bacteria and viruses is an expression of the polarity of blood and nerve. This sheds light on the increase of viral diseases, for in contrast to the bacterial "contagions of primitivity" (Kisskalt) of earlier days, in our own times the "contagions of civilization" (de Rudder) are increasing at a rapid rate. Obviously this change is not caused by the bacteria or viruses themselves. The key is provided by the dynamic that holds sway in the human being: the polarity of nervous system and blood-metabolic system. There is no doubt that in earlier centuries, human beings were more vital, stronger and more "full-blooded," more strongly connected with the metabolic system, whereas in recent times people have begun to live more and more within their nervous systems, one might almost say in their heads. It seems reasonable that such tendencies, which can extend over decades or even centuries, should have consequences in the physical constitution.

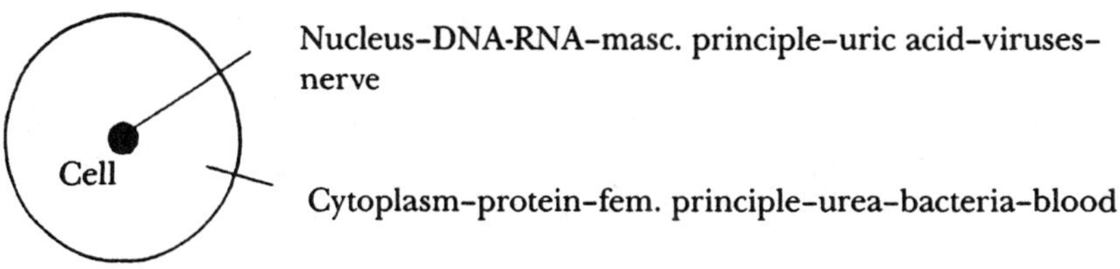

One direct result of the tipping of the balance between nervous system and metabolic system is a change in type of the most prevalent diseases. The association of inflammation and sclerosis with the ascending and descending halves of life, respectively, applies not only to individual lives, but also to the development of humanity as a whole. In earlier centuries, the inflammatory, acute, highly febrile illnesses predominated, while today they are far outweighed by the sclerotic, chronic, "cold" diseases.

This phenomenon has of course been generally noted, but its causes are not understood. In the words of Jores, "the chronic patient is the unsolved problem of contemporary medicine."[49]

49. A. Jores, Die Medizin in der Krise unserer Zeit (Bern:1961).

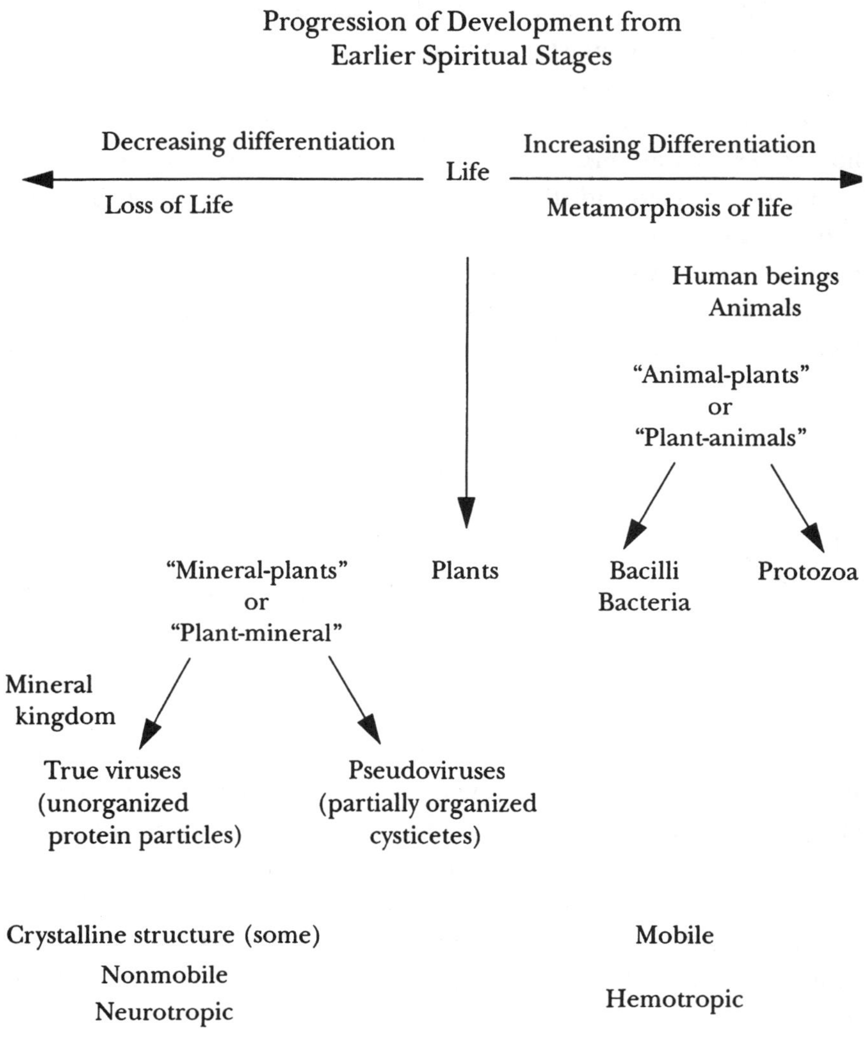

Figure 6: Viruses and Bacteria in the Kingdoms of Nature (after W. z. Linden)

From our point of view, the decline of febrile illness is by no means to be judged positively, for it has been bought at the expense of an inability to react, an anergy. Failure to comprehend the true nature of fever poses a considerable obstacle to a realistic understanding of illness.[50] Instead of coming to terms with an illness in a dramatic, short-term struggle followed by a new order, the organism incapable of fever is in a protracted state of "cold war," which it must eventually lose. The decline of bacterial illnesses may thus be seen as an expression of the decline in the human being's constitutional capacity for inflammation or fever.

Epochs as well as people have typical illnesses. Cancer, for example, cannot be understood in isolation, but only in terms of the absence of its counterpart, inflammation.

On the basis of the shift in disease types over the centuries, the cyclical infectious diseases and epidemics take on another dimension. Their frequency is subject to the alternations in the human constitution just described, but this does not exhaust their significance for human beings.

To a much greater extent than other diseases, the cyclical infectious diseases have a distinct temporal structure. Grote, and after him Höring, found that each disease has its own "law" governing the length of its phases and the overall course, and that this temporal structure is independent of the agents that provoke the disease. The latter, in fact, only trigger a response that is inherent in the organism. It is of course true that without bacteria or viruses there is no corresponding disease, but only conditionally so. The same "typical" disease can be produced in various ways; for example, pneumonia can be evoked either by pneumococci, viruses, or mycoplasms; dysentery can be produced by dysentery bacteria or by amoebae; diarrhea can be due to bacteria, toxins, or even psychosomatic influences. In short, many diseases can occur even in the absence of their usual pathogen. Moreover, Speransky succeeded in producing typical disease syndromes by directly stimulating the nervous system, in the complete absence of bacteria.[51] From this he concluded that infectious diseases are based on disturbances in the nervous system.

In all of these examples, the pathogen, whatever it may be, only initiates a process whose further development is determined by other factors. Speransky designates the bacteria not as initiators, but as indicators of pathology.[52] Even stimulation of the nervous system is not an "ultimate cause" of the illnesses produced; the latter are a problem of the

50. See F. Hoff, Fieber: Unspezifische Abwehrvorgänge und spezifische Therapie (Stuttgart: 1957).

51. A. D. Speransky, Grundlage einer Theorie der Medizin (Berlin: 1950).

52. Ibid.

organism as a whole. Nevertheless, we owe much to Speransky and others for having directed our attention to disorders in the organism as a factor in the genesis of infectious diseases.

Roloff calls the bacteria not provokers, but carriers of infection.[53] In this connection we may recall Letterer's distinction between infection and infectious disease: "Infection need not lead to infectious disease. The presence of infectious material is a matter of the tissue; infectious disease is a matter of the organism."[54] In essence, we have here the same situation as in a carcinoma: the proliferating cell is neither the cause of the disease nor the disease itself. Rather, the tumor is an indicator of the cancerous state of the organism. For decades people have attempted to gain insight into the causes of disease by ever more refined study of bacteria and tumors—a tragic situation, inasmuch as something is being sought where it cannot be found. In the future, the vitally important results that have already been achieved will have to be complemented with a study of the inherent principles and patterns of the organism.

The distinction between an infection and infectious disease, between a tumor and the disease of cancer, is one of utmost significance for both pathology and therapy, yet unfortunately it remains unrecognized today. One is a local phenomenon, the other a condition of the entire organism—a difference which is indicative of different therapeutic approaches. As long as the "pathogen" or tumor is seen as the cause of the disease, therapy will logically be directed at these and the organism will be neglected, to its detriment. When the organism is recognized as the higher reality, however, then treatment aimed at stimulating it will be the therapy proper—the causal, not the adjuvant therapy. This is of the greatest importance both for medical practice and particularly for prophylaxis. The two approaches are not mutually exclusive; one is not more correct or better than the other, and applied appropriately they can be complementary.

We have seen that the organism possesses a typical mode of reaction that, when activated, results in disease. In its premorbid state of sensitivity" (Hōring) the organism is susceptible to certain pathogens, which then initiate the corresponding illness. Clearly, however, pathogens are

53. Beitr. z. Klin. Tbc. 102 (1950):567.

54. Letterer, Die Medizinische (1953) 1.

not therefore unimportant or unnecessary. Without them diseases do not manifest "properly." For example, viral pneumonia runs a somewhat different course than bacterial pneumonia; nevertheless, both agents meet with a specifically susceptible organism. A different organism will react either not at all or with a latent or unapparent infection, or in some other way. In this connection it is interesting to note that the same virus that evokes the common cold in human beings produces cancer in hamsters.

Here we can discuss only fundamental principles, not the details of specific diseases. The question that seems most pertinent here is that of the significance of these phenomena, especially since the individual component—the fact of receptivity—is so obvious, regardless of all endemic or epidemic aspects. That these problems concern humankind specifically is clear not only from the fact that individual reactions are different, but also chiefly from the fact that certain diseases, such as measles, affect only human beings; what ought to be the same disease runs a different course in animals.

One key to understanding infectious diseases is contained in their general course and result. A susceptible organism responds to a pathogen with disease, which, after it has run its course, leaves an immunity to the pathogen. (We leave aside here the question of how long the immunity lasts as well as the fact that under some circumstances, a new infection with the same pathogen can occur despite immunity, albeit without the characteristic course.) Immunity, however, means that the organism has overcome an existing weakness or made up for a lack; it has become stronger. Thus the pathogenic agent evokes precisely the reactions that the organism "needs," putting it in a position to overcome the original disorder. The particular form in which the "environment" penetrates into human organisms is thus a mirror image, as it were, of what human beings need to accomplish; the environment helps us to develop our latent physical capabilities. This is a meaningful process of self-correction and evolution to higher stages; it is, in effect, a learning process. Of course, it is not customary to speak of "learning" at this level, but as we saw with infection, the same quality can manifest itself on many levels. It is not right to see the formation of immunity in purely organic terms. Through experience (in the widest sense of the term), we human beings acquire our own unique character. Disease gives us the opportunity to overcome something in the organic realm that we do not yet have the strength to overcome spiritually or mentally; a physical capacity can later be transformed into a spiritual one.

Illness exercises this function most obviously during the ascending half of life, in which "learning" in every sense is physiological, to be followed in later life by "utilization." The latter cannot take place without the former. Febrile illnesses are typical of childhood, while the descending half of life is dominated by degenerative-sclerotic diseases. Immunity is a developmental step that is significant for the entire remainder of life, and not just in terms of heightened resistance to disease. Thus we arrive from another angle at what was shown of the childhood diseases in an earlier volume, namely, that they are really aids to the overall development of the individuality.

It has been indicated at various points that the childhood diseases, which are cyclical infectious diseases, frequently restructure the constitution, so that after recovery a child will often appear to have been "reborn." The organism is recast by the disease, as it were, particularly by the fever. Through the specificity of its reactions the organism acquires precisely what it needs.

A true understanding of this phenomenon requires a careful consideration of the significance of warmth for the human mind and spirit. Since the human ego lives in warmth, fever indicates an intensified involvement of the ego in the organism. The role of fever is still greatly underestimated today. Its primary role as a defense against diseases is not fully acknowledged, not to mention its role as bearer of the ego and the related spiritual questions. We refer once again to the polarity of inflammatory illnesses and carcinoma discussed in Volume I, which is crucial to an understanding of the nature of infectious diseases. A view that limits itself to the physical course of a disease, no matter how correct and significant it may be, will comprehend only a small part of the disease process.

The infectious diseases demonstrate in a particularly clear manner that disease is not only due to past processes, but is also directed toward the future. Illness paves the way for future "achievements," stimulating human development by a unique "artifice of nature" (Goethe) to overcome the past and realize the future. Disease is thus, among other things, the means to an end; it is an indispensable helper that corrects individual imperfections, creating a new order and bringing about an enhancement of individual humanity.

Burdens and dangers are of course an unavoidable part of this process. No one can come to terms with life and the environment without taking risks. In childhood we all put this basic principle into practice on a physical level. Forces that we will need later on another level can accrue to us there or be taken away. Progress requires exertion and development risks; it is an illusion to believe otherwise.

In summary, the current conception of infectious disease is one-sided in that it takes into account essentially nothing but the "pathogenic agents" of infection. In fact these are not the cause of illness, but "merely" play a role in its development. The cause of illness lies in the organism. It was recognized early on that this is an epistemological problem, but this insight did not receive attention. Yet it is of tremendous practical significance for therapy and prophylaxis: If therapy continues to limit its purview to "pathogens," in the future we will continue to see diseases changing form and new ones arising against which the usual treatments are powerless. This is why it is so important now to look into the purpose and meaning of disease, as we have attempted to do in this book from various angles and for various diseases.

Therapy of Infectious Diseases

Therapeutic methods are always based on assumptions about disease, which is why these assumptions are so critically important. Antibiotic therapy, which still predominates in the treatment of infectious diseases, is based on the notion that bacteria causes disease. Conversely, freedom from bacteria is equated with health. That this is not so could have been anticipated by less prejudiced minds, but it took experience to demonstrate it, after which insight followed.

It is common knowledge that antibiotics have not accomplished all that was expected of them, and that they frequently have undesirable side effects. Even if we had an ideal antibiotic, one that could prevent bacterial growth without affecting the host organism, it would still deprive that organism of the opportunity to overcome the susceptibility that produced the disease in the first place. The disease is not allowed to run its proper course, and the organism is prone to relapses. We are confronted with a "completely irregular time-structure, a muting of the course, and multiple relapses resulting from antibiotic disturbance of the disease's temporal structure and immunizing effects" (Hõring).

Indiscriminate and premature application of antibiotics not only prevents the organism from reacting, it also lastingly upsets its relationship with endobiotic organisms. The increase in relapses is in part connected with this, as is the increase in fungal infections. The body's overall flora changes in an unfavorable way, including the development of resistance—an experience known since the time when gonorrhea was treated with sulfonamides. It is an experience that we have been reliving since the beginning of the penicillin era: Staphylococci, once extremely sensitive, are now resistant to penicillin at a rate of 85%. Another resulting phenomenon has been pseudomonas sepsis, the most frequent form of sepsis in our time. A shift from gram-positive cocci to gram-negative rods has also been observed.

The multiplication of resistant organisms has been considerably abetted by the uncritical use of broad-spectrum antibiotics. On the basis of all these negative effects, the prophylactic use of antibiotics is now generally discouraged. However, investigations by American authors as recently as the early 1970s showed that broad-spectrum antibiotics were applied either incorrectly or unnecessarily in up to fifty percent of internal medicine cases and up to sixty percent of surgical cases.[55]

The almost epidemic upsurge of fungal and yeast infections is to be seen in this context as well. Formerly the occurrence of candida was understood as an expression of general weakness, e.g. in premature infants. Today illnesses such as mycotic pneumonia (candida mycosis) and pneumocystis (interstitial pneumonia) occur following the use of cytostatics, immunosuppressives, corticosteroids, etc.—i.e., measures that weaken the immune system (a state that naturally prevails in the premature infant). These illnesses are characterized by chronic inflammation with little fever, reflecting the general state of weakness, in particular, weakness of the immune system. Although these relationships are generally known, therapy continues to be aimed at "pathogens" and "protection" from them instead of at the "weakness," which it ought to be the aim of therapy to transform into "strength."

This discrepancy between theory and practice is gradually being overcome, and is due to the usual delay between the conception of new ideas and their realization in practice. For a long time the bacteria-centered conception of disease allowed physicians to believe that in administering antibiotics they were doing everything possible in the area of causal therapy, and that to omit doing so was to commit malpractice. One obvious result of this was the emergence in hospitals of nosocomial (hospital-acquired) infections.

Studies in the U.S. have shown that approximately 5 to 6% of all hospital patients sustain a nosocomial infection, 8% of all hospital deaths must be attributed to it, and approximately 75,000 patients die of such infections annually in the U.S. alone.[56] It is further calculated that side effects of medications "rank among the top ten causes of hospitalization and account for more than fifty million inpatient days per year."[57]

---

55. Kunin, Tupasi, Craig, Annals of Internal Medicine 79 (1973):555, quoted in Daschner and Marget (note 52, below).

56. Proceedings of the International Conference on Nosocomial Infections (Center for Disease Control, 1970); quoted in Daschner and Marget (note 52, below). See also Eric Martin, Hazards of Medications (Philadelphia: Lippincott, 1971); Edwards C. Lambert, Modern Medical Mistakes (Ind. Univ. Press, 1978); Ivan Illich, Medical Nemesis, 1st American edition (New York: Pantheon Books, 1976).

57. M. Silverman and P. Lee, Pills, Profits, and Politics (Berkeley Univ. Press, 1974).

> Most hospital-acquired infections develop within 72 hours of admission, though some may not become manifest until after discharge. Two million hospital-acquired infections occur in the United States each year. Another four million infections are acquired in nursing homes. Nosocomial infections carry a mortality rate of 1% and contribute to death in 3.6% of admissions, placing them among the 10 leading causes of death. These infections prolong the hospital stay by three to 12 days and increase the total cost of medical care by more that $4 billion a year.[58]

In the Federal Republic of Germany, 500,000 persons suffer a nosocomial infection each year; of these, it is estimated that 25,000 die.[59]

It cannot be doubted:

> The danger to hospital patients from urinary tract infections, wound infections, respiratory infections, and sepsis—together the most common hospital infections—has essentially the following causes: the patients are endangered because they are in a hospital, that is, in a milieu of heightened germ exposure; they are further endangered simply because their resistance is lowered by illness; and finally, they are endangered because many of our therapeutic measures not only expose them to more germs (ultrasonic mist apparatuses, catheters, respirators), but also lower their resistance even further (e.g. cytostatics, corticosteroids, X-ray treatment, etc.).[60]

It is important to realize that this level of infection risk did not exist in earlier times, at least not to this extent, although the phenomenon of "hospitalism" has been known for a long time. In addition to the reduction of resistance through therapeutic measures there is the fact that human beings in a group become subject to special laws not applying to individuals. Future investigations will determine the extent to which the size (or enormity) of a hospital exerts a negative influence, as compared to the smaller hospitals of earlier times.

Added to these general considerations are the individual effects of antibiotic therapy, among which the most important and best known is immunosuppression. "Malignant tumors of various kinds grow unmistak-

58. N. C. Griffith and R. E. Schell, "Nosocomical Diseases," American Family Physician 35 (1987)6:179–186.
59. Antibiotika in der Praxis, 4. Jahrgang (Vienna:1978), p.66.
60. Daschner and Marget, MMW 118 (1976):545.

ably more rapidly when subjected to subtoxic doses of any antibiotic that has ever been in clinical use." The same holds true for tissue cultures in vitro.[61]

> The application of antibiotics, as is well known, is not a therapy in the proper sense of the word. It merely checks or eliminates the critical etiological factor, the bacteria. Depending on the efficacy of the treatment ... after the antibiotic is terminated the patient frequently relapses or becomes a carrier. Chemotherapy is therefore often no more than a support for the host in his confrontation with the pathogenic agents.[62]

A phenomenon less frequently noticed, for lack of the appropriate concepts, is the negative effect of antibiotics on light-metabolism. Among other things, antibiotics inhibit phosphorylation. (These relationships are treated thoroughly in another publication.[63])

Summing up, we may state that antibiotics negatively influence the organism's healing reactions, and are thus the opposite of a true remedy. This is not to say that they cannot save lives, but the same must be said here as was said about insulin: it can undoubtedly save and lengthen life, but does not heal diabetes, since it is only substitution therapy. To the extent that bacteria are only a symptom of the underlying disease, antibiotics act only symptomatically. They also reduce some of the effects of the organism's reaction to infection by suppressing immunity. If used at all, they should be used in such a way as to help the organism heal itself, not to achieve any obvious symptomatic effect. Of course, the organism may be so endangered that this is not possible; nevertheless, helping the organism heal itself should always be the physician's primary goal.

The use of antibiotics should therefore not be a first therapeutic step, but rather should be reserved for situations in which the organism is overtaxed. It is the physician's responsibility to determine when this is the case, based primarily on the patient's condition. The objection that "antibiotics should be used in every serious case" completely misses the point; it demonstrates a lack of understanding regarding illness, healing,

61. Kirsch and Rieck, Zentralblatt für Gynäkologie 77 (1955):1121.

62. W. Marget and M. Kienitz, Praxis der Antibiotika-Therapie im Kindesalter (Stuttgart: 1966).

63. O. Wolff, BEH (1953):104.

and the principles of effective therapy. "Serious cases" will generally not arise if the organism's own meaningful reactions are recognized and stimulated from the beginning and the organism is thereby guided through the disease; exceptions will be extremely rare and should not be generalized. Among other things, the problem of bacterial resistance would not have arisen had antibiotics always been used according to these principles.

The use of antibiotics can be compared to throwing a life ring to someone who has fallen into the water. Although even the best swimmer can find himself in a situation where a lifesaver is required, it is still better to teach people to swim than it is to rely on such devices. By no means is the lifesaver the "true" remedy to the problem of deaths by drowning.

For the physician, the decision as to whether and when a life-threatening situation is present must be made on a case-by-case basis and cannot be formalized. Furthermore, the two principles of assistance—helping the organism heal itself and saving it with antibiotics—by no means exclude one another. The common question today, which procedure is "superior" to the other, is wrongly conceived and inevitably leads to false conclusions.

For a long time the goal of treatment was specificity. For example, an antigen was to be countered by a particular antibody, or—following the results of sensitivity testing—a suitable antibiotic was to be put to use. Vaccinations are also based on this concept. Certainly this is a feasible approach. In the meantime, however, it has become clear that future progress is to be sought in the stimulation of nonspecific immunity.[64] Nonspecific measures stimulate the organism as a whole and act by way of the lymph system, the thymus, and so on.

A general example will help clarify the basic therapeutic principles we have been discussing. The measures cited in this example may be varied in accordance with the particular disease being treated.

We have seen that most cases of infectious disease are preceded by an enhanced disposition to infection. In many cases this is caused by chilling, to which the organism reacts by generating warmth. After a certain

64. W. Hauss, G. Junge-Hülsing, and U. Gerlach, Die unspezifische Mesenchymreaktion (Stuttgart: 1968). See also note 42.

latency period, this warmth manifests itself as fever, which is of course more than just a calorie-for-calorie replacement of lost body heat. Warmth, after all, is a constituent factor of the human being, and all influences upon the warmth organism have far-reaching effects.

During a period of relative hypothermia, the human being is more susceptible to infections. Depending on the constitutional situation, it may be bacteria or viruses that penetrate the organism and, having thus set the stage, evoke disease. The fever that results is a meaningful response designed not only to overcome foreign elements but also to restore the disturbed balance of forces.

Chilling has been mentioned here merely as an example. Many other factors, including stress or emotional trauma, can alter the disposition and cause the ego to react by producing a fever.

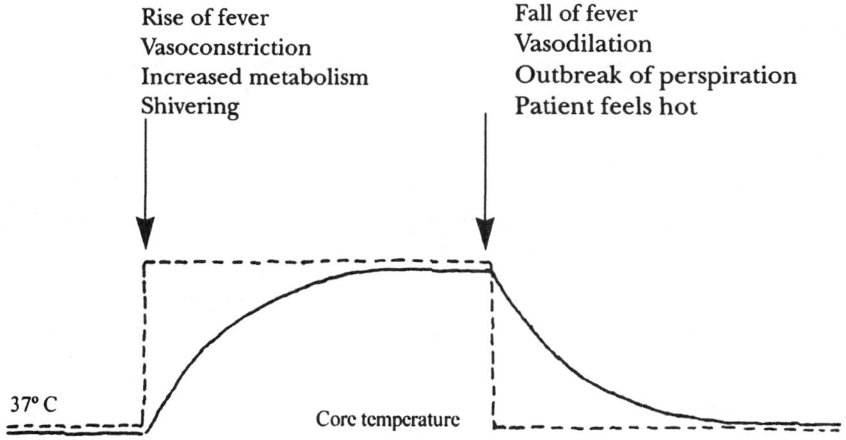

Figure 7. Physiological changes during rising and falling fever. Broken line: optimal value; solid line: actual value. (From H. Hensel, in *Kurzgefasstes Lexikon der Physiologie,* ed. by K. Wolf and D. Keidel, Stuttgart 1973).

Insight into the meaning of symptoms is the basis of therapy. It should be clear from all that has been said that to suppress fever as a general rule, as has been customary for a long time now, is counterproductive. Initially or prophylactically, the aim must be to assist or anticipate the organism's thermal reactions. This can be done with external applications of warmth, which is why a hot bath or sweating are among the oldest practical measures for the prevention of colds. These make the fever that would otherwise follow superfluous, since its goal has been anticipated. Using the nomenclature of Figure 7, the actual value is raised up to the optimal value immediately, so that the organism does not need to increase its metabolic activity and produce a fever.

It will be evident from their mode of operation that these measures are no longer appropriate when fever has already begun, since an excess of warmth would then result. Hot baths are therefore no longer indicated after fever has begun, though sweating is.

Medicinally, the initial stages of an infectious disease are treated with Aconitum napellus (monkshood). As discussed in volume I (p. 166f.), inflammations are preceded by a catabolic phase that originates in the nervous system. Hence almost all cyclical infectious diseases begin with a feeling of depletion, irritability (in the sense of an unhealthy wakefulness), pallor (vasoconstriction), chills and shivering, etc., all of which indicate the involvement of catabolism. The astral activity inherent in this process is mirrored in external nature by aconite, a plant that has a pronounced affinity to the nervous system, as witnessed by its strong analgesic effect (locally as an oil, in potentized form up to D30 for neuralgia). Aconite subdues excessive astral impulses; in potentized form, it enables the organism to recognize and overcome the disease and thereby develop its own forces. Hence aconite is indicated up to the point when the disease, sometimes with a crisis, takes a turn toward recovery. In many cases, often after a very high rise, the fever declines, accompanied by sweating. The disease process has now been overcome, and recovery begins. Up to this point the dynamic of aconite is appropriate; hence it is contained in such medications as Pneumodoron and Inludo.

A disease can also run a gradual rather than a dramatic course. In such cases, belladonna is indicated. It acts upon the anabolic aspect of inflammation and is in that sense the opposite of aconite. Red inflammations of organs, mucous membranes, or the whole organism indicate an excessive astral activity in the metabolic system or the blood rather than the nervous system. Such a situation can also be primary, as in scarlet fever. In these cases, belladonna is indicated from the beginning. The organism's reactions rather than the pathogen or a symptom are the key to deciding which remedy to apply.

Apis is an excellent complement to belladonna. The two together have proven very effective against local inflammations (tonsillitis, erysipelas, abscess, prostatitis, etc.), whether used as a liquid (Erysidoron I), injection, or locally (Bolus Eucalypti comp., Pasta Eucalypti comp.).

Since febrile phenomena are the outward expression of a new phase of the incarnation process, iron, as the incarnation metal, can be of some assistance, for example, in pneumonia. On the other hand, if the process of dissolution by warmth goes so far that body substance is not only "recast" but actually consumed, silver is indicated (especially D30 as injection). This keeps the consuming catabolic process in check. When, however, the process of dissolution requires stimulation, a sulfuric substance is given, such as Sulfur or Hepar Sulf., in conjunction with the external application of warmth. When the goal is to support the organism's formative forces, then quartz or a siliceous plant such as coneflower (Echinacea angustifolia) should be used. The latter is related to arnica, but is more active in the metabolism. Echinacea may be used together with Argentum (combined solution for injection) or alone (internally: full strength, or D3 for prolonged use; externally: Echinacin).

When immune weakness becomes chronic, mistletoe therapy is indicated. Dosage should begin low and rise gradually in accordance with the immune status. In addition, as mentioned, iron and Echinacea or an appropriate constitutional remedy are indicated. For venereal infections the remedy of choice is mercury.

All of the measures we have suggested support the organism's self-regulation. The reduction of fever does not in itself indicate a beneficial therapeutic effect. Antipyretic effects are merely symptomatic and say nothing about a treatment's significance for the course of a disease. At the same time it would be erroneous to see an enhancement of the febrile reaction as the sole effect of the medications just described. The disease process calls for a rise in body temperature only in the initial stages; equally important is control of that reaction, that is, limitation to the required degree and duration. The medications just described help with that phase of the disease process as well, and are thus true remedies rather than merely symptomatic medications.

Of course, febrile reactions can get out of hand and even become life-threatening (hyperthermia). In such cases a symptomatic procedure is justified. This may include physical measures such as moist calf compresses or abdominal compresses. In all cases, however, the aim should be merely to prevent excessive temperatures, not to restore a normal one.

Another essential factor in the therapy of infectious diseases is diet. During fever, but also during other toxic processes such an inflammation, suppuration, and tissue deterioration, protein consumption should be limited as much as possible. Here the organism is so busy reforming its own bodily protein and expelling microorganisms, which are also composed mostly of protein, that it must not be burdened with the additional task of breaking down protein. Care must also be taken to assure that the organs of detoxification, i.e. the liver and intestines, are functioning properly. Absence of hunger, for example during fever, expresses a healthy instinct and should be respected. In chronic infections, especially suppurations (e.g. osteomyelitis), a temporary, absolutely protein-free diet can have an excellent rebuilding effect, especially in combination with simultaneous or subsequent quartz therapy. Such a diet should last about four weeks.

Prophylaxis of Infectious Diseases

As shown above, the theory of infectious diseases can be expanded without negating the role of bacteria and viruses. To underestimate bacteria would be to regress to the age before Semmelweiss and Koch. Research results, once obtained, should be reasonably applied.

An example of such an application is surgical asepsis, a supplementation of the organism's natural defenses based on knowledge of the mechanisms of infection and the behavior of bacteria. Another example is antisepsis, which becomes increasingly necessary the more unusual the circumstances are. Hospitals, for example, are characterized by extreme conditions in the relationship between patients and the environment, as was mentioned above.

Of course, there are also irrational responses to our knowledge of bacteria, for example, fear of germs. The extension of antisepsis to every aspect of daily life merely upsets a person's normal relationship with the environment. In addition, it hurts the frequently beneficial saprophytes more than it does pathogenic germs or spores, and, like the indiscriminate use of antibiotics, effects a negative selection. Hygiene has here run amok.

The prophylaxis of infectious diseases is today usually equated with vaccination. The issues surrounding this problem are extraordinarily manifold, and far exceed the scope of this discussion. Even today these questions are seldom discussed without emotion, showing that convictions often play a greater role than insight.

Although vaccinations have caused dramatic decreases in the incidence of some diseases and in some cases even eliminated them entirely, the factors underlying the appearance of disease have not necessarily been overcome. The result, as in therapy, can be a relapse or, more insidiously, a suppression, which in fact represents the greater problem.

Here we are referring to more than just the continual appearance of new strains over the course of time. This phenomenon, vividly exemplified by influenza, should not be surprising when one considers the inexhaustible mutability of bacteria and viruses. Even a polyvalent approach can do little more than postpone susceptibility to a new form. Furthermore, if bacteria are prevented from provoking a disease, viruses can take their place (as in pneumonia).

The more serious consequence of suppression is the substitution of one kind of disease in human development for another. The infectious diseases are an opportunity for the human beings to develop in their relation with the world both physically and mentally. If the diseases do not occur at the proper time, then important changes in the constitution fail to take place and the organism is left in a state of relative weakness. This has its most serious effect on the balance between inflammatory and sclerotic diseases in the course of life, a balance that has become increasingly disturbed. More specifically, the prevention of relatively harmless diseases, such as the childhood diseases, prepares the ground for later, more severe illnesses, such as cancer. No statistical study is needed to recognize this: its reality has long since been established (see vol. I, pp. 187f.). The times demand that the meaning and duality of the disease process be recognized.

The realization that suppression of mild illness leads to a more sever one is far from new; it is as old as Plato, who clearly describes the effect of inappropriate treatment on the disease process: "If anyone, disregarding their [diseases'] appointed course, tries to subdue these with medicines, then mild diseases tend to become serious ones, and rare ones frequent. Wherefore we ought to manage them by our conduct of life, as far as a man can spare the time, and not stir up an intractable evil with medicines."[65]

Although these relationships are clearly recognized today (e.g. by Bock), no practical consequences result. "In modern therapy there is even the absurd phenomenon that the curable is made incurable by iatrogenic effects, e.g. by inducing resistance, sensitizing to allergies, inoculation and other side effect.[66] It should be added that it is not side effects that cause the problems, but intended effects, e.g. inappropriate fever reduction in minor infections and childhood diseases, as we have repeatedly shown.

The mere prevention of disease is no more a measure of a treatment's value than is fever reduction. The striving to exterminate disease at any price is motivated by the view of disease as an unnecessary interruption of the business of life. Such a view cannot be allowed to persist. Intelligent judgments will be impossible as long as the deeper meaning of disease, which the foregoing arguments have attempted to establish, is not generally recognized. This is particularly true of the childhood diseases, which in a very real sense mold the constitution of the developing human being. The substitution of sclerotic diseases for inflammatory ones, which is due in large part to inappropriate therapy, shows that the childhood diseases cannot be rendered harmless even when they are suppressed. Doubtless a certain risk is involved in letting them run their course; the necessity of that has already been discussed. Nevertheless, when the disease is prudently guided and supported through the appropriate therapy, the risk is small.

Every vaccination by its very nature places a strain on the organism, the magnitude of which can vary greatly and which must be weighed against the equally variable benefits. Well-intentioned investigators have frequently minimized the risks of inoculation in their zeal to protect against the supposed danger of the disease. A good example of this is the

---

65. Plato, Timaeus, 89 B and C

66. H.E. Bock, "Therapie des Unheilbaren," Schweiz. med. Wochenschrift 100: 2049-2056. Both quotes in G. Kienle, Arzneimittelsicherheit und Gesellschaft. Stuttgart/New York: 1974. This book provides a basic discussion of the problem of infection and of contemporary therapeutic thinking.

smallpox vaccination, which is documented by an extensive literature. Although this disease has totally disappeared, the literature is of heuristic value, especially since the vaccination has had considerable impact on the life of many individuals. "One must reckon with some form of brain damage in one out of every four thousand children vaccinated."[67] The lethal complications must also be considered.[68] And although it is asserted that the contagion was held in check by the vaccination, this factor, while doubtlessly real, is only a small part of the whole picture. More important were hygienic measures and the course of the disease itself, following its own inherent laws. The duration and strength of the protection afforded by the vaccination, which is by no means 100% effective, remain an open question. The true issues involved lie on a deeper level than the usual simplistic and seldom unbiased discussions might suggest. One may recall, for example, the phenomenon of the "developmental break" (Entwicklungsknick), in which previously acquired capacities are lost after inoculatory complications, an event that easily escapes notice, especially in childhood. Such things vary for each disease and for each vaccination.

Today the need to weigh risks against benefits is widely recognized, but the potential benefits of disease and the risk of being deprived of a chance to take a significant step in emotional and spiritual development are generally not. Present-day discussions ignore the core issues surrounding disease. Of course, most diseases pose a greater risk than the corresponding vaccinations, but it must also be realized that any developmental step, any gain in capacities, is necessarily coupled with exertion, and hence with the danger that the burden will be too great. Life without risk precludes any real development: this is a question of freedom. One hundred percent safety would leave no free space for the human being's development.

Vaccinations should not be categorically rejected, just as they should not be indiscriminately recommended. Still, one must realize that the

67. H. Doose and U. Eckel, DMW 93(1968):2263.

68. It is estimated that one out of every 62,500 smallpox vaccinations results in a fatality (Trüb, Posch, Richter, Med. Mschr. 26 (1972):118). Here again, such figures are dependent on time and other factors. For example, in the Federal Republic of Germany between 1956 and 1965, an average of twelve fatalities due to vaccination complications were registered per year, while for the period from 1961 through 1965 the average was 3.8 per year (Ehrengut, Deutsches Ärzteblatt Oct. 21, 1971, p. 2871).

regression of diphtheria, for example, is not due to the antitoxin serum nor did vaccination have any influence on fatalities due to pertussis, as those familiar with this area already know and generally admit.[69] The same applies to scarlet fever, which though it did not disappear, has completely lost its menace in recent decades. It is also true of the decline of tuberculosis, pneumonia, and likewise of most epidemics.

These facts have already been discussed in detail. However, it is indisputable that the regression of poliomyelitis was due to the oral vaccine (Sabin). In contrast to the vaccination by injection (Salk), this approach imitated the physiological mode of infection. Polio was limited to countries with a high standard of living, partly due to misguided notions of hygiene. The administration of weakened viruses imitates infection by the fecal-oral route, the mode of infection typical of more primitive living conditions. Despite this obvious success, however, it must be stressed that the modern constitutional oversensitivity of the nervous system remains completely unaltered (see the section on polio in chapter 3, page 147).

Even a highly effective, low-risk vaccine does not necessarily address the constitutional factors underlying disease. We must learn to distinguish between cases where a vaccine merely prevents a disease from manifesting—resulting in suppression and possible reappearance in another form—and those where the underlying disorder has in fact been overcome.

A comprehensive prophylaxis will thus not only consider the customary hygienic measures, but will subordinate them to a full understanding of the human being. It will not merely document physical and biochemical "successes," but will also take mind and spirit into account as concrete realities. To do so, however, it will have to see the phenomenon of disease in the whole context of human development.

69. F. Höring, editorial in MMW 17 (1976)

II

The Causes and Treatment of Cancer

ALEXANDRE LEROI & RITA LEROI
Revised by OTTO WOLFF

Organism and Cell

DURING THE INITIAL PHASES of embryonic development, an bilateral division of cells takes place, manifesting the fundamental principle of the cell: multiplication. The fundamental principle of the cell, namely, multiplication, now takes place. In this activity, however, the cell's part in the human body's development is then basically exhausted. The intensity of cell multiplication is so rapid during the early phase that the maternal organism would soon be overwhelmed and would have to perish were it not for the emergence of a second principle, namely, structuring forces.

Structuring forces hold the proliferating cell material in check. These forces organize the cell material spatially and differentiate it, thus limiting multiplication. The structuring of the embryo is initially brought about not by forces inherent in the embryo but by forces in its sheaths; these forces are the point of impact for the formative forces of the etheric body, the astral body and the ego. In the course of embryonic development, the connection between these formative forces and the embryo, and the permeation of the embryo by these forces, grow stronger, reaching a temporary culmination at birth.

The tension between cell principle and structuring forces is at its highest during embryonic development. The latter can be seen at work in the incessant changes of forms, the former in the rapid increase of size.

For our discussion it is significant that the development of the head, in terms of size and internal differentiation, is by far more advanced than all remaining development. The sense organs and central nervous system are already very nearly complete at birth (whereas the lung, for example, must increase twenty-twofold in volume between birth and maturity). The degree to which they have become a perfect replica of the human spiritual entity will not be attained by any other part of the body in its subsequent development. For this reason the ego and astral body, and to a lesser extent also the etheric body, can gradually withdraw from their *organ forming* activity in the nerve sense organization during postnatal development. Their gradual release is traceable by the emergence of mental and spiritual capacities in the growing human being. In this area the cell principle has been overcome: the ganglion cells are so strongly differentiated that they have lost their capacity to regenerate. Hence proliferative cell growth in this region is rare; it occurs only in the neuroglia active in the metabolism, and is only rarely malignant in the sense of metastasizing. Development has here come to rest; the tension between "pressing" cellular growth and formative forces no longer exists.

The digestive system, on the other hand, presents a different picture entirely. This system, as yet unfinished at birth, does adjust in the course of the first few years to conditions on earth, but never attains the differentiated structure of the nerve-sense system. It never finishes. Tension between cell growth and the supersensible human being remains in force here throughout life. Cell material is continuously destroyed, new material is formed and differentiated, and again used up by the activity of the organs. Here, the ego, astral body, and etheric body are organically active and involved, as they were in the entire organism during embryonic development. The correct balance between cell proliferation and organic structuring must be continuously reestablished. If the balance is upset in such a way that the higher constituents cannot become active, undifferentiated cell growth sets in. It is therefore understandable that this region, together with the reproductive organs (where special conditions obtain as well) accounts for almost half of all human cancers.

The organs of the thorax, which form the basis of the human rhythmic system, occupy a middle position both in terms of the tension between proliferation and structuring and of the incidences of cancers. The rapid increase in lung cancer observed in recent decades becomes comprehensible on the one hand through the lung's nature and the change in the form of pneumonia, as described in the chapter dealing with the lung. On the other hand, lung cancer is likewise largely due to environmental influences (e.g., cigarette smoke, automobile exhaust, etc.).

While embryology explains the relative frequency of malignant tumors in various parts of the body, an examination of life between birth and death leads to a comprehension of cancer in its relation to the aging process.

The urge to be active on earth leads the human individuality through birth into earthly existence. With the help of the parental zygote it builds itself a bodily sheath. To attain consciousness of its spiritual and emotional nature, however, it must eventually partially free itself again from the body. Perception of the outer world, ideation, thinking, remembering, the appearance of feelings in a person's consciousness are contingent on a certain degree of withdrawal by the higher constituents from their structuring activity in the physical organism. Catabolic and excretory processes are the physiological expression of the free activity of mind and spirit. In death, the spiritual individuality frees itself from the instrument that has made its earthly existence possible; it surrenders the body to destructive natural forces. Death is thus another milestone on the path to complete spiritualization.

Birth and death are merely special stages on the path to incarnation and spiritualization. The "birth forces" regenerate the body until the end of life; the "death forces" start breaking the body down at the very moment of birth. We have described how the ego, astral body, and etheric body fully form the head organization, then withdraw from the finished instrument and utilize it for mental activity. The head thus becomes the human being's pole of consciousness, or, from the point of view of the organism, the center of the death processes. In the metabolic region, the higher constituents further build up the body; the activity of the higher constituents that leads to birth is continued here. Tendencies toward hardening, deposition, and cold work down from the head pole into the organism. They are stopped by the life processes that press upward from the metabolic processes (see the descriptions both in vol. I of the English edition, as well as in the first volume of the German edition).

As it ages, the human organism becomes more "head-like" in character. The body cools and stiffens and blood vessels harden. The soul-spiritual part of the human being gradually withdraws from its anabolic activity in the body. Emotional life can begin to free itself more easily from its attachment to bodily processes, the possibility of unfolding a spiritual life becomes greater.

However, this withdrawal process can have pathological consequences as well. Everywhere in the body, its substance can begin to escape the higher constituents' structuring activity and be deposited; this is indicated in excessive fat formation, uric acid deposits, calculus formations etc.

The following situation then comes about in the organism. The cells—the body's basic substance that is endowed with autonomous life—have suffered a loss in regenerative capacity through decades of the action of formative forces upon them. The organs as a whole harden and become overly formed. The tension that existed in youth between the cell's proliferative tendency and the formative impulse of the higher constituents begins to slacken. A new equilibrium with less tension develops.

Just as substances become alienated from the organism and form concretions, the life of the cells in the organism can become independent. While regenerating, the cells then no longer develop correctly and begin to grow unchecked. It becomes obvious why cancer is a disease of age, and also why geriatric cancer is less malignant than cancer in young people.

Essential to an understanding of cancer is the fact that the tumor does not represent a part of the human organism as such; rather, it appears through a rebellion of the inherent cell element against the organism. A tumor is a living foreign substance within the organism. Its pathognomonic significance lies in the fact that the organism tolerates it, meaning, it does not resist it or recognize it as something foreign.

Now we first need to understand the role of the cell within the healthy organism, then we have to trace the disease process that finally leads to a process of independence of cell life within the organism. Microscopy has made it possible to ignore this larger organic context and focus on the problem of the "first malignant cell." Only thus could the riddle of the "egoistic cancer cell" arise. As long as we see in the cell the *cause* rather than the *condition* of the organism's existence, as long as we seek the *origin* of cancer in the first tumor cell, the problem of cancer cannot be solved.

> Cancer is no more a disease of cells than a traffic jam is a disease of cars. A lifetime study of the internal combustion engine would not help anyone to understand our traffic problems.... A traffic jam is due to a failure of the normal relationship between driven cars and their environment." In the same way "cancer is a disease of the organism and not a disease of the cells.[1]

As early as 1920, Rudolf Steiner drew attention to the relation of the cell to the organism:

> For what is the cell? It stubbornly asserts its own growth, its own life against that of the human being. If you look at the human being's overall form ... and then turn your attention to the cell, you will see that the cell destroys formative influences in the interest of unfolding its own life. The human organism is engaged in a constant struggle against the life of the cell. The views of cellular therapy and cellular pathology, namely, that cells are the basis of all life, and that the human organism is but a buildup of cells, could not be more crassly absurd. Rather, the human being is a totality connected with the cosmos and must continuously fight against the stubbornness of the cells. In essence, the cell continuously disturbs our organism instead of building it up.[2]

When these words were spoken more than seven decades ago, researchers were even more optimistic than they are now about describing the organism from the cell. When animal cells were first seen through the microscope, scientists imagined the entire pre-formed embryo to be inside the egg cell. When this theory proved untenable, the emphasis was shifted instead to the cell nucleus, and then to the chromosomes. Now genes are seen as the factor determining the growth of cells into an organism. But although the genes, that is the DNA structures, are the bearers of the hereditary process, they are in no way autonomous, meaning, they do not determine that process, nor do they change it through arbitrary mutation. Rather, they serve as "material" with which the human being's higher constituents seek to realize the intentions of that individuality within the hereditarily prescribed possibilities.

1. D. W. Smithers, *On the Nature of Neoplasia in Man.* Edinburgh and London 1964.
2. R. Steiner, *Spiritual Science and Medicine*, lecture 7.

Several well-known experiments demonstrate that the cell plays a passive rather than an active role in the development and functioning of the organism.

Spemann's brilliant experiments conducted at the beginning of this century highlight these relationships in many regards. For example, he showed that medial constriction or complete severance of a newt egg in the blastula stage results not in two half newts, but in two normal embryos. The formative forces of the organism shape the cellular material into two complete organisms. Interestingly, these well-formed embryos are only half the normal size, a further indication that the cells provide no more than the "raw material."

In experiments with mature newt gastrulae, it was possible surgically to exchange cells destined to form the medullar plate with cells destined for the epidermis. The substance destined for the medullar plate formed epidermis at its new location, while the substance destined for the epidermis formed a medullar plate.

It is, moreover, significant for our viewpoint that cells do not divide as long as they exercise their function, for example, as glandular cells. While incorporated into the functional order of the organism, they cannot pursue their own life. Functions usually thought to be cellular, such as bile secretion, are in reality life functions of the *organism.* Another interesting fact is that differentiated cells become morphologically and functionally undifferentiated outside the organism; no production of organ-specific secretions takes place in vitro. Tissue samples cultured under conditions favorable to growth generally dedifferentiate and show a tendency to proliferate. By contrast, unfavorable conditions often bring about renewed differentiation. Redifferentiation also occurs when tissue is successfully retransplanted into the organism.

C.A Braun[3] reports about an interesting set of experiments designed to test the possibility of transforming tumor cells back into normal ones by altering the environment in which the tumor grows. He used Crowngal tumors, which are produced on tobacco plants by a bacterium and in many ways resemble cancerous tumors. Braun found that when cells of a teratoma (a somewhat modified form of the Crowngal tumor) are grafted onto a healthy tobacco plant, they grow in a somewhat more

3. C. A. Braun, *Scientific American* 213 (1965), p. 75–83.

orderly fashion. Grafted from there to another healthy plant, they start to bring forth primitive leaves and shoots; the latter, when transplanted to a third plant, grow normally. Furthermore, seeds produced by these shoots germinate into healthy plants. Thus, through successive transplantations, the *tumor's proliferative growth* was gradually *checked.* By contrast, similar Crowngal tumor cells were cultured in vitro for over ten years without showing the slightest change.

In the same article, Braun describes tests on newts. The newts, after being injected subcutaneously with various carcinogens, developed large infiltrating and metastasizing tumors that quickly led to death. However, when small pieces of tail were removed and the animals' regenerative processes were thus stimulated—newts are known for their capacity to regenerate an injured or lost tail—tumors in the vicinity of the base of the tail suddenly stopped growing, and cancerous cells reverted back to normal cells. These experiments offer further evidence of the reciprocal relationship between cell and organism.

An impressive demonstration of the autonomous life led by malignant tumors is found in the experiments conducted by *Ehrlich* on the mouse carcinoma bearing his name:

> About seventy years ago *Hanau* discovered that a small percentage of spontaneous animal tumors can be transplanted to other animals of the same species, and that the process can be repeated ad infinitum. One of the oldest carcinomas being cultured in this way is the Ehrlich carcinoma, an adenocarcinoma of the mouse. A mouse that develops this carcinoma by inoculation survives an average of fourteen days. This carcinoma has been under continuous culture now for more than forty years [ninety as of this publication] and lives on today at various institutes. Rather than in mice, this tumor can also be cultured in vitro. *A. Fischer* (1939) cultured carcinoma cells (from Ehrlich's mouse carcinoma) continuously in this way for over twelve years, transferring them over eight thousand times, and upon retransplanting them into mice obtained the same carcinoma.[4]

This strikingly demonstrates that the tumor lives independently of the organism and that in the proper nutrient medium it can not only survive within limits but also reproduce itself indefinitely.

Just as we can observe how the formative forces of the human body overcome the cellular material in a series of distinct physiological stages by differentiating it and reducing its tendency to proliferate, so too we

4. K. H. Bauer, *Das Krebsproblem* (1949), p. 108.

see how a pathological emancipation of cells from the organism proceeds in diverse stages.

When a wound heals, a period of intense cell proliferation occurs, followed by a new balance of less intense cell division at the scar than that which existed earlier in the undamaged tissue. However, the balance can also be upset in favor of the cell principle. The result is "proud flesh," an as yet harmless deviation.

We encounter a different disturbance when benign tumors appear. An organ becomes larger; the suppression of cell proliferation has partly failed, but the ability of cells to differentiate has been maintained.

In malignant tumors, the disturbance is more radical. Here, the formative forces of the tissue have likewise failed, the cells dedifferentiate. Something takes place in the organism that is similar to what we observe in the in vitro culture of tissue outside the organism. Once again, the cell principle can freely develop, the tissue loses the pattern imposed on it by the organ.

We need to remember:

Malignant Tumor: Disturbance of form on level of tissue.
Benign New Formation: Disturbance of form on level of organ.
Malformation: Disturbance of form on level of organism.

Experimental cancer research has shown that the shift toward malignancy takes place within regenerating tissue, that is, in as yet undifferentiated cells. *Skarzynski* gives a striking description of one such process:

> In animal tests, a carcinogenic carbohydrate compound was locally applied. This first led to cellular damages with fatty degeneration and subsequently to formation of extensive necrotic foci. "The spreading cell damage and necrosis evoke regenerative processes, and for a time only inflammatory symptoms are observed that soon become chronic. At this stage, all newly produced cells and tissue are biologically identical to the ones destroyed. Only after some time do cells develop that show signs of a disturbance in chromatin balance; they are dedifferentiated and incompletely matured, with highly variegated nuclei, but still altogether benign. Only following a shorter or longer period, completely atypical tissue suddenly appears, with polymorphic cells and signs of a deep disturbance in chromatin balance. These cells multiply rampantly. The *nuclear instability* cited by

> *Borst* as a sign of malignant transformation now reaches the stage of a true *nuclear revolution (Rondini).* Thus the transition from quasi-dormant regenerative tissue into a rapidly growing tumor occurs quite suddenly.[5]

The moment the cell succeeds in freeing itself from the domination of the higher constituents, it becomes "external world" even inside the organism. The tumor follows its own laws of growth, respiration, and so on, and thus inevitably enters into opposition to the organism. Rudolf Steiner refers to these relationships as follows:

> It is not altogether right to speak of tumorous formations as 'new formations' [neoplasms]. It is valid at best in the quite trivial sense that they were not there before, but properly speaking they are not formations of the organism that lies within the cover of our skin. Rather, through a certain (cell) process, the physical body enters so strongly into opposition to the etheric body that it subordinates itself in a sense to the external world, to the hostile world of outer nature; in this way tumor formation opens the door to all kinds of outer influences.[6]

Organism and Environment

Up to this point we have considered the human organism's constituent forces in their relation to cells. In so doing, we have indicated the reasons for the frequency of cancers in the metabolic region as well as for the increasing incidence of cancer with advancing age. In order to understand the factors that initiate the cancerous process, we must now examine the relation of the human organism to nature.

Our bodily organization is subject on the one hand to the influence of our psychological and spiritual constituents and on the other to our natural and manmade environment. Man's soul-spiritual being and outer nature encounter each other in the bodily organization. Through the senses, breathing, and nutrition, our soul-spiritual being enters into relation with the environment. The organism has not originated

5. H. von Euler & B. Skarzynski, *Biologie der Tumoren* (1942), pp. 114–145.
6. Rudolf Steiner, *Spiritual Science and Medicine*, lecture 13.

through the environmental influences, rather, what approaches our body here tends only to destroy it when not suitably checked and transformed. When a direct continuation of these influences occurs, and if "nature" works unchecked with its own principles in the human body, it will destroy it in the end. In this way, diseases such as allergy, intoxication, infection, etc., appear.

On the other hand, human beings could not exist on earth were they not continually confronted with the surrounding world in the form of food, air, and sensations. Our organism thus needs two things to survive: first, as its life basis, it needs the influences of outer nature, which are hostile to it; second, it needs to overcome these, to metamorphose them through processes of decomposition that are based on the activity of the astral body.

Digestion, since it occurs on a coarse, material level, offers us the most obvious picture of the human being's relation to the natural world. We ingest food from the various kingdoms of nature, but as yet it does not penetrate the organism because the walls of the stomach and intestines prevent it from invading the organism proper. In the digestive organization with its glands we have a highly differentiated decomposition system for the ingested food (see vol. I, pp. 214ff and Ger. vol. I, page 163ff). This whole highly differentiated tract is necessary to divest ingested "nature" of its own forces: mechanical crushing, enzymes, acids and alkaloids etc. invade the food. If this divestiture is not successful and the substance does pass through the intestinal wall, poisoning of the organism occurs. Poisons are substances that maintain their characteristic quality in opposition to the [host] organism. The whole activity of the digestive glands can be viewed as the organism's material reaction to its being penetrated, through food, by external nature.

Overcoming these influences is a basic requisite of human existence. This always takes place through the metabolic system, either in a coarse, material way in digestion or more subtly in the metabolic activities of our nerve-sense organization. For not even light, sound, or warmth and so on may convey their effects unchanged into the organism without the latter constantly overcoming and balancing such "intoxications". The fact that a continuous, subconscious activity does take place is shown by the phenomenon of colored after-images: the human organism reacts with "green" to the perception of "red"; it responds to "yellow" with "violet" and so on. In this sense, it is possible to speak of light as being "digested" in the eye and likewise in the skin. A primitive defense mechanism arises through the skin's pigmentation. If the organism is not capable of this, injuries result.

In relation to the outer world, human beings are organized differently at the nerve-sense pole than they are at the metabolic pole. In the intestinal tract, the secretions generated in the glands are passed on to the food; they take hold of and pervade it. Only then does the encounter occur with the organism's inner nature, the blood, which flows through the capillary network on the inner surface of the intestine.

The relationships are different in the sense organs. Here, the blood has withdrawn from the surface. The development of the sense organs occurred through the participation of the formative forces of light, of sound and so on. We can observe how the capillary network spreads out only behind the organ, how the formation of the ear, for example, has obviously been sculpted from the outside into the bone. In the case of the eye, we see how the wall of bone forms behind the eye so that the eye lies outside the capsule of the skull. In the region of the senses we confront "organized outer world." Rudolf Steiner called the sense organs "gulfs of the outside world." The formative activity of the higher constituents predominates here in an extreme way over the cell material, just as it does in the entire head, as mentioned earlier (German vol. I, page 158). If this were not so, these locations would be particularly cancer prone.

This configuration of the higher constituents, which is the basis of the nerve-sense system, can extend pathologically beyond its own sphere. It then leads to catabolic tendencies that become evident in vascular sclerosis and kidney or gall stones. The latter result when forces of the human organization withdraw too early from waste products, allowing them to act according to purely physical laws while they are still within the organism. The crystalline structure of some concretions clearly attests to this.

A much more serious situation arises when portions of the body that are not on the way to being eliminated slip away from the higher human constituents. This can result from an overly powerful invasion by natural laws that makes it impossible for the higher constituents to penetrate certain parts of the body. In the metabolic region, we then confront a pathological situation, namely, a relationship of the higher constituents to the metabolic region that resembles the one we find in the sense organs in a physiological manner. We are then faced with a rudimentary "sense organ." The difference lies in the fact that with normal sense organ formation, cell material is differentiated and devitalized, whereas this is not the case in the metabolic region. This then leads directly to the possibility that cell material can begin rampantly to proliferate in the latter. On a number of occasions, Rudolf Steiner described the process underlying the development of cancer as the formation of a rudimentary sense organ at an improper location. One such description is quoted here:

> It can also happen that the dynamics, the forces active in a sense organ, forces that must be active there to a certain extent for the sense organ to come into being, become engaged at the wrong place. What is at work in a sense organ can likewise become engaged, transformed in some way, at another point. Let us take the activity of the ear. This activity, instead of occurring in the nerve-sense system, can (under conditions that can be described) be imposed upon another region, let us say somewhere in the metabolic system, where the latter joins the rhythmic system. An abnormal tendency toward a sense organ then arises at the wrong place. This appears as carcinoma, as cancer formation. Only by comprehending the human organization in this way can we recognize that in cancer we have, as it were, a dislocated tendency to form sense organs that extend over all systems.[7]

This observation leads us to an understanding of the causation of cancer by external agents, otherwise known as carcinogens. Perhaps the easiest situation to understand is one in which a cancerous growth appears as a result of repeated burns. In a burn, a part of the body is alienated from the organism by the destruction of tissue, it becomes "outer world." The organism then demarcates this zone, the intensified activity becomes evident through inflammation processes. Finally, the substance

7. Rudolf Steiner, *What Can the Art of Healing Learn through Spiritual Science?* (Spring Valley, N.Y.: Mercury Press, 1986), lectures 2 and 3.

that has become foreign to the body is cast off, the defect is repaired as best as possible according to the organism's inherent structural plan. During the healing phase, both organism and cell material are unusually active. For structure to be restored, initially undifferentiated cells must be differentiated into connective tissue, capillaries, epithelial cells, and so on. If a scar forms during the healing process, this is a sign that in this zone the original conditions are disturbed, that the organism's formative forces could not reform the affected area any more.

If injury through a burn occurs repeatedly, the moment can come when the cooperation between the organism's constituents is so disturbed that regenerative cell material is no longer seized and differentiated into the form. Experimental cancer research has shown that the transition from regenerating tissue to a carcinoma does not occur slowly but all at once, as described above. The locally proliferating cell damage and necrosis causes regeneration processes. For a while, infectious phenomena are observed that soon become chronic. In this process, the only cells and tissue to appear are those that are identical in their biological characteristics to the ones that were destroyed.

Through a reoccurring burn the affected area becomes increasingly impervious to the organism's formative forces, until the moment arrives when newly formed cell material escapes integration into the organism's form. The suppressed growth potential of the cells can work out unimpeded and very quickly. A rapidly growing tumor results. This is due as much to a disturbance of the balance between organism and cell brought about by repeated burns as it is to purely cellular processes.

The attempt to explain carcinogenesis in terms of the action of specific external factors on the cell has made the search for cancer-causing substances an important branch of cancer research. Endless efforts have been made to produce cancer artificially. What was sought was a specific effect on the cell mechanism that is common to all such substances and turns the benign cell into a malignant cell. This branch of research brought unexpected results. Within a few decades, hundreds of substances were discovered that were sooner or later capable of producing cancer. Chemically or physically, no common denominator for the great variety could be found. But they did seem to have one thing in common: they were found to be substances or radiation produced purely by human beings themselves and that "enter the organism of modern humans in the most various ways without encountering a natural defense or adaptive reaction... The original natural products or parent substances (e.g. in coal, in various kinds of dust, etc.) are not carcinogenic themselves. For the most part, cancer-producing substances are artificial products of technological processing.... The great majority of these substances have no relation to living substance whatsoever."[8]

Carcinogens (chemicals, radiation, viruses) produce certain alterations in the genome, which of themselves are not sufficient to cause malignant growth.[9] Only when particular promoters or cocarcinogens (certain hormones, chemicals, barbiturates, etc.) are present do affected cells progress from the stage of initiation to that of promotion. This transition, however, is reversible, provided the cocarcinogens have not yet acted for too long a time. Realization, that is, the irreversible progression from precancerous to an invasive tumor, occurs only as the result of the continued action of cancer-promoting agents. The whole process can extend over decades or occur quite suddenly. Its rapidity and extent depend on the overall state of the organism, the tumor's opponent, especially its immunological defenses. If these defenses are weakened, if the form-preserving forces of the ego organization slacken, then the unstable equilibrium between the organism and cellular multiplication shifts in favor of the latter.

This gives us an essential indication for the causes of carcinogenesis. The primary factor is not cell damage but rather a local disturbance of the order of the higher constituents. Whether this disturbance is caused by burns, radiation, chemicals, or by several factors working together is ultimately unimportant for the solution of the cancer problem. Such knowledge will have only prophylactic value. The truly crucial insight is that the organism is not in a position to "digest" the invading environment, so that "gulfs of the outside world" (Rudolf Steiner) develop in it.

The human organism and the environment in which it lives have a certain relationship with each other. Our organism is well adapted to handle the forces and substances that are ingested through sense

8. K. H. Bauer, *Das Krebsproblem* (Berlin, Göttingen, Heidelberg: 1963), p. 418.
9. E. Grundmann, "Die Kanzerogenese als Folge einer stufenweisen Gleichgewichtsstörung." Lecture at the annual meeting of the Deutsche Akademie der Naturforscher, Leopoldina, Halle (Saale), 1983.

organs, air, and food. For some decades, however, we have been exposed to an increasing number of influences against which our organism has no such natural defenses. We are able to produce synthetic substances that have been tested for toxicity, teratogeny, carcinogenesis and tolerance. But no matter how "safe" such substances appear, every use of them represents an incursion of the outer world into the organism, an incursion for which the organism is not prepared—in contrast with natural substances—and that it can therefore not absorb or only with difficulty. Yet human beings today are constantly exposed to such assaults. In food, we ingest hundreds of substances that have been added to our food through fertilization, pesticides, preservatives, and colorants, etc. By breathing, we take in gases from engine exhaust and so on. The insight is gradually dawning that even over-stimulation, particularly of eye and ear, represents a constant assault on the organism. In short, whether in a coarsely substantial or more delicate way, our organism is pervaded by foreign substances and alien processes that make a proper hold on our bodily instrument more difficult and alienate the body from man's soul-spiritual nature.

The cancer problem, therefore, is ultimately a question of properly taking hold of and penetrating the physical body with the human soul-spiritual entity or, expressed differently, a problem of proper incarnation. The potent influences of modern civilization act on the body from all sides, pervading it with substances and effects that bind it too strongly to the earth. We are alienated from the rhythmical element that unites us with cosmic processes. Artificial lights blur the rhythm of day and night; in nutrition, the annual rhythm is destroyed in nutrition through refrigeration, canning and rapid transport. This is correspondingly true of air conditioning homes. "Striding," the rhythmic movement of the limbs that is so important for the whole organism, is being forgotten because of modern means of transportation and frequently machine-dependent movements in work environments. The rhythmic system, the foundation of our emotional life, is constantly being disturbed. The metabolic-limb system is no longer thoroughly penetrated from within by the human ego, while the nerve-sense system is exposed to excessive demands.

What can be done in this situation, which perforce leads to an ever increasing disposition to cancer and ultimately to increased appearances of malignant tumors?

One key is *nutrition*. Both the food processing industry and agriculture contribute to the problem. The awareness exists that links to the problem of cancer exist here. There have been initial positive steps toward a healthy diet in many areas. The biodynamic method of agriculture inaugurated by Rudolf Steiner can make a significant contribution here once the public is fully aware of the nutritional problem.

Further help can come from the *educational system*. In current education, the children suffer from the fact that the forces of the nerve-sense system are overtaxed. This actually prevents human beings from being able to take hold of their rhythmic and metabolic-limb system in the proper ways. By training the artistic faculties of children, on the other hand, which produces an emotional life that is ego penetrated; through developing handwork skills that draw the perceptual all the way down into the children's limbs, a proper way of taking hold of the physical body is prepared. Waldorf School pedagogy is particularly suited to strengthening human beings at an early age, enabling them better to withstand the unavoidable negative influences of the modern environment.

Adults can likewise do a lot to counteract these pathological tendencies arising through today's civilization. An intensified onslaught of environmental factors must be counteracted by a strengthening of the human soul-spiritual nature. In the artistic domain, all art, and particularly *eurythmy*, is especially suited for this. In becoming involved in eurythmy, in this art of movement, the body turns into a means of expressing soul experiences that underlie poetry and music. Finally, the exercises, for example, that Rudolf Steiner describes in such books as *How to Know Higher Worlds* (Anthroposophic Press, 1994), will help human beings through strengthening their soul-spiritual activity to assert their individuality within their bodies and thus prevent the cell element, which frees itself, from posing a threat to the *human form*. Here, the *Exercise of Retrospection* (see vol. II, page 26) deserves special mention. The cell element's process of achieving independence only becomes possible if, within the totality of the organism, that is, the etheric body, a part is "left vacant," which is not directed by astral body and ego. This is the case when soul-spiritually something is repressed. Through retrospection, the possibility that a mental problem can invade the organic realm is prevented.

The prophylaxis of cancer is ultimately a social issue. It will become possible only when in nutrition, education, and our cultural life the necessities of life for the *human being* are centered in the wider sense around the requirements that will have to be put in place.

Mistletoe and Cancer

In 1920, Rudolf Steiner introduced the mistletoe plant, *Viscum album*, into cancer therapy, along with a spiritual scientific rationale for its use.[10] In this plant he recognized a remedy that, if suitably prepared, can be an aid for strengthening the organism in its control over the cell principle. For an understanding of how mistletoe's effectiveness in botanical, pharmacological, clinical, and spiritual scientific studies have cast light, reference is made to available literature here [11] as well as the concluding remarks.

From the previous commentaries it becomes clear that in cancerous diseases the relationship between the whole organism and the external world is altered in the sense that the latter can no longer be fully overcome. This allows the outer world to unfold its influences as nature (or subnature) in the realm of the organism itself. As a result, the body's cellular substrate can thus free itself from the organism's formative forces, a situation that in the end leads to such phenomena as proud flesh and infiltrative growth, etc., i.e., to cancerous tumors. The renowned pathologist *Siegmund* rightly designates the malignant tumor as a "catastrophe of form."[12] In malignant growth, the boundary between the organism and nature no longer lies merely on the skin, in the sense organs, the inner intestinal wall, the lumina of the glands, but is now transferred into the physical body itself at the border between the tumors and the

10. Cancer patients were first injected with mistletoe preparations in 1917 and 1918 (Dr. Ita Wegman) at the suggestion of Rudolf Steiner. In 1920, in a series of lectures for doctors (*Spiritual Science and Medicine*, repr. (London: Rudolf Steiner Press, 1975), this therapy was explained in terms of spiritual science.

11. D. Boie, *Mistel und Krebs* (Stuttgart: 1970). See also O. Wolff, *Die Mistel in der Krebsbehandlung*, 3rd ed. (Frankfurt: 1985). R. Leroi, *Misteltherapie* (Stuttgart, 1987).

12. W. Zabel, *Ganzheitsbehandlung der Geschwulsterkrankungen* (Stuttgart: 1953), p. 33.

surrounding tissue. This is why Rudolf Steiner stated that a tumor does not originate from the basis of the organism. The tumor has justifiably been called a parasite of the organism. Its metabolism and respiration differ from those of the organism on which it lives; this makes it comprehensible why processes *within* the tumor are not felt as pain.

Possibilities for resisting a tumor are few in a cancer patient. After all, the tumor shows the end of a collaboration between the cell principle and the formative forces, as was described above. The necessary balance can shift so that after a struggle of many years the organism finally is defeated by the cells' proliferating growth tendencies. It was shown that this is a matter for the organism, not for the cells. Through research in the area of immunology the view concerning cancerous disorders is shifting from considering the exclusively local to considering the totality of the organism. We are faced with an anergy in the organism. At an international cancer congress in Moscow in 1962, *Fould* claimed that tumors are only the third stage of cancer, and that twenty to thirty years may go by from the actual beginning of the illness to the appearance of tumors.[13] It can only be guessed how often over the years the organism may have succeeded in defeating or stalemating a cancerous transformation of its cells. It is known, however, that precancerous pockets of cells compose up to 30% of benign tumors. In dissections of the prostate in older men, cancer cells are frequently found, although the patients had not suffered from cancer. "*Druckrey* therefore assumes cancerous degeneration of cells to be no rarity. He speaks of it as a 'natural biological event' that very likely occurs at least once in everyone's life, and perhaps even more often. 'Not every cancer carrier,' he says, 'is a cancer patient.'[14] In this connection, the necessary distinction between infection and infectious disease must be pointed out (see page 42), which here corresponds to the distinction between cancer and cancerous diseases. This means that cancerous afflictions are a matter of the whole organism, whereas the question of which organ becomes involved in the affliction is a secondary, local problem. Here, damaging incursions such as smoking/lungs, burns/skin, food/stomach and intestines, and so on

13. W. Kahlert, *Krebs, ein Bericht über den internationalen Krebskongress 1962 in Moskau* (Stuttgart: 1962).
14. Meythaler & Truckenbrodt. "Körpereigene Abwehr und Krebs," *Ärztliche Praxis XV* (1963), Jan. 5 and 12, 1963.

can turn an organ into a locus minoris resistentiae, so that the affliction breaks out there as a tumor.

Our organism, however, can keep cancer cells latent and even destroy them. Inflammations surrounding the tumor, for example, are evidence of a defensive reaction. The power of inflammatory processes to counteract tumor formation is shown by the occasional spontaneous cures of cancer that take place after erysipelas or other febrile diseases. Similarly, malignant tumors have occasionally been made to disappear through hyperthermia. These relationships were presented in detail in vol. I, p. 190ff with corresponding references. In the relatively young discipline of immunology in which the defensive processes are studied, the significance of fever or the inflammatory reaction as a polar process to the cancerous tendency is again attracting much attention.

The approach indicated by Rudolf Steiner for combating cancer by injection with preparations of *Viscum album* (Iscador) aims at strengthening the organism's forces in its struggle against the cell's tendency toward autonomy.[15] The goal generally is to strengthen the influences of ego, astral body, and etheric body upon the physical body and locally to reincorporate the 'lost province' into the organism, or, failing that, to help the organism eliminate it.

As can be observed through changes in body temperature, Iscador treatment intensifies the processes of the *ego organization* in cancer patients. Several hours after the injection—sometimes longer—the patient's body temperature rises. This reaction is important for determining the appropriate dose, and the extent of this reaction should be monitored by rectal measurement. The intensity, delay in onset, and duration of the elevation in temperature vary widely. It is not always possible to measure this rise in temperature. Depending on the patient, the delay in onset varies from one hour to two days. Once elevated, the temperature may return rapidly to normal (see figure 1), or may decline slowly over several days (see figure 2). Optimally, the amount of the ele-

15. See *Guidelines for the Use of Iscador*, published by the Society for Cancer Research, CH-4144 Arlesheim, Switzerland, and D7070 Schwäbisch Gmünd. This brochure is distributed to physicians only. Iscador is the oldest and most thoroughly tested preparation of *Viscum album*. Later, a number of other mistletoe preparations were developed (see "Indications" beginning on page 391).

vation should be between 0.3º to 1.0ºC and return to normal in 24 to 48 hours.

Frequently the cancer patient's average temperature, which is often distinctly low, gradually rises over the course of treatment, despite the lack of a pronounced reaction after any of the individual injections (see figures 3 and 4).

Tumors that lie close to the skin offer the best opportunity to observe the temperature reaction, since the area around the tumor can then be monitored by thermography or dermal thermometry (see figure 5). Instead of a temperature reaction, local erythema can develop. This can last from a few hours to a few days. In most cases this requires a pause or generally a dose reduction.

Temperature Reaction During Treatment with Iscador Injections

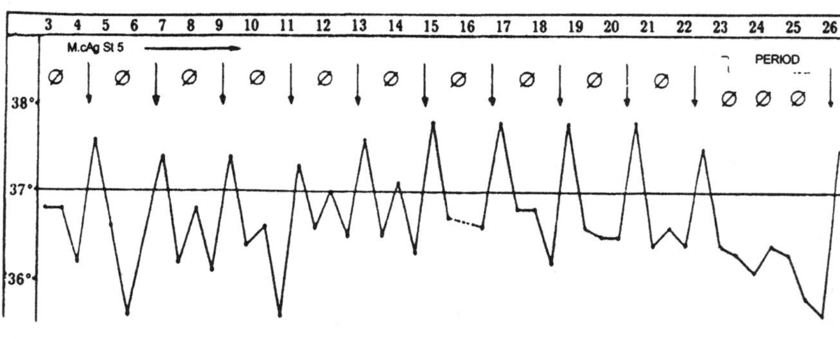

Figure 1. Pronounced (1.9º C) reaction of ordinary duration. Injections every other day. Reaction subsides after 24 hours.

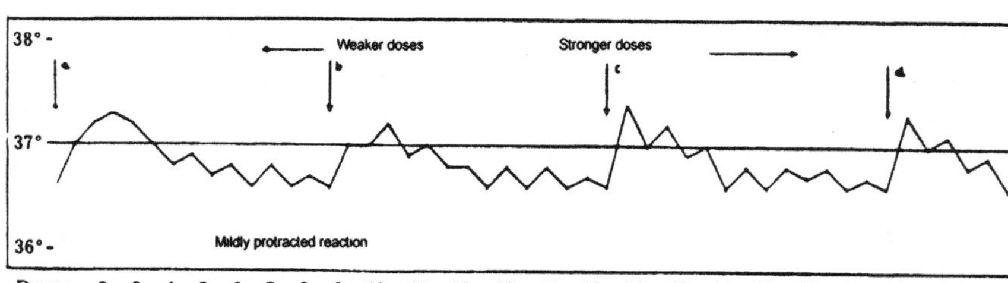

Figure 2. Strong (0.8º C) and slightly protracted reaction. Return to normal temperatures two days after injection.

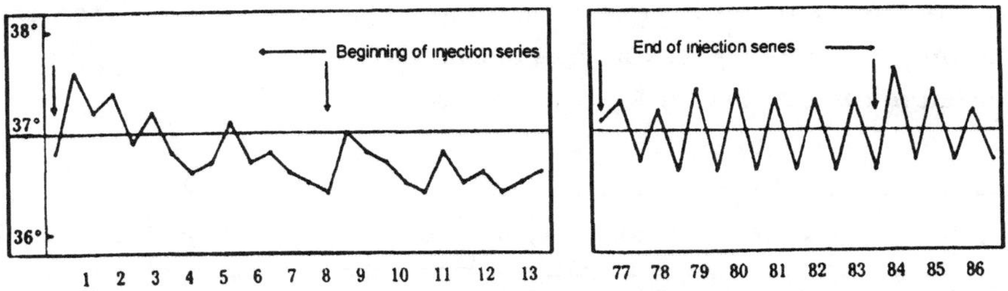

Figure 3. The temperature reaction in this case either did not occur or was not captured by the morning and afternoon auxiliary temperature measurement. The patient's average temperature was 0.2º C higher at the end than at the beginning. Furthermore, his daily variations in temperature assumed a more regular pattern.

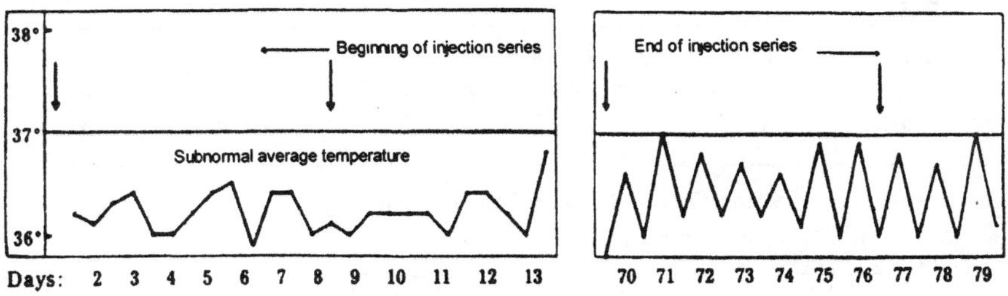

Figure 4. Temperature variations initially irregular, after treatment regular.

Just one hour after an injection—even if given as a test relatively far from the tumor—temperature differences of up to +2.0° could be observed as compared to the corresponding area on the healthy side of the body.

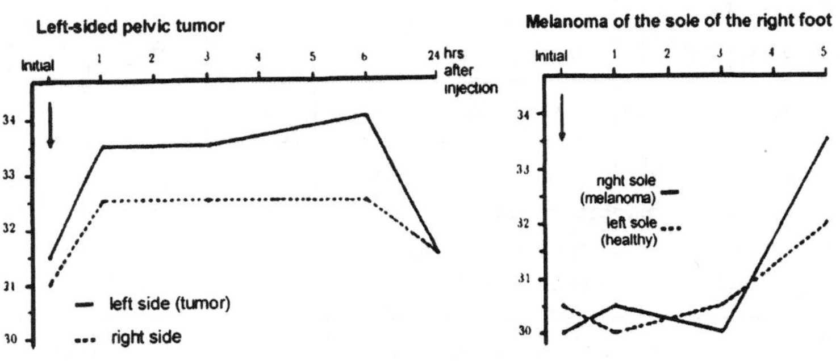

Figure 5. Skin temperature following injection of Iscador.

The tendency of the organism to have an inflammatory reaction to an Iscador injection can likewise be monitored by blood tests. Moreover, not only a temporary leukocytosis but moreover a pronounced shift to the left in cases of an overdose can be observed.

	Leuko	**Stab**	**Segm**	**Eo**	**Ba**	**Mono**	**Lympho**
Before inj.	5,650	5.5	67.6	2	0.5	3.0	21.5
1 hr. post	6,250	5.0	55.0	–	–	6.0	34.0
3 hrs. post	8,150	9.0	58.5	4.5	–	2.5	28.5
6 hrs. post	4,000	4.0	71.0	3.0	–	3.0	19.0
24 hrs. post	6,200	4.5	57.5	4.0	–	3.0	31.0
Desired reaction. Weak leukocytosis and shift to the left. Return to initial values after 24 hours.							

Table 1. Reactions to Iscador—Male with melanoma

	Leuko	**Stab**	**Segm**	**Eo**	**Ba**	**Mono**	**Lympho**
Before inj.	6,350	3.0	61.0	4.0	2.0	10.0	20.0
1 hr. post	7.850	6.5	76.0	1.5	–	5.5	10.5
3 hrs. post	10,550	6.0	71.0	1.0	–	9.0	13.0
6 hrs. post	12,000	1.0	78.0	1.0	–	7.0	13.0
24 hrs. post	6,150	2.0	60.0	1.5	–	10.6	26.0
Pronounced leukocytosis, mild shift to left. Return to initial values after 24 hours.							

Table 2. Reactions to Iscador—Female with breast cancer, resected

	Leuko	Stab	Segm	Eo	Ba	Mono	Lympho
Before inj.	8,700	6.5	79.5	0.5	0.5	2.5	10.5
1 hr. post	10,850	6.0	79.0	2.5	-	2.0	10.5
3 hrs. post	9,150	12.0	73.0	2.0	-	2.0	11.0
6 hrs. post	10,750	15.0	64.0	5.0	-	4.0	12.0
24 hrs. post	12,250	13.5	69.0	0.0	-	5.5	12.0
Overreaction with leukocytosis and shift to left even 24 hours after injection.							

Table 3. Reactions to Iscador—Female with malignant goiter

Observation of the temperature curve allows us to make inferences about the involvement of the ego organization as expressed in warmth processes. In cancer patients, the rhythm of the temperature curve, the rhythm of engagement and disengagement that is mirrored in a rise of temperature around three to four o'clock in the afternoon and a drop again in the early morning hours, is frequently disturbed. The curve tends to be flat and lacks pronounced maxima and minima. If it is possible to restore the proper rhythm in the course of treatment, this can be viewed as significant progress (see figures 3-4, beginning and end of injection series).

Another important result of a successful Iscador treatment is an improvement or disappearance of *sleeplessness,* which is frequently very difficult to treat.

The heightened intervention of the *astral organization* can be seen in an increase in excretion. Many patients spontaneously report that diuresis increases after Iscador injections. Treatment also often alleviates chronic constipation. Still other patients begin to perspire more.

The general stimulation of the *etheric body* becomes evident in weight gain, improved skin turgor, and the regression of existing cachexia. Often a positive reaction is noticeable soon after the initiation of mistletoe therapy. The patient feels better, sleeps better, has an improved appetite, has less constipation, etc. If these positive reactions do not arise and instead, the patient experiences fatigue and irritability on the day of or the day following the injection, it is usually due to an excessive dose. In such situations it is advisable to make a pause and continue subsequent treatment with a lower dose.

Seriously ill patients have repeatedly shown dramatic general improvement without any observable effect on the tumor. This indicates an initial activation of the organization of forces underlying the physical organism that is meant to enable it to engage in a battle against the tumor.

Surgeons frequently make two observations about patients who received Iscador treatment prior to tumor resection: 1. their tumors are well delimited. 2. the region of the tumor is strongly hyperemic. Both observations suggest that the organism has begun to defend itself against the tumor.

A number of clinicians have observed that cancer patients are often covered with verrucae; indeed, some have even attempted to find some diagnostic significance in this. Warts, after all, are epithelial proliferations that occasionally become malignant. A frequent side effect of Iscador treatment in postmenopausal women is a regression of the warts that commonly form during that period.

The following case history illustrates how the defense of the organism can be enhanced to the point where it influenced a generalized and already malignant hyperkeratosis:

> 1. Mr. R. A., 54 years old. Around the age of thirty, severe hyperkeratosis began to form on his hands and feet, causing chronic ulcerations on the fingers. Twenty-one years later, biopsy revealed a squamous cell cancer on one finger of each hand. Exploratory excision of a cubital gland somewhat later showed that metastasis had already occurred. The disease was still in full development when Iscador treatment began; dozens of new keratoses continually appeared on new areas of the skin. After approximately one year's treatment, the keratoses had regressed everywhere except on the soles of the feet that still felt like hard cardboard.
>
> Six months into the Iscador treatment, the little finger of the right hand was amputated. The histological study revealed a much calmer picture than the sample taken during the earlier biopsy.

The glands removed in resection of the antecubital and axillary lymph nodes were no longer malignant. (Physician: Dr. C. Zjupic) [16]

The following history, starting from a very poor prognosis, clearly illustrates Iscador's ability to inhibit and reduce tumors:

2. Mrs. M. S., 57 years old, came to the Lukas Klinik for Iscador treatment of a bleeding, radiologically confirmed stomach carcinoma and anemia. No operation was performed because of biopsies and X-rays indicating extensive bone metastases, as well as a decisional biopsy indicating skin metastases. After blood transfusions and a year-long treatment with Iscador, the skin metastases had completely regressed; the gastric bleeding had resolved, and the patient reported no more pain from the bone metastases. The patient remained in good condition almost three years and was able to work as usual. X-rays indicated a regression of the bone metastases. This previously well patient died quite suddenly during a uremic episode of undetermined origin. (Physician: Dr. E. Heymann) [17]

It has frequently been observed that relapses or metastases lose their malignant character after Iscador treatment. Two exemplary histories follow:

3. Mrs. M. B., 71 years old, had her left breast amputated and the axillary lymph nodes resected due to cancer. A second operation followed six months later: histologically confirmed recurrence at the operative site. After another three months, a third operation was performed to excise skin metastases at the scar site.

Iscador treatment followed. Nevertheless, after two months, multiple skin metastases appeared, and after another month firm infiltration on the lateral end of the scar.

Intensification of treatment. Within three weeks, the skin metastases disappeared; the infiltration of the lateral end of the scar formed into a semispherical tumor of 6 cm diameter; extirpation. The histological finding was of a benign fibroma. (Physician: Dr. R. von May) [18]

---

16. A. Leroi and R. Leroi-von May, *Die Iscador-Behandlung maligner Tumoren, BEH* (1952)3–4.
17. A. & R. Leroi, *Tumorbehandlung mit Viscum album, Erfahrungsheilkunde* 19 (1970)5.

4. Mrs. L. D., 33 years old, underwent surgery in 1954 for a right-sided, large cystic ovarian tumor. Histology revealed an ovarian carcinoma (Cystoma multiloculare adenomatosum papilliferum carcinomatosum). As the patient refused postoperative irradiation, adnexal resection alone was performed. Iscador treatment was begun after surgery and regularly continued. In 1956 and 1960, a fullness could be appreciated in the left adnexal region, but in both instances regressed upon more intensive treatment. In 1957, cone biopsy and dilation and curettage were performed for a cervical polyp and leukoplakia. Histology was benign. In 1963, renewed fullness in the region of the left ovary, this time persisting even after intensive treatment, but remaining stationary until spring of 1966. Then, after a period of severe job-related stress, the mass rapidly enlarged, causing the patient to go to surgery. A number of chocolate cysts and follicular cysts of the left ovary were found, without any sign of malignancy. The patient continued to work, now 30 years after the first operation. (Physician: Dr. R. Leroi-von May)[19]

In treating inoperable tumors, the doctor can judge the success of treatment only from the clinical course. Frequently a tumor that is inaccessible to direct observation will stop growing or regress, making it impossible to say to what extent it has histologically lost its malignant character as well. Two examples follow:

5. Mrs. Sch. H., 72 years old, of slender build, comes for an office visit on July 3, 1952, complaining of pain in the right auditory canal. She had been in treatment for some time for moderate hypertension and total cardiac arrhythmia. The pains in the auditory canal have been occurring for approximately six months. In the last three months there has been moderate lockjaw.

Findings: Otoscopically, the wall of the auditory canal appears slightly constricted from beneath. Oral cavity: a tumor-like, partially papillomatous neoplasm proceeds from the right posterior mandi-

18. A. Leroi & R. Leroi-von May, *Die Iscador-Behandlung maligner Tumoren II, BEH* (1953), p. 1.

19. R. Leroi-von May, *Fortschritte in der Iscador-Behandlung maligner Tumoren* II: *Aus der gynäkologischen Praxis, BEH* (1961), p. 231.

ble (wisdom tooth). Palpation reveals hard infiltration on the right side of the tongue. Induration of the sub-mandibular glands.

Diagnosis: Alveolar neoplasm, inoperable. Therapy: Iscador injections 2–3 times weekly.

July 7, 1953: Specialist's report... "I am surprised to find that after one year the patient's condition has hardly changed. The constriction of the right auditory canal found one year ago is hardly perceptible today. On the other hand, the tumor in the mouth has grown somewhat toward the lumen, but not in its downward and lateral continuation. Signs of decay with secondary infection are nowhere to be found. The patient's general condition seems good, better than one year ago." Dr. Sch.

The therapy is continued with one Iscador injection weekly. At the end of December 1954, after two years and four months of treatment, the patient died of a stroke. Beyond a minor feeling of tension in opening the mouth, the carcinoma caused no complaints. (Physician: Dr. A. Leroi)

6. Mrs. G. R., a 54-year-old with inoperable squamous cell carcinoma of the cervix, diagnosed 1949. X-ray and radium irradiation. Subsequent Iscador treatment initially had no success. Nine months later, the pelvis was filled with tumorous masses that had infiltrated and constricted the rectum. A colostomy was performed. At first, relief; then the patient complained of intense pain, which was unresponsive to analgesics. Daily intestinal and vaginal bleeding. Chordotomy was rejected by the surgeon due to extent of the disease and patient's poor general condition. Rather intense Iscador treatment was begun in November, 1950. After six weeks, all analgesics were discontinued; hemorrhages stopped. The patient became ambulatory. After three months, light housework was possible. After nine months, mountain walks up to five hours long. For nineteen years after the initiation of treatment the patient led the life of a healthy person. She then died of an intercurrent illness.[20]

20. A. Leroi, "Eine interne Behandlung malinger Tumoren," *Ars Medici* 8 (1955):545–556.

Of particular interest are treatments that lead to complete regression of the tumor. Palpation and X-rays tell us little about *how* the organism overcomes the tumor. Histories involving tumors that are accessible to direct observation, however, such as cancers of the bladder, are extremely interesting. Already in 1958 a study was published of patients who had come to the Lukas Clinic for treatment of bladder cancer between 1949 and 1955.[21] Despite the poor prognosis of bladder cancer, six out of fifteen patients survived more than five years, and some were still in good health after more than ten years.

In 1967, a further study was published on bladder and renal cancer.[22] A series of case histories showed that after less intensive treatment, tumors in the bladder spread, while after more intensive treatment they regressed. Among other things this study demonstrated the significance of proper dosage.

Two case histories of bladder cancer will be summarized, the first from the publication mentioned, the other from a patient who entered treatment later.

> 7. Mrs. T. H., a 49-year-old whose father died of bladder cancer, developed bladder pains and hematuria. A nut-sized bladder tumor was found cystoscopically near the right ureteral ostium; posterior bladder wall infiltrated with tumor masses. The primary tumor was fused with the posterior aspect of the pubic bone. No attempt was made to remove it. Biopsy: solid carcinoma. Radiation treatments interrupted due to poor tolerance. Patient was in a generally weakened condition with gripping pain in the bladder region. Iscador treatment. After the first injections, freedom from pain; after four months, weight gain of 7 kg. After eleven months the tumor had regressed, the bladder showing a half-dollar-sized radial alteration on the back wall (scar!), reddened. Several nodules in the vicinity, compatible with granular cystitis. One year later, renewed bladder pains, nocturia. Lower back pains, weight loss. Improvement after intensive Iscador treatment.

21. A. Leroi & R. Leroi-von May, *Behandlung malinger Blasentumoren mit Viscum album, Zeitschrift für Urologie* (1958) 9.
22. A. Leroi, *Fortschritte in der Iscador-Behandlung maligner Tumoren I: Gehirn und Haut, BEH* (1961)4.

A suspicious infiltrative recurrence appearing in the seventh year of treatment disappeared six months later. The patient was quite well in subsequent years. Today, twenty years after diagnosis of the inoperable tumor, she is symptom free and in good general condition. (Physician: Dr. A. Leroi)

8. Mr. R. F., a 34-year-old with a highly malignant anaplastic bladder carcinoma diagnosed in early 1964 by cystoscopy and biopsy. Patient refused both cystectomy and radiation and came to the Lukas Klinik for treatment, where an intensive Iscador treatment was begun. Cystoscopy at the beginning of treatment showed a rather compact, in parts coarsely villous tumor near the sphincter. Examination after three months: no increase in size. Six months after start of Iscador treatment, in July 1964, no tumor could be detected, only slight cystitis. Later examinations also yielded no pathological findings. Twenty years have now passed since the beginning of treatment. Iscador treatment continues. The patient is in good general condition and able to work. (Physician: Dr. R. Leroi)

The development of a solid bladder cancer has frequently been observed cystoscopically. It usually starts with granular cystitis, which then develops into papillomas. These degenerate and begin to infiltrate at the base. The villi disappear, and finally the compact tumor develops, sometimes ulcerating.

Summing up cystoscopic observations of bladder tumor regression due to Iscador therapy, a reversal of these stages of tumor development is being perceived. The compact tumor becomes papillomatous; coarse papillomas yield to a covering of fine papillae, and before final healing, conditions suggestive of granular cystitis can appear. The interesting implication of this is that Iscador treatment instigates a *physiological healing process.* If one follows *H. Siegmund* in describing cancer as a "catastrophe of form," it becomes apparent that Iscador restores the ability of the "form" to assert itself vis-à-vis the cell principle.

The treatment of tumors of the digestive and urogenital systems is a rewarding field for Iscador therapy. Even stomach and pancreas carcinomas, whose prognosis is usually poor, respond to treatment, as the following two examples illustrate:

9. Mrs. B.H., a 49-year-old, suffered for many years from recurrent stomach ulcers. In December, 1956, after considerable weight loss and the appearance of tarry stool, subtotal gastrectomy was performed, revealing a carcinoma of the stomach in two places, with infiltration into the muscularis. Quite soon thereafter, a recurrence was suspected. The patient was informed of the terminal prognosis. Iscador treatment was begun in May of 1957 and, particularly in the first years, carried out very intensively and regularly. She is still undergoing several treatments of Iscador a year. It is now twenty-seven years since the operation. The patient feels healthy. She has always worked. (Physician: Dr. Leroi) (Ibid.)

10. Mrs. B. D., a 59-year-old, showed symptoms of cholecystitis at the end of 1958. When she came for an office visit about one year later, symptoms of gastric stenosis were present, and she was admitted to the hospital for operation in April, 1960. An inoperable pancreas carcinoma was found, with metastases anterior to the spinal column. A gastroenterostomy was performed. Directly after her discharge from the hospital, treatment with Iscador was begun and continued without interruption. The patient recovered with striking rapidity and was able to work again within half a year. Today, seventeen years after the operation, she is symptom free and feels healthy. Except for a slight tenderness to the left of the navel, there are no pathological findings. (Dr. A. Schuetz)[23]

An example of an inoperable rectal carcinoma where the tumor regressed completely:

11. Mrs. G. P., 61 years old, was diagnosed by exploratory laparotomy with an inoperable adenocarcinoma of the rectum with lymph node metastases. Two and three-quarter years after this diagnosis, she came for Iscador treatment in very bad general condition; abdominal metastases were now externally palpable. Eleven months later she underwent an acute hernia repair. To everyone's surprise, no

23. A. Leroi, *Fortschritte in der Iscador-Behandlung maligner Tumoren III: Tumoren des Verdauungstraktes BEH* (1963) 3.

tumor could be found in the abdomen. The rectal tumor had resolved as well, and the patient was in good general condition. After nine months, a slowly worsening hemiplegia began. The cause was found to be a meningioma, which was resected and histologically verified. Unfortunately, the patient died of complications from the operation. Survival time after beginning of treatment with Iscador despite extensive metastases: three years (Physician: Dr. Schwenzer, case 26).[24]

Positive results have also been obtained in the treatment of *malignant melanomas.* One example:

12. Mr. K. F., 45 years old, developed a rapidly growing tumor overlying the tibia after a traumatic injury. The operation, with resection of the inguinal lymph nodes, revealed a malignant melanoma with inguinal metastases. Prognosis: at most six months. Iscador therapy was begun after the operation, but carried out very irregularly by the patient. About one year later, recurrence at the site of surgery, one deep metastasis above the groin, and a crop of about 80 skin metastases on the upper thigh. After this, treatment was intensive and regular. In the course of eight months, the tumors again regressed. The skin nodules were replaced by depigmented areas, some of which showed a small black point in the middle. The patient was well during subsequent years; he was altogether without symptoms, and died 1966 of a heart attack. (Physician: Dr. A. Leroi, case 10)[25]

These few short histories have been adduced to illustrate how Iscador works. Rather than directly destroying cancer cells, as is attempted with radiation and cytostatics and which could also be achieved under certain conditions by intratumoral injection of Iscador. Through such measures the patient is excluded, as it were, and is even a disturbing factor by virtue of intolerance and side-effects, which may actually be the desired pri-

24. A. & R. Leroi, "Tumorbehandlung mit Viscum album," Erfahrungsheilkunde 19 (1970)5.

25. A. Leroi, B. Wöhrmann, *Eine nichttoxische interne Krebsbehandlung mit Mistelextrakten, Ars Medici* (1965)9.

mary effect of treatment. Through conventional measures the tumor is meant to be destroyed; naturally, normal tissue will also be affected, just as in a surgical intervention skin and other tissues may well need to be damaged to a certain extent.

The decision to what extent a necessarily desirable damage must be tolerated is dependent on the patients condition and the experience of the therapist. The removal of a small tumor in a healthy person does not justify a disturbance of the immune system with massive chemotherapy. Rather, it would be more appropriate in this situation to immediately stimulate the organism to improve the immune system capacities as has been described.

Insofar, however, as the tumor is already highly aggressive and possibly inoperable, then it might well be indicated to block tumor growth for some time with chemotherapy or radiotherapy. At the same time, however, the immune system must be strengthened by an appropriate therapy. It then becomes a question of therapeutic judgment how long the organism can be subjected to the destructive treatment. It may well be the case that one or two cycles of chemotherapy are sufficient to retard the rapid growth or spread of a tumor until the immune system responds to the mistletoe treatment. In every case the organism must be stimulated to be active against the tumor to restrain its growth; otherwise the immune system weakness persists and recurrence or metastases are inevitable.

Although the conventional cytostatic treatment and the stimulation of the organism are based upon two entirely opposite principles, with proper application they could well complement each other. The tragedy that the stimulation of the organism is hardly contemplated or discussed in conventional medical circles, can be attributed to the predominant view that only the primary destructive principle is the valid, secure and certain mode of treatment. What is really important, however, is that the organism is supported in its battle against the cell principle. That it succeeds in doing so can be seen from the regression of a generalized hyperkeratosis, the loss of the malignant character of tumors, and the regression of metastases. How Iscador acts is revealed most clearly by its reversal of the stages leading to the formation of a bladder tumor.[26]

A malignant tumor is the end result of a disturbance of the total human organization, a disturbance that has certainly been present for many years. Tumors should be surgically removed wherever possible. After the operation, however, treatment is necessary to combat the formation of new tumors. Through such treatment, existing metastases can be checked in their development and the danger of recurrence can be minimized.[27]

The effectiveness of *followup treatment* with Iscador has been demonstrated by experiments on groups of patients with similar tumors. At the Women's Clinic of the University of Munich (headed by Prof. Dr. W. Bickenbach), a group of eighty-one patients with carcinoma of the cervix, stages I–III, received three years of followup treatment upon completion of radiotherapy. After five years it was found that the mortality in this group was about 40% lower than in clinic patients who had received no such followup treatment.[28]

In the surgical department of the city hospital of Vienna-Lainz (headed by Professor Dr. G. Salzer), groups of patients with cancer of the breast and stomach, rectum and colon received postoperative Iscador treatment. Significant reductions in mortality in contrast to control groups were observed.[29]

A random study of the effects of postoperative Iscador therapy on stomach cancer was conducted at the Ludwig Boltzmann Institute for Clinical Oncology in Vienna.[30]

Lymph node positive (advanced cases) and lymph node negative patients (early cases) were considered separately. Results from the first group were statistically significant (figure 6).

---

26. A. Leroi, & E. Wrede, *Fortschritte in der Iscador-Behandlung maligner Tumoren V: Nieren und harnableitende Organe, BEH* (1966 p.6 und 1967)p.5.
27. M. Günczler, *Fortschritte in der Iscador-Behandlung maligner Tumoren IV: Über die Iscador-Therapie des Mammakarzinoms*, BEH (1964).
28. C. Fellmer, K.E. Fellmer, Nachbehandlung bestrahlter Genitalkarzinome mit dem Viscum-album-Präparat 'Iscador', *Krebsarzt* (1966 Heft 3).
29. M. Günczler, G. Salzer, *Erfahrungen mit der eingeschränkten Radikaloperation und Iscador-Nachbehandlung beim Brustdrüsenkarzinom*, Krebsarzt (Heft 5, 1962); M. Günczler, Ch. Osika, G. *Salzer, Ergebnisse von Resektion und Nachbehandlung beim Magenkarzinom.* WiKliWo, Heft 6, 1968, p. 105; M. Günczler, G. Salzer, *Iscador-Therapie in der Nachbehandlung operierter Karzinome. Österreichische Ärztezeitung*, Heft 20, 1969.
30. G. Salzer, L. Havelec, *Adjuvante Iscador-Behandlung nach operiertem Magenkarzinom. Ergebnisse einer randomisierten Studie*, Krebsgeschehen 15, 106–110 (1983).

Even in *bronchogenic carcinoma*, the rising incidence of which is alarming, a comparative study of one group of thirty-seven patients showed a definite decrease in mortality in comparison with an untreated group of forty-one patients (see figure 7).[31]

Median survival time (days)	Lymphnode positive		Lymphnode negative	
	Iscador 660	Control 324	Iscador –	Control 1201

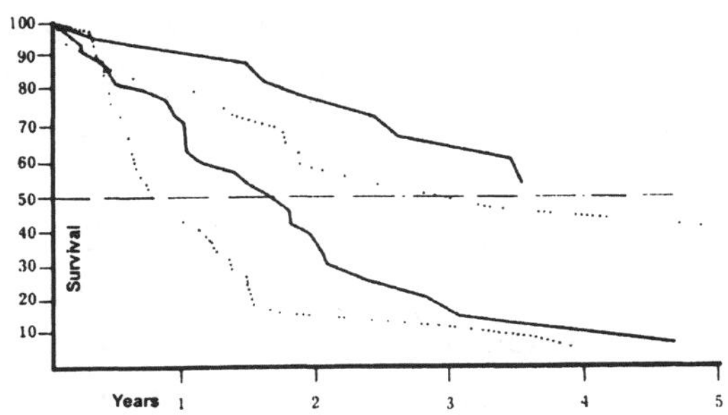

<u>LN Negative</u>
Iscador – 27 pat. —
Control – 38 pat. .....

<u>LN Positive</u>
Iscador – 35 pat. —
Control – 37 pat. .....

Figures 6. Postoperative survival rates for stomach cancer patients, lymph node positive and negative, with and without Iscador treatment.

31. G. Salzer, *Klinischer Versuch zur Verbesserung des Schicksals 'radikaloperierter' Bronchuskarzinom-Patienten*, Z.Erkr. Atm. 142, p. 127–131 (1975); G. Salzer, E. Danmayer, F. Wutzlhofer u. S. Frey: *Adjuvante Iskador-Behandlung operierter nicht kleinzelliger Bronchuskarzinome—Ergebnisse einer randomisierten Studie*, Dt. Zs. Onkol. 23, 4 (1991); G. Salzer, L. Havelec, *Rezidivprophylaxe bei op. Bronchus-Ca-Patienten mit dem Mistelpräparat Iscador*, Onkologie Bd. 1, Nr.6, 1978; O. Wolff, *Die Mistel in the Krebsbehandlung.* Frankfurt a.M., 3. Ed., 1985. R. Leroi, *Misteltherapie*, Stuttgart, 1987.

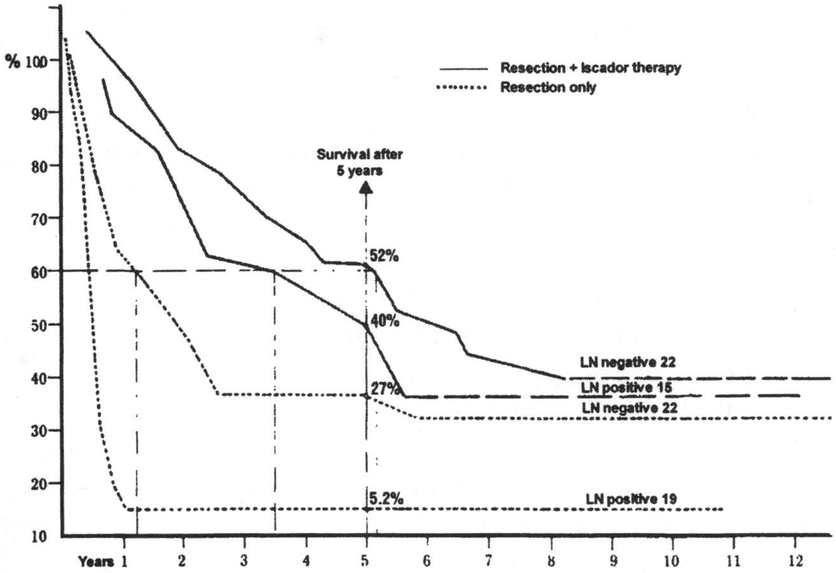

Figure 7. Survival rate of bronchogenic carcinoma patients.

Another aspect, which may in the future prove more significant than tumor treatment and postoperative treatment, is that of *cancer prophylaxis.* We are familiar with precanceroses such as leukoplakia, polyposis and others, but we have no 'hard' data for early diagnosis, that is to say, for definite recognition of cancer dispositions. This is quite natural since early conditions and dispositions are unstable and therefore much more influenceable than final stages as represented by a manifest carcinoma. According to studies up to this point, anybody with an anergic reactionary disposition is strongly cancer-endangered. This is always a matter of immune deficiency. It is often characterized by the lack of a febrile reaction or chronic lingering processes with only insignificant febrile reaction. It has been shown that mistletoe is able to strengthen the immune system. This is why mistletoe therapy is indicated in precanceroses and immune deficiencies and is particularly effective here. One of the reasons for the effect is its stimulation of the febrile reaction, the blood profile (see above), and the thymus gland (see below). For recognizing cancer dispositions, the patient's mental disposition and "repressions" (see above) can be of help in the anamnesis. In all this, a physician needs to observe the patient in his/her "totality," and in the synopsis of many, particularly "soft" data, to develop a sensitivity through experience when mistletoe treatment is indicated in weak, prophylactic doses.

On the basis of Rudolf Steiner's indications for its preparation, mistletoe has provided us with a remedy that strengthens the formative forces of the human organism and thus radically combats the processes that lead to the growth of cancerous tumors, as has been clinically proven.[32] The development of this remedy is still ongoing. But it has by now become an indispensable aid to countless physicians for treatment of inoperable tumors, for postoperative treatment, and for cancer prophylaxis. Work on the medication itself continues at the *Hiscia Institute* (Society for Cancer Research, Arlesheim, Switzerland). The advancing development of Iscador in the Research Institute *Hiscia* is evident above all in its increasing effect on tumors.

For the rest, monographs offer a comprehensive overview of experimental and clinical tests in the area of the treatment of cancer with mistletoe.[33]

Clinical results have now been confirmed by a series of experimental investigations.

Vester et al.[34] examined the pressed sap of the mistletoe over a period of years for tumor-inhibiting constituents and found that it contains three effective groups of substances:

1. Ether-soluble substances (not yet studied in detail)
2. Polysaccharides
3. Proteins

Biological experiments demonstrated that the cytostatic and cancerostatic effects of mistletoe protein are among the strongest yet observed. It is essential to note that the inhibiting influence of the mistletoe frac-

32. See footnotes on page 75 through page 92.
33. O. Wolff, *Die Mistel in the Krebsbehandlung*. Frankfurt a.M., 3. Ed., 1985. R. Leroi, *Misteltherapie*, Stuttgart, 1987.
34. F. Vester, L. Bohne, M. El-Fouly, *Zur Kenntnis der Inhaltsstoffe von Viscum album, IV. Biologisches Verhalten einzelner Proteinfraktionen*. Hoppe, Seyler's Z. physiol. Chem. Bd.349, 1968, p. 495.

tion extends *specifically to tumor cells* whereas in healthy spleen and thymus cells no retardation is noted in controls even with higher than therapeutic doses.[35] The malignant cells are inhibited in their development by proteins in doses that will affect healthy bone marrow cells only in a fourfold amount. Enormous significance is attributed to this fact insofar as it explains the clinically already known phenomenon that Iscador therapy is tumor-effective *without* side-effects on healthy cells.

In later studies[36] on animals, it was found that therapeutic doses of Iscador and mistletoe protein stimulate the thymus, the organ responsible for immunological prophylactic processes. What does this signify? The organization that can distinguish "self" from "not-self," that fends off foreign substances, and organically represents an instrument of the form-preserving human individuality is stimulated. (The significance of the thymus is described more closely in vol. I on page 25ff, and the role of the immune system in vol. I on pages 283ff).

Mistletoe treatment of cancer thus shows itself to be a therapy that, on the one hand, has potentially cytostatic effects, and on the other hand, activates the immune system. No other cytostatic drug can claim to have this twofold action.

In 1963 the *Lukas Klinik* (Arlesheim, Switzerland) was founded as a special clinic for treatment of tumors based on mistletoe therapy. In addition to drug therapy, the Lukas Klinik uses special diets, baths, massages, and artistic therapy. The aim of artistic therapy (curative painting and modeling, curative eurythmy and speech) is to stimulate the patients' inner life. In 1969, the Lukas Klinik was expanded, making room for a *continuing education center* for physicians who wish to receive training in medicine extended by spiritual science.

May it be possible in the not too distant future to fulfill the hope that Rudolf Steiner, out of deep insight into the disease process of cancer and

---

35. F. Vester, Über die kanzerostatische und immunogenen Eigenschaften von Mistelproteinen, Krebsgeschehen 1977, S. 106–114.
36. J. Nienhaus, M. Stoll u. F. Vester, *Thymus Stimulation and Cancer Prophylaxis by Viscum Proteins.* Experientia 26, (5), (1969); J. Nienhaus, R. Leroi, *Tumorhemmung und Thymusstimulation durch Mistelpräparate.* Elemente der Naturwissenschaft, Heft 2, 1970; J. Nienhaus, F. Vester, *Thymus Stimulation and Cancer Prophylaxix by Viscum Proteins.* Experientia 26/5, 1970; R. Rentea et al.: *Biologic Properties of Iscador®: A Viscum album Preparation. I. Hyperplesia of the Thymic Cortex and Accelerated Regeneration of Hemapoietic Cells following X-Irradiation.* Laboratory Investigation, Vol. 44, p. 43–48, (1981).

the corresponding therapeutic significance of mistletoe, expressed in the following words: "And in this way, through insight into the essential nature of this disease, there is no doubt at all that the remedy will be found that will gradually make the usual healing processes, the surgical processes, unnecessary."[37]

Conclusion

Mistletoe research and therapy are constantly advancing and have led to further results that will be reported here by way of an appendix.

It cannot be the aim of this chapter to offer a complete enumeration of research on mistletoe, since this has been done elsewhere.[38]

It is not justified today to dismiss earlier findings concerning influence on tumor processes—for example, the fact that mistletoe contains a significant amount of magnesium as well as arginine, choline, acetylcholine, gamma-amino-butyric acid, and so on. At least it is not justified in the case of magnesium and arginine. Independent of this, "attendant substances" of the so-called primary active substance play a modifying or potentiating role as cofactors. Proceeding from the assumption that the nature of a plant has been recognized as a "primary active principle," only a method of extraction that gently conserves the totality of the plant should be considered. Such a method is the basis of the preparations and experiences mentioned below.

According to pharmacological thinking today, one looks for "primary active substances" that one isolates or concentrates as much as possible. In so doing, one can in fact achieve correspondingly isolated and massive effects. But the danger always is that the overall *effectiveness,* meaning curative effect, is lost for the benefit of one result, meaning one effect.

Among the large number of substances contained in mistletoe, lectins and viscotoxins became the center of interest most recently. Research on them led to interesting experimental and clinical results.[39] To a large extent, they originate from the Research Institute Hiscia, the Association for Cancer Research, where Iscador® is manufactured.

---

37. See footnote on page 70.
38. See footnote on page 94.

Lectins are found in plants and animals. They are capable, for instance of aggulating blood group substances. Mistletoe lectins possess a strong affinity for tumor cells. We are dealing with a galactoside-specific lectin that facilitates 'recognition' of the tumor.

Mistletoe lectin I consists of two sub-units joined by non-covalent bonds. Each sub-unit in turn consists of two chains, A and B, that differ in character. The cytotoxic effect of lectin is based on the bond of the B-chain with carbohydrates of certain cell surfaces. This permits the A-chain to penetrate the cell membrane and enzymatically to impede the protosynthesis of the ribosomes. At the same time, the B-chain enhances the phagocytizing activity of macrophages.

This lectin likewise leads to stimulation of the forming of cytokines as well as an increase of NK-cells and moreover stimulation of cell-transmitting cytotoxicity of antibodies. This indicates a direction of effects that

---

39. H. Franz, *Inhaltsstoffe der Mistel als potentielle Arzneimittel.* Die Pharmazie, 40 p. 97–104 (1985); P. Luther et al., *Isolierung und Charakterisierung von Inhaltsstoffen der Mistel (Viscum album L.)*, II Wirkung von agglutinierenden und zytotoxischen Fraktionen auf Mäuse-Aszites-Tumorzellen. Acta biol. Med. germ. Bd. 36, 1977, p. 119–125; P. Luther et al., *Die Mistel in Botanik, Lektine, medizinische Anwendung,* Berlin 1987; H. Franz, H. et al., *A simple method for the preparation of two different chains of the mistletoe Lectin I.* Lectin-Biology, Biochemistry, Clinical Biochemistry, Vol 2, Berlin & New York, 1982; T. Hajto and K. Hostanska, *Effect of in vivo hyperthermia on human natural killer cells,* Clin. Tri J. 22, p. 514–520; T. Hajto and K. Hostanska, *An investigation of the ability of Viscum album-activated granulocytes to regulate natural killer cells in vivo.* Clin. Tri. J. 23, p.345–358 (1986); T. Hajto and Lanzrein, *Natural killer and antibody-dependent cell-mediated cytotoxicity activities and large granular lymphocyte frequencies in Viscum album-treated breast cancer patients.* Oncology 43, p. 93–97 (1986); G. Ribéreau-Gayon, M. L. Jung, S. Baudino, G. Sallé, J. P. Beck, *Effects of mistletoe extracts on cultured tumor cells.* Experientia 42, 594–599 (1986); T. Hajto, K. Hostanska, J.-J. Gabius, *Modulatory potency of the galactoside-specific lectin from mistletoe extract (Iscador) on the host defence system in vivo in rabbits and patients.* Cancer research 49, 4803–4806 (1989); T.Hajto and K. Hostanska, *Immunmodulierende Effekte der Misteltherapie,* Therapeutikon 3, 361–368 (1989); T. Hajto, K. Hostanska, J.-J. Gabius, *Zytokine als Lektin-induzierte Mediatoren in der Misteltherapie.* Therapeutikon 4 (3), 136–145, März 1990; M.-L. Jung, S. Baudino, G. Ribéreau-Gayon, J.-P. Beck, *Characterization of cytotoxic protein from mistletoe.* Cancer Letters 51, 103–108 (1990); T. Hajto, K. Hostanska, K. Frei, Ch. Rordorf and H. J. Gabius, *Increased secretion of tumor necrosis factor a, interleukin 6 by human mononuclear cells exposed to galactoside-specific lectin from clinically applied mistletoe extract.* Cancer research 50, 3322–3326, June 1990; T. Hajto, K. Hostanska, M. Fonalski, A. Kirsch, *Antitumorale Aktivität des immunmodulatorisch wirkenden-galactosidspezifischen Mistellektins bei der klinischen Anwendung von Mistelextrakten (Iscador),* Dt. Zs. f. Onkologie 23, 1 (1991); E. Kovacs, T. Hajto, K. Hostanska, *Improvement of DNA-repair in lymphocytes of breast cancer patients treated with Viscum album extract (Iscador),* Eurp. J. Cancer 27, 1672–1676 (1991); Synopsis: see Anthology *Mistletoe* Oncology 43, Suppl. 1., 1986.

demonstrates how mistletoe affects the immune system in a modulating, meaningful, and stimulating way.

As was pointed out, it will be necessary to recognize this lectin effect in connection with other mistletoe substances. It appears that a polarity exists in the viscotoxins.[40] This would definitely correspond to the previously mentioned polarity, typical for mistletoe, of a cytostatic *and* at the same time immune-stimulating effect. Such polarities can certainly be found in mistletoe as well as in cancer. Only by grasping this totality will it be possible to stimulate the organism with correspondingly prepared mistletoe in such a way that healing will thereby be effected.

In conclusion it can be said that Rudolf Steiner's ideas concerning his conception of malignant tumors as well as their therapy are receiving more and more confirmation. Unbiased physicians and researchers around the world are looking for a way of treating cancer that is in harmony with human nature, something that benefits cancer patients who are so urgently awaiting more help.

Several ways of manufacturing mistletoe preparations of cancer remedies are left open in Rudolf Steiner's indications mentioned earlier. Mistletoe preparations based on these indications by Rudolf Steiner and developed through the initiative of physicians are currently *Iscador* (manufactured by the Society for Cancer Research, CH-4144 Arlesheim, Switzerland, distributed by Weleda AG, D-7070 Schwäb. Gmünd, distributors in almost every country); *Iscucin* (Wala, D-7325 Eckwälden), *Viscum Abnoba* (Abnoba-Heilmittel GmbH, D-7530 Pforzheim), *Helixor* (Helixor-Heilmittel GmbH, D-7463 Rosenfeld); and *Isorel* (Novipharm, A-9210 Pörtschach, Austria; in Germany: Vysorel). The "Richtlinien für die Iscador-Behandlung" (Guidelines for Iscador Treatments) are available from Weleda AG.

40. K. Urech, *Mistelinhaltsstoffe und Krebskranheit*, Der Merkurstab 1992, S. page 445–453.

III

Pediatrics

WILHELM ZUR LINDEN
OTTO WOLFF

PEDIATRICS IS JUSTIFIED as a separate discipline within medicine because the developing child is subject to conditions that do not hold true for the adult. A detailed description of childhood development as an expression of the involvement of the various constituents of the human being has been given in Volume I.

As one example of the child's special nature, let us mention the infant's fluid metabolism, which is of great practical significance. In a fifteen-day-old infant, the body weight is 4.8% of the adult's weight, while the body surface is 25% of the adult value. Through the relatively large surface area a much greater insensible perspiration occurs, enhanced by a higher rate of respiration. The infant, as is well known, is much more "watery" than the adult; its fluid metabolism also proceeds four to five times more quickly. The infant, in a word, lives more in the realm of water and of the etheric than does the adult. However, its kidney function, which is governed by the astral body, is as yet undeveloped; glomerular filtration is lower than in the adult. Due to theses facts, any loss of water is cause for alarm (dehydration–exsiccosis–toxicosis), whereas excessive intake of fluids or salts can overwhelm the infant's regulatory capacity. Both must be avoided.

By taking into account the developing organism's special properties, medicine has been able to reduce infant and child mortality considerably. However, such success must not blind us to the possible long-range effects of modern medical treatments, especially in pediatrics. The child's organism and constitution have not yet reached their finished state; they are still being decisively shaped by such factors as the childhood diseases. In childhood, as in every other phase of development, medical and pedagogical measures must be carefully weighed in terms of their long-term implications.

Later we will discuss the extent to which a prematurely induced hardening tendency can manifest later as sclerosis, and how the routine suppression of febrile illnesses can upset the constitutional balance between the inflammatory and sclerotic tendencies. The current availability of powerful medications makes it more important than ever to inquire into the effects of such therapeutic measures on the course of life as a whole and on the personality. Nor should we be easily satisfied with short-term "cures." Intervening in the processes of development and disease changes the constitution, and such changes must be carefully weighed against all short-term benefits.

One factor that deeply influences and shapes the child's organism for the rest of its life is nutrition.

Infant Nutrition and Its Disorders

Breast-feeding

Breast-feeding is the least problematic and most desirable way to feed an infant, and mother's milk is the sole physiological food for the infant. Yet in recent decades breast-feeding has markedly declined. Many reasons can be cited for this. First, breast-feeding was considered too time-consuming for the routine of the modern hospital; more importantly, however, nutritionists were convinced that mother's milk was unnecessary, since synthetic formulas produced faster growth rates. Authorities interpreted this as an improvement, despite the fact that of all living creatures, human beings have the slowest natural development.[1] The situation has since changed, not least due to the energetic efforts of mothers who trust their instincts more than they do statistics.

Despite the renewed popularity of breast-feeding, however, medical authorities still judge infant development in purely quantitative terms. In doing so they display the demeaning attitude that Karl Jaspers described as reducing humanity "to the lowest common denominator: to vitality as physical prowess and to the triviality of consumption."[2]

As well as in physical development, mother's milk plays an important role in the child's soul-spiritual (including mental) development, which

1. Cf. F. A. Kipp, Die Evolution des Menschen im Hinblick auf seine lange Jugendzeit (Stuttgart:1980).
2. K. Jaspers, The Spiritual Situation of the Present (1931).

begins long before the awakening of the intellect. The spirit begins to incarnate during the embryonic period and continues to do so throughout childhood. This process should be smooth, and one important means of assuring this during infancy is mother's milk. Rudolf Steiner described milk as the "awakener of the human spirit in the child." Moreover, "ingesting milk is the first step in education. Nature educates children naturally."[3] Later education addresses the soul, in order to awaken the child's latent endowments.

Milk is secreted only after the mother has given birth and the placenta has been expelled. The flow of milk is triggered by the sucking stimulus, as well as by other stimuli rooted in the continuing close connection between mother and child.

The composition of mother's milk is remarkably attuned to the growing infant's nutritional needs, and changes in accordance with them. Of exceptional importance to the newborn is the colostrum. Rich in protein, it carries abundant etheric formative forces; it also contains high levels of antibodies that the newborn needs prior to developing its own immune system. The protein content of mother's milk decreases as lactation progresses, whereas the lactose content increases. Such changes are by no means accidental: they not only satisfy the infant's changing biological needs, but also subtly aid the incarnation of the child's soul-spiritual being into the "model" body provided by the parents.

Epidemiological studies conducted in hospitals have shown that breastfed children are less susceptible to diarrhea and respiratory tract infections than are bottle-fed children. They also rarely succumb to sepsis, hemorrhaging enterocolitis, abscessing staphylococcal pneumonias, or other severe infectious illnesses. Breast-feeding can also prevent allergies, or at least more or less permanently weaken a disposition toward them. This applies especially to cow's milk intolerance, pollinoses (e.g. hay fever), and asthma. Moreover, it was found that premature infants fed on mother's milk showed a higher intelligence quotient than those receiving formula.[4]

The specifically human protein in mother's milk transmits etheric formative forces from mother to child. Little work is required to digest this

3. R. Steiner, The Foundations of Human Experience, Hudson, NY: Anthroposophic Press, 1996, lecture 11 (previous translation, Study of Man, London: Rudolf Steiner Press, 1966).
4. Deutsche Forschungsgemeinschaft, Mitteilung XII (Weinheim: Verlag Chemie, 1984).

protein, a feature that clearly no formula can imitate. Protein not only primarily supports the etheric body, but also, through its nitrogen component, the astral body. Animal protein thus has a stronger "astralizing" influence on the child than mother's milk; the problems resulting from this will be discussed below.

Whereas protein stimulates the development of the etheric body, minerals are largely responsible for the formation of the physical body, particularly the skeletal system. The two most important minerals in this regard are calcium and phosphorus. Milk contains these and other minerals, and thus is a source of the salts so important to life, suffusing the child with earthly substance. The extraordinarily low mineral content of mother's milk (as compared to animal milks) allows mineralization to take place in a gradual and well-balanced way, a fact that receives much too little attention. Synthetic formulas have yet to match these values.

The astral body intervenes in the incarnation process through the fat in mother's milk. The percentage of unsaturated long-chain fatty acids is much higher in mother's milk than it is in animal milks, which expresses the internalization of warmth and other "imponderables" in the former. This fact in turn points to the ego organization; fats are one of the ways in which the child receives the formative forces of the ego organization. Unsaturated fatty acids are also important for the skin (especially in eczema) and for the liver (lipase activity).

Perhaps the most interesting fact about mother's milk is its high lactose content (7% as opposed to 4% for cow's milk). It is a commonplace that milk sugar is found only in milk. One form of it, galactose, has a very specific task to perform. It has a clear affinity to the nerve-sense system, that is, to the upper organization and to its structuring formative forces which are especially active in the child. Galactose is also present in significant amounts in connective tissue (acid mucopolysaccharides, chondroitin sulfate), and from there guides structuring impulses into the supporting tissue. Milk sugar, the physiological sugar of the child, thus helps the ego organization stimulate and guide the impulses of growth and, as time goes on, to awaken consciousness.

Sugar's sweet taste appeals to the ego and leads it directly into the depths of the organism. As Rudolf Steiner pointed out, the child "tastes" with the stomach as well as with the tongue, and involves the entire body in drinking, as the accompanying rhythmic movements reveal.

To summarize, mother's milk promotes the incarnation process in a comprehensive and balanced way, and is therefore the ideal nourishment for the growing child. It demands a minimum of digestive activity at a time when little can or should be demanded. Furthermore, it gives the child not only energy and substance, but also a delicately balanced complex of human formative forces, all suffused with maternal warmth.

Practical Advice For Breast-Feeding

Ideally, the child should be breast-fed for the first five months and gradually weaned over the next four. Breast-feeding beyond that time binds the child too long to the mother and to the forces of heredity. It thereby also impedes development toward individuality.

Even mothers who cannot completely satisfy their child at the breast should give as much milk as they can, no matter how small the amount. Galactostasis and mild puerperal mastitis do not present a real obstacle to breast-feeding. Studies have shown that lactagogue tea (Weleda) can significantly enhance milk secretion.[5]

Physical inability to nurse will always be present in a certain proportion of mothers. When present, it is seldom due to organic causes, but rather more often to disruptions of the natural mother-child relationship during birth and recovery. When this relationship is disturbed as little as possible, as, for example, when the child is kept in the mother's room ("rooming-in"), nursing is possible in 96.6% of all cases.[6] An understanding of these facts is essential for nurses, midwives, and hospital staffs.

Factors working against a high rate of breast-feeding include the administration of sedatives to the mother before birth, which depresses the newborn's sucking reflex.[7] This reflex peaks about twenty to thirty minutes after birth and recedes if it is not gratified at that time. Only after a long hiatus does it reappear. This fact is also seldom given due consideration.[8]

---

5. Unpublished studies conducted at the Gemeinschaftskrankenhaus Herdecke, Germany.
6. W. Hassauer, Jahrbuch der Psychohygiene 2 (1974):83; cf. also Cretius et al., Zentralblatt für Gyn. 87/17; DMW 90/162.
7. Kron et al., Ped. 37 (1966):1012–16.
8. Archavsky, Vopr. Pediatri 20 (1952): 45–53.

Another factor that has dissuaded many mothers from nursing is the DDT content of human milk, which is occasionally quite high. Despite this, the benefits of mother's milk can safely be said to outweigh the possible harmful effects of DDT, except in extreme cases.

Barring any special complications, the child should be laid to the mother's breast repeatedly on the first day so as to give the sucking stimulus a chance to operate. This also prevents pressure from building up in the mother's breasts. Of course, such closeness also has psychological benefits, for the mother as well as for the child.

The temperature in the delivery room should be kept at around 28ºC. At lower temperatures the infant is exposed to an abrupt and unnecessarily great loss of heat. Care should also be taken to preserve the vernix caseosa in the first bathing; this coating, which consists of high-grade lipoids, not only lubricates the child's passage through the birth canal, but also protects against heat loss. It is also very likely an important source of percutaneous nourishment, since it is absorbed by the skin in approximately three days. In our experience, maintaining sufficient warmth and preserving the vernix are generally sufficient to prevent icterus, one of the chief causes for the rapid fatigue at the breast frequently observed in newborns. Attention to the above measures will also protect most newborns from catching cold.

Another factor inhibiting normal lactation is the administration of labor-inducing drugs and of narcotics during delivery. Many cathartics also inhibit lactation and should therefore be replaced by enemas. The American practice of scheduling births for the morning hours, which necessitates the use of labor-inducing drugs, is just one more sign of the medical profession's decreasing sense of responsibility toward newborns.

Bottle-Feeding

Most pediatric researchers agree that even the very best synthetic formulas are no more than inadequate substitutes for mother's milk. The digestive processes and weight curve associated with breast-feeding set the standard for healthy development. Even thriving, however, is not in itself a sufficient indicator of nutritional quality; another important consideration is susceptibility to disease. Numerous studies in Sweden (Mannheimer), England (Sydown and Faxen; Robinson) and the United

States have shown that the mortality rate of bottle-fed children is two to three times as high as that of their breast-fed counterparts.[9] Breast-fed children also have a considerably lower mortality than bottle-fed children who show a comparable weight gain. It is thus reasonable to question "whether the weight gain achieved through specifically human nourishment is not in fact of a different nature than that achieved through cow's milk, which bears only a crude chemical similarity to human milk."[10]

In order to evaluate the effect of cow's milk on infant development, we must first address several fundamental questions. See table 1 for details of the relationship of growth rates in humans and various animal species to the chemical composition of their respective milks.

	Doubling of birth weight (days)	Growth rate (human = 1)	Casein	Albumin	Fat	Lactose	CaO MgO P_2O_5
Human	147	1	.60	.75	3.8	6.8	.08
Cow	47	3	2.85	.55	3.4	4.8	.46
Sheep	15	9	4.50	1.00	6.1	4.7	.60
Rabbit	6	14	13.50	2.00	10.5	2.0	1.90

(From König, Chemie der Nahrung und Genussmittel, and R. Höber, Lehrbuch der Physiologie des Menschen, Berlin, 4th edition 1928.)(From König, Chemie der Nahrung und Genussmittel, and R. Höber, Lehrbuch der Physiologie des Menschen, Berlin, 4th edition 1928.)

Table 1: Relationship of growth rate to composition of milk

A glance at this table shows that the casein and mineral levels of a milk are approximately proportional to the infant growth rate of the species from which it comes. Compared with all animals, the human being has the slowest growth:[11] It is the nature of human milk, with its comparatively low concentrations of casein and minerals, to promote growth in

9. R. Beckmann, MMW 106 (1964): 2325.
10. Ströder and Müller, Mediz. klin. 49 (1954):1356.

an extremely gentle and protracted way, preserving flexibility and thus permitting the development of specifically human capacities. The animal, by contrast, develops rapidly into a pre-established, relatively inflexible mold that leaves no room for the development of higher spiritual faculties.

Human infants need little protein. A diet of two-thirds cow's milk induces a nitrogen metabolism approximately three times that of a child fed with mother's milk. The bottle-fed infant thus becomes more strongly astralized.

If the pattern of growth rates shown in the table above means anything at all, then the highly touted accelerations of growth achieved with cow's milk cannot be seen as anything other than an animalization, as a deviation from the truly human course of development. This is just one aspect of the problem of acceleration so characteristic of modern times.

Diets other than human milk actually promote mineralization. This is already clear from the well-known but little-heeded fact that bottle-fed children retain much larger amounts of minerals than do breast-fed children.

	Ca	P	K	Na	Cl	Total
Breast-fed	.29	.27	.42	.26	.20	1.44
Bottle-fed	.40	.50	.93	.21	.26	2.30

(From Brock, Biologische Daten für den Kinderarzt, vol III, p. 219.)

Table 2: Mineral retention of healthy breast-fed and healthy bottle-fed infants. The values are relative to a 100g. weight gain, i.e., daily retention x four.

Researchers have of course attempted to reduce the mineral content of infant formulas, but even the most successful have only brought it down to slightly more than twice that of in human milk. Thus over a five month period, "a carbohydrate-enriched, two-third cow's milk formula would give an infant 900 g more foreign protein, almost 3.5 kg more unusable carbohydrates, 500 g more minerals, and 1.75 kg less fat than mother's milk.... In light of this it is not surprising that bottle-fed infants

11. Cf. F. A. Kipp, Die Evolution des Menschen im Hinblick auf seine lange Jugendzeit (Stuttgart: 1980).

usually weigh more than breast-fed children and often appear 'pasty' or overfed. Their rapid growth bears only a superficial resemblance to the breast-fed child's thriving; it is definitely not identical to it. The human infant thrives best on nourishment that is low in protein and minerals but high in lactose: mother's milk. Bottle-feeding unquestionably places greater stress on the infant's digestive, metabolic, and excretory functions."[12]

Through their higher mineral content, synthetic formulas favor mineralization, hardening, and rigidification in the child. That the minerals ingested become part of the body substance and are not just stored temporarily is proven by the fact that "even in a long-term metabolic study, special periods of elimination never occurred in the overmineralized bottle-fed infants."

Premature mineralization of the skeletal system and of tissue is directly connected to a higher level of wakefulness. The child's ego and astral body, which are at first exclusively occupied on a subconscious level with physical structuring, become active in consciousness once the internal organs have been formed and consolidated. This is the deeper reason for warning against premature mineralization.[13]

It goes without saying that bottle-feeding will be necessary in some cases; however, it must be used in such a way as to further the ultimate goals of nutrition. Nutrition specialists and pediatricians generally agree that a healthful food is one that is easily digestible, leads to weight gain, and promotes optimal organ function. Other effects considered desirable are a rosy complexion, good muscle turgor and tonus, a firm fat cushion, and resistance to infection and rickets. In addition, some authors mention contentment, a radiant look, and similar signs of well-being. Until now, however, little attention has been paid to the influence of nutrition on the child's physical constitution, and even less to its influence on the rhythm of development, which includes the emergence of such abilities as sitting up, standing, walking, and speaking, and such physical events as the closing of the anterior fontanel (which most often occurs too early). Psychologically it involves the rate at which the child

12. R. Beckmann, MMW 106 (1964): 2325.
13. The connection between consciousness and mineralization process has been portrayed at various points (see, for example, vol. 1, p.12f.: vol. 2, p. 118).

awakens out of dreamy awareness into a more focused consciousness. The increasing acceleration of such developmental events is generally not questioned; on the contrary, many take it as a sign of the superiority of modern civilization. Early consolidation and precocity are seen as desirable, compared to which the slow, harmonious growth of earlier times appears retarded and underdeveloped. Of course, nutrition is only one factor contributing to the overall phenomenon of developmental acceleration.

Health is nowadays so thoroughly equated with proper organ function and robustness that other considerations are completely ignored. However, food is more than just calories or raw material for tissue formation. Its primary function is to stimulate physiological activity, and a food is valuable to the extent that it is able to do this. With children, however, the influence of nutrition on the proper pace of incarnation must also be considered since it can be of decisive importance for all of later life. If a child is fed cow's milk instead of mother's milk, the entire subsequent process of incarnation is affected. In particular, the risk of premature sclerosis becomes greater.

We live today in an age of hasty scientific judgments. Physicians often do not consider the long-term effects of modern treatments, being satisfied instead with momentary "successes." However, the impressive growth rates obtained with some infant formulas are not a sufficient indicator of true nutritional quality. The child may be thriving and its organs physically well formed, but this is not enough. Organ formation is primarily an etheric, not a physical process and prepares the organs for use by the higher constituents. Defects in this process may not become apparent until adulthood. Rudolf Steiner specifically indicated that certain diseases occurring in the second half of life, such as liver ailments and gastrointestinal cancers, can ultimately be traced back to qualitatively inferior nutrition in infancy.[14] Such nutrition causes a child's liver to be structured too coarsely, hampering its ability to perceive food qualities and thus to properly detoxify the blood. The organism in effect becomes blind to its own metabolic processes. This phenomenon is repeatedly referred to in modern discussions of cancer.

14. R. Steiner, The Human Being in Body, Soul, and Spirit: Our Relationship to the Earth (Hudson, N.Y.: Anthroposophic Press, 1989), lecture 4.

Cancer patients suffer not just from anergy, but from the inability to recognize cancerous tissue as "not-self" and to mount an immune response against it. Some authors, while recognizing the significant role played by the liver in this process, nonetheless fail to see why the livers of cancer patients are incapable of playing that role.[15]

The etheric body and its formative forces must be recognized as the concrete realities underlying life processes. The etheric body has a definite temporal structure, which is reflected in the fact that certain periods in human development correspond to or mirror others. However, without the concept of the metamorphosis of formative forces discussed in various contexts in Volume I, these correspondences would be completely unintelligible. One need only consider the modern increase in degenerative illnesses, which can be traced back, at least in part, to defective nutrition in the first year of life.

Western countries offer ample illustrations of this. Almost all food consumed there has been extensively processed, and yet few people consider the effect that this has on susceptibility to disease, that is, on the etheric body. The food of Eastern countries, by contrast, is still largely natural and unadulterated.

With these points in mind we can examine the procedures used to make modern infant formulas, almost all of which are based on cow's milk.

Researchers first tried to bring the protein content of cow's milk formulas close to that of mother's milk by diluting the former with two parts gruel. The calories lost in this way were then made up with "equicaloric" additions of sugar. Due to disappointing results, skim milk was later substituted for whole milk, and beet sugar was substituted for milk sugar, since milk sugar caused diarrhea. Satisfactory results were eventually obtained after the addition of a second highly colloidal carbohydrate. Thus, by trial and error, a formula was eventually found that approximated mother's milk in caloric content and in volume, and that produced satisfactory weight gain in healthy, well-constituted infants. Nevertheless, it was plain that these infants lagged considerably behind their breast-fed counterparts in overall development.

Infant formulas have been even further enriched and modified in recent times, making possible not just equal, but even faster and greater

15. Casper Blond, Liver Damage as the Cause of Cancer, second edition (Bristol: 1960).

weight gains than with mother's milk. This has created the impression in lay circles that we now have formulas that are "better than nature." However, the passage quoted above bears repeating: "... it is not surprising that bottle-fed infants usually weigh more than breast-fed children and often appear 'pasty' or overfed. Their rapid growth bears only a superficial resemblance to the breast-fed child's thriving; it is definitely not identical to it."[16]

These newer formulas approximate the nutritional quality of mother's milk in a variety of ways. First, they are homogenized to increase digestibility. Cow's milk is pressed through fine jets under high pressure, resulting in the finest possible flocculation. This reduces the size of the milk's large fat-albumin globules, and allows the formation in the child's stomach of a fine curb similar to that produced with mother's milk. Children raised on homogenized milk without added carbohydrates developed normally. Today practically all commercially available milk is homogenized.

The fine protein flocculation sought through homogenization can also be obtained through the addition of carbohydrates (see below). Here, however, the advantage of finer curdling is offset by a disruption of formative forces, upon which the true nutritional value of a food is based.

A further method of refining flocculation is acidification with either lactic, citric, or adipic acid. This method also prevents the coagulation of casein and reduces the production of digestive juices, thus lightening the burden on the child's metabolism. Acidification also inhibits bacterial growth. This so-called "antidyspeptic security factor," however, takes effect only at impractically high levels of acidity (pH 4.5), and is thus a purely theoretical consideration. In practice, acidification overburdens the metabolism and tends to result in poorer development. In sensitive infants it can even temporarily impair kidney function through hyperchloremic acidosis. Acidification of the formula is thus unnecessary for normal infants, and the use of sour milk products has now been largely discontinued. Yet, it must be mentioned that in animal tests the addition of lactic acid to food greatly accelerated growth.[17] Whether this was caused by acidification as such or specifically by lactic acid is still unclear.

16. R. Beckmann, MMW 106 (1964): 2325.
17. H. Vollmer, Klinische Wochenschrift 6 (1927):1806.

Soured milk acidifies the upper portions of the intestine, but produces a stool that contains coliform bacteria and is relatively alkaline. Czerny-Keller malt soup, on the other hand, produces acid fermentation extending into the large intestine. However, as it tends to provoke diarrhea, it is used only as a special diet in cases of constipation. Children fed with mother's milk tend to have a much more acidic milieu in their lower intestine than do children fed with the customary cow's milk formulas, so that the breast-fed infant's stool has a slightly acidic smell.

In order to guide and structure the etheric body's activity in the large intestine, the astral body requires the acidic environment normal for that part of the digestive tract. The maintenance of this environment is in principle a task of the renal system. The infant's renal system, however, is not yet fully functional. An intestinal milieu that is alkaline and contains coliform flora hinders the astral body's structuring activity, which means that the etheric body then receives less than the normal and necessary amount of guidance. It may even be assumed that under these circumstances, astral influences are displaced into the nerve-sense organization, where they may give rise to the unhealthy levels of nerve-sense activity so characteristic of our times. Finally, the etheric body is unable to coordinate growth in a way corresponding to the astral body and ego. The change in the astral body's intervention also changes the nature of the ego's activity.

The presence of the acidophile bifidus bacteria in the stool of the breast-fed child is a reliable indicator of a properly acidic intestinal environment. Bifidus bacteria make up as much as 85% of the healthy breast-fed infant's intestinal flora and up to 40% of the healthy adult's. Bifidus bacteria protect the intestines from pathogenic germs by producing organic acids and play a crucial role in the formation of certain vitamins (B1, B2, K). However, the nature of intestinal flora is determined not only by diet but also by the activity of the higher constituents in the large intestine.

Intestinal flora can be adjusted favorably with a roasted preparation of butter and flour. Although this is hardly used anymore, its mode of action is instructive. The roasting process, which is analogous to caramelization, carries fermentation deep into the intestine. This preparation is particularly effective when used with sour milk instead of sweet. Infants fed this way exhibit excellent turgor, tonus, complexion, and immunity to infection. The addition of cystine or caramelized lactose (Bessau), of albumin and dextrin (dexamyl, after Adam), of beta-lactose (Malyoth), or of lactulose, produces the desired bifidus flora. Of these additives, lactulose, a beta-galactoside fructose (Petuely), is particularly effective. Whatever the method used, however, bifidus bacteria require a lactose-protein quotient of over 2.6 in order to grow.

The desire to find ever closer approximations to mother's milk has led in recent years to the development of so-called "modified milks." Their protein content is even lower than that of older formulas and sometimes completely derived from whey. Milk fat is almost entirely removed and replaced with vegetable oil in order to more closely approximate the proportion of unsaturated fatty acids in mother's milk. Mineral content is likewise reduced (especially calcium), resulting in an approximation of the Ca-P ratio of human milk. Nevertheless, the total mineral content is still higher than that of human milk, leading to the consequences described above. The sugar added in lactose, which is rendered more digestible by preserving a lactose-fat ratio of 2:1. This prevents the indigestion caused by the addition of lactose alone. Vitamins (and sometimes iron) are added to complete the formula, resulting in milk that is chemically and physiologically very close to mother's milk. The gradual changes in the composition of mother's milk over time (decrease in protein and increase in sugar and fat) are taken into account with the development of two types of formula.

These formulas are highly digestible, and further improvements hardly seem possible. However, such extensive, "perfected" modification is unnecessary, as shown by the satisfactory development of healthy children on older formulas.

Judgments of quality vary according to one's presuppositions. From the physiological and biochemical points of view, the modified formulas certainly represent an optimum. A more holistic evaluation, however, cannot ignore that these formulas are fabrications that begin with parts, not with the whole. Milk, like any other living substance, is more than the sum of its parts. Human milk originates in the mother's etheric body; it is therefore an integral whole and an all-embracing carrier of life processes. Its formative forces can never be completely captured by the imitative combination of ingredients, by the adjustment of the degree of saturation of fatty acids, the addition of vitamins, and so on.

Formative forces are a reality and should therefore be preserved whenever possible. Particular substances are only their vehicles, even if they are specific vehicles. Diluted fresh cow's milk, on the other hand, constitutes a whole, as do the carbohydrates that are added to it. Methods of preparation that respect the vital structure of formula ingredients are the key to preserving formative forces.

Milk Quality

Nutritional authorities still judge milk quality for the most part in exclusively chemical and bacteriological terms. Quality, however, is essentially imponderable. It eludes customary methods of measurements and acts on a level that transcends mere chemistry. Such matters as milk sources, methods of production, and processing are also usually dealt with on a purely quantitative level. A number of methods have been developed to remedy this lack and to address the question of formative forces, including copper chloride crystallization, the capillary dynamic method, and the droplet-picture method. These methods isolate the formative forces of an organic substance or foodstuff and enable us to make judgments about its quality.

Even calorie computation is not a purely quantitative problem. It is a common observation that children in an institutional environment require up to 50% more calories than children in a domestic environment. This points to the existence of "imponderables" that influence the utilization of food and that are hardly considered today.

A number of definitive nutritional experiments on animals illuminate the depth of the effect nutrition has on disposition, constitution, and heredity. Katase's classic investigations of the influence of nutrition on bone structure, tooth formation, and susceptibility to disease ought long since to have become familiar;[18] unfortunately, however, these studies and those that followed have not been given the attention they deserve, nor, for that matter, does anyone seem to have drawn the necessary conclusions from them.

In Katase's experiments, the effects of raw and variously processed foods on cats was investigated over a period of more than ten years. Cats fed on raw milk remained healthy and gave birth to normal offspring. By

18. A. Katase, "Der Einfluss der Ernährung auf die Konstitution des Organismus," Path. Inst. of the Med. Acad. of Osaka (1931).

contrast, those fed on processed milk began after only a few generations to miscarry, die younger, and fall victim to a variety of degenerative illnesses. They also exhibited skeletal, mandibular, and dental deformities. The frequency of these adverse effects was proportional to the degree of processing of the milk; pasteurized milk had the fewest detrimental effects, condensed had the most, and dried milk lay in between. Repetition of the experiments with white rats yielded the same results.[19]

Another particularly relevant set of experiments was described by Kollath in his basic work, *Der Vollwert der Nahrung.* Kollath investigated the effects of a diet based on isolated nutritional components.[20] In rats, such a diet disturbed the intestinal flora and calcium metabolism, causing various organs to calcify. It also caused premature aging, inefficacy of vitamins, and a wide variety of organ abnormalities. As might be expected, the diet affected young, developing animals the most. In no case could the effects be attributed to caloric undernourishment or vitamin deficiencies.

An interesting result of Kollath's experiments is that the effects of an inferior or fragmentary diet do not appear in the first generation. A diet of white rolls, for example, caused degenerative alterations only in the second and subsequent generations of rats. Furthermore, Pottenger found that the results of improper nourishment over two generations can be made good again only after four generations of a high-quality, fresh-food diet.[21]

Although animal experiments cannot be directly applied to human conditions, they still indicate that any judgment of the biological value of a foodstuff or diet must be based on much longer time periods than are customarily taken into account, and that strong initial growth and weight gain are not in themselves proof of real nutritional quality. A poor diet adversely affects the organism's formative forces, which are passed on to

---

19. F. M. Pottenger Jr., "The Effect of Heat-Processing of Food on the Dento-Facial Structures of Experimental Animals," American Journal of Orthodontic and Oral Surgery, 32 (1946):467–485. See also F. M. Pottenger Jr. and D. G. Simonsen. "The Influence of Heal Label Factors on Nutrition in Oral Development and Health," Journal of Lab. & Clin. Med. 25 (1939): Journal of the Southern Calif. State Dental Assoc. (1939)Nov.; W. A. Price, Nutrition and Physical Degeneration (New York;1939).
20. Kollath, Werner, Der Vollwert der Nahrung, vol. 1 (Stuttgart: 1950) and vol. 2 (Stuttgart: 1960).
21. See previous 2 footnotes.

subsequent generations. Adverse effects may become apparent only after many years, making the connection with the initial influences anything but obvious. This also explains why growing animals are the most susceptible to latent damage.

The significance of this for human infant nutrition is that dehydration and condensation of milk, which involve heating and exposure to a vacuum, denature milk protein and thus lower its biological value. A comparative study of premature infants, some fed with raw and others with sterilized human milk, showed that equal weight gains could be achieved only when the energy quotient of the sterile milk was 135–150 compared to 80–120 for raw milk. The lack in quality, in other words, had to be made up for with an increase in quantity, and even then the results were not identical, as witnessed by the lower mortality rate among the infants fed with raw milk.[22]

The denaturation caused by sterilization, however, is minor compared to that caused by condensation, which involves temperatures as high as 266ºF. The partial racemization of protein caused by this process, inferrable from the subsequent presence of d-amino acids, gives us a rough indication in chemical terms of how deep the effects of this treatment must be.[23] It is not hard to see that after so much processing the delicate formative forces that are the basis of quality in food have been completely destroyed. That vitamins, enzymes, and other valuable substances are also largely destroyed is a well-known fact.

The damage to formative forces must be even more extensive in ultra-pasteurized milk, a relatively new product that owes its imperishability to a short but very intense heating. The discussion surrounding this product's introduction clearly demonstrates the utter inadequacy of the criteria currently used to assess food quality. Shelf life, sterility, digestibility, and short-term nutritional trials tell only part of the story. Indeed, such labels as "bacteria-free," "germ-free," and "vitamin-rich" are overemphasized and contribute to a false sense of security, obscuring the true state of affairs and possible long-term harmful effects. Granted, sterile milk will not transmit infection, but neither does it support true health, as

22. Catel and Walituch, Monatsschrift für Kinderheilkunde 40 (1928)1–2.
23. Second Seminar of the Max Planck Institute for the Physiology of Nutrition, Dortmund, reported in Deutsche Molkereizeitung 73 (1952):880.

indicated in the higher mortality rate and greater severity of illness in children fed with it in the experiments mentioned above. Of course, this does not mean that we should stop guarding against bacterial contamination; however, sterility says nothing positive about a milk's quality—it only indicates the absence of something undesirable.

Interestingly, crystallization pictures corroborate Katase's finding that powdered milk is of higher quality than condensed milk. They also indicate that the formative forces of boiled milk can be partially restored by exposing the milk to diffuse sunlight in a shallow dish for approximately 20 minutes (W. zur Linden, H. Krueger, G. Schmidt, et al.). Ultraviolet irradiation, on the other hand, is unacceptable, since its effect is merely chemical and all one-sidedness upsets the milk's organic harmony.

The routine addition of vitamin D to milk is also unacceptable, for the reasons set forth in volume I (p. 36f.). Milk is "enriched" with vitamin D for the express purpose of preventing rickets in children. However, anyone else who drinks milk will also ingest the vitamin D, and in some of these it might promote premature sclerotization. Milk alone or cod liver oil could never have this effect, since in them, as in all natural products, vitamin D is balanced out by vitamin A, its polar opposite.[24] Should vitamin D supplements be necessary, a medically indicated, suitable daily dose is clearly preferable to the unphysiological use of megadoses.

The consumption of evaporated milk should be limited to times when no acceptable fresh milk is obtainable, and continued only as long as is absolutely necessary. Under no circumstances should evaporated milk be made a child's regular fare, as sometimes happens today.

Considerations of quality also extend to the carbohydrates added to milk. Grain that has been grown with production-oriented fertilizers, which destroy soil vitality, should be used only when nothing better is available. Decades of practical experience, on the other hand, have shown that children fed with biodynamically grown cereal products—commercially available in Europe under the "Demeter" label—thrive consistently. Even the crystallization method reveals that these carbohydrates contain a much higher degree of formative forces than more conventional products. Once again, it is the content of etheric formative

24. More detailed presentation in Wolff, BEH 7 (1954):175.

forces rather than of individual, chemically active substances that is decisive for infant nutrition.

Bottle-feeding for Healthy Infants

As already mentioned, even the bottle-fed child should be given as much mother's milk as is available. Badly dehydrated newborns should be offered a small amount of very weak fennel tea, in some cases as soon as several hours after birth. Depending on the child, actual feeding may begin approximately twelve hours after birth with a formula of one part milk to one part oat gruel. Even better than oat gruel, however, is Demeter-Holle cream of cereal.[25] The child should receive five feedings a day of approximately 20 g at first, and the amount per meal should be increased daily by 5–10 g. By the tenth day the amount needed per meal seldom exceeds 80–90 g (rule of thumb: body weight divided by 6 = daily food requirement). This increases to 140 g by the end of the first month, assuming one stays with the half-milk formula. Infants who drink comparatively little should begin to receive 2/3 milk already at this point; all other can wait until eight weeks.

In the third through fifth months, most children will consume daily about four meals of 200 g. Under no circumstances should more than 900 g be given per day. This corresponds to the amount a child would normally drink at the breast. However, some children may not be satisfied with this amount, due either to an abnormally high food requirement (premature birth, unusual size, or low birth weight) or inferior quality of the oat flakes or milk. In either case the composition of the formula should be changed so that the child can be satisfied with a total intake of no more than 900 g. The proportion of milk may be gradually increased in the tenth and twelfth weeks, so that by the beginning of the fourth month it is two-thirds. However, the total amount of cow's milk consumed by healthy children during their first year should not exceed 400 g per day. "Pasty" children and children at risk for rickets should

25. This often produces bloating, whereas the standard preparations, to which the children become accustomed in the hospital, are more readily digested. This is understandable, since the latter are formulated to require as little digestive work as possible, a valid principle for the first period of life. However, their ease of digestion must be weighed against their inferior nutritional value. Hence a slow and gradual transition to the preparation described here should be made as soon as individual conditions permit.

have even less. Undiluted milk should not be given at all during the first six months.

Each type of grain added to the formula influences a specific aspect of the child's being. Oats, the grain used first, tend to activate the child's movement organism. A relatively cosmic plant, oat contains large amounts of high-grade fat, which explains its beneficial influence on diabetes and on small-headed children, as well as its usefulness as a soporific (Avena sativa). If used exclusively for too long, however, oats may prevent the child from incarnating fully. Thus, by the fourth month, oat flakes should be supplemented with other grains in order to assure a well-rounded influence on the child's development. (Mixed preparations such as Holle Baby Food II satisfy this requirement.)

Barley not only contains large amounts of protein, but also contains silica, a mineral important for the development of the nervous system, the sense organs, and connective tissue.[26] It is mildly constipating. Rye, the universal bread grain, confers earthly solidity, but tends to be too heavy for infants and small children. Wheat is an all-purpose grain and easily digested but is insufficient by itself as a carbohydrate. Millet porridge and buckwheat are also excellent children's foods.

Although the caloric value of the cereal products used in milk formulas is minimal (3%), their clinical significance is considerable. For this reason it is important to choose products that contain an optimum of formative forces, such as grains produced by biodynamic cultivation. Obviously only whole grains will have the desired effect.

Added sugar normally amounts to 5% of the formula by weight. At three months, most infants will tolerate honey, a food of great importance for the formative forces. A pea-sized drop of honey, but no more, may be added to the bottle. Under no circumstances should honey be used to make up the entire sugar content of the formula. Honey should also not be heated over 120ºF.

Breast-fed children can subsist on milk alone for the first eight weeks. Bottle-fed infants, on the other hand, should begin to receive other foods after six weeks, for example, a teaspoon of juice twice a day (carrot or fruit juice depending on the season). The serving size may be gradu-

26. See G. Schmidt and U. Renzenbrink, Das Getreide als menschengemässe Nahrung (Dornach:1967).

ally increased. Such supplementation is more important in the colder months of the year and should then be increased more rapidly than in the summer.

The quality of the vegetable juices fed to children is critical. Vegetables fertilized with sewage or high-nitrogen fertilizers (e.g. spinach) are not only undesirable but can even cause illness or poisoning.

The next step—starting around the third month—is the introduction at the evening meal of whole-milk zwieback or porridge. The porridge may be sweetened with a little fruit juice, and should be fed by spoon.

In the fourth month, milk should be completely replaced at the midday meal by vegetable purees and fruit. The vegetables should of course be cooked. Steaming, which breaks down and "opens" the food, effecting a sort of predigestion, makes the child's digestive work easier. Cooking damages food only when it is done at too high a temperature, for too long, or repeatedly.

During the first six months, a child will normally receive five meals per day; only during the first six weeks may six meals be given. After three to four months the number of meals may be decreased to four; indeed, children will often do this themselves by sleeping through one of their meals.

To accustom children to a regular rhythm, feeding schedules should be adhered to as closely as possible. Of course, it can happen that a child will demand a different rhythm. Furthermore, no child should be expected to consume the same amount of food at every meal. Instead the child should drink only enough to be satisfied.

Children should begin to receive solid food at eight months, nine at the very latest. If one waits any longer than this, it may be difficult for the child to learn how to chew. Even children who as yet have no teeth can be given small pieces of bread with butter and jam or honey, a cookie, or a biscuit. The ingestion of solid food is an important milestone in the child's earthly development and should not be postponed.

By the age of nine months children will have learned to eat sitting up and to drink out of a cup. They eat at the same table as their parents and learn correct mealtime behavior by imitation. For the first two years, however, an adult diet is unsuitable for them.

Toward the end of the first year, the child's diet will have become so concentrated that the total quantity does not amount to much more than a liter. No more than 400 g of this total should be milk, including the milk used in gruel or porridge. Milk should also not be used as a thirst quencher. After the seventh month, it is best given undiluted, except perhaps for the addition of a small amount of chamomile tea or malt coffee, the latter of which facilitates the digestion of milk protein. To quench thirst, fruit juices or weak fennel or chamomile tea should be used.

An excess of protein, especially from eggs, in the child's diet before the age of three is not only unnecessary but also harmful. Protein digestion requires forces that in the child are occupied elsewhere and thus not yet available. Furthermore, protein specifically stimulates metabolic forces. This is undesirable for children, since their formative impulses normally issue from the head, not from the metabolism. To stimulate a child's metabolic system with protein is thus to accelerate development in an unhealthy way. Such considerations may explain Rudolf Steiner's remark that eating eggs spoils children's healthy instincts for food. This is not to deny that some children, especially ones with a pyknic constitution, may require meat in the diet as a protein supplement from about the third year on.

Potatoes are becoming an increasingly unacceptable food for children. Their quality is rapidly degenerating, and for reasons discussed in volume I (p. 226), they are of questionable value as a foodstuff. The fact that some nutritional authorities still recommend potatoes for children shows how little their evaluations are based on true quality. Whole grains, including rice, are an acceptable substitute.

Medications Supporting the Diet

Nutrition has lasting effects on the human constitution, never more so than during childhood. Knowledge of the effects of particular foodstuffs can therefore be a useful tool in guiding childhood development. Both diet and medications should be applied early on in a mutually supporting fashion to deal with constitutional peculiarities. One such peculiarity is the size of the head (discussed in vol. I, p. 105f). Large-headed children need root vegetables earlier and in greater amounts than small-headed children, because roots are rich in minerals and thus stimulate the formative forces. Salt may be added depending on the child's age. These effects are supported with medications such as lead (Plumbum praep. D10–D20, one pinch in the morning; for infants Plumbum salve, 0.1%, a pea-sized amount rubbed into the back of the head). Plumbum is given for two or at most four weeks, after which copper is given for two weeks to consolidate the effect of lead (Cuprum praep. D6, one pinch twice daily). Small-headed children should receive larger amounts of sugar in their milk, a dietary measure supported by silver medications.

The dietetic medications Calcon I and II were formulated in response to a specific suggestion by Rudolf Steiner and were originally given to compensate for malnutrition in times of famine. Calcon I is natural calcium phosphate (apatite) D6, with pumpkin blossoms. Calcon II contains 5% calcium carbonate from oyster shells, and oak bark. One pinch of Calcon I is given in the morning and one of Calcon II in the evening. Calcon is not meant to completely replace dietary calcium, but rather only to stimulate calcium assimilation. It also helps to better regulate calcium metabolism, leading to better utilization of food, healthier growth, and a calming of the nervous system. It should be administered over extended periods, with pauses of 2–4 weeks after every eight weeks of administration. It is intended neither as a therapy nor as a prophylaxis for rickets.

Breast-fed infants have no need for Calcon, but nursing mothers do. Remedies devised especially for the therapy and prophylaxis of rickets are Apatite/Phosphorus and Conchae/Quercus S (for infants) or K (for children).

The infant's anabolic processes may be stimulated with baths containing Prunus spinosa or Weleda children's bath. Cases of severe weakness may be treated with the so-called "nutritive bath" recommended by Rudolf Steiner, which contains the juice of half a lemon, half a liter of fresh milk, and one fresh beaten egg. This treatment can be useful for children as well.

Acute Nutritional Disorders in Infants

Infant indigestion is now considered an infectious disease engendered primarily by pathogenic coliform bacteria. These bacteria are transmitted by contamination. Bred in pure culture, they cause severe indigestion, which appears to prove the pathogenesis and mode of infection. Further confirmation of this etiology is seen in the effectiveness of antibiotic therapy. Despite this, some physicians admit that to regard dyspepsia as an infection neither explains nor solves the problem. Marget and Kienitz write: "We pediatricians in particular are quite far from being able to claim mastery over bacterial infections. The notion that a chemotherapeutical agent in sufficient dosage will eliminate the pathogens and thus achieve a cure does not explain the majority of successful cures, at least not in this simplified form. It is well known that the administration of antibiotics is not therapy in the proper sense of the word. It merely leads to a suppression or elimination of the critical etiological factor, the bacteria. Depending on the efficacy of the treatment, after the antibiotic is discontinued and the pathogenic agent disappears, the patient frequently has a relapse or becomes a carrier of the germ. Drug therapy is thus frequently only one means of supporting the host in the battle with the pathogen."[27]

The only conclusion that can be drawn from decades of experience with antibiotics is that there must be some other way to affect the disease process than by attempting merely to destroy bacteria. Moreover, if the theory of pathogenesis by infection were strictly true, it would follow that the danger of illness would be greater in the home environment than in the hospital, since the hospital is kept more sanitary. However, the opposite is the case. Furthermore, the course and origin of diseases contracted in hospitals frequently cannot be described as "normal." The clinical environment affects the child strongly enough to change his physiological responses, and the concentration of infants or ailing children in the hospital is a kind of "monoculture," an unphysiological condition that promotes the propagation of pathogens. This justifies thorough antiseptic measures. In the home, the presence or absence of bacteria is much less important than the child's susceptibility to disease.

27. W. Marget and M. Kienitz, Praxis der Antibiotikatherapie im Kindesalter (Stuttgart: 1966).

This is not to deny the importance of bacteria in the genesis of infantile dyspepsia. However, the role bacteria play is subsidiary rather than primary. A much more important factor is resistance, as was discussed in great detail in the chapter on infectious diseases, p. 8f.

The "house epidemics" of nurseries and other hospital settings are a striking example of "hospitalism," the genesis of disease through the very technological advances intended to prevent or cure it. Just how strongly the hospital environment influences children is apparent from the observation already mentioned, namely, that a 50% or greater increase in the energy quotient of food is often necessary to produce a weight gain comparable to that of a nonhospitalized child.[28]

Our previous discussion of the quality of food should have made clear that inferior food negatively influences organ development and resistance, as indicated by the bottle-fed child's greater susceptibility to disease. "Hospitalism" and inferior nutrition increase susceptibility to infections and lower resistance, thus endangering the child's mental as well as physical development. The goal of therapy must therefore be to strengthen the juvenile organism. Bacteria will then no longer be able to spread or exert deleterious influences.

All organic disturbances ultimately express a disharmony between the higher constituents of the human being. Anthroposophic medicine bases its therapy on a knowledge of the functions and relations of these constituents; their connections to the building blocks of nutrition, to metabolism, and to the various regions of the body were described in the chapter "Fundamentals of a Biochemistry and a Pathophysiology" in Volume I. From this standpoint, pediatric nutritional disorders fall naturally into two categories:

1. The ego organization and the closely allied astral body do not intervene with sufficient intensity in the digestive process, thus causing incomplete digestion and faulty absorption. Since the stream of nutrient substances does not deliver sufficient "material," organ development suffers. Ingested food retains an excessive similarity inside the organism to the force-structure of the outer world. It also remains in the intestine too

28. Fr. Lust and M. von Pfaundler, Krankheiten des Kindesalters: Diagnostik und Therapie in der Praxis, 24th ed. (Munich/Berlin/Vienna: 1971).

long, where it begins to rot and ferment as it would outside the organism, all with the help of bacteria. The pathogens among these bacteria produce toxic metabolic products, which the blood absorbs through the wall of the intestine. This leads to catarrh or inflammation, followed by flatulence and colics. Improperly or insufficiently digested food leaves the intestine as diarrhea.

Intestinal inflammation naturally calls for a bland or liquid diet, which, except in infants, should be preceded by an enema or by the drinking of a purgative tea. Rather than prescribe antidiarrheal remedies, a proper therapy will attempt to activate the ego organization and the astral body in the intestine. This is done primarily with Arsenicum album. Arsenic strengthens the astral body in the digestive tract. Dosage: 3 to 5 drops of D6-D4 liq., t.i.d., possibly more often depending on age and severity. A similar effect is produced by Veratrum album, the white hellebore, which for this reason has been called "vegetable arsenic." In most cases it is best to start with Veratrum (D4) and hold arsenic in reserve. Both medications counteract fluid loss, so that the decisive indicators are dehydration and accompanying thirst.

The activity of the higher constituents in the intestine can also be stimulated, though in a different way, with the bitter extracts of the roots of a variety of herbs:

Gentiana lutea, the yellow gentian, influences primarily the gastric nervous system, stimulating appetite and promoting absorption of nutrients in the small intestine. It thus has a weak antidyspeptic effect. Cichorium, Radix, the chicory root, acts primarily by way of the liver and bile metabolism. It enhances the digestibility of food and affects intermediate metabolism. Geum urbanum, bennet or yellow avens, has a considerably stronger influence on the small intestine than the two preceding medications, particularly in cases of fermentative dyspepsia (D1–D3). Chamomilla, Radix, the chamomile root, is indicated in cases of putrescent dyspepsia, the symptoms of which are green, watery, foul-smelling evacuations, and flatulent colics. When flatulence is the chief symptom, a proven preparation is Carbo Betulae 5%/Ol. aeth. Carvi 1%.

Ipecacuanha D3, D4, the ipecac root, is applied in cases of intestinal fermentation with watery, foamy, or bloody diarrhea. Its most important indication is intractable vomiting upon intake of even the smallest amount of tea or the like, without coated tongue. Evacuations are watery and forceful. In acute diarrhea with vomiting, the combined use of Ipecacuanha and Veratrum album in D4 in hourly alternation has proven successful. Both should be given with so little water that they can be almost entirely absorbed by the tongue. After four to five hours of this procedure, one can try giving a teaspoonful of tea, gradually increasing the intake of fluids while continuing the medication. Podophyllum peltatum, the may apple or duck's foot, is choleretic and a valuable remedy for profuse, watery diarrhea and for colitis.

The entire intestinal tract, to the extent that its functions are cellular and glandular, is subject to the influence of the mercury process. Mercury regulates the equilibrium between cells and the circulation of fluids, which explains its wide-ranging effectiveness against such digestive disorders as stomatitis, catarrhal inflammations of the liver, enteritic processes in the duodenum and jejunum, and various forms of colitis. Mercurius viv. nat. D4–D6 trit. influences mainly the upper portion of the digestive tract, including the small intestine, while the large intestine responds more to Mercurius dulc. D3 trit. (even in cases of ulceration). For infants, however, the latter remedy will be used only in extreme cases and then only for a few days (three, at most five times daily, a pea-sized amount).

Siderite D4 (native iron carbonate) may be prescribed in cases of incomplete digestion with excessive evacuations.

2. The other group of nutritional disorders develops when the ego organization and astral body are too strongly active in the digestive tract. Manifestations of this include accelerated peristalsis, flatulent colics, and spastic constipation. Intestinal atony or paralysis can result if the ego organization's activity far exceeds that of the astral body. The therapeutic goal in these cases should be to reduce or replace excessive astral or ego activity with the appropriate medication.

Carbo Betulae reduces overly strong activity on the part of the astral body in the intestines. As trit., D3–D6, it counteracts flatulence. An even stronger effect in this direction is achieved by Carbo animalis. Both remedies are appropriate for enteritis with thin, green evacuations, soreness, and putrid flatulence, as well as for hyperacid gastritis. Calcium carbonate in the form of Conchae verae also relieves the intestines of excessive astralization that manifests itself in acid, painful diarrhea. Colocynthis, the colocynth or bitter apple, is effective against excessive intestinal peristalsis that produces severe diarrhea and colics alternating with constipation. For strong colics, this remedy can be given as frequently as every 15 minutes in liquid form (D3–D4). Anagallis, the pimpernel, is indicated for spasmodic intestinal conditions not affecting digestive function (5% trit.). Belladonna, the deadly nightshade, also relieves intestinal spasms caused by an overactive astral body. It is the remedy of choice for pylorospasm. In keeping with the child's tender age, it is given in low potency (D3–D4), 1-3 drops in a little water or as globules, hourly or less often. Along with this, a warm chamomile compress is placed on the belly inside the diaper during and after mealtime, and if possible kept there until the next meal. Sometimes an abdominal compress with Cuprum praep. 0.1% ointment will suffice. In some cases it is necessary to administer a Belladonna D3 suppository once a day. Often Magnesite D4, a pinch five times daily, is most beneficial. Extremely severe cases, or cases brought late to treatment, call for a subcutaneous abdominal injection of Nicotiana tabac. D4–D5. Another possibility is injections of Nux vomica D6. With appropriate diet (small hourly doses of expressed mother's milk) and the above remedies, the majority of cases of pylorospasm can be cured. On the other hand, extreme hardening of the pyloric muscle will necessitate surgery. This is a relatively minor intervention if the child has not been dangerously weakened.

Some nutritional disorders of this second type call for metallic remedies. Cuprum sulfuricum, for example, when given per os, D3-D6, relieves spastic constipation and promotes absorption and nutrition. Cuprum praep. 0.1% ointment may be applied with a compress or rubbed directly into the abdomen.

The degeneration of an acute nutritional disorder into a chronic one can be prevented by influencing the organism's mode of reaction with the above remedies rather than by merely treating the symptoms. Chronic disorders are usually preceded by acute indigestion and consist in the inability to process food properly.

Chronic Nutritional and Developmental Disorders

The central factor in these disorders is usually a weakness of the etheric body, the higher constituent responsible for anabolic and developmental processes. Such a weakness can be either inherited or due to a qualitatively or quantitatively insufficient diet. Qualitative dietary deficiencies are currently the more common type. Chronic nutritional disorders can also be the sequela of another disease that, for reasons that may include faulty treatment, has not run its course, so that the underlying disharmony of the constituents of the human being persists. The childhood diseases are particularly important in this regard (see vol. I, p. 40f).

Developmental disorders of this type manifest as inanition, dystrophy, weakness of the connective tissue with the resulting static complaints, and anemia. They may also affect the mental life of the child, producing such symptoms as apathy and dullness or irritation and overexcitability. Such cases are frequently associated with an imbalanced diet, which can be as harmful as actual undernourishment. Such diets are increasingly common in affluent countries, where a high proportion of the food consumed in denatured ("malnutrition in the midst of plenty").

The psychological and physiological effects of such adulterated food is illustrated by the reaction some people have to food additives, such as artificial colorings, fragrances, flavor enhancers, and stabilizers. These food additives are extensively used, particularly in western countries: at the time of this writing, 2,764 additives were reported in use in the United States alone. Feingold connects food additives with the increase of hyperkinetic disturbances in children.[29] In the last ten years, the proportion of children in the U.S. who suffer from such disorders has shot up from 2 to 10%. Feingold personally treated several children who could not keep up in school because they were incapable of concentrating or sitting still, even though their intelligence was normal. These children improved dramatically after a few weeks on a totally additive-free diet. Putting the additives back in the diet frequently caused the children to become hyperkinetic again, sometimes in as little as a few hours after a meal. Aggressiveness and other serious emotional-behavioral

29. B. F. Feingold, 122nd session of the A.M.A., New York, June 3–27, 1973, reported in Selecta 46 (1973):4327.

problems occurred in some children due to allergic reactions to the additives.

Our food products also frequently contain pesticide residues, often in concentrations exceeding those considered dangerous (which in many cases is a highly arbitrary amount). Individual reactions to such substances vary widely; furthermore, it is an error to believe that if no negative effect can be proven, then none is present. Animal experiments are wholly inconclusive regarding the influence of such unphysiological substances on human beings, particularly on children.

Phosphates are another exogenous factor blamed for behavioral disorders. Believed to be harmless, they are added to many foods, including soft drinks and cured meat products.[30] Upon ingesting them, many children become aggressive or hyperactive, develop a short attention span, or exhibit some other behavioral disturbance (minimal cerebral dysfunction). Others become apathetic without any measurable loss of intelligence. All of these children display curiously inverted reactions to drugs: sedatives make them restless, whereas stimulants calm them. An understanding of the deeper nature of phosphorus makes all these facts comprehensible: phosphorus, by activating the ego, causes it to involve itself more strongly in the body. Potentized phosphorus is used for this very purpose in the appropriate therapeutic situations. A child's ego, however, is not yet constitutionally capable of controlling the astral body; for that reason it usually remains unconsciously active in the organism. If it does not, the result is uncontrollable restlessness, usually paired with sleepiness, lack of concentration, and attempts to gain attention through such inappropriate means as disruptiveness, clowning, or even vandalism.

Clearly, then, infants and children should be fed unadulterated foods whenever possible. If the milk and other available formula ingredients do not meet the suggested standards, the lack can be balanced out somewhat with various medications, chief among them being Calcon. Elixirs, such as Sandthorn (Weleda), should also be considered. These are used not so much for their vitamin content as for their forces of life and form, or light-forces. Finally, Gentiana should be mentioned for the stimulus it provides via the metabolism or intestine.

30. Hertha Hafer, Die heimliche Droge Nahrungsphosphat (Heidelberg: 1984). O. Wolff, das Hyperkinetische Syndrom, Merkurstab 1 (1993).

In some children, a constitutional treatment of the intestine with Digestodoron may also be necessary (or, correspondingly, the liver with Hepatodoron, and so on). Metals may be employed in specific ways to stimulate the anabolic or formative forces. Of particular significance in pediatric medicine is Argentum (silver), which lays the foundation for the formation of substance and its incorporation into the etheric body. The formation of the human body under the guiding influences of the cosmos, the process typical of childhood, is frequently disturbed, making silver a very useful remedy in pediatrics. A particularly well-proven pediatric remedy is Bryophyllum Argento cultum, a "vegetabilized" form of silver (see vol. I, pp. 311–312). It acts mildly yet relatively rapidly, particularly against disturbances in fluid balance, and against night terrors. Its effect is generally enlivening and regenerating.

Another remedy that stimulates the etheric body is magnesium. As Magnesium phosphoricum D4–D6, it particularly stimulates inner light-metabolism.

In addition to an enlivening effect, a plastic, forming one may also be required. Quartz or silica is indicated for weakness of the supportive or connective tissue, such as ligaments and cartilage. Kyphosis, scoliosis, and hernias are indications for Stannum (tin: for example, Stannum silicicum D6–D10). Among the processes that Stannum influences is the shaping of the internal organs, especially the brain, lungs, and liver. Stannum regulates fluid content and thus the firmness of the organs. Fluorine (as Fluorite D4–D6) has also proven effective in cases of extreme slackness of the joints (overextensibility).

The mineralization processes of the skeleton are guided by Plumbum (lead), which is thus indicated for rickets and craniotabes. Plumbum is also given for insufficient consolidation of the skin or mucous membranes, such as in exudative diathesis or hay fever. Lead has about the most profound effects of any remedy, so in children it must be used with great caution. In craniotabes, for example, lead may be used as Plumbum 0.1% ointment, rubbed into the back of the head, or as Plumbum praep. D20–D12, 1 pinch in the morning, for a few weeks at the most. Only in rare cases and only for older children will Plumbum be given in D6 or D8. A positive lead effect can be consolidated by copper, as described earlier.

Another metal frequently indicated in pediatric medicine is iron, the incarnation metal par excellence. The iron process and its relation to development are discussed in detail in Volume I, chapter 4. Iron is indicated not only for anemia, but also quite generally as an aid to incarnation. Urtica dioica Ferro culta 1% is particularly good for stimulating the inner iron process, though it is of course no substitute for dietary iron. Iron's effects are especially favorable following the administration of silver. Children who show too little movement and whose force of uprightness needs stimulation should be given Ferrum praep. D20 or Ferrum sidereum D20.

Rickets

The pathology, symptomatology, and essential nature of rickets as a disturbed process of incarnation are described in detail in volume I (pp. 34-40). The basic cause of rickets is a weakness of the ego organization, which is expressed in the characteristic anatomical and metabolic findings and in disturbances in light-metabolism. From this follows the necessary rationale for prophylaxis and treatment.

Rickets is not a pure avitaminosis. Vitamin D is less a vitamin than it is a light-activated hormone, and we now know that it becomes effective only after processing by the liver and kidneys. Administration of the isolated substance is thus substitution therapy at best, which may or may not be desirable.

Whenever vitamin D is administered, a number of things must be considered. First, the administration of a "ready-made" preparation relieves the growing organism of an activity that it should learn to perform by itself. In this case that means the formation of 7–dehydrocholesterol and the transformation of that into vitamin D by means of light. The child's light-organism is active in this process. Administering vitamin D makes it possible for the child to develop more quickly, which in rickets is desirable, as rachitic children are in a sense retarded. However, to use an analogy, it is as if one wished to spare children the effort of learning to walk and placed them from the start in a wheelchair or a car. Against this it must be stressed that what matters is not outwardly observable signs of development, but rather the abilities the children acquire in the process of mastering their bodies and of coming to terms with the world around them.

If rickets is a weakness of the tendency to incarnate, it is not hard to imagine how traumatic it must be for the incarnating human being to be suddenly wrenched down into the physical organism with a megadose of vitamin D, or to be veritably chained to the body by overly lengthy or overly high doses. Such considerations are lost on those who consider only physicochemical changes, X-rays, and short-term developmental "results."

In addition to the general drawbacks of administering synthetic vitamin D, we must also consider the possible long-term side effects, particularly of megadoses. When a powerful synthetic preparation of vitamin D first became available, the possibility of treating severe rickets was hailed by one author as one of the "greatest triumphs of medical research of all times and all lands" (Pfaundler, 1929); yet as early as 1927, the same author had warned instead of the dangers of using the same substance. Synthetic vitamin D was applied on a grand scale both therapeutically and prophylactically upon its introduction in 1931, and a drastic reduction of rickets was achieved. Since at that time vitamins were viewed as the very essence of health and life, it is not surprising that no one expressed reservations about possible overdoses or harmful side effects. Even experiments demonstrating the development of vascular calcifications in newborn rabbits whose mothers had received vitamin D during pregnancy was not enough to alert anyone to the dangers.[31]

After the Second World War, however, doctors began to notice symptoms of overdose and of hypersensitivity to vitamin D, including lack of appetite, malaise, vomiting, weight loss, headaches and stomach aches, thirst, emotional problems (ill temper, agitation, etc.), and renal disorders. Hypertension, nitrogen retention, hypercalcemia, and hyperphosphatemia were also observed. Fatalities were reported as early at 1946.[32] The so-called "idiopathic hypercalcemia" first reported in England in 1952 (Lightwood) reached nearly epidemic proportions and was only later recognized to be vitamin D poisoning.[33] In England at that time, one thousand units of vitamin D were being added to every liter of milk, which brought the average British child's daily dose to three or four thousand units (due to the vitamin D enrichment of other foods as well).

31. A. Junck, Virchows Archiv 283 (1932):265.

32. A summary of the toxic effects of vitamin D described through 1950 is found in G. Schönemann, BEH 4 (1951):261. A detailed presentation of these effects may be found in M. S. Seelig, "Vitamin D and Cardiovascular, Renal, and Brain Damage in Infancy and Childhood," Ann. New York Acad. Sci. 147 (1969):537.

33. Comprehensive survey in Hövels and Stephan, Ergebnisse der Inneren Medizin und Kinderheilkunde 18 (1962).

After vitaminization of food products was eliminated, hypercalcemia all but disappeared.

Later, in 1961, a significant correlation was found between hypercalcemia and supraventricular aortostenosis; this is now documented by an extensive literature. A similarly documented connection exists between hypercalcemia, vitamin D poisoning, and supravalvular aortostenosis. Idiopathic hypercalcemia is further associated with physical and mental retardation, a typical facies, multiple peripheral pulmonary stenoses, identical tooth deformities, and renal disorders caused by calcification. Ectopic calcification also occurs in the kidneys, heart, and aorta.[34]

Some researchers speak of a toxic effect of vitamin D shots on the tissues. "Elastic fibers lose their elasticity and are pushed out as the surrounding tissue swells. This swollen, necrotic tissue (the muscles are also swollen and anucleated) becomes the focus for calcium deposition."[35]

The dangers of megadoses of vitamin D as a prophylaxis for rickets have been emphasized by several researchers. Mai states that most infants who in present-day terms are "mildly rachitic" are not in any special need of treatment. "The undertreatment of rickets is quite possibly preferable to a later vascular or renal ailment."[36] Such warnings, however, are usually drowned out by the cries of those who want to hold fast to what they see as an indisputable public health advance. This only shows that such physicians have lost sight of the fundamental concepts of healing and that they consider only external data rather than the whole human being. Blinded by short-term results, they fail to realize that it is easier to remedy a developmental retardation than it is to reverse the aging process, which, once begun, is irreversible. The calcifications resulting from vitamin D administration are an example of such an aging process. A slight case of rickets is in fact less deleterious in the long run than a prematurely induced sclerosis. Where a therapy or prophylaxis also has harmful side effects, physicians must be guided by the principle of primum non nocere ("first, do no harm") and by a comprehensive understanding of human development from birth until death. With vitamin D, attention should be paid not only to the immediate

34. Junge-Hülsing et al., DMW 94 (1969):1877.
35. Wagner, et al., cited in Schönemann (see footnote 31).
36. Med. Klinik 50 (1955)26.

effects of hypercalcemia, but also to other effects on the organism as a whole, such as early vascular sclerosis, which may manifest only decades later.

For example, the pediatric pathologist Meyer asks "whether even correctly dosed, prophylactically administered amounts of vitamin D might not cause calcium depositions in the arteries of children, given certain individual preconditions. In this case vitamin D, as in animal tests, would take on the role of a 'calcifier' or 'sensitizer' (Selye) which even at minimal doses is capable of influencing calcium metabolism within a limited 'critical time period.' During this period, various factors influencing local tissue metabolism can become 'challengers' and cause calcium depositions in certain tissue portions. Other significant provoking factors besides chemical substances include mild mechanical injuries (Selye). Like a simple mechanical injury in an animal experiment, circulatory stress on the arteries could become a provoking factor during the mentioned critical period.... Calcium depositions occurring in early childhood are evidently not reversible. They thus represent a lasting injury to the vascular walls which, like other kinds of wall injury, can promote a later angiopathy."[37]

Furthermore a general, schematically applied prophylaxis is undesirable because it completely ignores individual requirements. This is the patent explanation for the fatalities that have resulted from the customary megadose. Clearly, concrete, individual circumstances, such as a hypersensitivity to vitamin D, must always be taken into account. But even when an intoxication is not lethal and the effects of hypercalcemia are reversible, the implications of the intervention for the patient's entire remaining development must be considered. A hardened organism is incapable of supporting mobility, especially of thoughts and emotions; at the very least it hinders the development of creativity and a spiritually oriented life. Intellectual thought may remain unaffected, since it is based wholly on the physical organization and on processes of mineralization, but there are limits even here, as shown by the general retardation—mental as well as physical—in D-hypervitaminosis.

Leading pediatricians now certainly all agree that megadose prophylaxis is wholly unphysiological, and that long-term, daily administration of small doses of vitamin D is preferable. However, even such doses are

37. W. Meyer, DMW 96 (1971):1093.

not entirely unproblematic, since we are not dealing here with a harmless vitamin, but rather with a highly specific and potent chemical substance. It has been pointed out repeatedly, and the vitamin D-resistant cases of rickets demonstrate, that vitamin D administration does not strike at the root of rickets because rickets is not a vitamin deficiency. Furthermore, all determinations of a so-called daily requirement are at best average values and of little use in individual cases. The customary dose may be toxic for children with constitutional tendencies toward sclerosis, whereby the toxicity lies less in an acute poisoning than in the worsening of the children's constitutions, with which they must live for the rest of their lives.

Significantly, vitamin D occurs in nature only in small quantities, which shows how carefully nature manages such highly active substances. The richest sources are fish liver oils, especially halibut. Also, natural vitamin D is always found together with vitamin A, its polar opposite, which synergistically limits it and balances its one-sidedness.[38] Cod liver oil has been known to be a harmless remedy for rickets since at least the end of the eighteenth century, when nothing was known about its constituent substances. Despite this, modern discussions of the prophylaxis and therapy of rickets give scarcely any consideration to alternatives to the application of synthetic vitamin D. This is not to recommend raw cod liver oil, which is often impractical for psychological reasons although some children actually enjoy taking it. However, it has none of the damaging side effects we have described. The effects of processes that "purify" cod liver oil or render it "flavorless" are unfortunately impossible to evaluate.

The form of vitamin D usually used by European physicians for the prophylaxis and therapy of rickets is vitamin D3, which is produced naturally by both humans and animals. In other countries (including the U.S.), milk is enriched with vitamin D2, which if formed by irradiation of ergosterol and occurs naturally in fungi but not in human beings. The two vitamins are similar, having the same "effect" with regard to ossification. However, now that the far-reaching physiological and even psychological effects that can result from the minimal steric alteration of a substance (as, for example, in the sexual hormones) are known, it is

38. See O. Wolff, BEH 7 (1954):175.

astonishing how recklessly the two forms of vitamin D are interchanged. This is merely one more example of a purely "results-oriented" thinking that ignores all other considerations.

As we have variously illustrated (see vol. I, p. 98f.), all infants today are threatened by an acceleration of normal development. Children not treated with vitamin D, by contrast, have an infancy of normal length; their static functions do not appear prematurely and the fontanel closes at the proper time. However, since the development of today's "normal" child is accelerated, truly healthy children are considered retarded. Normal school-age children lack vitality, are pale, restless, can concentrate only poorly, and are intellectually precocious; further, they are too coarsely material and too dense in their physical-etheric makeup. Obviously many factors contribute to this condition, but medicine need not be one of them.

The prophylaxis and therapy of rickets with artificial vitamin D is thus open to the following objections:

1. The treatment of rickets with vitamin D disregards the disease's essential nature. Rickets is not a vitamin deficiency, but a disorder of light-metabolism. Hence vitamin D cannot genuinely cure rickets.

2. The current routine dosages do not take individual differences into account. Stimulation of development can too easily go over into opposite: excessive and premature calcification, which is much graver than the original ailment.

3. Megadoses create such unphysiological conditions that they cannot be medically advocated.

4. The effects of vitamin D hypervitaminosis are so grave that the procedure contradicts the medical principle of non nocere. A hypersensitivity to vitamin D cannot be foreseen.

5. Acceleration and sclerosis should not be constitutionally favored by "prophylactic medication" at any time, but especially not in infancy.

6. In all cases where rickets is not actually present, the usual vitamin D prophylaxis constitutes an overdose. In the long term, this not only promotes the aging process, but also alters the quality of thinking and spiritual development. Thought becomes rigid and lacking in imagination, even though cruder intellectual functions are not affected.

The Prophylaxis of Rickets

Obviously we cannot simply refuse to use vitamin D3 and then wait for full-blown cases of rickets to develop. We must propose alternative solutions that have proven both effective and free from harmful side effects through decades of pediatric practice.

Prophylaxis should begin even before the child is born by seeing to it that the mother receives an adequate supply of iron and calcium, for example, with Urtica Ferro culta or Gentian-Anaemodoron, and then in the third or fourth month Calcon I and II, possibly Fluorite D6 trit. A teaspoon of honey should be taken daily; the diet should be varied from the point of view of formative forces.

The infant, in addition to proper food, needs light, an important factor in the prevention of rickets. In contrast to the turn of the century and before, however, the tendency today is to give too much of a good thing. A proper balance must be found.

The child's transition from the protection of the womb to the world outside must be gradual. Younger children must be protected from excessive cold. Protection from the effects of excessively bright light can be achieved with a light pink canopy; an additional layer of light blue may be used against brighter light. A child protected by such a canopy can be exposed to the sun much more safely. It has been found, moreover, that the indirect light from a clear sky is sufficient to prevent rickets, even in urban areas (Mai). Direct sunlight, by contrast, should be avoided, at least during the first weeks of life. If exposure to natural light is not possible, supplementation with artificial light sources should be considered. Full-spectrum light is preferable to simple ultraviolet, which, like synthetic vitamins, is unphysiological. Ultraviolet should be used only sparingly and after careful consideration of the reasons for using it.

The organism's capacity to manage and utilize light can be stimulated with phosphorus, which, particularly during the darker season, is given as Phosphorus D5 or D6, 3 drops in a little water before breakfast and the midday meal (not with a metal spoon!). Phosphorus, a bearer of light and of the ego, stimulates the ego and guides it into the metabolism. It thus addresses the fundamental disorder of the higher constituents that underlies rickets.

This effect of phosphorus can be carried specifically to the skeletal system by means of apatite, native calcium phosphate. A proven preparation is Apatite/Phosphorus comp. S (for infants), consisting of Apatite D8 and Phosphorus D6. Three to five drops are given daily in a little water before the first bottle. This mixture is complemented by Conchae/Quercus comp. S, a mixture of Conchae D10, Quercus Cortex D4, and Stannum D10. The last of these affects the fluid organism and thus the proper development of the brain, which in this phase can tend either toward hydrocephaly or its opposite. Both Apatite/Phosphorus and Conchae/Quercus were specially developed by pediatricians for the prophylaxis and therapy of rickets. At eight months, the "S" variant of both of these preparations should be replaced by the "K" ("K" being for small children, "S" for infants). Apatite/Phosphorus K contains the additional ingredient Ferrum sidereum D20, which stimulates the process of learning to walk upright. Conchae/Quercus comp. K contains Conchae D6 and Quercus Cortex D6. One pinch should be given in the evening.

The prescription and home administration of these preparations is extremely simple, so that compliance is practically assured. Other medications may of course be given as supplements or substitutes depending on the individual case.

Apatite and Conchae are also the main components of Calcon I and II. Although Calcon stimulates calcium metabolism and supplements the diet, it is not sufficient to prevent rickets. For this, Apatite and Conchae require different processing and supplementing, as in the preparations mentioned.

Breast-fed children are known to be less rickets-prone than bottle-fed children, with whom any overfeeding is to be absolutely avoided.

Another factor in the prophylaxis of rickets is a loving and caring environment, which facilitates the child's incarnation.

The Therapy of Rickets

Apatite/Phosphorus and Conchae/Quercus S or K are also used for actual cases of rickets. Each is given at least twice a day. Either can be supplemented or replaced with a more individualized treatment. For craniotabes, a pinch of Conchae D30 is given daily, supplemented in more severe cases with lead ointment (Plumbum met. 0.1%) applied to the back of the head. For the exudative diathesis that often accompanies rickets, a pinch of Plumbum met. praep. D20 can also be given in the morning. For disturbances of a more metabolic nature, one may lower the potency of lead to D8 or D10, 1 pinch in the morning for two weeks. All lead therapy should follow the guidelines set forth in volume II, p. 153f.

Bone deformations (for example, rachitic rosary or Harrison's groove) may be treated with Stannum praep. D8-D10, one pinch twice daily, in conjunction with Quartz D10 or D12 if desired. Stannum 0.4% gel or ointment may be applied locally. Related weaknesses of the connective tissue may be treated with Fluorite D6, later D10.

It is an interesting fact that craniotabes cannot be cured with phosphorus. Phosphorus does not harden bone; however, it does prevent the typical flattening and deformation, so that even though the back of the head remains soft, it also retains its normal roundness. At this point the bone can be relatively easily solidified by means of the indicated treatment.

A tendency toward hydrocephaly calls for Stannum, which is applied on the forehead as gel (0.4%) or ointment (5%). This is accompanied internally by Stannum D8, later D15, one pinch twice daily. In more severe cases, a subcutaneous injection of Stannum D8 should be given twice a week. It is important that these children, unlike those with pure rickets, be protected from all intense stimuli, especially direct sun or other strong light.

Where a hereditary disposition to rickets is present, or in cases of rickets that have been left untreated, a sulfur bath (Kalium sulfuratum 20%, one teaspoon) is given two to three times weekly.

Herb baths are another possible supportive measure; thyme and oak bark have proven particularly useful, as has the Weleda children's bath preparation.

The goal of these therapeutic measures is to heal rickets by means of the organism's own inherent forces. The rate of improvement is only of secondary importance, since even the most severe bone deformations can be made to heal relatively late in the child's development. The important thing is to synchronize the child's incarnation process with the normal rhythm of human development. Acceleration is just as dangerous for the child as is retardation; in fact, as mentioned above, a mild case of rickets, once healed, is less detrimental to the entire course of life than is a premature hardening with its effects on consciousness. The task of therapy, in other words, is not to turn a disease into its opposite, but to ensure a measured, proper development. This is especially true for the treatment of rickets.

Fundamentals of Infant and Child Therapy

Pediatrics arose as a separate discipline within medicine in response to the special nature of the child. With regard to medications, however, the child's difference from the adult is seldom given the degree of attention it deserves, even though bitter experience has shown how endangered infants are by age-specific side effects. Sulfonamides, caffeine, salicylates, morphine, and nitrofurantoin, to name just a few, are all absolutely contraindicated for newborns. No infant should be given methemoglobin-producing preparations (phenacetin, resorcinal, tar preparations, naphthaline) or vasoactive nose drops. Chloramphenicol, tetracycline, barbiturates, and steroid hormones such as cortisone, meprobamate, and thyroxine are extremely dangerous, since the child's detoxification is not yet fully developed. Failure to recognize the connection between the so-called gray syndrome (ashen skin, depressed temperature, perspiration, inappetency, death after few days) and the administration—most often prophylactic!—of chloramphenicol led to the deaths of an estimated four to five thousand infants between 1957–1959 in the U.S. alone.[39] Experiences such as these make it reasonable not to give new drugs to infants or neonates, just as we no longer give them to pregnant women since the thalidomide catastrophe.

To do justice to the child's special nature, we must recognize that development is more than just a physiological process. The physiological process is itself only the expression of the incarnation of a human spirit. Birth is a milestone not only in the sense that the infantile organism leaves the safety of the womb, but also in that the newborn's soul-spiritual nature connects with the physical body in an entirely new way. Doctors who base their practice on this thought will endeavor to remove as

39. H.M. Sutherland, "Die Chemotherapie bei Neugeborenen," Praxis der Antibiotikatherapie im Kindesalter, W. von Marget and M. Kienitz, eds. (Stuttgart: 1966).

many obstacles to the child's harmonious incarnation as possible. Among other things, they will assure an adequate temperature in the delivery room and refrain from administering any of the drugs mentioned above, which are totally foreign to human nature.[40] The inadequate detoxification, nuclear icterus, and Heinze body formation characteristic of this earliest period of life are only outward expressions of the defenselessness of a being still dwelling in another world. Deleterious influences can no doubt lastingly impair the incarnation process even when they produce no outwardly recognizable damage. Of all physicians, the pediatrician thus has an especially deep responsibility, one that today is seldom recognized because it cannot be deduced from merely physiological processes.

The same holds true for the treatment of childhood diseases. Childhood diseases, as discussed in volume I, are the process by which the incarnating soul-spiritual being of the child come to terms with inherited or prematurely aging physical substance. Through these diseases, a full and proper incarnation, and thus also the achievement of true selfhood and personality, become possible. Therapy must take these facts into account; otherwise, it neglects the very meaning of human existence.

The most important thing to note about the therapy of childhood diseases is that routine suppression of fever and agitation is not only superfluous, but also radically opposed to the child's developmental tendency. Fevers can be guided and held in check in ways that support rather than thwart the organism; calf and abdominal compresses are among the purely physical measures by which this may be achieved. Medications such as aconite, belladonna, and Argentum can also be used to guide different types of fever in a very nearly specific way, as will be discussed below.

40. See W. zur Linden, *When a Child is Born* (New York: Thorsons, 1984), which contains a detailed discussion of practical considerations. Also F. Leboyer, *Der sanfte Weg ins Leben* (Munich: 1974). The author urges that birth be allowed to take place as naturally as possible. This includes laying the newborn to the mother's breast immediately after birth, even before severance of the umbilical cord; also, the first breath is not forced, but rather is allowed to develop by itself. Proper respiration in later life, and with it free development, are greatly dependent on the first breath. All possibly traumatic stimuli should be excluded in the first few moments after birth, for their repercussions are deeper than is imagined today.

A most gratifying field of activity for the physician of older children is the medicinal guidance of their constitution. Here it is essential to work with the polarity characteristic of each stage of development and with the corresponding substances (see volume I, chapters two through five).

Measles Therapy

All unnecessary measures are to be avoided, especially the unnecessary use of antipyretics. Recently published clinical studies corroborate this suggestion: During a severe measles epidemic in an African hospital, the children in whom the illness took the most violent and highly febrile course (continua of 40–41°C lasting 3–4 days, heavy exanthem, pronounced discomfort) had the most favorable prognoses. Doctors soon surmised that the fever must activate the body's immune response and that the exanthem was an expedient excretory measure. Accordingly they divided the patients into two treatment groups of fifty-six each. The first received the usual treatment of sedatives, antipyretics, and antitussives. Of this group twenty (35%) died. The second group received no such medications, but malaria therapy, antibiotics, and blood transfusions were administered as required. Of this group four children (7%) died. In the first group, the most frequent cause of death was bronchopneumonia. In the second, many cases of bronchopneumonia were observed, but none were fatal.[41]

Aconitum napellus D4–D6 (or a combined preparation such as Ferrum phosph. comp.) is indicated for the very beginning of measles. Aconite noticeably limits and calms the nervous system, as evidenced, for example, by its analgesic effect. The nervous system is highly active in the initial phases of a febrile illness (the so-called "irritation phase"). In later phases, the metabolic system predominates; at that time, but not before, belladonna is the indicated remedy.

Severe, highly febrile measles with a strong flow of blood to the head may be treated with Belladonna D4 to D6 liq., 5 drops hourly (or with Erysidoron I, a combination of Apis D3 and Belladonna D3). Belladonna also relieves hacking cough, mitigates inflammation of the mucous membranes, and favorably influences conjunctivitis and rhinitis.

41. B. C. Witsenburg, BEH 28 (1975):116.

The most important treatment for measles is warmth, both emotional and physical. As described in volume I (p. 45), measles represents a reshaping of the etheric body by the ego. During this restructuring, the growing organism is exposed and defenseless, as manifested emotionally by the tendency of children with measles to whine and cling to their mothers. Mothers of such children must therefore be especially attentive, and in particular see to it that their children stay warm (woolen sweater despite high fever, warm drinks, etc.). The medicinal plant whose picture best corresponds to this situation is Pulsatilla.[42] The specific therapy for measles is Pulsatilla D12, 5 drops twice daily.

The cough typical of measles responds well to Belladonna D4-D6 (see above). It can also be brought under control with Ipecacuanha D4 and Bryonia D3 to D4 (both of which are components of Pertudoron I). Dry cough often responds well to Hyoscyamus D6–D4, depending on the child's age. The threat of pneumonia can be countered with injections of Ferrum phosph. D8 or with Pneumodoron I and II.

As long as neither codeine nor antipyretics are used, the chance of a measles pneumonia developing is very small. Measles croup is treated like a pseudo-croup (acute laryngitis): the principal remedy is Spongia tosta., Apis and belladonna, which are indicated for every local inflammation, complement this, as does Bryonia. These four medications together enable the astral body to reconnect itself properly rather than spasmodically with the upper respiratory passages. Every half hour at first, and thereafter less frequently, 3 to 5 drops (depending on age) of Bryonia/Spongia comp. should be given. Cuprum aceticum capsules (Wala) have approximately the same effect.

The exanthem of measles may appear either late or hardly at all, especially when an intercurrent illness is present or if the child has been previously inoculated against measles. In such cases a reaction can be stimulated with a few doses of Sulfur or Hepar sulf. D6 trit. Another possibility is to give an increasingly hot bath of 10 to 15 minutes duration, beginning at body temperature and gradually raising the water temperature until the patient begins to sweat, i.e. up to 102-104ºF. Sweating can be continued after the bath by wrapping the still wet patient in a bath towel. Before the bath it may be expedient in some cases to evacuate the intestines with a cleansing enema.

42. See W. Pelikan, Healing Plants I (Mercury Press, Spring Valley, NY: 2002)

Once the exanthem has begun, baths, moist compresses, and similar treatments should be avoided. Vapors of eucalyptus oil, turpentine oil, or rosemary bath oil near the bed help soothe the skin.

In cases of pronounced restlessness and high fever, the modified Kneipp's saltwater wash (1 tablespoon salt and 2 tablespoons vinegar added to a pint of warm water) of trunk and legs helps draw off the fever. The washing must be done in a matter of seconds so as not to expose the skin too long to the air; the skin, moistened and vigorously rubbed with a large washcloth, is left wet and then covered up again. The sickroom should be kept quiet and, if the patient is sensitive to light, dimly lit. The only nourishment febrile patients should receive is tea with sweetened fruit juice. Milk is permitted only for infants and then only highly diluted, at most half-strength.

After the exanthem has passed, the child may be given a thorough washing. It is correct in all cases to confine the child to bed for at least ten days after the onset of the exanthem. Only in extremely mild cases should the child be allowed to get up earlier, provided the exanthem has receded.

The procedures just described will prevent the occurrence of complications in almost all cases. As long as it is remembered that the mucous membranes remain susceptible after the fever and exanthem have passed, and if the recovering child is kept in bed, then otitis media or other sequelae will seldom occur.

The role of the exanthem in preventing complications in measles is illustrated by the fact that encephalitis, where present, disappears when the exanthem breaks out (Keller-Wiscott, Lehrbuch der Kinderheilkunde). This clearly implies that an exanthem should never be suppressed (as it inevitably is, for example, whenever fever is suppressed) and that the lungs and brain are relieved whenever a disease is drawn back out to the skin. Unfortunately this relationship is seldom perceived. However, since encephalitis is a serious disease that has severe, permanent effects and is hardly accessible to direct therapy, it is time that prophylaxis and therapy took account of these now clearly evident connections.

Ancient humoral medicine was aware of the value of "drawing a disease off to the skin," and applied methods ranging from dry brushing to the production of blisters with cantharides. Dry brushing will usually suffice, but more dramatic effects may be achieved with the local application of such irritants as mustard and horseradish (as a plaster and a compress, respectively).

The progression of disease processes from the skin inward to the lungs and brain was discussed in volume I (pp. 47–48). The complications of measles also follow this progression: pneumonia occurs first, then encephalitis. The aim of therapy must be to reverse this process, that is, to draw the disease back out from the lungs and brain to the skin, where it can harmlessly run its course.

Measles vaccinations are a sin against the deeper meaning of this disease and should not even be considered, even for infants. If a mother has had measles, her child has an inborn diaplacental immunity for the first three to five months of life. Moreover, a single episode of measles produces immunity in close to one hundred percent of all cases. Repeated cases of measles used to be extremely rare; after a live measles vaccination, however, recurrences are possible. Scarlet fever may be interrupted by measles and then run its normal course.

Scarlet Fever Therapy

This disease is changing in type (see chapter 1, Infectious Diseases). It occurs more frequently now, but is generally milder.

The chief remedy during the febrile stage is belladonna, initially D6 every half hour. If jaws and glands are sensitive to touch, Hepar-Sulfur D12 should be given twice daily as well. When coated tongue and oral fetor develop, a relatively rare occurrence in scarlet fever, belladonna should be complemented with Mercurius solubilis D12 (Hepar-Sulf. and Mercur. sol. should not be given simultaneously!). When a strong, generalized swelling of the glands is present, Mercurius cyanatus D4-D6 should be substituted for Mercur. sol. For sore throat, see below regarding treatment with Erysidoron I and Bolus Eucalypti. Circulatory problems are relatively rare in children, but when present can be treated with Cardiodoron.

Complications can be prevented with Apis D12; however, the use of Apis is not recommended for the initial stages. Vaucheria D3 to D6, 3 to 5 drops daily, is a specific for scarlet fever. According to Rudolf Steiner, the algae in Vaucheria restore the harmony between the astral and etheric bodies.[43] The diet of a scarlet fever patient should be low in salt and protein.

43. R. Steiner, CE, lecture 10.

Barring complications, treatment with antibiotics is unnecessary. Antibiotics will often shorten the course of the illness, but they also thereby increase the chance of a relapse. They are also inadvisable for the reasons cited in the chapter on childhood diseases in volume I. Complications, when they occur at all, usually appear in the third week. The therapy described here, however, is usually sufficient to prevent them. One complication is scarlatinal nephritis, which responds well to Hepar sulfuris calc. D6. Otitis is another, and may be treated with Echinacea 10-30% per os and locally or with Lachesis, preferably in the form of Lachesis cps. glob. (Wala), approximately 10 globules every half hour. Close observation is necessary, since the complications of scarlet fever can be extremely dangerous; in fact, antibiotics will sometimes be unavoidable. Bed rest is absolutely indicated, its length varying according to the severity of the case. Complications are merely the outward manifestation of an inner crisis, with which the patient must be allowed to come to terms undisturbed.

Diphtheria and Purulent Throat Inflammations

Coating and exudates are formations that have evaded the guidance of the organism as a whole. The appropriate remedy for their reintegration is mercury. Mercury can be used in all cases "where secretory processes occur within the organism and must be brought back under the organism's control."[44] Furthermore, mercury is related in a special way to the glandular system.

The compound of mercury and sulfur occurring in cinnabar (natural mercury sulfide) is ideal for the treatment of diphtheria and of simple, chronic, or recurrent tonsillitis. In acute cases (catarrhal angina), one tablet (D6) is given at least every two hours. Apis D3/Belladonna D3 or Erysidoron I, when alternated hourly with Cinnabar, have also proven effective, as have the combined preparations Cinnabar comp. (Weleda) and Apis/Belladonna c. Mercur (Wala). Apis and belladonna are indicated for all local inflammations, especially swelling of the mucosae.

Cinnabar should not be administered in cases of purulent tonsillitis or of Vincent's disease (trench mouth), since its sulfur component can

44. Steiner/Wegman, FT.

favor a tonsillar abscess. In these conditions, which like diphtheria are more toxic than inflammatory, Mercurius cyanatus D4 (or D6) liq. is given in place of cinnabar.

Toxins can be absorbed by a suspension of Bolus Eucalypti comp. either gargled or swallowed. When swallowing is difficult, gargling should be avoided and the patient should be confined to bed. In such cases, Carbo Coffea (charred coffee–Weleda) can be blown onto the tonsils or applied with a cotton swab. Externally, a warm paste of Eucalyptus comp. should be applied.

In order to avoid favoring additional toxin formation, the acute patient's diet should be kept largely free of protein. Raw juices are the preferred fare. A daily enema, or at least sufficient purging, may be necessary for detoxification.

Chronically recurrent sore throat can be controlled with Cinnabar D6, later D20 (one tablet two to three times daily for several weeks). Constitutional therapy is also advisable (detoxification, bitters, cleansing of the intestines, constitutional remedies, Kneipp's applications, etc.). In toxic diphtheria, cardiac remedies are given early on (Cardiodoron or injections of Aurum D10, Arnica D10, or Lachesis D15), especially if the patient complains of upper abdominal pains.

Carriers of diphtheria bacilli are rare today, but a proven treatment is to smear the tonsils at least three times a day with unheated honey. A thin solution of honey in warm water can also be used to irrigate the nasal passages in nasal diphtheria. Bolus Eucalypti comp. and Carbo Coffea may be used as snuff.

For the prophylaxis of diphtheria, Rudolf Steiner recommended rosemary baths.

Poliomyelitis

Infantile paralysis, once a terrifying "epidemic of civilization" (de Rudder) appears to have been at least temporarily banished, so that a discussion of it might appear no longer pertinent. The disease, we are told, will eventually be "exterminated" by use of the oral vaccine and other means. Close examination, however, shows that the fundamental questions raised by polio, in particular that of its etiology, still remain unsolved. Our prophylactic successes have only obscured this fact.

The concern surrounding poliomyelitis shows how significant one's view of the nature of a disease can be for its prophylaxis and therapy. As one would expect, those whose concept of the disease centers around the virus concentrate on preventing infection, and consider treatment a success when this goal is achieved. By contrast, those who see the disease within a larger context recognize that the mere prevention of infection does not solve all the problems, as the chapter on infectious diseases demonstrates. In what follows we shall discuss the most important problems related to polio that are still unsolved.

Polio is indisputably a "disease of civilization." Civilization must therefore be a pathogenic factor, favoring not only the dissemination but even the proliferation of neurotropic viruses. The cause of proliferation must lie in a weakening of the resistance of the nervous system. This is why only relatively few people acquired the disease despite the ubiquitous presence of the virus during the epidemics.

People likely to contract polio are doubtless distinguished by low vitality, either at the time of infection or chronically. An overtaxing of the nerve-sense system by the influences of civilization weakens the etheric body. This is why susceptible people are so easily overwhelmed by sensory stimuli. Whether chronic or acute, this situation is not affected by the vaccine: the nerves are susceptible even if the virus is prevented from reaching them. All the vaccine does, therefore, is to prevent an underlying pathology from becoming manifest.

It follows that the causes of polio have not been eliminated even though the disease now scarcely occurs. The disease has not really disappeared, it is merely prevented from appearing, that is, it has been suppressed. The effects of this will become apparent only after many years.

If civilization continues to exert its pathogenic influence or even intensifies that influence—as can be observed just about everywhere in the modern world—then the nerve-sense system's heightened susceptibility will become apparent in other ways, perhaps in an increase in encephalitis or in degenerative diseases such as multiple sclerosis.

Two factors that have been shown to affect a person's disposition to poliomyelitis are overexertion and chilling. Sandler discovered further that polio viruses can penetrate into the nervous system only when the organism is in a hypoglycemic state, as it frequently is following the consumption of sugar.[45] He therefore recommended total abstinence from sugar during vulnerable periods, a suggestion that was successful in practice, but has since been ignored.

Preventing the disposition to polio, however, solves only one part of the problem; the other part is the nervous system's constitutional hypersensitivity. Increased nerve-sense activity in any organ enhances sensation, leading ultimately to pain, lowered vitality, dehydration, and overforming, that is, to degeneration in the broadest sense. In the limbs and muscles this translates into painful movement and eventual paralysis.

As is known, the first symptoms of polio after it emerges from latency are irritations of the meninges. The inflammatory alterations accompanying this are minimal and hence do not justify the interpretation of the disease as mainly inflammatory. On the contrary, all of the symptoms, including pains, losses of sensation and motor control, the alteration of reflexes, sweating, insomnia, and mental symptoms, are enhanced nerve-sense processes. This is especially clear in the case of insomnia.

Human physiology is governed by the interplay of brain and metabolism. The metabolic system frequently responds to an overactive nerve-sense organization by producing fever and inflammatory phenomena, as happens in poliomyelitis. The metabolic pole's reaction, if it is forceful enough, halts the disease process and brings about a spontaneous healing. Otherwise, catabolism and devitalization prevail, resulting in devastating paralysis.

Antipyretics, although they eliminate the unpleasantness of the inflammatory symptoms, also suppress the metabolic reaction, thereby

45. B. P. Sandler, Diet Prevents Polio (Milwaukee: Lee Foundation for Nutritional Research, 1951).

intensifying the underlying disorder. As might be expected, follow-up studies have demonstrated the fruitlessness of this approach.

The paralytic stage of polio is clear proof that the formative processes of the head pole have won out over the liquefying, dissolving forces of the metabolic pole. Vital activity in the limbs is reduced to a minimum and sensitivity is enhanced.

The inflammations accompanying infantile paralysis are therefore defensive reactions rather than the primary disorder. They are directed not only at the virus but also at the enhanced mental processes characteristic of this disease. Polio consists of a particular relationship of consciousness to the world: patients are inwardly defenseless against external stimuli. Their perceptual oversensitivity opens them to damages that ultimately extend into the physical. A hereditary weakness of the nervous system may contribute to this oversensitivity. Furthermore, the damages of hypoglycemia already described tend to affect such sensitive people the most. As long as their constitutional oversensitivity can be compensated for by the rhythmic system, it will remain latent; however, further burdens on the nervous system, such as a predisposing illness, will force the latent process into a critical stage. At that point, favorable conditions are created for the virus to take hold. Infection will then draw the functional disturbance into physical manifestation.

Infantile paralysis is thus based not on an inflammatory process but rather on the opposite of inflammation, namely, on a disturbed process of consciousness. This distinction is more than semantic; it changes our entire understanding of polio and explains its primarily catabolic, degenerative character. From this understanding flow certain consequences for therapy.

Rudolf Steiner once indicated that paralytic ailments are closely connected with deteriorations in the quality of soil used for agriculture. Soil in industrialized countries is contaminated with many substances. These substances enter the ground water and affect the health and development of plants, animals, and human beings. Our increasingly unecological methods of agriculture and the pollution of rivers by industry are the main contributors to this problem.

The type of cell most affected by the decreased vitality of agricultural products is the one that by its very nature is least vital: the nerve. Nerve cells are also specifically affected by lead, which, because it was added to gasoline for so many years as an antiknock compound, persists in small amounts in the air and soil of industrialized countries. The levels are of course not sufficient to cause acute poisoning, but the issue of long-term, more insidious effects must also be considered.

The problems raised by the phenomenon of polio thus continue to exist. Modern physicians must seek out the roots of this disease and recognize the signs of the times, in order to prevail against a civilization that is increasingly inimical to the human spirit and to life.

Poliomyelitis Therapy

A brief outline of therapy is sketched here because although there are currently no cases, the situation could change. Furthermore, variants of this therapy are valid for other kinds of paralysis.

Poliomyelitis, as just described, is essentially a degenerative process, not, as its name suggests, an inflammation. The inflammations that accompany polio are more or less feeble attempts by the organism to overcome the primary, devitalizing tendency. For this reason, all measures that tend to "cool" the organism must be avoided, including antipyretics, antibiotics, and X-rays. Warmth, on the other hand, is the basis for all forms of polio therapy.

At the onset of paralysis, injections of Scorodite D30 should be given daily or every other day, 0.5-1.0 ml, depending on age and severity of the case, i.v. or s.c. in the paralyzed limb. Cerebellum D4 liq., 5 drops three times daily, should be given as well. With bulbar symptoms, similar doses of brain stem D4 liq. should also be given. Phosphorus D6 liq. is also administered, 5 drops three times daily.

Polio patients should also receive a low-protein, vegetarian diet consisting as much as possible of unadulterated, fresh food. Good evacuation of the intestines and bladder is also important. Hot steam compresses on the bladder may be used to alleviate urine retention.

In both the preparalytic and the paralytic stages of polio, treatment is accompanied by a daily, full-immersion, rising-temperature bath of 10 to 20 minutes duration. Thirty grams of soda are added to the bath water, and the temperature of the bath gradually raised to 97–102°F, higher if possible. The skin should be gently brushed in the bath. When respiratory paralysis threatens or when bathing is not possible for other reasons, steam compresses with soda may be used instead. The latter should be placed under the recumbent patient's spine for about 20 minutes several times a day. The compress cloth, folded several times, is brought to the bedside in a bowl of boiling hot water containing one teaspoon of soda to every two quarts water. It is removed with the handle of a wooden spoon and wrung out with a hand towel, and then laid almost dry beneath the patient, as hot as can be tolerated.

If no noticeable improvement in the patient's condition occurs within the first few days, Scorodite D30 should be injected less often (two to three times weekly) and replaced on the injection-free days with Arnica D20. Arnica should be injected in alternation with an organ preparation whose choice will depend on the chief seat of the paralysis: Medulla oblongata c. Stib. D6 or Medulla spinalis c. Stib. D6, s.c. Higher potencies should be used in acute cases. Nursing care is especially important.

For older paralyses with muscular atrophy, Arnica, Planta tota D6 and Prunus spin. D6 are injected alternately on four days of the week s.c.; also, Scorodite D30 should be injected once a week for 8 to 12 weeks. Phosphorus D6, 5 drops three times daily, and Plantago primula c. Hyoscyamo 5%, 5–10 drops three times daily, are given internally. For severe atrophy, injections of Musculus D6, 0.5–1.0 ml i.m. or s.c., should be given several times weekly.

It is advisable in treatments of long duration to occasionally stop all medication for one day and to give Sulfur D30 once in the morning on those days to stimulate a reaction.

Poor circulation and sluggishness in the extremities can be counteracted with an herbal bath of arnica or hay flowers two to three times a week. Two tablespoons of 20% arnica essence are added to each bath, and the water temperature is kept between 97º and 102ºF. Alternatively, a hyperthermic or Schlenz bath may be given. In this type of bath, the temperature of the water is gradually raised to 106ºF.

Nursing care, such as proper positioning, prevention of contractions, and the application of compresses, is extremely important.

The recommendation on the part of some French physicians of prophylactic and therapeutic administration of magnesium (2% MgCl, 60-120 ml every 6 hours) appears to be well founded.[46]

Pertussis (Whooping Cough)

Unless complications arise, this illness, although it takes a dramatic course, is relatively harmless. Chief among the complications is pneumonia, although bronchiectasis formation can also occur and dormant tubercular foci can be reactivated. Neurological complications include encephalitis, cramps, and paralyses. The disease course depends heavily on constitutional factors (neuropathy, exudative diathesis), as well as on age and on the physical and therapeutic environment (noise level, degree of care, atmospheric conditions, etc.). Infants in particular are at risk from cerebral hypoxia, which can lead to genuine, life-threatening seizures.

The most obvious symptom is the coughing spell. While some authors believe this to be set off by difficulties in inhalation, Steiner indicated that the main factor is really an impairment of exhalation. Whichever is true, the patient's convulsive efforts to expel air are obviously an attempt to exhale as thoroughly as possible. As in asthma, spasms occur that inhibit normal respiratory functions.

Unlike the cough of bronchitis, which can occur during inhalation or exhalation without any appreciable disturbance of either, the pertussis cough does not allow any inhalation to occur during the cough itself. A spasm spreads from the bronchioles and the bronchial musculature to the glottis, which eventually closes completely. The bronchial tubes are also affected. The spasm indicates an "entrapment" (Steiner) of the astral body in the lungs. The body's violent effort to expel air through the constricted glottis can also involve the digestive tract, resulting in vomiting. When the paroxysm subsides, the rush of air into the opening respiratory passages produces the familiar "crowing" inspirium of whooping cough.

Certain constitutional types are at special risk for pertussis, in particular children with neuropathy or exudative diathesis. Both types are characterized by a disturbance of the interaction of the air organism with the water organism, that is, of the astral body with the etheric body. Either the impulses of the astral body are too strong and the etheric body too

---

46. For description of results obtained with the therapy described here see M. Schotte, Hippokrates (1945)15; W. zur Linden, Hippokrates (1940):505; M. Schotte, Korrespondenzblatt für Ärzte (1949, special issue); W. zur Linden, Hippokrates (1952):529; T. Böckheler, BEH 6 (1935):149.

weak (neuropathy), or the formative forces of the astral body and the ego organization intervene too weakly in the etheric body (exudative diathesis), leading to an insufficient "aeration" of the water organism. This can be expressed outwardly in swollen facial features.

The function of pertussis in the child's development is to eliminate either kind of constitutional imbalance. After the disease has run its course, the nervous system is enlivened by etheric impulses and the astral body incarnates more thoroughly, structuring the etheric and thus better forming the entire organism. Pertussis is therefore a particularly good example of how childhood diseases, when allowed to run their proper course, can actually enhance the child's health and development. Children who have recovered from pertussis looks healthier than before, have an unparalleled appetite, and are better balanced emotionally. In a word, they are properly incarnated for someone of their age.

Such recoveries are the therapeutic ideal toward which physicians should strive with all the childhood diseases. These diseases are, and should be treated as, a struggle on the part of the child's spiritual individuality to overcome the forces of heredity inherent in the "template body" (Steiner) bequeathed by the parents.

As mentioned, the real danger of pertussis lies in its complications, which appear only when the disease is prevented from running its proper course. The intelligent doctor will therefore never attempt to suppress symptoms, since the organic process underlying them will simply be shifted, producing complications or the disposition to a later and seemingly unrelated illness. Pertussis vaccination is a case in point. Infants do not tolerate this vaccine well, so much so that after the first year it is contraindicated due to the high rate of complications (encephalopathies between 1:6,000 and 1:60,000).[47]

The therapy proposed here strives to manage rather than suppress symptoms, to guide them toward a true recovery while keeping them from endangering the child. Symptoms are merely expressions of the disease process and become superfluous once the latter is addressed.

Nursing care is an important part of the therapy for whooping cough. Anxious mothers should be reassured that while whooping cough is seri-

---

47. O. Goetz, Med. Klin. 70 (1975):914. See also W. Ehrengut, DMW 99 (1974):2307, 2273; Monatsschrift der Kinderheilkunde 125 (1977):908; Lancet (1978) Feb.:370.

ous and requires diligent observation and care, the symptoms can be made tolerable and any danger to the child's life can be largely overcome.

Change of milieu is indicated only when the child does not respond to the measures indicated below. A mountain climate can bring relief, but great changes in altitude can also aggravate the illness. In earlier times children were often placed in a horse or cow stall; presumably the ambient nitrogen (in the form of ammonia) beneficially affected the air organism. Daily walks outdoors are advisable, though rapid walking would be avoided. On windy days patients should be confined to their rooms, which should be well ventilated.

The diet is kept light and meals small. Milk consumption should be limited. One possibility is to dilute milk with a cough tea (Sytra tea), malt coffee, or Fachinger or Emser mineral water. Children who show little desire for food usually come through the coughing phase most easily, and later demonstrate surprisingly healthy appetite. Weight losses are temporary and of no import (except in infants). Salt loss through vomiting, however, should be compensated through the diet.

Irradiation with artificial light (preferably full-spectrum) can sometimes be beneficial, especially for plump, phlegmatic children. Ultraviolet light is usually too great a stress on the nerves of neurasthenic children.

On the psychological level, excessive leniency must be avoided, as this undermines the child's will to resist the disease. Overexcitable children in particular may need to be handled with some sternness, since this is the only way to get them to face the coughing attacks in a calm and reasonable fashion. Otherwise it is not uncommon for them to use the attacks as a way of forcing their will upon their families and caregivers.

Children who are not disturbed by it may be given a half bath in the late afternoon. The temperature of the bath should be raised gradually over ten minutes from 97º to 101ºF, and then raised more slowly to about 104ºF. Total length of bath: up to one hour. After the bath the child should be left wet but also wrapped in a warm towel; if coughing or agitation sets in, the towel should be immediately loosened, although care must be taken to avoid chilling. Brushing of the back during the bath is extremely beneficial. Bath additives such as blackthorn (Weleda) or thyme have also proven valuable.

The main medications for whooping cough are Pertudoron I and II. These preparations were developed in the 1920s specifically for this disease. Their main component is the sundew, Drosera rotundifolia, a so-called "carnivorous" plant that grows in moorlands and swampy areas.[48] The glands on the upper side of the sundew's leaves secrete protein-digesting enzymes, indicating a digestive function otherwise observed only in animals. The localization of this function in the leaf suggests a close connection between it and the human rhythmic system; astral impulses that normally affect only the blossom are here shifted into the leaf, corresponding to the astral body's excessive involvement in the respiratory system in pertussis.

Another ingredient of Pertudoron is Veratrum album (the white hellebore). In this plant, as in other members of the lily family, growth is initially concentrated on the rootstock and corm, but then suddenly leaps into an intense blossoming process that overwhelms the plant's etheric forming, resulting in excessive alkaloid formation (e.g., veratrine), and hence in potent nerve and muscle poisons. Veratrum is rightly designated by the homeopathic school as "vegetable arsenic." Like arsenic, it tones and stimulates, and because it harmoniously reintegrates the astral body, it also relieves spasms.

Cinchona, Cortex (cinchona bark) and ipecacuanha, two other ingredients of Pertudoron, are both members of the large Rubiaceae family. This family harbors astral impulses to a degree matched only by the Leguminosae. This is expressed by the Rubiaceae's ability to assimilate nitrogen directly from the air. Like the Leguminosae, they do this through symbiosis with nitrogen-fixing bacteria; however, whereas the Leguminosae fix nitrogen in their roots, the Rubiaceae do it in their leaves, thereby expressing, like the sundew, a special affinity to the human rhythmic system. Many Rubiaceae also have antipyretic barks, especially the cinchona tree. A strong involvement of astral forces is also indicated by high levels of tannin in the bark, as well as by the high alkaloid content of root, bark, and to a lesser extent, of the leaves. Like the sundew, cinchona stimulates the proper integration of the astral body into the respiratory organs.

Ipecacuanha, a remedy known to the Indians, contains the alkaloid emetine. This substance, since it alleviates diarrhea, vomiting, and pulmonary dryness and spasms, evidently acts by way of the vagus. In home-

48. See Pelikan, "Fleischfressende Pflanzen als Heilpflanzen," BEH 3 (1950):90.

opathy it has proven effective against all of these symptoms. The same is true of Coccus cacti, the cochineal insect, and Mephitis, the secretion of the perineal gland of the skunk, two more ingredients of Pertudoron. These preparations from the animal kingdom were included on the basis of homeopathic provings.

The final ingredient is belladonna, whose spasmolytic effect is well known. The spiritual-scientific rationale for the use of belladonna is presented in detail on p. 358 in volume I and in various other places.

In addition to these ingredients, Pertudoron II contains Cuprum aceticum, a critical remedy for pertussis. Copper is always indicated when the astral body cannot integrate properly and instead imitates the dynamic of the nervous system, i.e., causes contractions and spasms. The acetic acid component directs copper's effect to the rhythmic system. Copper also stimulates the renal system, the ultimate regulator of the air organism.

These remedies all support one another: on the one hand, they help the astral body reintegrate itself properly by releasing it from the lungs, where it is overly active ("trapped"); on the other hand, they help structure the etheric body and thereby regulate body fluids.

Pertudoron I and II are normally given in hourly alternation, 1 to 2 drops each for neonates, 3 for infants, 5 for older children, and 8 to 10 for adults, always with a little water. Any increase in dosage hampers the effect. Thus, particularly with Pertudoron II, dosages should be adhered to exactly and never increased, no matter how severe the coughing spells. One may experiment with less frequent doses or change the potency and give Cuprum aceticum D4. Pertudoron's effect cannot be judged with certainty until two or three nights have passed.

In the early phase, remedies should be given at night at well as during the day if at all possible. The period of severe coughing spells will then usually last only 8 to 14 days and pass rapidly into the recovery phase. Pertudoron I and II should be administered until the cough is altogether eliminated, each 2 to 3 times daily.

A highly beneficial and proven measure is the injection of Formica D40 or D60 (lower potencies do not have the desired effect). In most cases, a single subcutaneous injection suffices to bring about a turn toward recovery (repeated after one week; smaller children 0.5 ml).

Although many parents will not understand the need to allow the disease to run its full course and will consequently demand a faster recovery, anthroposophic physicians must attempt to increase the public's understanding and acceptance of their therapeutic approach. The goal is not "the elimination of symptoms at any prince," but rather a true healing. This includes taking advantage of the chance offered by every disease to further healthy development of body and soul, a chance that the childhood diseases offer as no others.

IV

Gynecology and Obstetrics

ERICH JOSEPH THIEL
OTTO WOLFF

GYNECOLOGY EXISTS as a separate discipline because of the special nature of the female organism, which is distinguished from the male by its ability to gestate an embryo. This is determined by emotional and spiritual as well as by physiological factors. The constitutional differences between male and female, which have been described at length elsewhere, may be summarized by saying that the male incarnates more strongly, whereas the female retains a closer connection with the cosmos. For that reason the female is more closely connected to fluidity and to life, while the male is connected to the solid and mineral, a fact expressed, for example, in his heavier bone structure. Only because of her special anatomical and physiological characteristics is the female capable of receiving the primarily cosmic human embryo.

Physiology of the Menses

The menstrual cycle is the physiological prerequisite of gestation. Its processes are well known and need not be discussed here; they are essentially glandular and stand in a variable relationship to the higher human constituents. Glandular processes in general are related to the etheric body; however, the manner of a gland's activity and secretions is determined by the astral body and the ego organization, which act differently in each organ system. The hormones produced in this way serve as "messengers" of the higher constituents and influence the various processes occurring in the organism.

During the first half of the menstrual cycle, the etheric body's anabolic activity obviously predominates, a fact expressed in the growth of the uterine lining. The hormone responsible for this process is estrogen, which is produced in the ovarian follicles. Estrogen's purely upbuilding effects are evident in the development of the genitalia and of secondary sex characteristics during puberty as well, that is, subcutaneous fat build-up, development of the breasts, etc.

The second half of the menstrual cycle is characterized by a kind of "ripening." The uterine membrane ceases to grow and begins to secrete. The analog of this in the plant kingdom is the transition of the fruit from growth, which is conditioned by the etheric, to ripening, in which new qualities such as aroma, color, and sweetness emerge. The same process occurs in the human organism through the action of the bile process upon substances produced by the liver. Cholesterol, for example, is transformed by this process into provitamin D, cholic acids, adrenocortical hormones, and sex hormones. In all of these processes, existing substances are transformed by a mild catabolism to serve a higher function. In this, the action of the astral body is apparent. However, since catabolism is not carried out here to its conclusion, the astral body merely modifies the activity of the etheric. In Volume I, the sex hormones were used to demonstrate the astral body's modification of etheric activity both in the direction of anabolism (estrogen) and of maturation (progesterone). The embryo requires not only anabolism but also ripened human substances as a basis for its development.

One sign of astral influence upon the menstrual cycle may be seen in fluctuations of the arsenic content of the endometrium and the blood.[1] This content increases during the proliferative phase, stabilizes, and then markedly increases again just before menstruation, after which it falls off. As has been described elsewhere, arsenic is a carrier of astral impulses, as evidenced by its toning and strengthening effect.

The rise in basal temperature that occurs about a day after ovulation is a sign of the ego organization's intensified involvement in the other three essential constituents during the second half of the menstrual cycle, specifically in the metabolism. That the ego organization's involvement in the uterus continues throughout pregnancy is evidenced by the sustained elevation of the pregnant woman's basal temperature.

1. Guthmann and Henrich, *Archiv für Gynäkologie* 172 (1942):360.

That the ego organization plays a dominant role in menstruation is supported by the fact that nothing truly corresponding to menstruation occurs anywhere in the animal kingdom. The sexual cycles of the higher mammals (e.g., estrus) are governed by an annual rhythm, not by an ego organization. Even the rhesus monkey's bleedings, which occur every 28 days, are not true menstruations, since they are not always preceded by an ovulation. Ovulations occur for these animals only in winter, which is the only time they can conceive.[2]

The third phase of the menstrual cycle, which occurs only in the absence of conception, is menstruation proper, i.e., the expulsion of the endometrium. This massive catabolic and excretory process is conditioned by a more intense involvement not only of the astral body, but also of the ego organization. "Everything that enters the realm of the ego organization dies."[3] In keeping with this, during this phase most excretory processes are enhanced, such as diuresis and bowel movements, frequently also as a reaction to preceding congestion. After this, the ego organization gradually withdraws, the basal temperature falls, and the astral body brings excretion to a close. Another sign of the ego organization's increased involvement at the beginning of menstruation and in pregnancy is a heightened sensitivity to light.

As is well known, the hormonal regulation of the menstrual cycle is subject to the pituitary gland, which secretes follicle-stimulating and luteinizing hormones. The anterior lobe of the pituitary is the organ of the totality of the etheric body, and transmits astral impulses received primarily in the posterior lobe (the neurohypophysis). The anterior lobe also responds to the pineal body, which is more open to the spiritual and to the past. As the organ of the etheric body, the anterior lobe is subordinate to the pineal body's impulses. The result of a premature discontinuation of these impulses, that is, a loss of the incarnating human being's connection to the past, is early puberty.

The menstrual cycle's primary function is to prepare a substrate for the development of a human embryo. The organ in which this occurs is the uterus, which participates both in the metabolic-limb and in the rhythmic system. The connection to the former is evident in the uterus's

2. Franken, "Menstrualzyklus und Ovulationen," *DMW* (1951):229.

3. Steiner/Wegman, *FT*, chapter 9.

musculature and in its strong involvement in alkaline, anabolic organic processes (e.g., potassium metabolism), that to the latter in the uterus's cyclical physiology and in its anatomical and embryological relationships to the heart.[4]

The woman's monthly loss of blood obviously also involves a loss of iron, the metal characterized elsewhere as the metal of incarnation. Iron establishes a concrete connection to physical reality. The woman's lower levels of iron thus leave her more open to cosmic influences, a spiritual necessity in view of her reproductive function. Except in pathological cases, these lower levels of iron in women are not due to menstruation; if they were, amenorrheic, postmenopausal, and pregnant women would have higher iron levels than menstruating women, which they do not. Lower levels of iron have to do with the female constitution.

The cosmic influence to which the female genital system is most open is that of the moon, the heavenly body that governs regeneration and reproduction. The menstrual cycle, for example, is influenced by the lunar cycle, even though it is on the average a bit longer (29.5 as opposed to 27.3 days). Extreme individual deviations from this norm as well as complete emancipations from a cycle are expressions of what Friedrich Husemann termed "the physiology of freedom."

Pathology and Therapy of Menstrual Disorders

The development of the female reproductive system is governed by individual constitutional factors, namely, by interactions of the pituitary gland, ovaries, and uterus. A healthy person's physical development is initially a function of the etheric body, although the astral body and ego organization exert a guiding influence.

At puberty, part of the astral body frees itself from its previous structuring activity in the metabolism, while another part connects more strongly with the sex organs, causing growth and the emergence of primary and secondary sex characteristics. If the genitalia are underdeveloped, the result will be a juvenile or in some cases even an infantile habitus or hypoplasia. In such cases the etheric body has not sufficiently

4. See J. Rohen, *BEH* 1/8:22; Thiel, *BEH* 2/5–6:196; Päde, *BEH* 2/9–10:333.

prepared the ground for the astral activation of sexual development. The result of this in women is *primary amenorrhea,* a constitutional condition that as such bears the mark of the ego.

The therapeutic possibilities in this condition are limited by the essentially irremediable underdevelopment. The first medication to consider is Argentum, due to the nature of the silver process (described elsewhere) and to the moon's relation to the menstrual cycle. It is best to start with Bryophyllum Argento cultum and then continue with injections of Argentum D6. Both of these may be complemented with abdominal applications of Argentum 0.4% salve.

Secondary amenorrhea is caused by withdrawal of the higher constituents from the etheric-physical organization, sometimes in response to emotional trauma or to a change of milieu. To that extent it has much in common with both pregnancy and menopause, and can display symptoms of both, such as morning sickness and swollen breasts, or hot flashes, palpitations, and sleep disorders. Outwardly, the withdrawal of the higher constituents frequently manifests itself in a kind of formlessness, a failure of the ego and astral body to completely penetrate the water organism. Women and girls in whom this occurs not only grow fat but also have a moist, "bulging" appearance, and tire easily. Constitutionally, here it is a question of medicines like Pulsatilla D12-30, Kalium carbonicum D6 and bile stimulants like Chelidonium Ferro cultum D2.

In some cases, on the other hand, the ego and astral body withdraw so completely that they take part of the etheric body with them. The result is an overall weakening of development that presents the opposite picture from the one just described: instead of bloating, the patient becomes anorexic. *Anorexia nervosa* shows that the will to incarnate has been lost. Medications that stimulate anabolism, such as Argentum, Ferrum, and Prunus, can be of help here, but only if the patient's ego can be stimulated to reconnect with the body and the world.

Argentum is also recommended for secondary amenorrhea, especially in patients who are hypoplastic or who have suffered an emotional trauma. In the latter case, Oxalis should also be administered. Otherwise, Mucilago Levistici is the most important medication for secondary amenorrhea. Plant mucilage, especially that of the lovage (*Levisticum officinalis*) is a compound intermediate between sugar and starch, and as such strengthens the activity of the ego organization in metabolism. Similarly, vegetable gums, being morphologically as yet entirely undifferentiated, are completely open to environmental forces and thus to the intervention of the higher constituents. Potentized preparations of animal organs, used either together or in alternation with Mucilago Levistici, can direct it toward the locus of pathology. Here the appropriate preparation is Ovarium D3–D6, which in some cases may be complemented with Argentum.

Another group of medications essential to the treatment of amenorrhea is derived from plants of the Labiatae family, specifically lemon balm and marjoram (discussed in greater detail below), which can be applied both internally and externally, either as teas, additives to foot or sitz baths, salves, or as vaginal suppositories. Many other medications can be used depending on the situation. Injections of Tormentilla D30, for example, can precipitate a delayed menstruation.

A basic constitutional therapy should be carried out simultaneously with the specific treatment, especially in cases of hypomenorrhea or oligomenorrhea. The chief remedies to be considered are phosphorus and Pulsatilla. Phosphorus D5, seven drops in the morning and at midday, is specifically indicated when the higher constituents have withdrawn from the lower organization.[5] It helps the ego and astral body reintegrate themselves into the fluid and etheric processes of the metabolism. In such cases, the usual phosphorus symptoms (i.e., tallness and thinness, nervous weakness and hypersensitivity, early but weak and protracted menses) will be accompanied by a more or less pronounced leukorrhea. The indications for Pulsatilla (especially D12–D20) can be deduced from its homeopathic proving, in which the emotional symptoms are the most significant: whining, indecisiveness, dependence, vulnerability, and lateness of everything including period. Other measures that can be of some help are sitz baths with either sulfur or marjoram/lemon balm, or external stimulation of the calves with either brushing or mustard compresses.

Coincident constipation will sometimes resolve itself once menstruation resumes. At other times it will have to be treated along with the amenorrhea. The two conditions occur frequently together and have similar causes.

---

5. Steiner, *SM,* lecture 5.

Another method that can be quite helpful is dry cupping in the area of the lower back. Experience has shown that the effect of the medications already discussed is enhanced if they are injected subcutaneously in the area where blood has been drawn to the surface by cupping. Injections of a milliliter of the patient's own blood (drawn from a vein) together with the remedy of choice can be helpful for hypoplastics or asthenics, whereas the opposite constitutional type can benefit from phlebotomy (100 ml).

Not every case of amenorrhea requires specific treatment. For example, in cases of exhaustion (including mental exhaustion bordering on shock), cachexia, and severe anemia, the primary condition rather than the accompanying amenorrhea should be treated. The medication most generally recommended here is Prunus spinosa.

Successful treatment of amenorrhea should be followed up with a Menodoron treatment extending over several months. Menodoron harmonizes and stabilizes the entire menstrual process, so that even relapses can be quickly corrected with the appropriate therapy. It is indicated for all menstrual disorders, including excessive or deficient flow, irregular periods, and the accompanying subjective symptoms. Menodoron is a combination of decoctions of blossoms and other above ground parts of *Urtica dioica* (stinging nettle), *Achillea millefolium* (yarrow), *Capsella bursa-pastoris* (shepherd's purse), *Origanum majoranae* (marjoram), and the bark of *Quercus robur* (English oak). These ingredients, each of which will be discussed below, are subjected to pharmaceutical processes that bring out the full effect of their therapeutic substances.

Menodoron is one of the so-called "typical remedies"[6] composed by Rudolf Steiner. Rather than combining similar ingredients, these remedies unite opposites. In Menodoron, these opposites are united through a mediating, rhythmic process known as "digestion" (see volume I, p. 306). Menodoron should therefore be considered the basic and proven remedy for all menstrual complaints.

6. See O. Wolff, *Remedies for Typical Diseases* (Spring Valley, N.Y.: Mercury Press, 1996.)

Urtica dioica (Stinging Nettle)

Essential here is the dynamic-active form in which iron is present. Urtica's remediation of profuse and debilitating meno- and metrorrhagia is thus readily comprehensible, since even normal menstruation, like phlebotomy, provokes an increase in the production of red blood cells. Urtica urens is an important component of the combination Berberis/ Urtica, which is used in the conservative treatment of uterine myomas and bleeding myomas.

Another important substance in Urtica is the irritant responsible for its name. This substance, which resembles certain snake venoms, is composed of volatile acids and toxalbumins. It is produced by only two plant families in the world, the Losaceae and the Urticaceae, and is more powerful in members of the latter family that grow close to the equator. Clearly, then, the stinging nettle toxin is related to warmth. The toxalbumins, proteinous substances, are responsible for stinging nettle's tendency to rot quickly. Above-ground parts of the plant, when cut up and compressed, soon develop an intense, sulfurous odor. This by itself is an indication of Urtica's relation to the same kind of sulfurous protein decomposition processes that occur in some pathologies of the menstrual process. The additional presence in Urtica of high levels of silica, particularly in the stinging hairs, strengthens and regulates the plant's protein process.

Achillea millefolium (Yarrow)

Yarrow has been used for centuries by both lay practitioners and physicians as a styptic. Unlike Urtica, which acts mainly via the iron component of blood, Achillea tends more to harmonize the blood's metabolic processes. It also contains significant amounts of sulfur, but in a more chemically stable form than Urtica. The juice of the above ground parts of Achillea keeps for a long time without preservatives. This is due to the combination of a strong potassium process with the sulfur process; yarrow ashes contain up to 48% potassium salts. Through these, the plant holds its protein processes in check, a fact expressed outwardly in its well-formed leaves and its mechanical resilience. This also accounts for yarrow's positive therapeutic effect on the overactive protein processes found in polymenorrhea and in meno- and metrorrhagia. The organism's need for potassium is proportional to its metabolism and processes of regeneration, both of which are high after blood loss.

The upper part of the yarrow plant also contains an essential oil whose pigment is the same as that found in the essential oil of chamomile. The essential oil of yarrow counters inflammation and spasms.

Capsella bursa-pastoris (Shepherd's Purse)

Yet a third variation of the sulfur process appears in shepherd's purse. Sulfur is present physically in the form of thiols and allyl isothiocyanate (allyl mustard oil). Capsella is a member of the Cruciferae, a family that has a special affinity to sulfur. However, it also contains high levels of potassium, sodium, and silica. These make up 10% of the plant ash and counteract the sulfur process and keep it in check. An interesting fact is that these substances are concentrated to an unusually high degree in the leaves and stem of the shepherd's purse. In the majority of plants they are found mostly in the root. Thus, forces of the root are here raised into the above-ground part of the plant and restrain the sulfur processes associated with the blossom and fruit, which, interestingly enough, grow almost directly out of the root: the leaves are confined to a rosette at the base of the stem, which thus carries almost exclusively flowers and fruits.

Capsella blossoms throughout its vegetative period, indicating an inexhaustible vitality. It accounts for Menodoron's invigorating and toning effect in cases of menstrual debility. It also normalizes the overactive blood and protein processes of disturbed menstruation.

Capsella also contains significant amounts of iron (2–3%). It thus approaches the hemoactive iron process of stinging nettle. Perhaps more important, however, is its acetylcholine content. Acetylcholine fulfills two essential physiological functions: first, it stimulates rhythmic activity of the involuntary muscles; second, it facilitates those contractions by dilating blood vessels and thus increasing blood flow through the muscles. Through acetylcholine, Capsella exercises a direct influence upon the uterine muscle.

This influence is supported by another component that is similar to secalin and has a styptic effect. Because of it, shepherd's purse, together with Potentilla tormentilla, has proven effective as a styptic in cases of genital bleeding of both menstrual and nonmenstrual genesis.

Quercus robur (English oak)

The two components of this plant that are of therapeutic significance for Menodoron are lime and tannic acid. Oaks absorb a high proportion of calcium salts from the ground and store them, primarily in their thick bark. Oak bark ash, the form in which the oak goes into Menodoron, contains up to 95% calcium salts. Calcium's significance for blood coagulation is common knowledge. Here, however, mineral calcium has gone through a vegetable process and thus become organized in a specific way.

Oak bark in a dry state contains up to 20% tannins, a fact that accounts for its economic and medical utility. Tannins are valued in medicine as astringents, and can be used effectively for bleeding, inflammations, exudates, and edema.

Origanum majorana (Marjoram)

Marjoram is characterized to a greater extent than any of the preceding plants by its dynamic qualities, in particular that of warmth. It is one of several characteristic members of the Labiatae family that have a particularly strong affinity to warmth. It grows only in a hot, dry environment, and "distills" the warmth of the sun in its essential oils, which impart its strong, spicy aroma. Many of the plants of this family are similarly fiery and aromatic and hence used as seasonings: savory, basil, lemon balm, mint, and sage, to name a few.

The role of chilling in the genesis of dysmenorrhea is well known. A great many women who do not experience any of the symptoms of chilling nevertheless have a debilitated "warmth organism."

Essential oils are antispasmodic, which accounts for their effectiveness against the complaints of spasmodic dysmenorrhea. The ingredient of Menodoron that contributes essential oils is the seed of the marjoram plant, making Menodoron the first medication ever to use that part of the plant. Marjoram seed is characterized by high levels of fats and oils.

The fatty oils of a plant such as marjoram, which is strongly permeated with warmth processes, aid the antispasmodic action of the essential oils by stimulating the production of warmth in the involuntary muscles of the uterus, acting, to use a gross analogy, as a sort of "internal hot water bottle."

Marjoram shares a specific action on the uterus with other representatives of its family, which are the lemon balm (*Melissa officinalis*), lavender, germander (*Teucrium scorodonia*), and dead nettle (*Lamium album*). The organ-specificity of these plants has been treated in greater detail by Pelikan[7] and Simonis.[8]

Because both excessive and deficient menstruation are due to the same mental and physical causes, Menodoron may be used to treat both. The same applies to both delayed and premature periods. Indeed, Menodoron by itself is frequently sufficient, since its ingredients and composition enable it to influence every aspect of the interaction of the higher members that governs the menstrual process. Its effectiveness has been repeatedly demonstrated for nearly half a century in many parts of the world.

Menodoron should be taken between periods, not during menstruation, over a longer period of time (approx. three months).

Profuse menstrual bleeding is a special therapeutic problem that indicates a lack of activity on the part of the ego organization. This lack can be remedied with a healing substance until the normal organ process reconstitutes itself from within. One such substance is calcium.[9] Calcium should be given during menstruation by injection, or, less optimally, by mouth. A particularly effective form of calcium for this purpose is Corallium rubrum, in which calcium has been modified by the metabolism of an animal, the coral. Potentized preparations of natural calcium carbonate (Marmor) or calcium sulfate may also be given.

Calcium's effects can be enhanced by the concurrent application of antimony. Antimony influences the formative forces of the blood and hence the processes of coagulation and bleeding. The most useful combinations are Corallium rubrum D6/Stibium D6 or Marmor D6/Stibium D6 (injected), several ampules intravenously if necessary. In addition to coral calcium, the ointment Corallium comp. contains an extract of tormentil root and is best applied to the calves, an important therapeutic site for all ailments of the lower abdomen.

---

7. W. Pelikan, *Healing Plants*,Vol.I, (Mercury Press, Spring Valley:1997.)
8. W. C. Simonis, *Die unbekannte Heilpflanze* (1955).
9. Steiner/Wegman, *FT*, chapter 17.

The most important vegetable remedy for excessive menstrual bleeding is Potentilla tormentilla, the tormentil. The rhizome of this rosaceous plant is massive and produces substances that in other plants are produced only by the above-ground parts: glycosides, gums, tannins, astringents, acids, and a bright red pigment. For menstrual bleeding, Tormentilla can be used in low potencies (D3) either injected or internally, preferably in combination with Capsella bursa-pastoris. It is particularly helpful for juvenile metrorrhagia.

Profuse or prolonged menstrual bleeding may be treated with Hamamelis (original tincture or distilled, 10%) and injections of Berberis vulgaris D4. Both medications are indicated for sluggish, dark menstruations, which occur particularly in the presence of inflammation (endometritis or metritis). The same kind of flow is observed in menopausal women whose uterus is swollen and tender but not yet myomatous.

The most important use of Berberis and Hamamelis is in the treatment of uterine myomas, discussed below. Profuse or prolonged menstrual bleeding can also be a sign of weak kidney radiation. When circulation tends to stagnate in the lower extremities, the remedy of choice is Urtica dioica D3. Even more effective than this, however, is the "model" of Urtica (see vol. I, p. 312), namely Solutio Ferri comp., particularly in the combination ampule with Glandula suprarenalis. The injection is best made in the upper right thigh.

Persistent secondary amenorrhea can give way to an increased and protracted blood flow, i.e., to menorrhagia, which in turn can lead to a cystic hyperplasia. The latter, in which the normal and periodic breakdown phases cease to occur, is usually caused by a persistence of the follicle. The mucous membranes of the uterus proliferate excessively and an unusual number of cysts are formed. In keeping with the above discussion, we may assume that here the etheric body suffers from a lack of structuring. The formation of retention cysts indicates that a kind of maturation process does occur, but the ego organization's grip on the astral and etheric bodies is too weak to initiate the third, desquamation phase at the proper time. The conditions in question therefore tend to occur at the beginning and end of a woman's reproductive life (i.e., at puberty and at menopause), when the ego organization has either not yet learned to control the menstrual process or can no longer do so. By contrast, "around the age of thirty-five," in the middle of life, "the ego organization has a strong affinity to the rest of the organism."[10] In the pathological conditions just described, "the ego organization does not deliver enough strength to reign in the menstrual process it has initiated."[11] Signs of this weakness of the ego organization in the metabolic realm include dizziness, orthostatic hypotension, fainting spells, and memory loss. These symptoms can occur in conjunction with the described conditions or during normal menstruation. The appropriate response is to strengthen the ego organization with such remedies as Saccharum sacchari or Saccharum tostum, for "sugar acts directly upon the ego organization and strengthens it inwardly."[12]

Another indication for this condition is Berberis. Prophylactic doses of Iscador may also be indicated, depending on the case. When Iscador is used, the cellular proliferation, although benign, receives new formative forces from mistletoe.

Endometriosis is one step closer to actual tumor formation. This disease occurs most frequently between the ages of twenty-eight and thirty, i.e. shortly before the time of the ego organization's strongest connection with the menstrual cycle (around the age of thirty-five). Endometriosis is also a case of a partial failure of the ego organization. The astral body attempts to make up for the absence of the latter's excretory activity, leading to intense pains. Significantly, women of asthenic constitution, in whom the upper organization is emphasized, tend more toward this disorder than do women with "excessive etheric energy." As our culture as a whole tends toward an emphasis on the head at the expense of the rest of the body, endometriosis has accordingly become more prevalent over the last few decades. The ego organization's failure to permeate the lower or metabolic pole, which is obvious in endometriosis, has also become apparent in an increase in urinary tract infections, complaints about cold feet, diseases of the hepatobiliary system, and other metabolic disorders.

When surgery is not yet indicated or not possible, the treatment of endometriosis should consist of the hemostyptic use of a calcium remedy (for example, Corallium rubrum/Stibium, combination ampule) and

10. Steiner/Wegman, *FT*, chapter 19, eighth case.
11. Steiner/Wegman, *FT*, chapter 19, eighth case.
12. Steiner/Wegman, *FT*, chapter 20.

the stimulation of genital function with silver (e.g., Bryophyllum Argento cultum D2, then Argentum praep. D6). Mercury in lower potency may also be indicated in some cases, either in addition or subsequent to silver treatment, to limit the hyperplasia and lead it over into maturation and secretion. In cases where the uterus is emphasized, mercury should be administered premenstrually; where the ovary is emphasized, around the time of ovulation (intermenstrual pain). The lack of metabolic formative forces can be countered with silica, specifically with Equisetum Silicea cultum D2. Rarer, "vital" types may also require a short course of injections of Plumbum D6–D8 in order to check proliferation. As with hyperplasia (discussed above) and myomas (below), mistletoe therapy is also indicated, for example, Iscador M St 5, twice weekly for a total of seven to fourteen injections, in alternation with the therapy already mentioned. Berberis, Radix/Urtica should be applied in alternation with the main therapy (see the discussions of the treatment of myomas, p. 158f.).

The painful cramps of endometriosis can frequently be held within tolerable limits by the therapy for dysmenorrhea discussed below. Profuse flow can be managed with the appropriate medications, such as Tormentilla, Capsella, or Agnus castus.

The conventional treatment of endometriosis with progesterone frequently relieves symptoms, since it initiates the lacking maturation and secretory processes, but only for the duration of treatment, since it is merely substitution therapy. Curative eurythmy and painting offer special therapeutic possibilities.

Dysmenorrhea

Dysmenorrhea can have many causes. In every case, however, the cramps associated with it are a sign of excessive astral activity of the nerve-sense type, as has been discussed before. Pain is an intensification of consciousness at the wrong location. The astral body's hyperactivity may be due to a weakness of the etheric substrate, in which case the relatively strong astral body "pierces through" into the physical, causing cramps. This is most frequent in women of an asthenic build or constitution, for whom Argentum is indicated, particularly when their reproductive function tends to be below normal. Copper is preferable in cases of generalized cramps combined with insufficient blood supply, especially in dark-haired or dark-skinned patients. The most effective form of copper for this application is Chamomilla Cupro culta although copper ointment on the lower abdomen or the calves is also helpful. Calf cramps in particular respond well to the natural compound of copper with arsenic, olivenite (D6, preferably as injection).

The constitutionally opposite situation occurs in robust, vital women whose etheric body is strong but somewhat too "dense." In such women, the astral body forces its way into the etheric, once more producing cramps, usually in conjunction with delayed or weak menstrual periods. Tormentilla D30 is practically a specific for this condition; limited phlebotomy is also helpful.

As with all other menstrual disorders, the basic treatment of dysmenorrhea should be with Menodoron (see above). For some forms of dysmenorrhea, Menodoron has to be supplemented, at least in the initial stages, in order for it to have its full effect. This is the case, for example, when dysmenorrhea is combined with migraine. If there is a predisposition to the latter, it should be treated in accordance with its essential nature (see List of Indications at end of this volume). Some forms of migraine occur only during menstruation, when processes that should take place in the metabolic region are displaced into the nerve-sense system as a result of deficient control by the ego organization. Such migraines tend to inhibit consciousness and are very common nowadays. The remedy for this will usually be Tormentilla D30, as it will be for similar complains during menopause or after a premenopausal hysterectomy (in the latter case preferably D15). Tormentilla can also help restore a normal menstrual cycle in cases of infrequent periods. The homeopathic remedies Cimicifuga and Sepia are also useful, provided they are used according to the symptom complex of their provings.

Acute menstrual cramps can frequently be relieved by an injection of Oxalis D2 or D3, as can other cramps of the smooth musculature. Oxalic acid energizes the etheric system in the digestive and genital systems.

Belladonna's generalized antispasmodic qualities can also be put to use here. Fair-skinned patients sometimes respond better to Chamomilla, especially injections of Chamomilla Cupro culta D3. In cases where it is difficult to decide which remedy is more appropriate, it is best to use a combination (Belladonna/Chamomilla).

Ammi Visnaga comp. suppositories (Wala) also bring rapid relief from cramps. Fast and lasting relief can also occasionally be achieved by brushing the inside of the nose with Gencydo 1% liquid or Berberis, Fructus 20%.

Pains in the lower back during menstruation may be due to a disturbed iron process. Acute cases, to the extent that they do not respond to the stinging nettle contained in Menodoron, may be treated with injections of Ferrum sidereum. Chronic lower back pains may also be an indication for Kalium carbonicum D6, particularly when there are also edema, leukorrhea, or liver symptoms. Of course, vertebral problems may also play a role. Cupping is indicated in all cases.

Premenstrual Syndrome (PMS)

This disorder deserves special mention, as it seems to be on the increase. It affects approximately one third of all menstruating women in varying degrees of severity. The most prominent complaints are of swelling and tension caused by fluid retention. The emotional symptoms include irritability, nervousness, aggressiveness, and depression, all of which are manifestations of congestion corresponding to the congestion in the patient's fluid organism. Once menstruation begins, the retained fluids are eliminated, and the mental symptoms correspondingly relieved.

As mentioned above, the ego organization is more active in the second half of the menstrual cycle; PMS therefore indicates a lack in the ego organization's activity. At the same time, the retention of fluids points to a disorder of the hepatobiliary system, which controls the fluid organism. As in the disorders just discussed, the normal maturation processes of the menstrual cycle are too weak or delayed. Fluid retention is overcome only when the ego organization and astral body intervene more forcefully, i.e. in the desquamative phase. The depression that frequently attends PMS is a further indication of a liver disorder.

The therapy of PMS includes a stimulation of the fluid organism with Kalium carbonicum D6 (10 drops t.i.d.); the potency is increased to D10 when D6 starts to become less effective. A general remedy for disorders of the second half of the menstrual cycle is Agnus castus liquid (full strength to D4). Congested bile processes can be set back in motion with Chelidonium D3 or Chelidonium Ferro cultum D2. Equisetum Silicea cultum D2 has a formative and diuretic effect. Specific metabolic disorders can be treated with the appropriate medications, for instance, gastric digestive disturbances with Ignatia D4-D6, disorders of the reproductive organs with Cimicifuga D3. The basic medication will of course be Menodoron, which can be given during the first half of the cycle, the other medications being given individually or together as indicated in the second half. In many, cases primrose oil (which is rich in gamma-linoleic acid) is recommended. The effect is often very good and obvious.[13]

Uterine Myomas

This disease is characterized by a benign local proliferation of smooth muscle and/or fibrous tissue. The etheric body dominates and carries an essentially necessary regenerative and constructive activity to an extreme. The proliferation may or may not be extensive enough to form actual leiomyomas. Other possible outcomes are a concentric enlargement of the entire uterus or the formation of multiple growths in the various layers of the uterine wall. Myomas form when the astral body and ego organization fail to structure and limit the etheric body's activity, with the result that menstrual periods become longer. If the ego organization's guidance collapses completely, menorrhagia can yield to metrorrhagia or to menometrorrhagia, i.e. uncontrolled, continuous uterine bleeding.

A conservative therapy is possible as long as myomas have not become too large or the patient has not been excessively weakened by increased menstrual flow. The two main remedies here are *Berberis vulgaris* and *Urtica urens.*

Urtica was described above as one of the ingredients of Menodoron. The outer form of Berberis (the barberry) suggests great vitality and pent-up forces of growth. The undersides of the leaves are almost always

13. See O. Wolff "gamma-Linolensäure und Omega3-Fettsäuren" Mercurstab 1994 S. 165-170.

populated with fungi of the family Ustilaginaceae, which indicates the action of lunar influences.[14] Astral influences are in general quite pronounced in this plant: the flowering impulse is strong and extends down to the root, which is correspondingly yellow. An alkaloid similar to the hemostatic hydrastine is formed in the root. Alkaloids always indicate the presence of strong astral forces.[15]

Myomas respond to remedies derived from the entire barberry, such as Berberis, Planta tota D2/Urtica urens D3 aa, initially as injection and then later orally as a liquid. The root of the barberry (Berberis, Radix D3 or D4) has a greater effect upon such inflammatory processes as bleeding due to endometritis. Berberis, Radix is also best given first as injection and then later as liquid.

Myomas will occasionally shrink as a result of therapy, but not always.[16] A more important and highly frequent result is control and normalization of bleeding, which allows the patient to forgo an operation. If this can be sustained until menopause, no further treatment is necessary thereafter.

Another useful remedy for myomal bleeding is the original tincture of Hamamelis (20 drops 5 times daily), especially where the flow is sluggish and dark.

As with other benign growths, mistletoe preparations are indicated for myomas in careful or prophylactic doses (e.g., Iscador M c. Argentum St. 5, two injections weekly, 0.001 or 0.01 mg.).

Ovarian Cysts

Simple ovarian cysts (not dermoid) are also amenable to a conservative treatment as long as they are not too large. Due to the danger of rapid growth, the condition of the cyst will have to be checked more frequently than that of a uterine myoma. The possibility of spontaneous remission in the case of follicular cysts must also be considered.

The chief remedy for these growths is tin, which organizes fluids and

14. G. Grohmann, *Die Pflanze,* vol. 1 (Stuttgart).
15. W. Pelikan, *Healing Plants,* vol. I (Mercury Press, Spring Valley:1998)
16. See Volkmann, *BEH* 18 (1965):61.

thus also affects local fluid production and accumulation. It has been applied successfully in the form of Mixtura Stanni comp., a combined remedy invented by Rudolf Steiner (Stannum/Acidum nitricum/ Cuprum/Alumen). Cuprum stimulates venous drainage and alum (Aluminum potassium sulfate) is an astringent.

Further remedies that should be considered are Vespa Crabro, Apis, and Lachesis. Apis is especially called for with right-sided, Lachesis with left-sided cysts. Each can be given internally or injected with various potencies of Ovaria. Another combination remedy is Magnesium sulfuricum/Ovaria comp. (Wala).

Inflammations of the Genital Tract

Inflammations are generally regarded as infections. Of course, hematogenous and invasive bacterial infections exist, but the question is why they occur. This question is dealt with at great length in the chapter on infectious diseases. To summarize, bacteria are by no means the cause of a disease, but rather only proliferate in an organism that has already been weakened. Antibacterial therapy therefore does not solve the essential problem of infectious disease, despite the occasionally dramatic improvement that such therapy can produce in acute cases. Indeed, the result of antibacterial therapy is frequently a transition to more chronic forms of the disease or the spreading of the disease to further sites (e.g. chronic adnexitis).

A chronic inflammation must be judged differently than an acute one. In particular, the ego organization is much less involved in the former; it has so to speak "lost interest" in the inflamed area. Instead of the catabolic processes typical of acute inflammations, fibrous structures form; the result can be adhesions and infertility. Chronic inflammation with cellular proliferation also expresses an increase in uncontrolled etheric activity, due mainly to the weakness of the ego organization.

The chief therapeutic measure indicated in this situation is the application of warmth, either with rising-temperatures sitz baths, diathermy, or, less effectively, hot-water bottles. Common sense also dictates the wearing of warm clothing, the avoidance of undergarments made of synthetic fibers, and so on. The cold feet that usually accompany chronic inflammations are a sign of disturbances in the warmth organism, the treatment of which is the condition for the effectiveness of all other therapy. A possible remedy is Apis, for example, injections of Apis/Bryonia or Apis/Belladonna.

The structuring of protein can be influenced with antimony or stibnite. The best remedy is Antimonite/Echinacea comp., injected or orally as liquid; Echinacea increases resistance.

Argentum in higher potencies is indicated for all acute febrile conditions up through sepsis. It is contained in Antimonite/Echinacea comp. but is most useful by itself in acute cases of parametritis and pelvic inflammatory disease. Its effects can be complemented in such cases with Echinacea, Quartz, or Lachesis, all of which are injected once or twice daily. (The combined ampule Argentum/Echinacea may also be administered intravenously, five to seven ml.).

A "scar treatment" consisting of local injections of Argentum D6 + Vespa Crabro D4 + Tabacum D6 may be applied when adhesions or complete blockages have already occurred. Naturally the usual physical, resorptive, and general measures should not be ignored. Art therapy and curative eurythmy can also be extremely helpful.

Leukorrhea (Vaginal Discharge)

So-called physiological leukorrhea calls for constitutional therapy. Leukorrheas that indicate a loss of integrity of the water organism are usually thin, profuse, and frequently accompanied by lower back pains. A helpful remedy in such cases is Kalium carbonicum, especially where hepatic congestion or subtle indications of a liver disturbance are also present. Phosphorus can also be helpful in influencing the constitution, particularly in cases of chronic inflammation, since it draws the ego into the metabolism and activates it there.

Mercury is the chief remedy for inflammatory leukorrheas and catarrhs of various genesis. Possible forms include Mercurius viv. nat. D6 and Apis/Belladonna c. Mercur. Vaginal tablets of Mercurius vivus/Ol. aether. Eucalypti have proven especially effective.

Acute vaginitis with purulent, fetid, and burning discharge and occasional ulceration frequently responds well to creosote, which is obtained from beech wood by dry distillation. Creosote burns and corrodes, causes proteins to coagulate, and prevents putrefaction, which accounts for the effectiveness of smoking as a way of preserving meats. Creosote was formerly used as an astringent for various inflammations of internal organs or mucous membranes and for tuberculosis. Here it is best applied as liquid, D4 or injection, D6.

Vaginitis is frequently combined with cystitis, since both derive either from colds or from a local warmth deficit. In addition to heat therapy, treatment with mercury and silver is possible, e.g. Thuja comp. Painful or difficult urination is usually relieved by Cantharis D4.

Cervicitis and Endocervical Eversion

Acute inflammations of the cervix and portio vaginalis usually involve the surrounding tissues as well, the vagina, uterus, and adnexa, and should therefore be treated as general infections of the genital tract (see section above). Trichomoniasis, mycosis, and similar inflammatory diseases are usually diagnosed on the basis of microscopic examination of a drop of the secretion and require specific treatment. Such treatment should, however, be followed by a more general treatment designed to build and strengthen immunity. In some cases, the more general treatment suffices to eradicate a disease all by itself. The remedies that constitute such treatment are in the form of vaginal tablets or suppositories, including Marjoram/Melissa, which effects a general readjustment of disturbed warmth-processes in the lower organization, and Argentum/Quercus comp., which applies to more strongly exudative, liquefying conditions. Milder disorders respond well to insertions of yogurt in the vagina every night for about one or two weeks. Sitz baths with the addition of marjoram-melissa tea, Mercurialis perennis 20%, calendula essence, or even just vinegar, can occasionally resolve even chronic, resistant inflammations of the vulva, vagina, and portio vaginalis.

Simple endocervical eversion or metaplastic processes in the so-called transformation zone of the cervix are now considered to be physiological occurrences of the reproductive phase of a woman's life. However, various irritations or more general disruptions can frequently aggravate these processes into chronic cervicitis, which is often accompanied by hypersecretion of the endocervical glands and in isolated cases can even impair fertility.

The constitutional therapy described above does not always produce satisfactory results. If this is the case, and if cytological analysis has ruled out an excessive dysplastic alteration (which would call for a prophylactic treatment with mistletoe), the technique of cryocauterization should be considered. It is not very traumatic and leaves no scars that might impair later function. The strengthening therapy described above can then be applied.

Descensus

Uterine descensus and prolapse are due to a predominance of forces of weight over those of buoyancy, though of course a weakness of connective tissue also plays a role. The history also usually reveals external stresses, such as pregnancies and births, which can have occurred several years earlier. However, young nulliparas who have no history of such "mechanical" injuries can also develop a descensus.

The connective tissue can, depending on the case, be strengthened with silica, primarily as Equisetum Silicea cultum. For younger patients, silver is also important (internally or as an ointment). Older patients do best with tin, since they lack the structuring forces that tin can provide. Stannum silicicum or Arandisit, each of which also contains the formative forces of quartz, may also be used. Operations will be unavoidable in some cases.

Infertility

Infertility that is not due to any of the possible pathological causes, which cannot be discussed here, can be treated with a method developed by Rudolf Steiner. This method has proven particularly effective with delicately built or even frail women with somewhat translucent skin and a more differentiated psyche. Internally these women receive Alumen/Berberis comp. (composed of Christmas rose, barberry fruits, and alum), externally three different compresses at various times of the day. Specifically, a blackthorn (Prunus spinosa) compress is applied to the hips in the morning, a horseradish compress to the lower abdomen in the afternoon, and in the evening a compress with Cuprum praep. ointment to the calves. For the sake of convenience, blackthorn and horseradish can be applied as ointments (Prunus spinosa and Cochlearia armoracia 10%).

Some patients will of course require constitutional therapy. Included in this should be a mental-emotional regimen, art therapy, and curative eurythmy. It should also be kept in mind that conception is more than a merely biological event; it is also determined by the incarnating human being, who chooses the optimal time.

Climacteric

The climacteric is no more a pathological condition than is puberty. However, the possible unpleasant side effects are more numerous, and they can and should be treated. Menopause is only one among many events of the climacteric period, just as menarche is only one among many events of puberty.

As part of the general excarnation process of increasing age, the astral body begins to withdraw from the organic activity of the lower organization into which it entered during puberty. Significantly, the timing of both puberty and menopause has changed from earlier times. Early puberty as a sign of developmental acceleration has been discussed at length in an earlier volume (see vol. I, p. 98f.). Menopause, by contrast, occurs later than it used to. The average female reproductive phase is thus longer. Part of the reason for this is certainly better nutrition. However, these facts also express a more intense connection of the ego and astral body with the etheric and physical bodies.

The astral body withdraws from the woman more suddenly and drastically than it does from the man. The woman's being is thus more strongly divided into ego and astral body on the one hand and physical and etheric body on the other. This division, normal for the human being throughout life, becomes more profound in the climacteric. The result is a splitting of mental life between the extremes of nervousness, restlessness, cramps, and insomnia on the one hand and impaired consciousness on the other. The dissociation can also lead either to a predominance or a weakness of the etheric body.

A predominant etheric body can express itself in the growth of connective tissue, the ovarial parenchyma, the fallopian tube musculature, or the uterine lining. In the blood and tissue fluids, a mild lymphocytosis develops and the ratio of potassium to calcium increases.

In response to this uncontrolled increase in etheric activity, the astral body attempts to integrate itself again more strongly. This gives rise to a tendency toward functional or organic sclerosis throughout the genital system and in the circulatory system. People in the climacteric frequently experience temporary increases in blood pressure, a sign of the astral body's increased activity. Such people may seem as if they fear to lose something in the astral body's withdrawal; instead of directing their activity toward spiritual matters, for which this metamorphosis gives them the opportunity, they cling all the more strongly to the body. This tendency frequently remains subconscious but can also enter the person's awareness.

The signs of a weakened etheric body include disturbances in fluid metabolism; edemas are possible if the liver does not process water properly. However, a relative "drying out" is also possible, which can lead to arthrosis and spondylarthrosis. Women are more susceptible to this than are men, especially in the climacteric and typically in the lower parts of the skeleton, in the pelvis, lower spine, and knees. The subjective symptoms do not always correspond to the radiological findings. Another sign of weakened etheric body is the loss of tone that leads to descensus, prolapse, and ptosis. Tissue tone and turgor, which in the young create the impression of firmness and luminescence, are, after all, a function of the etheric body.

A weakness of the etheric in relation to the physical body ultimately results in depositions that can no longer be resorbed, i.e. in sclerosis. For this reason such sclerotic diseases as heart attack and angina pectoris usually affect women only after menopause. Arthrosis and spondylarthrosis also tend to progress more quickly during this period, especially in cases of obesity.

Another expression of the sclerotic tendency is osteoporosis, even though this disease is essentially a decalcification. Apart from this, the larger problem is a disorder of calcium metabolism, whereby bone calcium is dissolved and redeposited in blood vessels or other organs. The goal of therapy is therefore not to eliminate the calcium, but to redirect it to its proper place, to the skeletal system. This can be achieved, for example, with Fluorite D4, which usually relieves the subjective symptoms and strengthens connective tissue (e.g. in cases of varices or ptoses). Agaricus comp./Phosphorus as injection or liquid helps by influencing the osteoporosis itself.

A certain decalcification occurs in old age, i.e., the bones become weaker. This is more or less true for every organ. But the deterioration of bone thickness is not the actual problem. Rather, the problem lies in loss in the *organic* substances of the bones. These organic substances give the bones their elasticity, while, as is generally known, hardness affects brittleness. Among the organic substances it is a matter above all of galactosamine chrondroitin sulfate, the formation of which is to be understood as interwoven with the effect of silica. Calcium binds human beings to the earth; silica is a cosmic substance (see volume II, the chapter on mineral remedies). Therefore, in old age a certain diminution of calcium as well as a sufficient supply of silica is necessary because older human beings should now prepare their way to the cosmos according with their interests in life (correspondingly, the embryo and the child are still relatively rich in silica which changes to calcium in the course of incarnation).

Silica may be provided, for example, in the form of Equisetum (Silicea cultum D2). The formation of organic bone substance (collagen) can be prescribed through potentiated organ preparations (Cartilago) or more specifically through preparations using shark cartilage rich in proline which may also found in collagen and in cereal proteins.

Natural foods and appropriate physical activity are essential; a simultaneous antisclerotic therapy may also be necessary. High doses of calcium, particularly in combination with vitamin D, can produce a symptomatic improvement of the osteoporosis but at the same time worsen the arteriosclerosis.

The relationship between the etheric and physical bodies is the same as that between buoyancy and weight. The dissociation of the essential constituents that occurs in the climacteric exposes the organism, particularly the lower part, to the influence of weight. Latent tendencies toward descensus and prolapse frequently become manifest now for the first time, even though the initiating stresses—pregnancy and childbirth—may have occurred years ago. The occurrence of varices and hemorrhoids are another sign of the increased influence of weight, this time on the blood. Of course there are gradations between this and weak kidney radiation, since the latter is a lack of anabolic activity of the astral body within the etheric body.

The changing relationship between buoyancy and weight manifests itself mentally as well. Every possible gradation exists, from mild mood disturbances and impairments of the sense of vitality to the well-defined clinical syndromes of climacteric neurosis and depression, sleep disorders, anxiety, and loss of appetite.

A cardinal symptom of the climacteric is hot flashes. This is obviously an extension of metabolic activity toward the upper part of the organism. It is also a symptom of an arrhythmic, uncontrolled kidney radiation, which is at times too strong and at others too weak, indicating the frustrated efforts of the astral body to reintegrate itself for a time into the body, from which it should slowly be withdrawing itself. The hot flash per se is usually a reaction of the astral body to a preceding withdrawal, whose symptoms may include weakness, exhaustion, nausea, and hypotonia. The astral body awkwardly attempts to reintegrate itself, producing the hot flash and the accompanying perspiration.

Underlying all these symptoms is the ego organization, which, if it is strong enough, executes the "change of life" at the proper time and without serious side effects. If, on the other hand, "the relatively independent part of the ego organization that regulates the reproductive organs"[17] is exhausted, the astral and etheric bodies cannot withdraw properly or at the right time. The result is that, as with many menstrual anomalies, the ego organization is not strong enough to lead the menstrual process to is proper resolution. This gives rise to climacteric metrorrhagia, which displays the irregularity and unpredictability of many climacteric hemorrhages.

A very nearly specific remedy for these disorders of the physical-etheric and emotional realms is gold. Since the process in question is an excarnation, an opening toward the spirit, a higher potency (D20 or D30) is usually indicated. Lower potencies, by contrast, tend to encourage incarnation (useful, for example, when a miscarriage threatens). Only when cardiac symptoms or pronounced circulatory disorders are

17. Steiner/Wegman, *FT,* chapter 19, ninth case.

present is it advisable to switch to D10 or D15; hypertonias, however, respond best to higher potencies. The first symptom to disappear as a result of Aurum therapy is nervous insomnia. This therapy is best applied initially by injection and then later orally. In cases where depression is also present, it is best to use Hypericum Auro cultum.

Among the remedies available for treatment of hot flashes and migraine-like conditions are Potentilla tormentilla and Sanguinaria canadensis. The former is a member of the rose family; the latter belongs to the family of the Papaveraceae. Both are characterized by a spreading of the blossoming process to the root; each has a thick rhizome containing milky, red sap. In nature, such reddenings indicate a reaction against excessive astralization. In this case, the reddening is in the root, which corresponds to the nerve-sense system. The root can thus be used to contain the excessive astral processes responsible for congestion, hot flashes, migraine-like conditions, and redness in the upper organization. The one indication common to all these symptoms is their transitoriness.

Belladonna is to be preferred for people with dark complexion and a relatively "dry" constitution; it is especially effective in combination with Lachesis. The alternation of Sanguinaria with Belladonna/Lachesis can be helpful, especially when symptoms recur over long periods, as often happens during the climacteric.

Marjoram and Melissa are also important remedies due to their intense relationship to warmth. They can be prescribed as vaginal tablets or as a tea added to the bath. Mood disturbances respond well to Sepia, provided the proper symptom complex is present. Fearfulness is best treated with Aconitum (D30 or higher).

The vegetabilized metal Melissa Cupro culta deserves special mention. Copper's warming, antispasmodic effect is complemented in this remedy by the similar effects of Melissa, making this a particularly useful combination. This remedy should be used at the beginning of therapy in menopause, as also in other conditions.

The use of potentized extracts of ovary in combination with other remedies helps guide the effects of the latter to the organs of regeneration. Examples of such combinations include Ovarium comp., which contains Bidor and Stibium in addition to ovary. This remedy influences both the threefold function of the organism and the protein process.

Another combination is Sepia comp., which in addition to Sepia contains Conchae and Ignatia and is indicated particularly for hot flashes and mental symptoms. Flores Sambuci comp. contains larch resin and elderberry and not only influences hot flashes but also vitalizes hardening processes.

Arsenic may also be indicated, particularly in cases of general loss of vitality and poor overall condition. The variability of the arsenic content of the blood and the uterine lining over the course of the menstrual cycle was discussed above. Arsenic levels increase in polymenor-rhea and decrease in oligo- and amenorrhea. In the climacteric, the arsenic content is especially low. When applied as a remedy, arsenic "tones" and strengthens the astral body (see vol. II, p. 134f).

As long as the only problem with climacteric menses is their irregularity, normalizing them is not so important. Menodoron should be tried in any case. Furthermore, the timing of menopause varies from woman to woman. In younger women and women of the appropriate constitution, however, it is desirable to treat diminished ovarial function with the therapy described for amenorrhea.

Profuse and protracted or even continuous periods during the climacteric are a sign that the ego organization needs support. The chief medicines for this are calcium and Stibium (for example, in the combination Corallium rubrum/Stibium, several ampules i.v.), as described above for treatment of menstrual anomalies.

A remedy with wide application to climacteric symptoms is Cimicifuga, known in folk medicine and in homeopathy. It is a typically "female" remedy and especially effective in women of a nervous constitution who tend toward excitability, cramps, rheumatic pains, and muscular hypertension. Its indication in amenorrhea and PMS has already been mentioned. The original tincture is often more effective in the climacteric than the otherwise sufficient D3. When mental symptoms such as depression or restlessness are also prominent, the combination of Cimicifuga with Hypericum or Hypericum Auro cultum is recommended.

Since conventional medical thinking concerning the change of life focuses upon chemical changes and emphasizes the concept of a "hormonal deficit," hormones are nowadays used liberally to relieve or eliminate symptoms. However, only seldom, for example, after an ovariectomy, is there a true deficit. The climacteric woman suffers no more from a "deficit" of sexual hormones than does the female child. The goal is not to artificially prolong a biological process by hormonal substitution, but rather to help women make the transition into a phase of life whose concerns transcend biology. The climacteric may be seen as a further maturation process in addition to puberty; however, unlike puberty, the most important new possibilities are spiritual and emotional rather than biological. Healthy human development demands that these new possibilities be actively realized and the previous phase of life be allowed to come to its natural conclusion. Art therapy is thus particularly important during this transition.

The "matronly type" of former times grew naturally into a new set of emotional and spiritual responsibilities within the extended family. This smooth transition strengthened her ego organization and mitigated the effects of menopause. In our times, however, the physician must avoid nostalgic illusions and help guide his or her female patients from biological to spiritual productivity in keeping with their individual needs.

Pregnancy and Childbirth

Pregnancy, like the climacteric, can hardly be called a pathological condition. Nevertheless, it is also not the woman's normal state. A woman's subjective condition may vary widely from one pregnancy to another.

Pregnancy demands that the mother's etheric, formative forces connect more strongly with her corporeality in order to nurture the growing embryo. In some cases the child's organism can monopolize the mother's etheric forces to the point where it literally "runs her life." Even after giving birth to the child, such a mother may recover only with great difficulty or not at all; her etheric constitution can be permanently weakened. In many cases, however, the opposite occurs: the mother benefits from her etheric body's intensified connection with the physical. This beneficial change in constitution can persist long after the child is born. The effect a pregnancy has upon the mother depends not only on her but also, primarily, on the incarnating ego of the child, which forces the mother to make extensive adjustments.

After conception, the female organism serves as the nutritive ground for a being whose entire life consists at first of growth and differentiation. The younger the embryo, the more pronounced these processes are. As has been repeatedly pointed out, anabolic processes are associated with an alkaline environment, whereas acid formation is a sign of the intervention of the catabolizing astral body. For this reason the uterus, cervical mucosae, amniotic fluid, and sperm are all alkaline. The uterus, being the most muscular organ of the female body, contains high levels of potassium, the bearer of vegetative etheric forces.

Anabolic processes also require a fluid environment, i.e., the fluid organism. A maternal fluid organism that is not properly mastered allows fluids to follow gravity, which over the course of months can lead to anything from a mild swelling of the ankles to a generalized edema. Kalium carbonicum D6 is frequently indicated in such cases.

The embryo is shaped by the incarnating ego from without. Silica, since it is always the bearer of structuring forces, mediates this process. For this reason, the embryo and its environment are unusually rich in silica, the amnion having the highest concentration of all. Structuring forces proceed from the periphery through the nervous system and into the various organs. This principle is demonstrated most strikingly by the extremities: the hand is formed before the forearm, and both precede the formation of the upper arm.

If silica represents cosmic formative forces, calcium is the substance that binds us to the earth. Accordingly, the silica content of our bodies decreases from the very first moment of life until we die, whereas the calcium content increases. The deposition of calcium, in contrast to organ formation, proceeds from within outwards: starting at the shoulder blade, it progresses to the upper arm, forearm, and finally to the hand. A young child's age can be determined by an X-ray of his hand because infant's and toddler's hands are still not entirely calcified.

Medical advice concerning what a pregnant woman should and should not do has tended to focus almost exclusively on diet and external hygiene, which, although unquestionably important, leave out emotional and spiritual considerations that are at least as important. The incarnation of the child must be treated as a spiritual reality; the accompanying physical processes make sense only in light of this. Rudolf Steiner advised pregnant women to occupy themselves less with abstractions than with artistic and pictorial things, which is understandable when we consider that the mother's etheric forces, which would be diminished by our usual, abstract thinking, are required for the child's development in the womb. In this regard, pregnancy is similar to the "pre-logical" state of childhood, in which the forces of thought are still actively forming the physical organism and have not yet assumed an independent, conscious existence.

Pregnancy is the most intimate relationship between two human individuals. However, it transpires on the organic and hence largely unconscious level. The encounter between two egos places high demand on the mother's ego organization. The vomiting that accompanies morning sickness is essentially a defensive reaction to a "foreign" life. Only after the expectant mother has "developed a tolerance" to that life, usually after the first few months, do vomiting and nausea begin to disappear. The complete uniqueness of the relationship between mother and child is indicated by the fact that the same woman can experience different degrees of morning sickness in different pregnancies, if she experiences it at all. Another indication of the woman's changed situation are changes in appetite and cravings, which are also doubtlessly dictated by the needs of the gestating embryo.

This encounter with another life must ultimately be directed by the mother's ego organization. As mentioned above, the ego organization's increased activity during pregnancy is indicated in the mother's rise in body temperature, whereas during menstruation the temperature falls. To support the ego organization in this challenging situation, sugar, the bearer of the ego organization, may be applied in potentized form as Saccharum sacchari D10.

A further remedy for morning sickness is mercury. According to Rudolf Steiner, this substance "is active in reproductive processes within the organism that practically separate its being from itself."[18]

The involvement of the ego organization in pregnancy can also be inferred from the changes in iron levels and metabolism. Iron, as has frequently been mentioned, is the metal that allows human beings to assert themselves on earth, the "metal of incarnation." In the final months of pregnancy, the fetus, in anticipation of the adventure of birth and the

18. Steiner/Wegman, *FT,* chapter 20, fifth case; see also Steiner, *GG,* lecture 8.

associated dangers, lays claim to a large portion of the mother's iron. A sufficient supply is therefore important in pregnancy even in the absence of anemia. The light-component of iron exists in isolated form in cerium, which for hyperemesis is indicated as Cerite (most effectively: 2 ampules intravenously; in milder cases, subcutaneous injection D4–D6 or triturate).

The demands placed upon the ego organization in the area of the uterus can also lead to bone disorders in the rest of the organism. A certain "vitalization of the bones" is quite normal in pregnancy; histology reveals conditions reminiscent of embryonic and childhood bone-formation in all parts of the expectant mother's skeleton. Closely related to the bones are the teeth, not merely by virtue of the substances they have in common (calcium, magnesium, and fluorine), but also by the fact that the teeth are also "vitalized" during pregnancy, another sign of the etheric body's intensified connection with the physical. In other words, the teeth become less "mineral"; they begin to resemble milk teeth, which in an adult is a pathological state. This corresponds to the changes in the mental life of the expectant mother that were touched upon earlier. That the dental damages of pregnancy and lactation are due to more than just a calcium deficiency is clear from the fact that the bones, a much larger reservoir of calcium, are affected much less frequently than are the teeth.

From this we may infer that the therapeutic administration of calcium will not suffice. In addition to Calcon, other substances will be necessary that can draw the overactive etheric body out of the teeth and preserve their mineral character. Such substances are Aesculus, Cortex, an extract of horse chestnut bark, and chlorophyll, which stimulates the management of magnesium. Particularly when there are weaknesses of connective tissue, fluorine, the dynamic opposite of magnesium, may also be indicated in the form of fluorspar. Naturally, the preceding remedies in conjunction with Stibium are also useful in treating hemorrhoids and the varicose veins of pregnancy.

An impending miscarriage or premature birth is an indication for Aurum D6, best injected daily. As mentioned earlier, gold in lower potencies favors incarnation. Additional indications are bedrest and such antispasmodic medications as Ammi visnaga comp. or Chamomilla/Nicotiana. For habitual abortion, gold therapy can be supplemented with Berberis, Fructus D3, best injected in the calves. Incipient hemorrhages can be treated with a remedy already frequently mentioned, Corallium rubrum/Stibium. A pinch of Bryophyllum 50% trit. can be given as frequently as once an hour (or injected as 5%).[19] Bryophyllum, the kalanchoe, possesses an extraordinary vitality, as manifested in its nearly unlimited reproductive capacity.

Toward the end of pregnancy a particular form of toxicosis can occur, toxemia of pregnancy, which can worsen into eclampsia. Warning signs of an impending attack include headache, visual disturbances ranging from blurriness or clouded vision to temporary amaurosis, deepened respiration, edema, massive proteinuria, oliguria to anuria, and hypertension. These symptoms indicate an obvious impairment of renal activity. Acidosis is also usually present, indicating excessive but failed attempts of the astral body to integrate itself. In particular, the astral body fails to reach the renal system, which explains anuria and the retention of nitrogenous substances. As with epilepsy, convulsions can result from this, in this case the convulsions of eclampsia.

The goal of therapy here is to properly incorporate the astral body into the renal system and simultaneously to strengthen the etheric body so that it is ready to receive the astral body. The latter aim is achieved primarily with magnesium, administered as injections of Magnesium phosphoricum D6, possibly with Tabacum D10. Organic compounds of magnesium (Mg-asparatate, -gluconate, -ascorbinate, -orotate) may also be given in acute cases, possibly even intravenously, although intravenous administration should be restricted to situations where observation is possible. A tendency to convulsions may be counteracted with several doses per day of Belladonna in low potency. Cuprum has the same effect and may be given as Cuprum/Ren. Olivenite, a natural compound of copper and arsenic, should also be considered. Albuminuria should be treated according to the description given in the kidney chapter in Volume II, for example, with Ferrum sidereum/Pancreas or potentized arsenic. Salt intake should of course be limited. In view of the dangers of eclampsia, preparations should also be made for a possible Caesarian section.

19. W. Hassauer, "Bryophyllum: Ein neuer Weg in der tokolytischen Therapie," *Erfahrungsheilkunde* (1985) Sept.

Childbirth

Obstetrics is a highly specialized discipline whose established practices and techniques the physician does well to respect. On the other hand, it should not be forgotten "that birth is a physiological process and that obstetric practice should deviate from the natural process only when absolutely necessary. The greatest error to which modern obstetrics has succumbed is the tendency to expedite birth unnecessarily."[20]

In light of this, the physician's job is to foresee and, if possible, to forestall possible complications and dangers. Techniques for relaxation and mental preparedness, which have become increasingly popular, should be welcomed, but tranquilizers should be avoided. During delivery it may be desirable to administer Belladonna D3, possibly with Chamomilla.

Recovery is enhanced at first by Arnica and then primarily by Argentum, which facilitates the reintegration of the higher constituents. Argentum is also effective in helping prevent postpartum psychoses.

The new mother should always be encouraged to consider breastfeeding as an indispensable aid to the child in its first months of life. This topic is discussed at greater length in the chapter on pediatrics. Milk production can be stimulated with lactagogue tea and oil. (Weleda).

Useful books on the subject of pregnancy and childbirth include *When a Child is Born* by Wilhelm zur Linden,[21] *Conception, Birth, & Early Childhood* by Norbert Glas,[22] and *A Guide to Child Health* by Wolfgang Goebel and Michaela Gloeckler.[23]

---

20. Martius, *DMW* 79 (1954):1505.
21. Wilhelm zur Linden, M.D., *A Child is Born: Pregnancy, Birth: First Childhood* (London: Rudolf Steiner Press, 1998).
22. Norbert Glas, M.D., *Conception, Birth, and Early Childhood* (Spring Valley, N.Y.: Anthroposophic Press, 1983).
23. Wolfgang Goebel and Michaela Gloeckler, A Guide to Child Health (Hudson, N.Y.: Anthroposophic Press, 1992)

V

The Skin and Its Diseases

KURT MAGERSTÄDT
GEORG GRÄFLIN
Supplemented by OTTO WOLFF

The Threefold Structure of the Skin

CONTEMPORARY DERMATOLOGY in most cases focuses on the organ of the skin in isolation. Diagnoses are deliberately restricted to descriptive ones. Therapy thus assumes a symptomatic character and the effect of externally and internally applied medications is frequently suppressive. While such therapy produces results, it is not causal. More than other organs, the skin is a reflection of the whole organism. In evaluating diseases of the skin, the diagnosis should ultimately lead to questioning the whole organism, something to which therapy should supply the answer. What direction must we take in order to rediscover the whole human being in the organ of the skin?

One approach to holistic research is the threefold nature of the human organism, which Rudolf Steiner described on many occasions as a functional, dynamic process. It has provided the foundation for many aspects of this study as well. The *dynamics* at work in the skin are threefold:

1. Through the countless nerves embedded in the skin, we perceive warmth, cold, light, and chemical qualities, for example those of baths and ointments. Particularly in the senses of touch and warmth, the skin serves as an organ of perception. The skin is our largest *sense organ.*

2. At the opposite pole to the nervous system's structural inflexibility, the skin is host to an active and autonomous *metabolism.* The germinal layer continually builds up skin and degenerates in the direction of horny skin. In the course of a person's lifetime, many pounds of skin, hair, and nails are produced and sloughed off. Millions of sebaceous and sweat glands serve the human warmth and fluid organisms through differentiated secretions.

3. Through the *rhythmic movement* of blood and lymph, a constant stream of nutrients reaches the skin from within, making it a mirror of nutritional disorders, poisonings, and pathologies of inner organs. It indicates not only our genetic background and internal conditions, but moreover mental states become perceptible through changes in skin color. Shame makes the face blush, fright and anxiety cause the blood to leave, the skin pales and becomes merely "sense." Sudden rage drives the blood upward and out, reddens the face, makes it feel hot, and causes us to "lose our heads."

The function of the skin as a *respiratory organ* does not merely extend to the well known absorption of gaseous components. Rudolf Steiner described how the skin continually assimilates rarefied substances and then condenses them into bodily substance, a process in which the sense organs are likewise involved. This indication could shed light on metabolic functions that proceed from the skin and sense organs, functions about which almost nothing is known today.

Results from our functional observation are likewise confirmed by the anatomical/microscopic structure of the skin in all its details. Three basic layers can be distinguished. The skin is differentiated in epidermis, corium and *tela subcutanea*. The archetypal phenomenon of threefoldness thus becomes apparent anatomically. It can lead us to diagnoses and processes.

The subcutaneous cell tissue, *tela subcutanea* or *subcutis*, contains glands and fatty tissue in more or less pronounced ways depending on the anatomical location, *bursae subcutaneae* and hair bulbs. The tender *perimysium* that envelops the fibers and fascicles of the facial muscles is directly connected with this subcutaneous layer. The subcutis corresponds to the human *metabolic-limb-system*, where movement, transformation of substance, secretion and excretion take place.

The derma, *corium*, represents the rhythmic system of the skin-organ. Here, arteries and veins are concentrated next to lymph vessels in networks of loops and anastomoses. In some cases, they are arranged and entwined with each other in three or four superimposed layers. They are capable of holding up to one third of the blood during pronounced conditions of blood circulation. Here, in the corium, the skin's living peripheral *organ of blood and circulation* is present. Therapy makes use of this physiological-anatomical fact through such hydrotherapeutic measures as wet compresses and hyperthermic baths.

In the case of the outermost layer, the *epidermis,* the most interesting feature is its extensive final innervation of countless interepithelial, sensory nerves and their relationship to the central nervous system. Furthermore, they are particularly abundant in the *stratum germinativum.* The encounter between blood and nerve in the papillae, where tactile corpuscles (Meissner and Vater-Pacini) and vascular loops lie in close proximity, is interesting. Skin, hair, and nails are interspersed with silica, which serves as the material foundation of our sensitivity to warmth, light, and touch (See Ger. vol. I, p. 152ff). Here, the skin turns into *sense organ.*

Anatomists distinguish four layers in the epidermis, two in the corium, and the subcutaneous cell tissue. Ultimately, the skin thus has seven layers.

The Polarity of Skin Diseases

The polarity of inflammation and sclerosis has proven fruitful and is repeatedly mentioned by general pathologists, (see vol. I, pp. 163ff), and it is rediscovered in the polar phenomena of weeping, vesicular eczema as opposed to the dry, squamous form. We think, for example, of pemphigus neonatorum as contrasted with ichthyosis. In the first case, phosphor combined with oyster shells is therapeutically effective; in the second, sulfur in medium potency combined with antimony can be the remedies.

Let us first examine these two polar processes, reflected as they are in the skin, from another angle. The first relates to the protein metabolism in its relationship to the blood, the second the salt metabolism in its relationship to the nervous system. Both are important for the skin. Disturbances of protein metabolism proceed centrifugally, as does the blood. They penetrate through the skin layers from within to the surface. They often lead to inflammatory exanthemata, at times accompanied by fever. We think, for instance, of acute episodes of urticaria, allergies, serum disorders, and exudative diathesis.

Many *inflammatory* and *weeping eczemas* are best understood as disorders of the entire protein metabolism. Their treatment is therefore chiefly dietetic. We prescribe a diet with skim milk that is low in fat but enriched with calcium salts. In illnesses of a centrifugal nature, which can be based on protein disorders, we find symptoms of overactive metabolism, in a manner of speaking, an untimely childhood condition of exudation. This can even lead to purulent forms. The patient's sulfur process is disturbed. Up to 40% and more of such cases occur in children between 7 and 8 years of age. In such disorders, a short-term diet of raw foods is indicated. This generates a sphere of influence similar to that of silica in the skin. With such a diet, the whole organism, all the way to the periphery, is drawn into the task of moderating the metabolic process. A raw diet with subsequent quartz medication (D12) has proven consistently effective, particularly in chronic suppuration.

The relationships between inflammatory skin diseases and the internal organs is described by Rudolf Steiner as follows: "Inflammatory phenomena of the skin are the result of abnormal activity there on the part of the astral body and the ego organization, which have withdrawn from activities they ought to be performing in organs situated more toward the inside.... These in turn cease to perform the processes for which they are responsible because of their lowered sensitivity. One result of this can be abnormal conditions in the liver process, and digestion can then be influenced in an improper manner. When silica is introduced into the organism, the activities of the astral and ego organisms that have moved out to the skin are relieved, so that these organisms are freed for their internal activity, and recovery begins."[1]

Dry eczema, which is more or less "mineral" in orientation, presents us with a different picture. Here the important process is salt metabolism and the associated centripetal current of the nervous system. Illnesses of this kind are characterized by desiccating, cracking, flaking, and nervous itching of the skin. Here, suboptimal functioning and premature aging appear. The salt process is disturbed.

Because of their common ectodermal origin, the central nervous system, the sense organs, and the skin all have the same function. In them, life processes retreat to make room for forming of consciousness. More passive reflections arise, less activity is developed. Ultimately we owe our self-awareness to these mirroring processes. The skin mirrors both internal and external influences and the brain is a mirroring organ of sense

1. Steiner/Wegman, FT, chapter 15.

impressions of the environment. The process manifested in this sphere is that of silver in high potency. In low potency, argentum manifests its inherent polarity by stimulating reproduction processes. All life radiates outward as does the reproductive process of silver that likewise concerns the skin.[2] Here, the human being is continually renewed from the inside out. We continually shed our skin, as it were.

The skin strikingly illustrates the transition from life processes to those of desiccating mortification. The stratum germinativum with its nuclei-containing cells is still full of life. The succeeding upper layers lose their nuclei and become increasingly keratinized. Still more devitalized are the hair and nails, which die and mineralize as they move outward. Observation of these processes reveals the participation of silica in the formation of the ectoderm. The effect of silica leads to rigidified forms of the outer layers of skin, in which are stored the end plates of the cutaneous nerves. The skin's organized suffusion with silica forms the physical foundation for its activity as a sense organ. This activity also illustrates the salt process.

Therapy of Certain Skin Diseases

We begin the therapeutic section of this chapter with a qualitative examination of two remedies suggested by Rudolf Steiner: calcium derived from oyster shells (*Conchae*, see vol. II, p. 131), and birch bark (*Betula, Cortex*).

"The structuring of the organism is essentially a transformation of proteinous substance, through which the latter is brought into interaction with mineralizing forces such as are contained, for example, in calcium. An example of this process is shell formation in oysters. The oyster must rid itself of the forces represented by the shell in order to preserve the quality of its proteinous substance. A similarity exists as well in the shell development of eggs. The oyster secretes calcareous substance in order to exclude it from the protein process."[3]

All invertebrate shellfish expel calcium as dead substance in order to maintain their life in a kind of albuminous exudation. Here we reen-

2. See R. Steiner, GA 313, lecture 8.
3. Steiner/Wegman, *FT*, chapter 16.

counter the same polarity of life and death. The excretion of calcium is "nature's device for having abundant life" (Goethe). The enclosing shells preserve the animal organism from dissolution. Muschelkalk [shell lime] and Jurassic formations are fossil remains of an animal-like stage of the living earth organism. The tabular and layered structure of calcium deposits observable in many quarries corresponds on a grand scale to the structure of the oyster shell. Mineralogically speaking, calcium is not only the mineral that has the widest variety of forms in the countless combinations of its crystallization, it likewise lends form to the entire animal kingdom in shells, supportive structures and bones, including the human skeleton, molded as it is by the ego.

When human metabolism becomes so intense that it appears in the skin as wet or vesicular eczema, then oyster shell, processed as a remedy, can correct the imbalance. Calcium that has imbued itself with the oyster's shell-forming power arrests the excessive metabolic processes of exudative eczema. It heals the skin with its isolating, form-giving power in the same way that it prevents the oyster from dissolving.

The *birch* concentrates the protein processes in leaf formation, particularly that of the young leaves. Salt processes (potash salts) are assigned unilaterally to the white bark. In a unique way, the birch is thus able to separate salt and sulfur processes, which in most herbaceous plants are completely blended together.[4]

The therapeutic effect of birch leaves is observed in the case of a disturbed protein metabolism particularly in uric acid diathesis and concretions. A decoction of the bark acts on the skin's surface as a salt process. Dry, fissuring and flaking eczema, pruritus as an atrophying process in senility, are healed with preparations derived from the bark.

In animal (oyster) and plant (birch), sulfur and salt processes are separated. Both eliminate minerals as the result of inner albuminization processes, in the first case calcium carbonate, in the second, potassium carbonate. This external polarity of forces leads to healing effects in the diseased organism.

Skin diseases in particular may require therapy on several different levels. The golden rule in therapy according to R. Steiner is to "attack, break down, and eliminate the pathological process." Under certain cir-

4. See R. Steiner, *SM*, lecture 15.

cumstances, attempts to stimulate excretion with birch leaves may not work if the pathological deposits have not yet been sufficiently dissolved. In that case, one may first have to treat the disorder as such. This can be accomplished by various means, through medication, through baths and so on, either simultaneously or in succession.

Dermatodoron is unique among the available medications for the treatment of skin diseases. It consists of *Lysimachia nummularia,* the moneywort, compounded by a special pharmaceutical process with *Solanum dulcamara,* the bittersweet or woody nightshade.[5] These two plants are strikingly similar, yet in important respects also polar opposites. Through their common traits they influence the skin as an organ; through their difference they affect opposing processes.

Both plants show a clear relationship to silica. The ashes of *Solanum dulcamara* contain 18% silica by weight, while those of *Lysimachia nummularia* contain as much as 27%. The significance of silica for the skin was described above. We may assume that the form in which silica is present in each plant is imbued with that plant's essential nature and thus receives its effective tendency. Both plants like moist, shady locations and do not have a real tendency for growing upright. In this, an essential relationship to the skin is indicated. Furthermore, both plants contain a substantial amount of tannin. It is needless to mention that tannins have an astringent effect, especially in cases of skin diseases. But it goes without saying that they must be viewed in the overall context of their interactions with silica, glycosides, and saponins.

A closer study of these two plants demonstrates that in the processed form as Dermatodoron, they represent a universal remedy that supports skin formation as such. Dermatodoron is not indicated against any particular skin disease. Accordingly, Dermatodoron is especially valuable in the treatment of childhood eczema. Here it may be desirable to combine internal application of the liquid (5 to 10 drops t.i.d.) with external application of the salve or gel. The effectiveness of Dermatodoron is exemplified by several case histories:

5. A thorough description of these plants is given by W. Daems in *Korrespondenzblätter für Ärzte,* No. 72, (1969).

A thirty-month-old boy has suffered for about two years from a continually deteriorating, impetiginized eczema merging into neurodermatitis, now covering his entire body, except for his head and neck. Previous treatment with corticosteroid ointment recently ceased to be of help. An initial switch to Calcon, Chelidonium, Argentum, Thuja, and Calendula/Stibium oil likewise failed to bring improvement. A short time after beginning generous applications of Dermatodoron salve, oral administration of Calcon I and II, Phosphorus D5 (5 drops b.i.d.), Cichorium (planta tota) D3 (5 drops five times daily), and injections of Stibium D6/Arsenicum album D4 (0.3 ml), the eczema began to flake heavily and after three weeks was practically cured. The lichenified patches inside the elbows and knees healed completely after 18 months. Followup observation: 2½ years (Dr. Boie).

Injections of Dermatodoron seem to act more rapidly and intensely than external or oral administration:

A 50-year-old woman has suffered from "sensitive skin" since childhood. The skin is thin and extremely tender. Even wind produces an unpleasant irritation. Dermatodoron as salve and drops fails to alter the condition. After eight injections, the patient is able to expose her skin to the elements. It strikes her that her skin as a whole feels improved (Dr. Wolff).

Psoriasis vulgaris in a 40-year-old woman; annually recurring episodes with considerable spreading of the process; particularly unpleasant on the scalp, with loss of hair. Spreading ceases immediately after thrice-weekly injections of Dermatodoron are begun. This is the first time that an episode could be stopped, despite previous treatment in many clinics. Normally, (other) therapies took effect only when the episode had passed its climax (Dr. P. Baerens).

The treatment of hundreds of *burns* of all degrees may perhaps best be illustrated by the author's own experience in treating bombing victims in 1944. *Combudoron* liquid, which contains *Urtica urens* and *Arnica montana,* was added to large barrels of boiled water, which had been collected in advance. This brought the concentration to 3–5%. Countless burns of all degrees were treated with wet compresses upon admission. As these measures seemed to be contrary to standard practices, first-aid personnel first had to be convinced of the positive effect of the new prescription. The supply of burn dressings was soon exhausted in any case, and all burns were treated according to this method. Burn victims were especially grateful for the *pain relief* afforded by this treatment. Subsequent dressings with Combudoron ointment, followed later by Wecesin powder, resulted in satisfactory healings. Even large abrasions and pronounced *venous hemorrhages* respond well to Combudoron dressings.

Exudative Diathesis

A series of case histories may serve to exemplify the therapy of particular dermatological illnesses:

1. Boy, aged 3, with chronic episodes of weeping eczema distributed over entire body, especially on the head (sparse hair), rims of the eyelids, and auditory passages. A tendency toward catarrh with difficulty in breathing, frequent thirst, mild constipation, tendency for acid vomiting, painfully swollen lymph glands, cold, sweaty hands and feet.

Therapy: Predominantly vegetarian diet, though not exclusively raw that includes almond milk and skim milk.

Drug therapy: Conchae verae D30, 10 drops in the morning on an empty stomach, Nicotiana D6, Quercus D3 aa, 10 drops before midday meal, Veronica D3, Prunus spin. D3 aa, 10 drops in the evening; abdominal and spleen massages with Cuprum met. 0.1%, ointment.

Following general recovery within two months: Dermatodoron, 5 drops t.i.d.; Chamomilla, Flos/Juniperus communis, Summitates/ Sambucus nigra, Flos/Urtica dioica, Folium/Viola tricolor, equal amounts of herba as tea with additions of bran; Calcon I and II. Symptom free after three months.

2. Five-year-old girl, a skinny, pale, dark-haired child whose skin appears dirty despite exceptionally good care at home; suffers from chronic episodes of eczema. Extensive eczema, especially between fingers and on arms and legs; lesions have a fetid odor. Strikingly warm head and cold extremities, distended abdomen. Poor sleep because of itching. Belching with tendency to vomit in the morning; belches smell of rotten eggs.

Therapy: Sulfur D30; Conchae D10 aa, 10 drops in the morning on empty stomach; Cuprum sulf. comp., 1 tablet t.i.d. before meals; Phosphorus D6/Malva D6 aa, 10 drops before bed; abdominal massages with Cuprum met. praep. 0.1% ointment. For general strengthening after recovery: Nutritive baths (see vol. II, pp. 39ff), Calcon I and II, Cuprum sulf. comp. continued. Later, as followup therapy: Dermatodoron liquid (5 drops t.i.d.) and salve. All symptoms are gone after three months; weight gain of eight pounds.

Cases Requiring Birch Bark and Quartz Remedies

1. Tall, stately woman, early sixties, has suffered for seven years from episodes of eczema, particularly on face and hands. Her skin is leathery and has some rhagades. The anamnesis reveals a history of liver problems. Some years earlier a gall bladder resection was performed.

Therapy: Quartz D20, Tartatus stib. D6 aa, a pinch t.i.d. before meals; Hepatodoron, 1 tablet t.i.d. after meals; birch leaf and strawberry leaf tea in equal parts. Followup treatment: Betula, Cortex; injections, Scleron and Hepatodoron.

2. Fifty-year-old patient with generalized eczema and tendency to purulent skin infections. He suffers from constipation and lack of appetite, complains of instinctive restlessness and headache, meteorism, and renal insufficiency. Hospitalized five months for his skin condition and discharged unimproved at his own request.

Therapy: Carbo Betulae D20, 10 drops in the morning on empty stomach; Sol. Siliceae comp. D3–D6, Graphites D6 + Argent. met. praep. D6 aa, a pinch t.i.d. before meals; Mezereum D6, Phosphorus D6, Malva D6 aa dil. before sleep; raw food diet. Largely recovered after four weeks; completely healed after two months.

We have described the sulfur and salt processes of the skin and their disorders, and now we must consider the *mercury* process and its disorders. *Acne vulgaris* belongs among the latter. It is an inflammation of the sebaceous glands, hence appears anywhere where sebaceous glands are located. Several factors favor the development of comedo and their inflammatory transformation into papules, pustules and nodules: An over-active function of the sebaceous glands with seborrhea; a hornification disturbance with hyperkeratosis in the excretory duct of the sebaceous gland of the follicle and subsequent colonization with bacteria and fungi. Acne in all its forms is an illness of the entire organism; specifically, it involves a disturbance in fat metabolism. Acne affects women more frequently than men and is limited essentially to the developmental period between age twelve and the early twenties. Treatment should always be constitutional. In addition, the type of bedrock that predominates in the region where the patient lives has proven significant in the choice of remedies. Calcium preparations are most effective in areas with siliceous bedrock, whereas high potencies of silica are preferred for areas with limestone bedrock. This applies to the treatment of all eczema. As observation of the patient's overall metabolism is important, regulation of the diet is the main concern. Furthermore, attention must be paid to the localization of eruptions: for example, asthenic types tend to be affected on the chest and back.

1. Forty-year-old man returns from wartime captivity with dystrophy and barber's rash (Tinea profunda barbae). Thick purulent secretions in the hairs of beard and on the temples accompanied by intense pain.

Therapy: Mercurius viv. nat. D 30; Quartz D20, Vaucheria D6 (inj.); Erysidoron II internally; calendula blossom compresses. After improvement: Mercurius vivus 0.1% ointment; Thuja D10, Plantago maj. D3(DHU) and Graphites D8, each 10 drops t.i.d.; Quartz D15, Mercurius viv. nat. D15 (inj.).

The following case history shows the importance of the overall constitution and its appropriate therapy:

2. Obese, dark-haired woman, twenty years old, with indurating form of acne, especially on face, chest, and back; weak menses at long intervals. Tendency to unpleasant body odor.

Therapy: Conchae D30, Tormentilla D30 aa, 10 drops in the morning; Nux vomica D4, Plantago maj. D3 (DHU), 5–10 drops before lunch; Sulfur D6, a pinch in the evening; dietary supervision and sulfur baths. With improvement of the menses (mainly owing to Tormentilla D30), the acne gradually fades away after 3 months of treatment.

3. Nine-year-old girl suffers from *Epidermolysis bullosa hereditaria*. Her parents decide to attempt treatment despite attestation by university clinic that relief is impossible. Three months of Dermatodoron produce no change in the patient's condition. Switch to Betula, Cortex D1, 15 drops t.i.d. Marked improvement after three months; after six months, patient begins participating in outdoor activities and sports, which she had previously been unable to do (Dr. Wolff).

Nail Diseases

The variations in nails is interesting and much can be observed and indicated from them. They grow out of the lunula or half-moon, where life and sensation predominate. Each temperament has its own nail form. The ridges that run lengthwise and crosswise, differences in substance, and white spots become significant. Brittle nails in young people grow better after doses of copper and calcium preparations; brittle nails are caused by a general weakness of vitality. White spots often disappear after spleen massages with copper salve. Children whose nails are so sensitive that they dislike having them cut require high quartz potencies. As it grows outward, the nail leaves the vital sphere of the lunula and gradually becomes lifeless and cornified. Brittle nails in older people are a sign of incipient sclerosis. Here Scleron and Betula Cortex injections are indicated.

In principle, nail development represents densified hair development—we could also say, densified skin formation—primary formative processes are applicable here as well. They can be recognized in silicic acid (see vol. II, pp. 118ff). Moreover, it is not only formative development as a whole that is connected to silicic acid processes but also elasticity as well. But brittle nails may not be just an indication of a premature aging process but may likewise exist in the case of hyperthyroidism as well as in disturbances of parathyroidism. This calls to mind clubbed fingers caused by chronic lack of oxygen in diseases of heart and lung. In conclusion, koilonychia [spoon nails] in cases of anemia deserves mention. When iron is low, lengthwise and crosswise ridges as well as brittle nails and formation of cracks in the skin can be observed. Here too, nail or skin development respectively can diagnostically indicate disturbances of the whole organization that must be treated accordingly.

Woman, late forties, with onychomycosis, fingers 3 and 4, right hand and right foot. Nails are thickened and raised, feel rough and break easily. At other spots they are thin and atrophic. The ailment is chronic and resists all treatment.

Therapy: Thuja D30, 10 drops in the morning; Plantago maj. D6 dil. (DHU); Sepia D6 dil. and Cinnabar D4 trit., 3 times 5 drops or a pinch t.i.d. before meals. Essentially healed after six months.

Hyperkeratoses

In the remainder of this chapter we shall discuss several specific phenomena and diseases that can be comprehended in terms of the polarity between inflammation and sclerosis.

In elderly people, the upper half of the face and bald spots on the scalp frequently show crumbling and occasionally firmly attached skin growths, *senile hyperkeratoses.*. Nowadays, these are called actinic keratoses, meaning, conditioned by radiation. Doubtlessly, these appear more frequently on skin that is exposed to light. Still, their characteristic is that they appear with the onset of age (particularly among males). For this reason the term senile hyperkeratosis is appropriate. We are obviously dealing with excessive cornification, hardening which is oftentimes typical of the aging process. At the same time, this is connected with intensified new formation in the epidermal region. Here, we are confronted with the fundamental condition that becomes evident here in the epidermal area but, in reallocated form, in the cellular region in cancer (page 77ff). When too much activity is developed on the part of the nerve-sense-organization in a centripetal direction, that is, when too much of the processes of the outer world are pushed into the human being and are not sufficiently "digested," then tumorous excrescences develop that crumble.[6]

> A 72-year-old man, whose forehead and bald spot have been strewn for many years with crumbling hyperkeratoses, suddenly falls ill of violent herpes zoster of the left nervus frontalis. Temperature remains subfebrile for five days; Wecesin-talc powder aa causes the blisters to dry up. Six weeks later the Herpes zoster, and with it most of the hyperkeratoses, have disappeared. The remaining hyperkeratoses heal without recurrence after treatment with 2 tablets t.i.d. of Sulfur D6, prescribed for stimulation of patient's senile, reduced metabolism.

We cannot always count on such assistance as in the above case history, where a second disease came to the physician's aid, showing him that healing can be achieved through the establishment of a healthy bal-

---

6. Hyperkeratoses that appear with advancing age as warts are precancerous. See in particular the chapter, "Causes and Treatment of Carcinoma," p. 369ff.

ance, namely, how an inflammatory disease can arrest the sclerotic tendency (see vol. I, "Inflammation and Sclerosis").

> The pretty face of a slim, lively, 49-year-old woman is disfigured in the upper third by many brownish, raised *hyperkeratoses.* Patient reports four years of unsuccessful inpatient and outpatient treatment by specialists. Marked improvement after daily warm chamomile compresses and massages of Phosphorus oil D3 for local metabolic stimulation; however, despite 2 tablets t.i.d. of Sulfur D6/D3 and 10 drops t.i.d. of Formica D3/D1, relapses cannot be avoided. Two years later, the patient's first *basal* cell carcinoma appears on the forehead. Excision with a sharp spoon and a series of Iscador treatments (Iscador Pini cum Hg., strengths 5,4,3,2 thrice weekly). Nevertheless, six months later two new basal cell tumors develop on the forehead, as does a *scaly epithelioma* on the right temple. All the tumors are excised. Patient is put on an anti-arteriosclerotic, lacto-vegetarian diet with large amounts of greens, grains, and fruits. Every morning and noon 2 tablets of Scleron. The remaining hyperkeratotic foci disappear after being covered with 5% Antimonite ointment and a plastic foil bandage. No recurrence.

Formica's therapeutic dissolving effect is described in detail in the chapter, Animal Remedies, volume II, pp. 182ff (for Iscador treatment see above, page 77).

It should be specifically noted here that in other patients with skin cancer, treatment with Iscador injections alone brought about the spontaneous disappearance of hyperkeratoses. The female patient mentioned above received Scleron (Plumbum mellitum) in order to bring the sclerotic process under control. The remedy Scleron is described in detail in vol. II on p. 422f. This is a preparation that intervenes in the physiological processes of aging in such a way that it guides the catabolic aging processes into the proper direction, surrendering them to strength of spirit and to the destiny of the ego. Periodic courses of treatment with Scleron should ideally be made available to all persons past the age of 40 to 45 as a prophylaxis against sclerosis and cancer (but not without pauses in between!).

Stibium or antimonite (natural antimony sulfide) play an important part in dermatological therapy. According to spiritual science, antimony is a synthesis of the three metals silver, mercury, and copper (see "The Seven Metals", vol. II, pp. 145ff). Given orally or by injection, antimonite has a strong formative effect within, particularly on pathologically intensified protein processes that lead to cutaneous exudates.

Antimonite ointments have the opposite effect. They have a radiating effect, drawing in the etheric body that is active in the fluid organism. They are prescribed mainly to loosen and revitalize circumscribed, lichenified, chronic eczema, verrucous neurodermatitis, isolated remnant psoriatic foci, hyperkeratoses, and seborrheic warts.

Rudolf Steiner even recommended Antimonite oint. (1%) for the treatment of ichthyosis vulgaris, the ointment being applied behind the knees, inside the elbows, and under the arms (though these areas are not affected) and inside the nose.[7]

Apart from the various forms of eczema and pyodermia, *psoriasis* is the skin disease most frequently encountered by physicians. An irregularly dominant, hereditary disease, psoriasis recurs chronically, usually throughout the patient's life. Mild cases affect primarily the extensor surface of the extremities and, when the face is involved, the forehead near the hairline.

The erythema of psoriasis indicates a hypertrophy of the epidermis caused by an intensified activity of the blood. However, the newly formed epithelial cells cannot form "normal skin" because powerful nerve processes deaden them into a thick layer of white scales. On the almost microscopically small field of the epidermis, the psoriatic efflorescence is seen as the macroscopic form of an excess both of growth *and* of death processes.

The aim of therapy, after checking these excesses, is to establish a new and calmer state of equilibrium. The balance between silver's vitalizing effect and lead's hardening effect is represented by gold. In elderly, arteriosclerotic psoriatics who have crusts of white scales, the condition must first be loosened with daily injections of Plumbum mellitum D20 and Betula, Cortex D2 (possibly as the combination ampule Arnica/Betula comp.). This clears the way for subsequent daily injections of Aurum met. praep. D20 or D15. Thin, nervous psoriatics concurrently receive Formica D5, 5–10 drops t.i.d., and one injection of Bryophyllum Mercurio cultum D2 in the evening.

The combination of hyperuricemia with tormenting itch is treated with a vegetarian, low-salt diet, along with sulfur baths every other day. A cup of corn meal should be stirred into each bath.

7. *Krankengeschichtensammlung*, published by Degenaar.

Overweight, lipemic but nondiabetic psoriatics, even those with generalized outbreaks, respond quickly to a strict fasting cure. Satisfactory long-term results can be achieved with an individualized, minimal diet.

The pain of chronic psoriatic arthritis has proven amenable to injections of Stannum met. praep. D10–D12 near the joints and to compresses of Oleum Petrae crudum 1%. At the same time, the liver should be treated intensively with Hepatodoron and with bitters, such as Artemisia comp., Absinthium 10%, Abrotanum D1 or D2, or artichoke preparations.

The rare but dangerous pustular psoriasis, which often conceals a tetany, should be controlled with daily injections of Apis D3/Belladonna D3 aa, with Mercurius viv. nat. D15 Trit., Conchae D6 Trit. aa, 1 teaspoon five times daily, and possibly also with Calcium e Quercu (Wala) i.v.

An exanthem after tonsillitis or flu in children and adolescents is a prognostically favorable sign. The spontaneous regression of the pathological process can be intensified by acidification of the organism through medication and diet (see p. 89). Remaining foci can be eliminated with 5% Antimonite ointment under an airtight bandage.

In the corium, the rhythmic layer of the skin, the invasion of sclerotic or inflammatory processes must be viewed as being much more discrete. A pale, anemic papule develops in place of the red, hyperemic, inflamed papule. Long-term emotional stresses "act upon the rhythmic part of the organism, and from there upon the rest of the organism."[8]

The following history can illustrate the dermatosis arising in this way:

> The 18-year-old patient has anxiety concerning exams. Large-headed, imaginative, and somewhat adipose, he has great difficulty with math and science. For weeks he has felt tired but has trouble falling asleep. Mornings he is exhausted, fidgety, and cannot concentrate. The spells of itching on his head, neck and elbows have been getting worse now for a week. Although no eruption is visible on his skin, he is sent in by his mother for consultation.
>
> Oblique lighting of the affected parts reveals many pale, small, flesh-colored polyhedral papules that scarcely protrude above the surface, the first manifestations of a neurodermatitis that could ultimately lead to verrucous thickenings on the lichenified skin.
>
> In case of the above patient, the mental symptoms suggested a therapy of 5 drops of Acidum phosphoricum D5 in the early and

8. R. Steiner, *GG GA 313.*

> midmorning and 10 drops of Stibium met. praep. D10 at noon and in the evening. The former made the patient feel more refreshed, whereas the latter effected a "strengthening of memory, elevation of the creative forces of the soul, and inner coherence of the emotional disposition," making concentrated study possible.[9] The itching spells grew less frequent. The neurodermatitis disappeared after the patient passed his exam. Follow-up treatment with Prunus Elixir for strengthening of the etheric body.

Neurodermatitis, also called atopic dermatitis or endogenous eczema, is the bronchial asthma of the skin. The dreadful attacks of itching, which completely fill the patient's awareness and make him scratch himself until he bleeds, correspond to acute attacks of asthma, while generalized chronic neurodermatitis corresponds to the status asthmaticus. Just as the asthmatic frequently tends toward physical and emotional hypersensitivity (instantaneous allergy of a humoral nature) owing to the over-activity of the astral body in the dynamic of the nerve-sense system, this is equally frequent in the neurodermatitis sufferer.

In the original terminology, neurodermatitis, the nervous component is expressed directly, whereas in the more modern nomenclature, "endogenous eczema," implies nothing about the obvious relationship to the nerve-sense system. The "more modern" designations become increasingly abstract and lose any relation to evident realities. Examples mentioned of this were actinic keratosis instead of geriatric keratosis (see above), likewise tuberculosis instead of consumption (see p. 205).

Primarily, in neurodermatitis, the fact is that the astral body is too strongly involved with the dynamics of the nervous system, something that leads to processes of consciousness in the periphery which in turn are expressed in itching. Secondarily, the blood process intervenes in this area in order to arrest the principally degenerative nerve-sense-process, something which then leads to the inflammatory reaction of the eczema.

Bronchial asthma and neurodermatitis are alternating manifestations of an excessive involvement of the astral body in the rhythmic domain. Hence therapy for this skin disease is guided by the same fundamental principle as was described for bronchial asthma (see p. 207ff).

Thin, melancholic, or pronouncedly intellectual neurodermatitis patients are effectively treated with a daily regimen of Prunus spinosa

9. Steiner/Wegman, *FT,* chapter 20.

30%, 5 drops t.i.d., and Formica D5, possibly as low as D1, 5 drops t.i.d.. Patients whose condition tends to improve in summer and worsen in winter should drink a cup of marjoram-melissa tea in the morning, since this has a warming, mildly sudorific effect. Itching attacks that occur in the evening and at night call for 5 to 10 drops of Arsenicum album D30 every hour or half hour beginning in the late afternoon or several subcutaneous injections of Arsenicum album D30 or D20. Baths with lavender admixtures and bran have a relieving, calming effect. Diet is important here as well and should contain large amounts of green salads and dishes made with fresh, coarsely ground grains.

Owing to the clearly allergic component, the exclusion of allergens (frequently lactoprotein or wheat) is effective, but it goes without saying that this is no causal therapy. In such cases, the attempt should be made to direct the astral body into the metabolism so that protein can be properly catabolized. As mentioned before, this can be accomplished with arsenic, better with Scorodit, or Pancreas cum ferrum sidereum, as well as the bitters referred to above. It has meanwhile become known that the mental component must likewise be taken into consideration and that it plays an important role, although it is not sufficiently considered owing to medications that work too quickly. This is important particularly in children. And it is actually true quite frequently that pediatrics must begin with treatment of the parents.

> A 37-year-old teacher with a 19-year history of lichenified generalized neurodermatitis localized especially on the head, neck, and upper thorax, treated unsuccessfully with steroids and antihistamines in dermatological clinics at home and abroad, received red beet juice, two to three tenths of a liter in the morning, as his sole prescription. The great vitality of the red beet root repels overactive astrality in the upper organization. Six months later the patient was free of his severe chronic skin disease.

Cases of chronic bronchial asthma and chronic generalized neurodermatitis that resist both internal and external therapy may be cured by a long-term change of milieu and climate.

At this point, a secret of localization should be indicated that is revealed by neurodermatitis, hyperkeratoses, and skin cancers. Why do these last appear most often in the upper third of the face? This is because it is the site of the strongest catabolic or death forces. The brain's white matter represents the most lifeless and physical human substance. The physiological process at work here is a significant factor in carcinogenesis (see p. 51ff).

Generalized neurodermatitis also tends to affect primarily the head, neck, the upper third of the thorax, and the insides of the elbows and knees. We see in this not only a disease of the upper region of the body. Rather, in the epiphyseal development of the long bone, we can recognize a "head-development" in miniature. The affected regions of the body are thus those in which the head or death forces act more strongly than their polar opposites, the anabolic or blood processes.

A pathological process of the corium that lies on the border between tumorous and inflammatory diseases is that of *lichen ruber planus*. The exanthematic eruption of the small red papules, which are often mistaken for a generalized subcutaneous eczema, shows a dominance of the blood impulse, as do the erythrodermic and the rarer pemphigoid forms. Small, flat, annular foci, consisting of wax-like shiny nodules about 1–2 mm high, show the dominance of the nerve-impulse, as do the frequent milky-blue alterations of the lingual and oral mucosae. This impulse becomes especially evident in *lichen ruber verrucosus* and in paroxysms of itching.

> *Therapy* for the pale papules and nodules consists of daily injections of Arsenicum album D20 and of 5 drops of Arsenicum album D30 taken several times in the evening; for fresh eruptions and the erythematous form, daily injections of Stibium arsenicosum D6 and a large pinch of Stibium arsenicosum D4 trit., five times daily. Small, firm, and verrucous foci are treated with Stibium met. praep. 0.4% ointment, applied as occlusive dressing.
>
> Caution: Sulfur ointments and baths can cause erythroderma.

When death forces stream with great vehemence into the deeper cutis and subcutis, into *the metabolic part* of the skin, severe syndromes such as *sclerema neonatorum* can result. This illness begins in the lower extremities in the first weeks of life, spreads to the trunk, and along with lowered body temperature leads to death in a short time. Dissection merely reveals a stearin-like hardness of the fatty tissue and an edematous accumulation of protein-rich fluid in the deeper layers of the skin. Etiology, pathology, as well as an effective therapy are not yet known today.

The chief symptoms are rigidity and hypothermia. Fever is therefore desirable, for example, by therapy with an irritant. In addition, the hardening can be addressed with a daily injection of Plumbum mellitum D30, possibly D60, in the morning, and injections of Argentite D10 in the evening. Hot elderflower baths of the legs and lower trunk help support this therapy.

Adolescent and adult scleroderma appears in two forms of eminently different prognosis:

1. *Localized scleroderma*, also called morphea, causes little more than a cosmetic impairment.

Therapy: in the first week, Galenite (lead sulfide) D20 injected all around the affected area; second week and after: Iscador Pini strength 5, increasing to 5%, one to three times weekly. Local inflammatory reactions are desired! Mustard plasters, applied near the morphea, not only heal through the "burning" hyperemia; they also stimulate the sulfur process locally, inhibiting protein breakdown and opening physical processes more to healing etheric ones.

2. *Progressive scleroderma* with sclerodactyly, rigidity of facial muscles, microstomia, dysphagia, arthrosis, myocardial fibrosis, and pulmonary sclerosis is a chronic disease that often leads to early and complete invalidism. Here, in the subcutis, the most pronounced sclerotic alterations are found: depositions of calcium phosphate and carbonate and genuine bone formation. These are clear signs of a potent death process. Only early diagnosis and intensive therapy can save the patient from irreparable damage. Such therapy includes injections of Plumbum mellitum D20 or D30 and of Betula, Cortex D2 (1%), possibly as the combination ampule Arnica/Betula comp. These remedies counteract the sclerosis and mineralization. Moreover, silver in the form of Argentum met. praep. or Argentite D6 or D10 revitalizes. Lavandula D3 is also indicated, as it "acts toward the periphery of the human organism in such a way as to drive out the astral body, making the astral body lose its power over the physical body."[10] Baths conducive for raising body temperature with sulfur, rosemary, or elderflowers followed by sweating in a dry towel

10. R. Steiner, *SM,* lecture 10.

wrap for half an hour to an hour are essential. Iscador Pini strength 5, increasing to 5%, may be used to maintain a weak but continuous state of fever, possibly with the help of irritant therapy. Ultimately, as in all depositions, the dissolving effect of Formica in increasing and decreasing dosage (D3–D30, see vol. II, p. 188) is indicated. An antisclerotic diet should be observed.

Inflammation is a constantly present process in the healthy human being, especially in certain organs (see "The Gastrointestinal Tract", vol. I, pp. 210ff). It is carried more or less strongly by the blood or the blood vessels to the body's utmost periphery. As well as elsewhere, in the skin too, this process causes dissolution or encapsulation of penetrating foreign bodies, foreign accumulations (deposits) developing within the body. If this process occurs in intense and generalized ways, it results in fever.

The lactating breast is an example of increased but normal glandular activity. Only a small congestion in milk flow is required before *mastitis* sets in, sometimes explosively, with classic clinical signs of inflammation, often accompanied by chills.

> Five days after giving birth to her first child, a boy, a 25-year-old woman develops a left-sided mastitis, which quickly subsides after injections of penicillin in the women's clinic. Several painful relapses occur at home in the following weeks which the family doctor suppresses with antibiotics in each case. Diarrhea occurs; milk flow decreases. After changing doctors, arnica compresses on the reddened swellings are prescribed, internally twelve drops of Erysidoron 1 hourly, and a lacto-vegetarian diet with generous amounts of much yogurt. Strict bed rest is observed. After two days the patient is without fever and is allowed to leave her bed. Five days later the erythema over the infiltrates has disappeared. The diarrhea ceases and the infant can once again be completely breast-fed. No relapse in the following months of nursing; Erysidoron 1 is continued, 12 drops five times daily, later reduced to 12 drops t.i.d.

Apis is well complemented by belladonna. This combination can be designated the remedy of choice for every kind of local inflammation. The bee's relationship to light and warmth (see vol. II, Animal Remedies, pp. 186f) stimulates the ego to warm the body in an organized manner. Belladonna (see vol. I, p. 358) stimulates the astral body to hold the excessively active etheric body in check.

Using apis and belladonna is a harmless form of prophylaxis against relapses that proves effective against easily recurring skin inflammations such as erysipelas, secondarily infected eczema, and impetigo contagiosa. It is even useful in treating severe cases of a relapse, as the following case history shows:

> A 23-year-old business clerk has suffered for years from a chronic, predominantly visceral *lupus erythematosus* with noninfectious endocarditis of the mitral valve, insidious nephritis, moderately severe polyarthritic deformities and impairment of mobility of the finger joints. After exposure to intense sunlight, the patient develops an extensive, partly bullous exanthema with bright red patches along with chills, subsequent high fever, and a left-sided exudative pleuritis.
>
> *Therapy*: mid-mornings and evenings, an injection of Argentum met. praep. D30; 12 drops of Apis D3/Belladonna D3 once every half-hour; 10 drops of Cardiodoron five times daily; pectoral compresses with Equisetum tea. After five days, the patient is subfebrile, and the vesicular exanthem regresses. Doses are reduced, and a pinch t.i.d. of Stannum met. praep. D10 powder is added. Three weeks later the skin is everywhere intact. Cautious application of mustard plasters. Ten weeks later, chest X-ray shows a small remaining exudate; after six months, only pleuritic adhesions are detectable. Since then the patient has remained fully able to work, having no lupus efflorescences nor albuminuria along with counterbalanced mitral defect. Long-term medications: morning and noon, twelve drops of Erysidoron 1 with a two-week interruption after every eight weeks of administration.

Inflammatory *photosensitization disorders*, which are becoming ever more frequent, are quickly eliminated when the cause has been found. Owing to skin contact, tar, some plants like Psoralea in Umbelliferae, optical brighteners in washing powders or clothing have photosensitization effects. In cases of internal use, sulfonamides, oral antidiabetics, and other derivatives of sulfonyl urea, as well as phenothiazine and ACE-blockers, griseofulvin, etc. likewise have photosensitization effects.

The following case history shows a different etiology:

> A 26-year-old, blond housewife suffers from a polymorphic photosensitization. For two years, she has been able to tend her garden only when she wears a long-sleeved blouse, gloves, and a wide-

brimmed straw hat as protection against the sun. Otherwise, the exposed skin develops an itching, burning, erythematous and bullous dermatitis. Clinical examination showed no pellagra or porphyria, no disorder of tryptophan metabolism, and no iron deficiency. Internal anti-photoallergenics, such as Nivaquin tablets, caused nausea, as did antihistamines; external sunscreens with Contralun ointment or Nivea-ultra irritated the skin after repeated use. Homeopaths had prescribed quartz among other remedies without success. The anamnesis revealed that ever since an emotional trauma two and a half years ago, the patient has slept poorly and often awakened suddenly from nightmares; since that time she has suffered from peripheral inflammatory tendencies. This is the triad of which Rudolf Steiner said "that the astral body and the ego do not 'sit' right in the physical body; here phosphorus is called for, as it tends to guide the ego and the astral body properly back into the etheric body."[11]

The patient receives Phosphorus D5, 5 drops in the early and late morning. After two weeks she feels fresher, but still sleeps quite restlessly; the light sensitivity has improved considerably. Further prescription: 10 drops of Phosphorus D30 in the evening, possibly several times during the night. Since then the patient has slept soundly. One month later the low potencies of phosphorus in the morning can be discontinued; the photosensitization has completely regressed.

The chief effect of phosphorus in low potency (D5) is to draw the ego to the body, while in high potency (D30) it allows the ego and astral body to dissociate themselves at night from the etheric and physical bodies, so that in the morning they are able to penetrate both all the more strongly. For this reason low potencies of phosphorus are given in the morning and high ones in the evening.

Reddish-blond patients whose excessive sulfur processes predispose them to peripheral inflammations, pyodermia, folliculitis, and photosensitization require Nontronite D3 Trit. powder (Ferrum silicicum) in order to reinforce the therapy with low potencies of phosphorus. In patients with constitutionally intensified photosensitization, Hypericum D4 is often effective if taken on a regular basis (about 3 times 10 drops) for an extended period (approximately three weeks) prior to exposure to light.

11. R. Steiner, *SM*, lecture 4.

A painful chronic skin inflammation that greatly impairs the patient's freedom is *furunculosis.*

> A 42-year-old adipose taxi driver has been unable to work for weeks owing to recurring furunculosis. The disease began eighteen months ago, and in spite of many megadoses of antibiotics, sulfonamides, and vitamins, and a number of vaccine, diet, and fasting cures, he continually suffers from three to four furuncles on the trunk, buttocks, and upper thighs. There is no diabetes. As he is the father of a family of seven, financial considerations preclude any change of occupation.
>
> *Therapy*: low-fat, low-oil diet, plenty of fruit, fruit juices, vegetables. Daily walk of thirty minutes duration, later vigorous running; this eliminates constipation. Internally: 12 drops of Erysidoron 1 every hour. Externally: 10% Calendula ointment; full Formica baths (one teaspoon Formica 5% in a bath lasting 15 to 20 minutes), every day during the first week and thereafter every other day. After one month the patient is able to work again. At any given time he still has one to two furuncles, but they are smaller and less painful. Daily for six successive days: one injection of Ipecacuanha, Radix D4, then a week's pause: only one new furuncle forms. Six more injections: since then the patient is symptom free. Long-term medication (interrupted only during vacation): daily 15 drops of Erysidoron 1 and Ipecacuanha, Radix D3.

Furuncles form because of an "excess of etheric activity."[12]

When not properly penetrated by the ego, the etheric excess becomes free and causes inflammations. When obesity as well as inflammation is present, "highly diluted formic acid in the form of baths" is indicated, because in this way "the ego is kept near, the human form is permeated by the ego" and is thus held together.[13]

In the ipecacuanha root, a human secret is manifested in the vegetable realm. The ipecacuanha's rhizomes greedily attract cosmic astral forces much more so than belladonna and nightshade plants. Ring-shaped protuberances, in essence tumors, form in regular succession along the root. The toxins contained in these allow the ipecacuanha, which grows rampant in tropical jungles, to hold its potent, "inflammatory" etheric forces in check. The plant's high vitality is clear from its ability to regenerate

12. Steiner/Wegman, *FT,* chapter 8.
13. R. Steiner, *SM,* lecture 14.

from small pieces of root, stem, and leaf stalk. Thus the plant demonstrates a controlled vitality.

The anti-inflammatory root forces of the ipecacuanha also have a healing influence on another eminently painful, chronically recurrent dermatosis: *Hidradenitis suppurativa,* (Acne inversa), which not only can appear on the armpit, but likewise inguinally or in the rima ani.

In these as in furunculosis, use of the patient's own urine (Herz, K. and Abele, J.: Die Eigenharnbehandlung, 7th edition, Heidelberg 1986) is quite effective.[14] As the organ of the astral body, the kidneys' (see p. 54ff) task is elimination of nitrogen substances. Rudolf Steiner called urine the "mummy of the astral body." If these substances are returned to the organism, the latter is in fact given an image of its own astral body's activity. From such a "picture," the organism can possibly recognize and correct its lack or excess of activity. The above quoted "excess of etheric activity" can be brought under control through introduction of the astral substance, urine (a few injections of 1 ml).

In patients with an etherically weak constitutions, sloe fruits, above all, are indicated because of their astringent nature (sugar-free pure sloe juice, daily about 1/3 of a bottle or Prunus, Fructus D3 injection).

The skin is subject to a bewildering variety of ailments that are sometimes temporary, sometimes stubbornly persistent. The task of clearly understanding its pathology and therapy is enormous and requires great devotion and enthusiasm.

14. K. Herz and J. Abele, *Die Eigenharnbehandlung,* 7th edition (Heidelberg: 1986).

VI

Eye Diseases and Refractive Disorders

ILSE KNAUER

EYE THERAPY ACCORDING TO the insights of spiritual science is possible only when the eye is seen in connection with the human being as a whole. In addition to its physical connection with the rest of the organism through blood vessels, lymph vessels, and nerves, the eye is also connected with the higher human constituents—etheric body, astral body, and I organization.

A weakness of the etheric body due to fatigue or illness will express itself in the eye as dullness, greater sensitivity to light, and loss of visual acuity. Joy, sorrow, and pain live in the astral body and are reflected in the luster of the eye, in the pupil's expansions and contractions, in tears. Pain and fear cause the pupils to dilate. The pupils also dilate when the spirit and soul are unable to take proper hold of the body, which is why children often have wide pupils, especially if they are nearsighted: nearsightedness comes about through the reluctance of the higher constituents to integrate themselves into the physical.[1] Older people, by contrast, have narrow pupils.

When the ego organization is weakened, binocular coordination is disturbed; the extraocular muscles, the eye's movement apparatus, are affected. One consequence of this is strabismus, which is treated later in the chapter; here we may simply point out that strabismus is more than just a local disorder. It manifests itself in the entire human being, as can be observed particularly in curative eurythmy. Walking becomes less coordinated; the leg corresponding to the uncoordinated eye is less controlled; if the eye tends to turn inward, so does the leg. Patients who have one of their eyes weakened or blinded by illness tend to veer off to the side of their healthy eye. This is a clear indication that the eye is related

1. R. Steiner, *SM,* lecture 5.

to the ego organization, since the ego organization manifests itself in walking. The limbs on the side of a weakened eye are less sensitive, less vital, and less permeable.

It is this interconnection that allows curative eurythmy to affect the eyes with exercises involving the arms, fingers, feet, and toes. The fingers and toes especially, being the utmost extensions of the limbs, are strongly connected etherically with the eyes.

The following phenomena as well may show just how extensively the eye is connected with the entire organism. First, congenital eye defects are often accompanied by deformities in the fingers and toes. Nearsightedness is usually associated with flat feet. Rudolf Steiner's suggestions for the treatment of nearsightedness included applications of Cochlearia ointment on the top of the foot and of mustard plasters on the soles or calves.

The eye is shaped by the forces of the entire universe; more than any other organ of the human being, it is an image of the cosmos. its spherical shape is repeated and varied in almost every aspect of its structure: in the sclera, choroid, and retina, in the iris with its circular and radiate muscles, and in the pupil. Lens fibers can be point-like, encompassing, or radiating. The ophthalmic artery issues forth from the center of the optic nerve and divides in the retina into a number of branches that eventually return to the optic disc as veins. The number of branches is most often four, symbolizing the relation of blood to nerve or pulse to respiration, which (in healthy people) stands in a 4:1 ratio. The vorticose veins emerge from the sclera in a stellar form.

The following may be said of the healthy eye: "If you imagine the entire firmament, with its stars that radiate their light onto the earth, and now imagine the same in miniature, what you have is the interior of the human eye. The eye is actually a whole world in miniature.... The eye is inwardly like space illuminated by stars, whose light does not go into the brain but is felt in the soul."[2]

In certain pathological states, for example, in synchisis scintillans, ophthalmoscopic observation reveals a twinkling and glittering in the vitreous body, as in a starry sky. Retinitis pigmentosa is characterized by

2. R. Steiner, *Health and Illness*, vol. 2 (Hudson, N.Y.: Anthroposophic Press, 1983), lecture 5.

black, star-shaped pigment granules on the retina that look like burned-out stars.

Because the eye is so intimately connected with the rest of the organism, generalized illnesses affect it. For example, diabetes is frequently accompanied by retinal bleeding, a sign that the ego organization's activity has shifted in an unhealthy way into the nerve-sense system (see vol. I, pp. 237-46).

Since insulin treatment does not halt diabetes retinopathy, for the sake of the eye a holistic treatment of diabetes is necessary, that is, a strengthening of the ego organization in the metabolism. Treatments include rosemary or equisetum baths; internally: Belladonna D6, Hyoscyamus D4, Betula fol. 10%, Caryophyllum D3, Stibium D6, Prunus (Summitates) D2–D5, Phosphorus D5. Retinal hemorrhages call for injections of Retina D10 and Arnica D15, with Stibium 0.4% ointment around the eye and Capsella bursa-pastoris D4 as eyedrops. All diabetics—even those without retinal bleeding—should be given injections of Retina D10. Diabetes is also characterized by patchy retinal degeneration, which is the effect of an astral body that is not sufficiently controlled by the ego organization.

Another generalized illness that affects the eye is chronic nephritis. Nephritis frequently results in hypertensive retinopathy, which indicates an excessive activity of the astral body in the eye. As has been discussed elsewhere, the renal system's role is to permeate the body from within with material forces, while the nerves and senses, which act from the outside inward, have the task of forming the organs. If the kidney's activity, known as "kidney radiation," is too strong, then cramps, inflammation, and catabolism result. In the eye, this overactivity manifests itself in star-figure edema at the macula lutea, arteriolar constriction, and tortuosity of the retinal veins. If, by contrast, kidney radiation is too weak, then the eye is undersupplied with blood and etheric forces, resulting in some cases in retinal detachment or—in older patients—retinal degeneration. In these disorders of kidney radiation, the urine need reveal no pathological finding.

Other eye disorders, such as conjunctivitis, photosensitivity, and heterophoria, can be rooted in functional disturbances of the liver, kidney, stomach, or abdomen.

Just how strong the relations are between the eye and the fluid organism, that is, the etheric body, is shown by experiments concerning the "energetic portion of the visual path" (Hollwich; see vol. I, p. 290). Light affects not only fluid balance but also the functioning of the autonomic nervous system, carbohydrate metabolism, and the diurnal rhythm.[3] When the eye absorbs light, melatonin secretion in the epiphysis is reduced and the gonads are stimulated, which is why laying hens are kept under strong light.

Heart disease can provoke or aggravate a left-sided glaucoma, which is why left-sided glaucoma patients should always receive cardiac therapy as well, especially in the presence of hypotension.

The fundamentally threefold structure of the human organism is reflected in the eye. The *sclera* is the eye's metabolic system, even though it becomes clearer toward the front in the cornea, which is transparent. The eye's nerve-sense system is represented by the *retina* with its network of optic nerve fibers. The *choroid, iris, ciliary body,* and *vitreous body* belong to the rhythmic system.

The development of the eye in the embryo is most revealing, proceeding as it does out of a definite duality. Cornea and lens are formed from without, from the ectoderm. The posterior part of the eye, including the vitreous body, grows toward them from within. The posterior part of the eye corresponds more to life, while the anterior part is more "inorganic" in character. The pupil and the iris, which are located between the two parts, act as a kind of bridge.

The anterior portion of the eye, including the iris and lens, can be regarded as the more active, "speaking" part, and is thus comparable to the larynx. The posterior portion, including the retina, is more receptive, and is thus analogous to the ear. Like larynx and ear, the anterior and posterior parts of the eye form a functional whole.[4]

In what follows, individual diseases are considered and therapeutic suggestions made on the basis of insight into their nature. This is the procedure that any rational therapy must pursue.

---

3. See also Hollwich, *Klin. Monatsblätter zur Augenheilkunde* 142 (1943) and 149 (1966) and *The Influence of Ocular Light Perception on Metabolism in Man and Animal* (New York: 1979).

4. See R. Steiner, *Light* (Forest Row, U.K.: Steiner Schools Fellowship, 1981), lecture 8.

Scleritis

Inflammations of the sclera, the metabolic portion of the eye, are very painful and often stubborn. Warm compresses with Species Ophthalmica (Weleda) or healing clay, internally Graphites D6, Mercur D6, and Belladonna D20 are well-proven remedies. Rheumatic inflammations call for injections and eyedrops of Formica, Vespa Crabro, or Apis (see the section on animal remedies in vol. II, p. 182f), as well as Stannum D8 eyedrops. Due to the eye's kinship with the periphery and the skin, sulfur baths are also helpful.

Conjunctivitis

The conjunctivae are also part of the eye's metabolic system, and are clearly related to the mucosae. Many mucosal inflammations—particularly of the nose and throat, but also of the stomach, intestine, and abdomen—can induce conjunctivitis. Here we may also mention Reiter's syndrome, one of whose three major symptoms is conjunctivitis; the other two are polyarthritis and urethritis. Other factors that favor conjunctivitis are colds, insomnia, overexertion, weakness due to illness, shift work under poor, artificial lighting, and any weakening of the etheric body in general. Prunus spinosa eyedrops are helpful in cases of generalized weakening of the etheric body, as are injections of Iris bovis D4. Iris bovis not only supports the iris but also stimulates the patient's entire light metabolism. It is also particularly effective against conjunctivitis in glaucoma patients, in whom pilocarpine or other miotic agents may easily cause conjunctival irritation.

Acute conjunctivitis is effectively treated with Euphrasia and Mercurialis eyedrops; chemical burns or flash injuries call for Combudoron eyedrops applied as frequently as possible.

Purulent conjunctivitis is best treated with Argentum nitricum eyedrops (D4). The silver regenerates the etheric body, while the nitrogen stimulates the astral body to activity. Calendula D4 eyedrops (at least four times daily) can also produce rapid healing. When conjunctivitis is accompanies by a marginal keratitis, Echinacea/Quartz eyedrops (Wala) are indicated; these have also proven valuable for wearers of contact lenses.

An infant whose purulent conjunctivitis resisted all previous treatments was finally healed with compresses of Resina Laricis comp. Emulsio (Weleda), 15 drops to 2 tablespoons of water.

Dry conjunctivae respond well to Echinacea 5% ointment or to Stibium 0.4% ointment, applied on the eyelids in the evening. Follicular conjunctivitis may be treated with Cuprum sulfuricum eyedrops (D6); the same remedy is used for inflammations of the bulbar conjunctiva, especially on the left eye. It also helps counteract excessive watering of the eyes. In moderate, chronic cases of conjunctivitis, Dioptase D8 (native copper silicate) eyedrops may also be given. These are also recommended for photosensitivity. Eyestrain due to difficulties in near vision responds very well to eyedrops of Argentum/Corpus vitreum.

Mercurius vivus is indicated as an ointment (0.1%) or as eyedrops (D6), as is Cinnabar D20 internally, especially when the right eye is affected. The right eye is more closely related to understanding, the left to personal interest in things seen.[5]

The eye irritations of hay fever may be treated with Gencydo eyedrops as well as injections. Twice-weekly injections of Aurum D30/Equisetum D20 aa have also proven effective. For Morax-Axenfeld conjunctivitis, the customary zinc eyedrops are indicated (Zincum sulfuricum 0.01:10.0). Finally, it must be considered that incorrect eyeglasses can provoke conjunctivitis.

Neoplasms in the conjunctivae are rare. When they do occur, they are associated with pigment formation, which is thus a sign of possible malignancy.

> In an 8-year-old boy I found a circumscribed vascular neoplasm on the temporal side of the conjunctiva of the left eye, associated with pigment accumulations and conjunctival congestion. On strong suspicion of malignancy, the eye was to be enucleated. Treatment with Iscador P c. Hg along with Chelidonium eyedrops and Solutio siliceae comp. D15 liq. (Weleda) caused the symptoms to regress, making the operation unnecessary.

5. See R. Steiner, *Speech and Drama* 2nd ed. (Hudson, N.Y.: Anthroposophic Press, 1985).

Diseases of the Eyelid

Blepharitis and styes are indicative of a general illness. Blepharitis indicates a scrofulous constitution or a general eczematosis. Here a constitutional treatment is called for, naturally one that is gauged to the individual circumstances. Therapy with Conchae D6 trit. has proven effective, as has external application of Antimonite 0.4% ointment or Euphrasia comp. ointment on the rims of the eyelids.

Styes usually indicate a general furunculosis and should be treated as such, for example, with Erysidoron I and II, Sulfur iodatum, Mercur, and/or Quartz. Hot compresses of fennel tea and Species ophthalmica (Weleda) should be applied externally. Internally: Belladonna D10 and blackthorn (sloe) elixir; as eyedrops: Euphrasia D3 or Echinacea D3; subcutaneous injections in the nape of the neck with Gencydo 1%. Ointments that can be used include Euphrasia comp., Mercur viv. 0.1%, and Echinacea 1%. (Mercurius and Echinacea ointments should not contact the eye.)

Chalazions are a kind of benign tumor that develop due to occlusions of certain sebaceous glands of the eyelid. Treatment: Viscum Pini 5% ointment is applied externally, and internally Staphisagria D3 or Fluorite D10. Operative excision of the chalazion is appropriate when it is so large that it impedes eye movement; however, internal treatment should still be carried out to reduce the likelihood of a recurrence.

Keratitis

The cornea is without blood vessels and therefore poorly nourished. Keratitis and corneal ulcers are so difficult to heal because the cornea is the most devitalized part of the eye. The indication here is for hot compresses with Species ophthalmica, injections of Quartz D12 with Stibium D6, Belladonna D20, and internally Conchae D6 and Aethiops antimonialis D8. Hot foot baths with Equisetum tea are also beneficial. The use of atropine eyedrops (1/2%) or scopolamine (1/4%) will sometimes be unavoidable. Euphrasia or Quartz D6 eyedrops are indicated in any event.

Anabolism can be stimulated and the sense organs strengthened with quartz, ideally in conjunction with larch resin. Chronic cases therefore call for injections of Quartz D30 + Resina Laricis D5.

Corneal spots have been effectively treated with eye compresses or ointment of Resina Laricis comp. Emulsio, as well as with Quartz D12, injections or powder. Quartz D30 may also be injected with Resina Laricis D5.

Iritis

The sequelae of iritis, which include posterior synechia, keratic precipitates, opacities of the vitreous body, and secondary glaucoma, can impair vision considerably. Since the iris belongs to the eye's rhythmic system, the condition of the patient's heart and circulation must also be taken into consideration. Cardiovascular disorders can impede the healing of iritis, as can abdominal illnesses, especially endometritis and prolapses. Iritis can also follow pregnancy. One case did not respond to therapy until a uterine fibroid treatment with Berberis had been carried out. The uterus is the rhythmic part of the abdomen and is related to the heart. Iritis associated with rheumatic fever or tuberculosis cannot be treated in isolation from these.

Hot compresses of Species ophthalmica (Weleda) are indicated for every case of iritis and iridocyclitis. Species ophthalmica is a tea consisting of Euphrasia, Foeniculum, Plantago lanceolata, and Erythrea centaurium.

Euphrasia or eyebright is a member of the Scrofulariaceae and grows as a parasite from the roots of meadow grasses. In keeping with its parasitic character, its root is inconspicuous. Among other substances it contains tannins, bitter substances, and a blue pigment, all of which speak for its astringency. This quality allows it to counteract uncontrolled inflammatory processes in the sense organs. Eyebright has been known to folk medicine since ancient times. Melanchthon (1497–1560) is supposed to have suffered once from a "flux of the eyes" and been visited in a dream by a protective spirit in the form of a physician who recommended this plant to him. In two days he is said to have been healed.

Foeniculum, the fennel, belongs to the Umbelliferae (see vol. I, p. 338). These plants thrive in light-filled air, which they distill into their volatile oils. Fennel also contains the silica process, which is of great significance for the eyes. Fennel should be preferred to chamomile for eye compresses, since chamomile's effects are directed more toward the metabolic system.

Plantago lanceolata, the ribwort plantain, and *Erythrea centaurium,* the centaury, are well-known vulnerary herbs, especially for the mucosae.

Indispensable for the treatment of iritis are atropine and scopolamine. By dilating the pupils they protect against the formation of posterior synechiae. If used with the remedies described here they will not need to be used quite as often as in conventional practice.

A highly significant remedy in iritis treatment is Sanguinaria/Spongia D15, which was developed by Rudolf Steiner. Steiner suggested this remedy to a woman who was suffering from severe iridocyclitis. Sanguinaria/Spongia is particularly effective when injected subcutaneously in the shoulder or temple. In stubborn cases it may be combined with injections of Cissus/Ossa D6, even when no secondary glaucoma is present.

Spongia is a sea sponge whose processes of nourishment and respiration are still unified; the separation between etheric foundation and astral penetration that occurs in higher animals is less pronounced here. This, together with Spongia's iodine content, accounts for its specific therapeutic action. Spongia cleanses the upper organization, which aids not only in iritis, but also in vitreous body opacities and keratic precipitates. *Sanguinaria canadensis,* the bloodroot, is a papaveraceous North American plant whose bright red root sap indicates a strong connection to blood and to the iron process, while the white blossom suggests the purification of blood processes that have penetrated too strongly into the senses. Sanguinaria D15 can be administered internally for the often agonizing symptom of *muscae volitantes* ("floaters" or "spots before the eyes"); Sanguinaria/Spongia eyedrops are used at the same time. By virtue of its ingredients, Sanguinaria/Spongia D15 not only influences iridocyclitic inflammations, but also clears opacities of the vitreous body, loosens posterior synechiae, and regulates intraocular pressure.

Iritis is an inflammation that involves misdirected protein processes, including a possible rheumatic component. For this reason it cannot be treated effectively without iron, which acts upon light metabolism via magnesium. Both iron and magnesium are compounded with iris in the preparation Uvea comp. Their effect is complemented by Hyoscyamus, which bears a special relationship to the rhythmic system and is more specifically indicated for the iris than is belladonna. Acute iridocyclitis calls for injections of Uvea comp. D30; relapses may be prevented by injections of D15 or eyedrops of D6.

> A 43-year-old male patient with a history of rheumatism has suffered for the past six years from recurrent iritis, which is being treated by specialists with cortisone and antiphlogistics. Patient receives a total of 9 injections, each consisting of 2 ampules of Uvea comp. D15 and a milliliter of his own blood. He also receives Uvea comp. eyedrops. During two years of post-treatment observation, no recurrence. The patient reports a beneficial effect on his rheumatic symptoms as well. (Dr. Matthiolus)

Another remedy indicated for iritis is Belladonna D10–D30, particularly injections of Belladonna D20. Belladonna D30 is effective for episodes of intense pain. Belladonna is examined as a medicinal plant in vol. I, p. 358.

Posterior synechia may be treated with combined injections of Formica D15 and Iris bovis D4 in the temple or shoulder; stubborn cases respond to injections of Nicotiana D10, Argentite D30, Apis D6, Iris bovis D4, and Lachesis D10 (s.c. in the upper arm).

The sequelae of iridocyclitis, including opacities of the vitreous body, have responded well to Belladonna/Betula/Formica eyedrops.

An important remedy for iritis and iridocyclitis is Absinthium D1/Resina Laricis D3 aa liquid (10 drops t.i.d.), which was first recommended by Rudolf Steiner for a woman with severe iridocyclitis. The woman's vision was seriously impaired by adhesions of the iris to the anterior capsule of the lens and by numerous opacities of the vitreous body. In addition to the remedy just mentioned, this patient received Cardiodoron, although no cardiac or circulatory disorders were diagnosed. This prescription becomes understandable when one recalls that the iris belongs to the eye's rhythmic system, and that Cardiodoron stimulates rhythmic processes throughout the body.

Resina Laricis is larch resin; it is highly aromatic. The larch, although a conifer, is not an evergreen: like deciduous, broadleaf trees, it sheds it leaves (actually needles) in the autumn. Compared to the other conifers, it has a very soft and delicate appearance. Resins are the tree's inmost sap of life. Solid but not opaque, they vitalize the etheric body. The resin of the larch, a tree wholly integrated into the rhythm of the seasons, counteracts all hardening tendencies.

In the preparation Resina Laricis comp. (emulsion and ointment), the effect of larch resin is intensified by pineapple. This fruit, with its hard rind but aromatic and watery interior, acts against hardening, muscular spasm, and opacification. Resina Laricis comp., Emulsio may be used as a bath additive to supplement the therapy of any degenerative process, since the periphery of the human being, including the skin, is closely related to the eyes, as has been repeatedly indicated (1–2 tbsp. to a full bath).

Children with recurrent iritis frequently require a constitutional therapy with iron, e.g., Ferrum ustum D4, Ferrum ustum comp., or Scorodite D6, in order to stimulate their incarnation process.

Drug therapy of iritis can be supplemented with curative eurythmy, which in this case helps especially to prevent relapses. Possible exercises are: *L M G A U,* sympathy-antipathy, expansion and contraction, and rhythms.

Choroiditis

The choroid, like the iris and the ciliary body, can be assigned to the rhythmic portion of the eye, since it is the eye's circulatory system and blood organ. Inflammation is usually associated with a tubercular disposition (disseminated choroiditis). Foci are scattered over the entire membrane. Scar formation and accumulations of dense black pigment can be observed, which can impair vision considerably. Choroiditis patients usually have too "watery" a constitution, so that their structuring forces must be stimulated. Heart therapy should also be considered.

Drug therapy will seek mainly to influence constitution and tubercular disposition with Phosphorus, Ferrum, and Quartz. Proven remedies include Phosphorus D10 liq., Ferrum praep. D10 trit., Conchae verae D6, Quartz D12, and Chrysolith D12. Injections of Resina Laricis D6/ Retina D4 are indicated when the foci lie in the macula; in the acute stage, Chrysolith comp. is indicated. Further constitutional therapy may also be necessary, for example, with Bidor or other remedies.

Curative eurythmic treatment will include the exercises *B S U, L M* (behind the head), rhythms, sympathy-antipathy, and *I* (pronounced ee as in "bee").

Diseases of the Retina

Retinal Degeneration

This is the most frequent illness of the retina, and usually involves the choroid. It is a premature aging process and results from vascular sclerosis, myopia, diabetes, and/or renal disease. Although it usually afflicts the elderly, it can cause considerable visual impairments even in childhood. The most troublesome form is central macular degeneration, which results in central scotoma and makes focusing practically impossible. Although healing is out of the question here, treatment can halt the progress of the condition or bring minor improvement. Obviously, the treatment will be long-term; an example is twice-weekly subcutaneous injections of Resina Laricis D6/Retina D4 in the shoulder or in the temple. These can also be combined with Arnica D15 or Plumbum mellitum D20, which are indicated when vascular scleroses are involved. Capsella bursa-pastoris D4 eyedrops are beneficial; Capsella counteracts both hemorrhages and hardening. Curative eurythmy is very important: *L M G U*, done at least some of the time with the fingers and feet, and L M around the head.

The illness underlying hypertensive retinopathy with star-figure edema in the macula lutea is life-threatening; treatment of the kidney is critical. Useful local remedies are Capsella D4 eyedrops and Equisetum 10% ointment around the eyes.

Retinal Hemorrhages

Arteriosclerosis of the retinal vessels can lead to retinal bleeding. Treatment of the underlying disease will naturally be the primary concern. Here, injections of Arnica D15 may be given in conjunction with Retina D6 or Resina Laricis D6/Retina D4 aa, Plumbum mellitum D20 (or Arnica/Betula comp. inj.), also Ferrum c. aceticum praep. trit. D4 to D10, and as eyedrops, Capsella D4. The latter is effective in all cases of internal hemorrhaging.

A further cause of retinal bleeding can be thrombosis of the central retinal vein or one of its branches. Eyedrops of Borago D3 and Ruta graveolens D3 may be recommended for this, as may internal administration of Kalium aceticum c. Stibio D6 and the already mentioned injections of Arnica D15/Retina D6.

Juvenile retinal hemorrhages are notoriously difficult to treat. They often result in near-total blindness. In such cases kidney radiation is usually too strong, in which case Chamomilla, Radix is indicated, preferably as subcutaneous injection D3 in the upper thigh. Arnica compresses bring immediately felt relief. Hamamelis 10% or Stibium 0.4% ointment should be applied around the eyes. Effective injections and internal medications include Marmor/Stibium and Corallium rubrum D6/ Stibium D6. Stibium, as discussed in Volume II (pp. 132ff), has a styptic effect. Subcutaneous injections of Spongia/Sanguinaria D15 in the shoulder help clarify the vitreous body and improve vision.

Retinal Detachment

This develops primarily in myopia, which is discussed below. The chief cause of retinal detachment is a weakness of the etheric body, which allows tissues to fall out of their connection with the structural whole. The ego organization, whose task it is to regulate the whole, is also too weak, which favors detachment. The proximate cause can be emotional traum or physical overexertion. The primary remedy is Prunus spinosa (the sloe). The fruit of this plant does not achieve its full effectiveness until after the first frost. Cold connects the life ether more strongly with it. The fruit's tart flavor is another expression of its astringent, concentrating power. An ointment of 10% Prunus, Fructus should be applied around the eyes. Injections of Prunus, Fructus D3 should also be given, preferably together with Retina D6, D10, or a combination ampule of Resina Laricis/Retina, subcutaneously in the temple or shoulder with subsequent bandaging of the eye. By means of the organ preparation Retina, the concentrating power of the sloe is guided to the patient's retina, where it stimulates and strengthens the etheric body and works against the retina's tendency to fall out of the etheric whole.

Operative treatment of retinal detachment, which results in scar formation at the side of the tear, is successful about 75% of the time. Surgery, no matter what its results, should be followed up with the treatment just sketched in order to avoid relapse: the degenerated retina is in need of life-forces, and the ego forces must be strengthened. The eye tolerates each subsequent operation increasingly poorly, since all operative interventions by their very nature weaken the etheric body.

My own experience has shown that the described therapy can significantly improve postoperative patient's vision and alleviate their subjective complaints.

In cases that were detected early, I have also seen recoveries brought about by light pricking of the calves with needles dipped in fresh fish bile, a treatment once recommended by Steiner. As fresh fish bile is often difficult to obtain, it can easily be replaced by Fel piscis D6 injected s.c. in the calf or application of Fel piscis 0.5% ointment to the same area. The ointment can also be applied directly to the eyelids. Due to its warming effect, it is generally useful for encouraging proper scar formation. Fish gall is mentioned in the Old Testament story of Tobias as being a potent eye remedy.

Curative eurythmy can be an important supplement to the treatment of retinal detachment, provided it is carried out carefully and competently. It helps prevent postoperative recurrence of retinal detachment. Effective exercises in my own experience are *L* and *M* done behind the head, *N* and *M* from front to back, and *E* with arms and feet, whereby the separate E's are connected in the horizontal. This is complemented by the antipathy exercise, which strengthens the back and ego activity and gives a feeling for the space behind the body.

Atrophy of the Optic Nerve

This condition arises either primarily or as a consequence of optic neuritis and can be counted among the hardening and degenerative ocular diseases. It responds to injections of Arnica D15, D20, in alternation with Lamina/Retina comp., an organ preparation containing Nervus opticus, Corpora Quadrigemina, and Retina. Particularly good results can be obtained in younger patients. Other remedies must also be given depending on the case, such as Nervus opticus cps. eyedrops (Wala) and Chrysolith comp., D12, D20, inj. and per os.

Cataract

Although gray cataract is primarily a disease of later life, it can appear as early as middle age if severe myopia, general sclerosis, or diabetes is present. It results from depositions in the lens, which appear in diffuse or regular forms in the center or as spokes in the periphery. Advanced cases are now usually treated with surgery, after which the patient may regain normal visual acuity with the aid of cataract glasses.

A nonoperative therapy makes sense only in the earliest stages, when the process can sometimes be arrested or even remedied. Rudolf Steiner indicated that intravenous injections of high potencies of belladonna can counteract cataract formation, provided the disease is not too far advanced. My experience has shown subcutaneous and subconjunctival injections of Belladonna, Radix D10–D20 to be effective. The effect is even stronger when the Belladonna is combined with Lens/Resina Laricis (combination ampule, Weleda). Subconjunctival injections should be followed by application of a pressure bandage for one hour, and no anesthesia should be given. Lens/Resina Laricis may be injected simultaneously in the forearm. For background on Belladonna as a curative plant, see vol. I, p. 358. Belladonna is also indicated as eyedrops (D6, D12), 1 to 2 drops in the eye twice daily, or internally D6 or D10.

Belladonna's effect is enhanced by Formica and Betula. The combination of these three is available as eyedrops (Weleda). In any form, this combination is an established remedy for all processes of deposition and hardening.

According to an indication of Rudolf Steiner, lamellar cataract can be treated with injections of phosphorochalcite (D6 trit.). Resina Laricis comp. ointment or gel is indicated for every kind of cataract. Still better are compresses of the emulsion (15 drops to 2 tablespoons of water). Such compresses are especially effective in the evening, as they sometimes also promote sleep.

Opacities of the Vitreous Body

These accompany severe myopia and senile liquefaction of the vitreous body. They can also develop as a consequence of iridocyclitis. All of these conditions represent degenerations of the eye's etheric body.

During iritic inflammation, injections of Sanguinaria/Spongia D15 are recommended; the same remedy may be used internally or as eyedrops. Chronic cases respond to subcutaneous injections of Corpus vitreum/Stannum, Corpus vitreum/Succinum, or Argentum/Corpus vitreum (see below) in the temple or shoulder; internal application of Chrysolith D12 trit. and Sanguinaria D15; eyedrops of Stannum D8/Succinum D6 or Argentum/Corpus vitreum; and eye compresses of Resina Laricis comp., Emulsio (see above).

Glaucoma

It is important to recognize glaucoma early, for often it causes no symptoms, especially when only one eye is affected, so that patients seek treatment too late. This is typical of simple chronic glaucoma.

Acute glaucoma is much more dramatic, leading in some cases to blindness within a few hours. It is accompanied by intense pain in the head, nausea, reddening of the eyeball, dilated pupils, and seeing colored rings around lights.

There are many theories as to the cause of the increased intraocular pressure.[6] Up to the eighteenth century, the dominant view was that of Galen, who attributed glaucoma to a desiccation of the lens. It was not until 1844 that Mackenzie first spoke of an increased accumulation of watery fluid in the interior of the eye and swelling of the vitreous body. The invention of the ophthalmoscope by Helmholtz in 1851 led to Albrecht von Graefe's discovery of the glaucomatous excavation of the optic disc in 1855. Von Graefe spoke of a diffuse liquefaction of the corpus vitreum, and traced the heightened intraocular pressure to a degeneration of the secretory nerves. His performance of an iridectomy in glaucoma—the first ever—caused a sensation, and in many cases brought improvement. Today the most important factor in glaucoma is believed to be the pressure. The tendency is to locate the cause in compressions or obstructions of Schlemm's canal, through which aqueous humor flows out of the anterior chamber. Other researchers, however, theorize that the cause may be a decreased permeability of the hyaloid

6. Cf. P. A. Jaensch, "Zur Geschichte der Glaukomtherapie," *Beihefte der klin. Monatsblätter für Augenheilkunde* (1952) 21. More recent experimental findings are reported in Lütjen-Drecoll (ed.), *Basic Aspects of Glaucoma Research* (Stuttgart/New York: 1982).

membrane of the vitreous body (Nordenson) or age-dependent changes in the vitreous stroma (Thiel).

Thus it is still true that "we do not know the underlying cause of primary glaucoma; hence our therapy can only be aimed at normalizing the pressure. In acute glaucoma, this will restore the best possible functioning, and in chronic glaucoma at least maintain or perhaps somewhat improve the status quo. Lowering intraocular pressure arrests progressive functional degeneration in all but prolonged, chronic glaucomas where there is severe impairment of the visual field. In these latter cases, even very low pressure values fail to help."[7]

This last circumstance shows that the heightened pressure in the eye is not the only factor in the genesis of glaucoma—quite apart from the fact that the cause of the pressure has still not been unequivocally determined.

In 1923, Steiner pointed to the vitreous body as the cause of glaucoma.[8] He spoke of the vitreous body's becoming too physical, and of a hypertrophy of its activity. In this view, the etheric body is no longer able to thoroughly penetrate the vitreous body.

Little is known today of the specific function of the vitreous body. A measurable correlate of an excessive "physicalization" of the vitreous body is hard to find, since glaucoma does not change the vitreous body's outer appearance; it remains transparent. Hence the physicalization to which Steiner refers cannot consist in metabolic depositions, as it does in cataract; rather, we must assume that the vitality of the vitreous body is impaired. Steiner indicates that compared to the lens, which is relatively "dead," the vitreous body is imbued with vitality. This squares well with the well-known fact that glaucoma can be provoked by emotional agitation, anxiety, overwork, and other stressful situations. Such situations weaken the etheric body or even partially dislodge it. This etiology is similar to that of cancer (see chapter 2); in fact, Steiner once compared glaucoma to a tumorous process. He claimed further that deficient exhalation is a factor in glaucoma, a claim that has now been experimentally verified; hyperventilation has been shown to markedly lower intraocular pressure, whereas hypoventilation causes it to rise, as does constriction

7. Goldmann, in textbook by Amsler-Brückner (1954).

8. See R. Steiner, *Physiology and Therapeutics* (Spring Valley, N.Y.: Mercury Press, 1986).

of the veins in the neck. "In addition to the known correlation between venous or intrathoracic pressure and intraocular pressure, it has been found that intraocular pressure also depends upon the CO_2 pressure of arterial blood."[9]

As a remedy, Steiner indicated calcium carbonate from bone ash, mixed with the sap of aerial roots. The goal of this combination is to specifically stimulate the respiratory process, whereby "exhalation" is understood in a comprehensive sense and includes a better structuring of the fluid organism.

The first preparation created on the bases of these indications was Cinis ossis/Philodendron. This preparation failed to achieve the desired level of effectiveness. Nevertheless, with extended use it did succeed in lowering pressure and improving vision. In some cases it also had an analgesic effect. One patient had a splinter in the sclera. The splinter could not be removed; the affected eye went blind, and the patient experienced intense pain. No glaucoma was present. Despite the blindness, the patient did not wish to have the eye removed. Immediately after the patient took Cinis ossis/Philodendron, the pains abated, making it possible to leave the eye in place. Pains often arise due to congestions of the astral body; when "exhalation" is stimulated, the astral body can dissociate itself.

A more effective preparation is Cissus/Ossa (amp. D6; trit. D3, D6). What distinguishes it from other preparations is the source plant, *Cissus gongyloides,* whose aerial roots come closer to Steiner's intentions. In addition, the bone calcium is obtained by different means, and the bones used are those of birds.

Another remedy indicated for glaucoma is Stannum, which has a formative effect, specifically on the semifluid-solid state. Stannum eyedrops (D8) have proven helpful, as have injections of Stannum D12-20. Still more efficaceous is Corpus vitreum/Stannum, in which tin is joined with the vitreous body through a special pharmaceutical process. Together with Cissus/Ossa, this remedy should be injected two to three times weekly, subcutaneously in the upper arm.

---

9. Meyer and Opitz, in *Klin. Monatsbl. Augenheilkunde* 156 (1970):730.

It is interesting to observe that a frequent side effect of glaucoma therapy with Stannum is an increase in diuresis. This is a sign that the higher members are gaining greater control over the fluid organism.

The excessive "physicalization" of the vitreous body can be counteracted with silver. A useful preparation here is Argentum/Corpus vitreum (Weleda), through which the effect of silver is carried directly to the vitreous body. This preparation is therefore also indicated for opacities of the vitreous body (injection and eyedrops). It also influences acute states of pain. Further, it helps against premature presbyopia and asthenopia. A different approach is taken with Trabeculum comp., which like several previously mentioned preparations was a result of collaboration between O. Wolff and opthalmologists. Trabeculum comp. acts on the irido-corneal angle and is designed to release adhesions, congestion, etc. in Schlemm's canal. Thus it is particularly indicated in secondary glaucoma, also in combination with other preparations we have mentioned. In chronic cases, Resina Laricis comp. is also indicated, both as ointment and in compresses (emulsion). Warm compresses with Jura Fango (Bad Boll) can also be helpful. A small amount of the black powder is stirred in hot water to form a paste. This is spread on a cloth and laid upon the closed eye, the entire compress then being covered with a dry woolen cloth.

A holistic treatment of glaucoma should pay special attention to the liver and kidney. The liver controls the fluid balance of the entire organism, and hence of the eye as well; glaucoma treatment may therefore be supplemented with treatment of the liver using such remedies as Kalium carbonicum D6 or Hepatodoron. The kidney bears the same relation to the air organism as the liver does to the water organism: it controls overall aeration. Kidney remedies indicated for glaucoma include Equisetum D15, Carbo Betulae (or Carbo Equiseti) D5, D20, and Formica D15.

Another remedy that has proven effective in my own experience is amber (Corpus vitr. D6/Succinum D6 eyedrops). Amber is fossil pine resin from the Tertiary period, and has thus undergone millennia of hardening and clarification. Relics from earlier states of the earth are often particularly effective therapeutically, since they engage the organism's forces of youth. This is what distinguishes amber from larch resin (Resina laricis), which is derived from a fresh living substance and thus affects vitality. Amber, by contrast, deals more with the eye's permeability to light. It is indicated not only for glaucoma, but also for opacities of the vitreous body and of the lens. A good combination is Stannum/Succinum eyedrops (best applied three times daily).

Iscador, thought originally developed for the treatment of cancer, is sometimes also indicated for glaucoma. Rudolf Steiner regarded glaucoma as a tumor process that does not reach its full potential. He described the pathology of glaucoma as polar to inflammatory processes in the ear. Eye and ear are polar in their structure, just as the disease tendencies of sclerosis and cancer are the polar opposites of inflammation. A colleague who was unacquainted with this idea once called glaucoma the "cancer of the eye." This "tumor formation in the fluid element" of the eye can therefore be approached with the appropriate constitutional treatment.

Though doctors recognize today that constitutional treatment can beneficially influence glaucoma, their insight is very seldom implemented in practice. For example, studies have confirmed that concurrent heart therapy improves the chances of success of measures directed specifically at glaucoma.

Another important factor to consider is the patient's overall metabolic situation. It is known that glaucoma scarcely ever develops in the presence of acidosis, and that alkalosis promotes it (almost no vitamin C is found in the aqueous humor of glaucoma patients). The logical response is to promote acidosis either through diet or through medications.

Curative eurythmy is another important component of glaucoma treatment. With it one can achieve better results than with remedies alone. The sounds to use are *L M A U, D, S,* and *G* in various modifications (see the section on curative eurythmy in volume II, pp. 85–111).

Refractive Disorders[10]

Refractive disorders, although not diseases per se, can contribute to eye disease when they are progressive. This is especially true of myopia. They can be remedied symptomatically with eyeglasses, but this does not solve the root problem. Eyeglasses also cannot prevent the pathological sequelae of myopia and other refractive disorders. If vision were an altogether passive process, then every myopic with the same dioptric index would have the same unaided visual acuity. That this is not true indicates sufficiently that the eye is not passive like a camera.

Seeing is an active process in which the human being lives and expresses the self. The eye is suffused with life; it encounters the passively inflowing light with an etheric and astral activity that streams out to the object being seen. The higher constituents have a much looser connection to the body in the head than they do in the middle organization or in the metabolism. This is especially true in the eye. In seeing we are not "in" our bodies; our egos and astral bodies live in the object seen. By acting as a kind of mirror, the eye raises the object seen into consciousness; it provides the mind with an image of that with which it communes outside the body.[11]

Refractive disorders cannot be understood apart from the context of the eye's overall development.[12] They are commonly believed to be due to an improper length of the eyeball, the nearsighted eye being generally too long, the farsighted too short. This is in fact the case in what is known as axial myopia. However, it need not be true in every case, especially in milder ones. The axial length of approximately nine-tenths of all myopic eyes six diopters and under is different from what one would expect based on the refraction. About two-thirds of all myopias over six diopters are pure axial myopias. The length of the eyeball can thus play a significant role, but does not always correspond exactly to the eye's

10. This section was written in collaboration with O. Wolff.

11. See R. Steiner, *Occult Reading and Occult Hearing* (London: Rudolf Steiner Press, 1975), lecture 1.

12. Cf. H. Brunke, "Zur Problematik der Kurzsichtigkeit," *BEH* 27 (1974):173. Many of the indications that follow are taken from this essay. Also: Grube, *BEH* 28 (1975):152; Brunke, *BEH* 28 (1975):175; Knauer, *BEH* 29 (1976):14.

refractive state. Other and equally important factors are the refractive indices of the cornea and lens.

These two factors—eyeball length and refractive index—are balanced against each other as the eye grows, so that images are focused on the retina regardless of the absolute length of the eye. Therefore, when an anomaly appears, the cause need not lie only in the globe length, but can also lie in the refractive medium. Disorders in either can be balanced out to a certain extent by the superordinate ordering principle. Only when this is no longer possible, that is, when the higher constituents are not sufficiently integrated, does an anomaly develop. This is spoken of today as a "failure of the correlation mechanism" (Spooner).[13] Eyeball length and refractive power must be matched to one another through a process of active correlation; otherwise, a refractive error develops.

It is also possible, however, for transitory refractive disorders to occur once the eye has reached its final form. Known as transitory ametropias, that is, myopias or hyperopias of limited duration, these disorders cannot be based on the eye's physical structure. Rather, they are functional disorders, developing because the eye is a living, active organism penetrated by the supersensible constituents of the human being. They are often triggered by traumas, allergies, and various medications, including sulfonamides and arsenic. It is interesting to note that when the transitory ametropia is a myopia, blood sugar levels tend to be *increasing*, whereas when it is a hyperopia, blood sugar levels tend to be *decreasing*. As has been discussed in several places in this book, sugar is the bearer of the ego organization, which integrates the organism's various functions and systems. It may therefore also be assumed that the ego organization is responsible for the harmonizing of eyeball length and refractive index. In this light it is clear why transitory ametropias occur after traumas: the higher constituents are temporarily dislodged from the body and can no longer integrate themselves properly. Allergy is analogous. Here, foreign processes gain the upper hand over the "self." Arsenic, as was shown repeatedly in Volume I, represents the astral body, which, if overly stimulated through arsenic, obstructs the healthy organizing activity of the ego. Sulfonamides evidently have the same affect.

13. Spooner, in *Der Augenarzt* (Stuttgart: Karl Velhagen, 1959).

In sum, it can be said that a refractive error develops when the ordering principle fails, that is, when the ego is too weak to correlate the refractive medium and the eyeball length with one another. Hyperopia nad myopia are thus not a matter of globe length alone, but of two largely contrary variants of ocular development, as will be described in some detail.

All organs, including the eye, are formed by the etheric body, which is in turn influenced by the astral body and ego. The specific connections become clearer when we consider that nearsightedness generally first appears between the ages of 9 and 14 and continues up to about the age of 30. Farsightedness, by contrast, can be congenital or become apparent in infancy, especially when combined with cross-eye, as it often is. The eye of the myopic is therefore evidently still healthy during the first years of life, whereas the eye-forming impulse of the hyperopic is too weak from the start. This is further evidenced by the fact that in axial hyperopia the eye does not grow sufficiently in length.

Myopia

Myopia is a more pressing problem today than hyperopia. Several investigations show that nearsightedness is on the increase. Significantly, however, this increase is occurring only in industrialized countries and not among primitive peoples. Furthermore, city-dwellers are more prone to be myopic than people in rural areas. The educated classes of Europe display a higher proportion of nearsightedness than other classes; this is in complete contrast to the situation in India. Between 1927 and 1951, myopia increased by 19.45% among vocationally-oriented and by 25.26% among university-bound students in Sweden despite considerable prophylactic and hygienic measures. In Germany, the proportion of myopes among elementary school pupils was 4.38%, among secondary school students 13.03%, and among university students 41.31% (Thiel, 1953).[14] Numerous investigations of this correlation exist, and the interpretations are equally numerous.

As early as 1867, in a study that in retrospect seems very modern, Cohn examines over ten thousand schoolchildren in Breslau in an

14. Thiel, in *Der Augenarzt*; Spooner, in *Der Augenarzt* (Stuttgart: Karl Velhagen, 1959).

attempt to establish statistical evidence for the concept of school-myopia.[15] Cohn postulates an increase of myopia due to reading and studying. Later researchers rejected such exogenous influences, holding instead that myopia is exclusively hereditary.[16]

Today we know that such a view is one-sided. More recent studies have confirmed the relation found by Cohn between myopia and schooling.[17] A correlation also exists between myopia and height. In London, for example, nearsighted fifteen-year-old pupils were found to be taller on the average than nonmyopic pupils of the same age.[18] Correlations have also been found between myopia and the time of menarche in female pupils (Scholz).[19] This establishes a link to the problem of acceleration, which, as we will see in due course, plays a significant role in the development of myopia. "The considerable differences in frequency of myopia that exist between young people of different types of schooling develop only after they have started school.... Of all the factors investigated, the type of education has the closest relation to the incidence of nearsightedness" (Scholz).[20]

Psychological studies reveal that "nearsighted pupils are hardworking and attentive in class, have more academic hobbies and take less interest in sports" although "they are not markedly more intelligent than children with normal vision."[21] They are frequently bookworms who seem happy remaining still for long periods of time; their movement organism sometimes seems atrophied. They take interest in little things and have more concentration and persistence than hyperopes, one reason being that they are simply not troubled by a strong urge to move.

These traits are related to the fact that myopes tend to "look inward" rather than outward. Their interests are predominately mental. They are only loosely connected to the physical, the material, the earthly. They are desk workers rather than born craftspeople.

15. H. Cohn, *Die Hygiene des Auges in den Schulen* (Vienna: 1883).
16. A. Steiger, *Die Entstehung der sphärischen Refraktionen des menschlichen Auges* (Berlin: 1913).
17. D. Scholtz, in *Das Öffentliche Gesundheitswesen* 32 (1970):530.
18. Douglas, Ross, Simpson, *Journal of the Royal Statistical Society* A 130 (1967):479.
19. Scholz, in *Der Augenarzt*; Spooner, in *Der Augenarzt* (Stuttgart: Karl Velhagen, 1959).
20. Scholz, in *Der Augenarzt*.
21. Douglas, Ross, Simpson, *Journal of the Royal Statistical Society* A 130 (1967):479.

These facts become more comprehensible when it is recognized that seeing produces an etheric framework throughout the human being.[22] This framework is shifted more into the periphery in farsighted people and more toward the inside in nearsighted people. Thus the myope is generally more "inward-oriented," while the hyperope tends to be more outwardly active.

Naturally the accentuation of the head pole in the nearsighted can manifest itself in various ways. The ideas presented here are intended to help understand the myopic constitution, not to make categorical statements about *all* myopes. For example, the constitutional emphasis on the nerve-sense-pole is expressed in some myopes by attention to minutia, by a tendency to analyze, or by neurasthenia rather than by reading or intellectual interest. As discussed in Volume I (pp. 201), the entire "upper organization" of the human being is overburdened in this condition. A constitutional preference for the nerve-sense-pole along with a general reluctance to incarnate can express itself in various ways. One characteristic symptom of it, however, is myopia.

Summarizing these findings, one can speak of a stronger accentuation of the head pole in the nearsighted; their life is centered more in the nerve-sense-system. In such people the higher constituents take hold of the metabolic-limb-system only relatively weakly.

The question arises why such a state of affairs should adversely affect the eye, our chief sense organ. According to Rudolf Steiner, "nearsighted people are those in whom the ego and astral body retain a certain 'aloofness' toward the physical body; nearsightedness is one of the most telling signs that a person's soul and spirit are unwilling to integrate themselves into the physical."[23] When myopia develops relatively late in life, the disposition toward it may have been present earlier. In such cases the higher constituents do what is necessary in the early stages of the eye's formation but then begin to withdraw, early enough, apparently, to cause a structural disorder. Such a withdrawal is normal in old age, but by then the eyes are already fully formed.

It is possible to be even more specific about the role of the higher constituents in myopia. Although all of the myopic's higher constituents

22. R. Steiner, *SM*, lecture 14.
23. R. Steiner, *SM*, lecture 5.

are a bit too loosely connected with the physical body, in the eye it is chiefly the etheric body that is too weak and that disengages itself too early, whereas the astral body intervenes more strongly. This is borne out by the fact that the sclera of the myopic eye is unusually thin, sometimes only a third of the normal thickness. Electron microscopy revealed tissue development in the sclera to be poor. The vitreous body is prone to premature degeneration. The lens opacifies and becomes more physical relatively early. Retinal degeneration is also frequent; the optic nerve can begin to atrophy. Even the choroid, the metabolic part of the eye, can begin to deteriorate, either in the area of the retinal cones or more extensively. The parallels between myopic and senile degeneration are currently undisputed. A correlation has also been established between retinitis pigmentosa, an explicitly degenerative eye ailment, and myopia.

All these phenomena attest to a devitalization of the eye, which allows us to infer that the etheric body is too weak in relation to the physical body but at the same time more strongly bound to it.

In was mentioned above that the failure of length and refractive index to develop in the proper proportion to one another may be seen as the result of insufficient activity on the part of the ego during the eye's formation. This usually does not become apparent, however, until about the age of 9. Before that, the myopic child's ego appears to be just as completely absorbed in anabolism and organ formation as is the normal child's ego. Around the age of 9, however, the ego fails to make the normal descent into the metabolic system (see vol. I, pp. 61–63), producing definite changes in the etheric and astral bodies. The etheric body, relatively unrestrained by the astral body and ego, becomes "hyperactive," resulting in accelerated and somewhat uncoordinated growth. In the eye this can give rise to an axial myopia. The myopic eye is thus a special case of acceleration, which is due to a deficient involvement of the higher constituents in the physical body.

The activity of the astral body in the human organism may be symbolized by a figure eight. That is to say, the influence it has on the upper organization tends to be the opposite of its influence on the lower.[24] Thus, if the astral body intervenes too weakly in the lower organization,

24. See R. Steiner, *Physiologisch-Therapeutisches auf Grundlage der Geisteswissenschaft: Zur Therapie und Hygiene* (GA 314), lecture of Jan. 1, 1924.

it will connect itself all the more intensely with the nerve-sense-system, the phenomenon observable in myopia. In myopia, the astral body binds itself more strongly to the eye, weakening the etheric body and causing the etheric body to withdraw prematurely. Because of this, the myopic sees well only at short distances; the astral body is too tightly bound to venture out any further. According to Steiner, the visual process creates an etheric framework throughout the body. This is in contrast to the ego's activity, which creates a *physical* framework.[25] In the myopic, the etheric framework is more closely bound to the physical framework than in individuals with normal vision.

Unlike the astral body, the etheric body operates uniformly in the upper and lower organizations; hence it can be pictured as an ellipse.[26] The dotted line represents the etheric body in myopia.

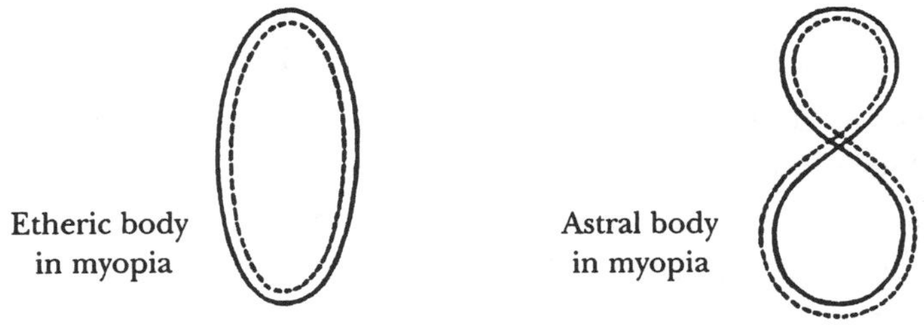

Figure 14

These facts also shed light on why myopia does not become manifest until relatively late, and why the degenerative phenomena described above appear even later.

Not long after myopia becomes manifest, but before devitalization sets in, the etheric body begins to withdraw, causing the eye to become more rigid. By this time the damage has already been done; prophylaxis and therapy must begin earlier.

The prevailing opinion that myopia is largely hereditary confirms that its cause lies in the etheric body. Of course, myopia is aggravated by the increasing intellectualization of life in industrialized countries. Intellec-

25. R. Steiner, *SM*, lecture 14.

26. See R. Steiner, *Physiologisch-Therapeutisches auf Grundlage der Geisteswissenschaft: Zur Therapie und Hygiene, op. cit.*

tualization favors the nerve-sense-system's catabolic processes and prevents the ego from properly incarnating into the metabolic-limb-system (cf. "Diabetes", volume I, pp. 237ff).

The true prophylaxis of myopia lies in healthy living, especially for children. To counter intellectualization, which shifts the child's forces toward the nerve-sense-system, we must not only intensify incarnation into the limbs, but also harmonize the child's thinking, feeling, and willing. One means of achieving this is the Waldorf method of education. Children must be encouraged to feel interest in and love for their surroundings, not to analyze them intellectually.

A chief remedy in the treatment of myopia is belladonna. Steiner once characterized this plant as desiring "to have the same view of the world that the beings reigning over the plant kingdom have. This striving to perceive is manifested ... and develops into something akin to the human eye."[27] This general relation to the eye as such also makes belladonna appropriate for hyperopia.

Children of highly myopic parents can be helped with potentized belladonna (eyedrops: D12; internally: D20) and quartz ointment around the eyes up to the age of 3; internally, Scorodite or Vivianite D6 helps promote incarnation. In older children, belladonna cannot counteract myopia per se, but it can help prevent the associated degenerative phenomena, such as retinal degeneration and opacities of the lens and vitreous body.

Curative eurythmy is another important part of the therapy of myopia, since it re-establishes harmony and stimulates the higher constituents to integrate themselves more intensely in the metabolism. Myopic patients must be united more strongly with their limbs, while their astral body must be released from the eye and their etheric body strengthened. The appropriate therapy to achieve these ends involves rhythms, rod exercises, and sound sequences such as *L M F U, L M F I,* or *L R D I,* depending on constitution. *L* was described by Rudolf Steiner as "formative power overcoming matter"; it liberates and releases, stimulating etheric forces. *M* penetrates with understanding into the surrounding world. *F* encourages exhalation guided by wisdom and stimulates renal activity. *I* (pronounced *ee* as in "bee") strengthens the ego organization,

27. R. Steiner, *SM,* lecture 19.

balance, and the back (nearsighted children are frequently kyphotic). The vowel *U* is important because it affects exhalation in the upper organization; it also affects the legs, which is important inasmuch as nearsighted people are often flat-footed. Consonants should be done with the fingers and toes, vowels with the arms and feet.

Another possibility for the treatment of myopia is color therapy. Looking at blue, with an occasional glace at red for contrast, is beneficial. Blue releases and vitalizes the eye and extends the visual beam. Steiner described blue as drawing us out into the world and helping us overcome egoism.[28] Short intervals of red activate and intensify this effect. The alternation of pink and green has proven beneficial for amblyopia and retinal degeneration. One of Steiner's therapeutic indications for myopia was that mustard packs be applied twice a day to the soles of the feet, and that the patient stare at the same time without glasses into a sky-blue box, imagining that the blue is penetrating through his eyes right down into his feet. Mustard plaster draws the astral body more strongly down into the metabolism and the feet. The same effect can be achieved with phosphorus, Scorodite, Levico, or Urtica dioica. Cuprum praep. ointment, 0.4%, may also be applied to the feet.

Hyperopia

The genesis of hyperopia was described above. Frequently the correlation between eye length and refraction, which should be maintained by the ego, breaks down even earlier here than in myopia. The convergent strabismus (cross-eye) that frequently accompanies hyperopia will be discussed below in greater detail.

Both myopia and hyperopia are based on a disturbance of the ego's activity; however, the disturbances are polar opposites of each other. In myopia, the eye's refractive index is too high; in hyperopia, it is too low. This is because the myope's higher constituents connect too strongly with the physical part of his eye, whereas the hyperope's constituents connect too loosely. In hyperopes, therefore, the etheric body does not

---

28. See R. Steiner, *Art as Seen in the Light of Mystery Wisdom* (London: Rudolf Steiner Press, 1996), lecture 5.

sufficiently penetrate the vitreous body, so that the latter becomes too physical. This is similar to what happens in glaucoma.

In contrast to the nearsighted, constitutionally farsighted people tend to be oriented toward the outer world and to be more active in their limbs. This gives rise to a certain urge to move. The healthy balance between the nerve-sense-system and limb-metabolic-system is upset here in favor of the latter. However, just as the intensified growth characteristic of myopia is not really healthy, the metabolic processes and limb activity of hyperopia are insufficiently formed. Proper organ formation requires a harmonious equilibrium between formative tendencies proceeding from the nervous system and the material processes originating in the lower organism. Interestingly, neonates, whose eyes are as yet imperfectly formed, are hyperopic.

Since near vision is more difficult for the hyperopic child, cramps of the eye muscles and convergent strabismus often occur. In later life the severely hyperopic are disposed toward glaucoma, a sign that they have not completely mastered their metabolism. As we have said, glaucoma develops because the etheric body does not thoroughly penetrate the vitreous body, leaving it open to purely physical influences. The remedy to be applied here is Equisetum/Tabacum ointment around the eye. Equisetum contains a strong silica process, which has a formative effect on the metabolism, while Nicotiana mitigates deformities. Other advisable medications are Argentum D6 and Conchae D6, Levico, and eyedrops of Argentum/Corpus vitreum. Argentum enlivens the etheric body, and the Argentum/Corpus vitr. eyedrops are particularly beneficial in this respect. Levico is also indicated for its cuprum and arsenic content.

The curative eurythmy of hyperopia will tend to use plosive sounds, which have a formative effect, such as *B* and *N*. This is in contrast to myopia, where mainly fricatives are used. Of the vowels, *A* and *E* may be used. *M* should be performed more from without inward. Of the rhythms, dactyls and trochees are to be preferred to iambs.

A third refractive disorder of the eye besides myopia and hyperopia is astigmatism. Here the cornea loses its spherical, cosmic shape; deformed by the astral body, it approximates more earthly forms. An improvement is possible only during the first years of childhood, while the cornea is still malleable. Possible remedies include Conchae D6 powder and, even more important, Tabacum D6 salve and D10 liquid. Conchae influences exhalation and spherical forms, while Tabacum corrects deformities. In curative eurythmy, the sounds *L S I B D* are appropriate. Astigmatisms induced by pregnancy are easier to treat and correct.

Strabismus

As a rule, the hyperope's eyes turn inward and the myope's outward. In both cases, the ego can no longer integrate the images on both retinas into one. It has lost the power to direct and guide the eyes.

Convergent strabismus (esotropia or cross-eyes) intensifies for hyperopes in near vision, since in addition to the normal accommodation they must also overcome their hyperopia. This can easily cause cramps of the eye muscles. Convergent strabismus generally appears in the first few years of life, though it can also be congenital. Emotional trauma, accident, serious illness, severe indigestion, or any other major stress during this period can contribute to convergent strabismus, since this is when the organs are developing most rapidly. Emotionally unstable children seem to be particularly susceptible.

Prepubertal children whose strabismic eye is also amblyopic should have the intact eye covered periodically so that the amblyopic eye receives more exercise. However, the intact eye should not be covered for excessively long periods, since this might impair binocular vision. A good rule of thumb is three days uncovered for every week covered. The amblyopic eye's visual acuity is considerably improved in this way, while extramacular vision can regress. The retarded eye may be stimulated with compresses of Resina Laricis comp. Emulsio as well as with twice-weekly subcutaneous injections of Arnica D20 mixed with Lamina/Retina comp.

Medications used for convergent strabismus should relieve spasms and strengthen the ego. Such medications include Argentum D6, Magnesium phosphoricum D6, and Conchae D6–D15. Levico D3 is appropriate for both convergent and divergent strabismus. Organ preparations are also indicated, such as Cerebellum, which guides the effect of the other medications to the centers of coordination of the appropriate muscles. Injections of Lamina/Retina and Cerebellum D6 have proven effective in diplopia (double vision).

The decision whether to operate and when is seldom an easy one. The best time is doubtless between the ages of six and twelve. Special attention should be given to follow-up treatment with curative eurythmy and medication.

An especially important therapy for convergent strabismus is curative eurythmy. An exercise designed especially for coordinative disorders of the eyes involves the vowel sound *I* (ee as in "bee") and is done with the fourth finger and the foot. The finger is first moved forward at eye-height, then out toward the side, and then back to the body. This is done on each side separately and then on both sides together. The same is done with the outer toes. This exercise can be complemented with the sounds *L M H A G*, and with *B* behind the head. Rod exercises may also be done, as well as contraction and expansion, rhythms, and the devotional *A*.

Divergent strabismus usually accompanies myopia or blindness in one eye that develops later in life due to illness. It is treated with the same medications that are used for myopia: Phosphorus D5, Scorodite, and Formica, but also Equisetum comp. oil applied around the eyes. In curative eurythmy, the *I* exercise described above is performed with the index or middle finger, whereby the *I* is drawn inward from the outside.

Children for whom exercises with orthoptic apparatuses are prescribed should also receive curative eurythmy.

In treating paralysis or weakness of the extraocular muscles, the therapy already described should be supplemented with an organ preparation of the appropriate nerve, for example, Arnica D20 + Nervus oculomotorus or abducens D3 or D4.

A phenomenon related to strabismus is heterophoria or latent strabismus. Esophoria, the tendency of the eyes to turn inward, frequently causes painful headaches, especially in hyperopics. Prismatic lenses often help relieve this condition. Metabolic organ disorders are frequently a contributing factor. An improvement can often be achieved with mustard footbaths, Agaricus muscarius D10 internally, and Tabacum D10 or Levico D3 s.c. in the upper thigh. In one of my own patients, heterophoria regressed only after correction of a retroflexion of the uterus.

The various therapies presented here are only a beginning; much still has to be elaborated. Further development will hinge upon a recognition of the eye as more than just a physical apparatus. Its spiritual function and significance for the entire human being will also have to be recognized.

Rudolf Steiner was prevented by illness and by his subsequent death from delivering a course of lectures on the physiology of the senses that he had intended to give in 1924. However, the seeds of a comprehensive physiology of the senses based upon the essential nature of the human being are present in his earlier work. Only on such a basis can a rational therapy of the eyes be developed.

VII

Diseases of the Spine and Joints

OTTO WOLFF

THE INCREASE IN COMPLAINTS and diseases of the spine and joints makes it imperative that the nature of the spine and joints be understood. Since the nature of an organ expresses itself in function, we must begin with function in order to understand the organ's physiology and pathology.

The function of the spine is to make our upright, typically human posture possible. Standing upright is a peculiarly human activity. Of course, other vertebrates possess spines with similar parts, but they do not use them in the same way. Human beings must constantly maintain balance against the influence of gravity, whereas animals are bound to the earth by their posture. Our posture, like speaking and thinking, is a characteristic expression of human spiritual activity.

This difference in spinal function results in a dynamic difference as well. Many researchers hold that the "wear and tear" to which the human spine is subjected is due to the added burden of the head and shoulder blades. The pathology of the human spine has even been called "the price we pay for the privilege of walking upright."[1] As reasonable as this may seem, it must also be pointed out that in earlier times people carried, and in some parts of the world still do carry, heavy loads on their heads without any "wear or tear" appearing in their spines; in fact, were the load itself responsible, then beasts of burden would have to show similar changes, which they do not. A further argument against simple mechanical pressure as the cause of spinal disorders is the increased incidence of such disorders in young people in industrialized countries.

Upright posture is the key to understanding the physiology and pathology of the human spine. It is an essential feature of the human being and as such expresses the ego organization, the universal constitu-

1. See Fritz Reischauer, *Untersuchungen über den lumbalen und cervikalen Wirbelbandscheibenverfall* (Stuttgart: Thieme, 1949).

ent that raises human beings above the animals. The physical vehicle of the ego organization is silica; for that reason, silica is an important remedy in the therapy of spinal diseases. Like speech and thought, the ego organization is a potential that all human beings are born with. The extent to which and, above all, how we take advantage of that potential is an individual question, an expression of our ego, our personal, spiritual core, and hence also of our individual destiny. The genius of the language has captured these truths in pictorial form: we speak of upright and of spineless people, of having backbone, of being stiff-necked, and so on, all expressions of bodily traits that are in turn expressions of character.

Uprightness must be achieved through a struggle with gravity and through adjustment to the surroundings. The infant's attempts to raise the head are the first expression of the ego's activity. The spine of embryos and infants is kyphotic, that is, curved outward toward the back. This expresses an extreme introversion, an internalization of formative forces, which during the first stages of incarnation is necessary. Later, in the child, the spine becomes practically straight, leaving room for the development of the opposite kind of curvature, lordosis. Lordosis expresses buoyancy and openness toward the world, traits that should predominate in children. Healthy children jump for joy; weight is a foreign experience to them, though this changes as they grow older. However, today's children seldom experience buoyancy the way they should; they are frequently depressed and "weighed down," often by excessive and premature demands in school.

In healthy adults, the spine strikes a balance between kyphosis and lordosis. It rhythmically combines weight and buoyancy, oppressive sadness and uplifting joy. This fact alone offers insight into the pathology of the spine; more essential than mechanical stresses on the spine are the emotional and spiritual stresses to which the human being is subjected. This insight affects our understanding not only of chronic disorders, but also of therapy.

The forces of buoyancy observable in the healthy child derive from the etheric body, which in the child is still fully devoted to growth and constructive activity. By contrast, in adults, the ego predominates, fighting its battle with the forces of gravity. However, it naturally does so in conjunction with the etheric body. The effects of this confrontation with gravity are apparent in the gradual increase in size of the lower vertebrae with increasing age. The infant's vertebrae are all approximately the same size. But, the downward pull of gravity and the struggle to overcome it in the upright posture eventually cause the lower vertebrae to grow larger.

A similar development can be observed in the hands and feet. In the young child and even more so in the embryo, the hands and feet are small in relation to the trunk, but grow markedly faster than the trunk, and certainly much faster than the head, throughout childhood. This growth accelerates at two points in the child's development, at about the age of six and later just before puberty. Inasmuch as they are followed by the change of teeth and by puberty, these "spurts" represent distinct phases of the child's incarnation.

Even the growth of the hands and feet shows the conflict between weight and uprightness. This is particularly obvious in the sole of the foot, which in young children is flat but later develops an arch in response to the weight exerted by the ankle. Only the human being possesses an arched sole; even animals who walk on their soles, such as bears, do not have an arch. The arch of the foot expresses the overcoming of gravity, and is the norm in terms of which common deviations can be understood. Flat feet have succumbed completely to the forces of gravity, whereas high-arched feet express an overly strong tendency to leave the earth.

The dynamic at work in the spine naturally requires physical material suited to the relevant mechanical stresses. This material consists of bone, cartilage, and connective tissue. Bone, down to its most detailed structure, expresses the activity of the ego organization, the constituent that makes uprightness possible. The special features of cartilage are discussed below. Connective tissue not only connects parts and organs with one another and fills spaces, but since it is rich in silica, the physical vehicle of the ego organization, it also acts as a conduit for formative forces. The significance of silica in the body has only begun to be noticed in recent years.[2] Modern diets are usually quite low in silica, since extensive refinement of grains and other foods removes the parts richest in that nutrient. Furthermore, artificial fertilizers shift the mineral content of plants toward potassium, phosphorus, and nitrogen and away from

2. Voronkow, Zelchan, and Lukewitz, *Silizium und Leben* (East Berlin: 1975).

magnesium, silica, and other trace minerals. The lack of these minerals in the diet can of course be compensated for with nutritional supplementation; however, this leaves untouched the question of how the substances are used. In the case of silica, this is a matter of the ego organization. For example, although a postural anomaly may be due to a dietary deficiency of silica and the resulting faulty development of supportive tissue, it may also be due primarily to an impairment of the activity of the ego organization by overstimulation of the astral body. Such overstimulation is common today and reflects the influence of environmental forces inimical to human spiritual activity and self-assertion. Therapy must therefore consider both the nutritional and the spiritual aspects of the problem.

The Joints

A joint makes possible the movement of two bones in relation to one another. The connection between bones is also partly established by muscles. With that we have characterized all three principles that underlie the mobility of the human skeleton: bone, which develops from the mineralizing influences proper to the forces of lead; muscle, which expresses the will embodied in motion and thus the dynamic of iron; and cartilage, which makes the normal interplay of the bones possible and by its gelatinous character exhibits the influence of the tin process, which mediates between iron and lead.

Bone, joint, and muscle are thus products of the three trans-solar planets, Saturn, Jupiter, and Mars, whose influences have come to rest in the metals lead, tin, and iron, respectively. By virtue of these relationships, each of these three metals can be used to affect and stimulate the formation of the corresponding tissue.

Of course, not all disorders of bone, cartilage, and muscle are to be treated solely with these three remedies or basic principles. Silica, for example, also plays a role in the formation of bone and connective tissue and can thus be used in therapy.

Many muscle and joint diseases belong to the so-called rheumatic family of diseases. As important as it may be to distinguish the various diseases within this family, it is still more important to recognize the underlying tendencies that produce them.

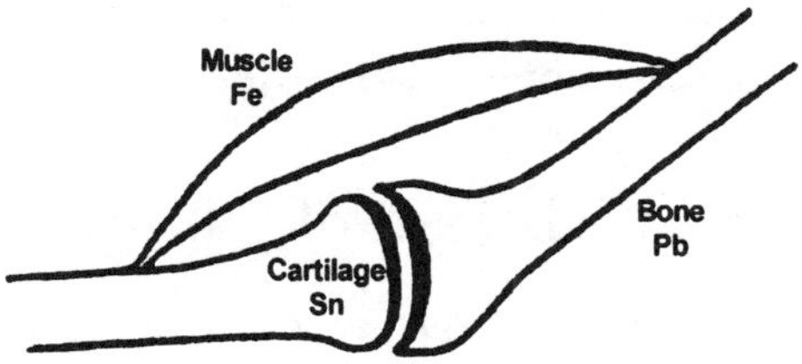

Figure 15

Specialists admit that despite extensive research, the real causes of the rheumatic diseases remain unknown. Conventional therapy is therefore considered successful if it eases pain and checks inflammation. However, no matter how impressed patients may be by the fast relief of their symptoms, physicians must still judge whether such measures contribute to real healing or only bring temporary improvement. This they can do only if they recognize the disease's underlying tendency.

Rheumatic diseases indisputably involve processes of deposition and are thus metabolic in nature. The question whether the deposits are recognizably mineral, such as uric acid in gout, or of a more organic nature, such an intra-articular nodules in rheumatism, is only secondary. Both types are a sign of insufficiently regulated metabolism tending toward deposition, at times to the point of mineralization. The rheumatic diseases are thus primarily sclerotic. The inflammatory symptoms that often accompany them are merely secondary; they represent an imperfect attempt by the organism to dissolve the deposits. That this is so is shown by the tendency of rheumatics to seek out dry warmth, which favors not only dissolution but also restructuring.

The fact that a physiological reaction is meaningful does not mean, however, that it cannot begin to do more harm than good, especially when it persists. The limiting of inflammation can thus limit the disease process even though it cannot heal it. The question always arises, however, to what extent the primary disease process, which is sclerotic, is thereby only pushed onto a different plane.

Gout, with its actual deposits of uric acid crystals, has been discussed elsewhere (see vol. I, p. 280). The deposits that are clearly the most prominent feature of this disease are due to the dynamic of the nerve-sense system, as evidenced by another symptom, insomnia. As in other rheumatic diseases, the inflammation found in gout is merely secondary and represents a futile attempt to dissolve deposits.

Suggestions for the Therapy of Joint Diseases

In addition to the important distinction between joint diseases that are primarily degenerative and sclerotic and those that are mainly inflammatory, within the latter group the further distinction needs to be made between acute and chronic phases.

Acute rheumatic arthritis (rheumatic fever) is essentially characterized by edema, which is why the main therapeutic goal has always been to draw off the accumulated fluid. In earlier times perspiration was induced and preparations made from willow bark were administered. Later, willow bark was found to contain salicylic acid and its ester, so that from then on salicylate preparations were given for rheumatic fever. The same compounds are found in the meadowsweet, *Spiraea ulmaria.* Both the willow and the meadowsweet are known for their ability to transpire large amounts of water from the soil into the air, and as such are "remedies" for a particular condition of the earth, namely, the accumulation of water beneath the surface. Earlier peoples intuitively understood the similarity between this condition and rheumatic fever and thus chose the remedy accordingly.

The essential feature of rheumatoid arthritis (chronic polyarthritis), by contrast, is a disturbance of protein metabolism. This is evident in the agglutination of the rheumatoid factor in serodiagnosis. The presence of auto-antibodies indicates a disturbance of the immune system, that is, of protein metabolism. As will be discussed below, the defects in protein synthesis are coupled with impaired catabolism.

Although rheumatic fever and rheumatoid arthritis differ both symptomatically and serologically, intermediate forms exist. Rheumatic fever is a disturbance of the mercury process, rheumatoid arthritis of the iron process, which correspond to fluid and protein metabolism, respectively, as will be discussed later. The organ that mediates between these two processes is the liver, which governs both the water organism and protein synthesis. Clearly, then, the obvious disturbances underlying rheumatic diseases should be treated by way of the liver, that is, by way of the metabolism. To put it another way, the stresses on the metabolism must be relieved. However, the emphasis in conventional therapy upon antipyretic and analgesic measures usually causes the dietary approach to be neglected.

Treatment of Acute Rheumatic Diseases

The rheumatic's diet should be salt-free during acute phases, since sodium regulates water. The best prescription is a juice fast lasting a few days. Furthermore, although it is generally recognized that protein tends to stimulate warmth production and hence also inflammation, in the case of rheumatism this knowledge is seldom applied. Of course, not all proteins are equally undesirable for rheumatic patients; meat and eggs are worse than dairy products. Pork stimulates inflammation most consistently of all; therefore, rheumatics should avoid it completely. Meat of any kind also tends to acidify the metabolism, which only worsens the rheumatic's usual acidosis. Depending upon severity and acuteness, a practically protein-free diet may be advisable for a time, as it tends to gradually lessen severity. As long as excesses are avoided, the protein content from plant sources may be disregarded. The patient should then be eased into a lactovegetarian diet. However, protein should not be reintroduced into the diet too quickly, since apparent failures can be attributed to too rapid a return to a "normal" diet.

The correct application of dietary principles is an indispensable condition for the effectiveness of all other therapy. Stresses on the metabolism must be relieved before the metabolism can be made healthy again.

One remedy that helps deal with edema is mercury, which can dissolve congestion. Low potencies should be used. For example, daily injections of Mercur viv. nat. D6 may be given, or a pinch of Mercur solubilis D4 five times daily. These remedies should be applied only for the duration of the edema. Since mercury is the antagonist or opponent of tin, which regulates the formation of joints, prolonged administration of mercury can retard regeneration. During acute phases, however, tin is completely contraindicated. Its task is to organize, vitalize, and shape fluids, in other words, to counteract degenerative and arthrotic processes.

Another remedy indicated for acute inflammations is bryony, a plant that exhibits a hypertrophic root process. Its formative force can be put to use in injections of Bryonia D3 or in Rheumadoron 1, of which it is an ingredient. The effect of bryony in Rheumadoron is complemented by aconite, a medicinal plant that has been discussed repeatedly. Aconite is indicated in all acute conditions during which the body generates warmth to overcome a preceding temperature loss or some other condition. Arnica, another component of Rheumadoron, has been discussed frequently for its formative, restructuring power. Rheumadoron 1 is complemented by Rheumadoron 2, whose constituents, Colchicum and Sabina, have proven effective in potenized form against both gout and arthritis. Doses of Rheumadoron 1 and 2 in hourly alternation are the basis for the treatment of all acute diseases of the joints.

Treatment of Chronic Rheumatic Diseases

Chronic rheumatic diseases, such as rheumatoid arthritis, also require a dietary treatment. A strict low-protein diet should be prescribed at first and only gradually replaced with a diet containing more protein.

A chronic stage is usually a sign that the organism has surrendered to the disease process. (See vol. I, pp. 173ff.) This surrender can be the result of repeated suppression of acute phases, for example, with antipyretics. Fever is a sign that the ego is attempting to restructure the organism, and when fever is too often suppressed, the ego withdraws. The result is a state of constant, smoldering tension, in which metabolic processes elude the ego's control and assume a life of their own. When a chronic condition develops in this way, it can usually be overcome by directing it back into the acute phase and by allowing the latter to run its course. Earlier physicians were well acquainted with this principle, which explains their attempts to provoke local inflammations by such means as irritating salves. In recent times these procedures have been readopted and modernized by Baunscheidt, Aschner, and others; however, the medical community as a whole has failed to recognize their value.[3] Not only do they run counter to the conventional philosophy of suppressing inflammation, they usually also cause the patient some temporary discomfort. Since patients expect rapid symptomatic relief, most are less than enthusiastic about procedures that temporarily exacerbate their symptoms.

---

3. B. Aschner, *Technik der Konstitutionstherapie* (Ulm: 1961).

It has been known for centuries that beekeepers, who are frequently stung, almost never suffer from rheumatic diseases. Bee stings, as is known, cause a local inflammation, which, when often repeated, effects a lasting change of the metabolism in the direction of a permeation of warmth and light. A similar rationale underlies the therapeutic use of Formica from ants (see volume II, pp. 187f). Due to the close connection of ants to the earth, remedies prepared from them dissolve indurations and deposits more effectively than do bee remedies. The bee's connection to light and warmth, rather than to the earth, is obvious. Apis and Formica are thus essential remedies for rheumatic diseases of the acute and the chronic type, respectively.

Although some chronic joint diseases result from the suppression of acute conditions, others are idiopathic. One such disease, rheumatoid arthritis, is connected with both the constitution and the disposition, factors profoundly connected with individual destiny. A contributing factor may be early influences upon the constitution that only later cause disease. Rudolf Steiner indicated to teachers that "external compulsions" enforced upon children, especially when they are learning to walk and to balance themselves, can predispose them to rheumatic diseases later in life.[4] The same influences can also cause a constitutional weakness in the organization of fluids. This weakness can manifest early in life as hydrocephalus or as its opposite, which is rarely seen nowadays. Later, it can manifest as a tendency to pleurisy, which, if not treated properly, can in turn metamorphose into a predisposition to diseases of the joints.[5] Although these three types of diseases appear unrelated, they are all stages of the same underlying process. Common to all is a faulty organization of fluids, which is related to the Jupiter-tin process (see volume II, p. 165f.). Hydrocephalus, pleurisy, and degenerative diseases of the joints are thus all indications for Stannum.

With the exception of uric acid deposits in gout, the "deposits" in rheumatic diseases are organic formations comparable to benign tumors. Both gout and rheumatism, however, are disorders of metabolic regulation. The former emphasizes catabolic processes (uric acid as an end product of purine metabolism), the latter anabolic processes

4. R. Steiner, *A Modern Art of Education* (Hudson, NY: Anthroposophic Press, 1999), lecture 6.

5. R. Steiner, *SM*, lecture 7.

(hypertrophy of cartilage in the joints, proliferations). In rheumatic diseases, tissue formation occurs in areas of normally low vitality, such as the surfaces of a joint. Clearly the balance between catabolism and anabolism has been disturbed.

As has been discussed elsewhere, an essential requirement of this balance in sentient organisms is that every anabolic process be preceded by a catabolic one.[6] The tissue formations characteristic of rheumatism are thus the result of faulty catabolism.

The dynamic that coordinates these two processes is that of iron. Iron catabolizes as well as builds up and organizes. Its catabolic effect may be seen in oxidation, while its anabolic effect may be inferred from the deficient anabolism characteristic of anemics. Other features of the iron dynamic are activity, force of will, and a healthy immune system, all of which are lacking in the organism beset by chronic disease. Rheumatic deposits may thus be seen as the result of a misdirected iron process. Although the qualities mentioned describe the organism rather than the soul, a primarily psychological resignation can gradually sink down into the body and thus fade from conscious awareness. In such cases the very opposite of resignation may appear in the soul as a kind of compensation.

Potentized iron is one means of stimulating physiological activity in rheumatics and of regulating their protein metabolism. Substantial doses of iron would be useless, since what is needed is not nutritional supplementation of a lack of iron, but rather iron's inner dynamic, which is released only by potentization. Varying the potency from D6 up to D30 and back down has proven particularly effective.[7] Sulfur administered in bath form also stimulates physiological activity, but should be used with caution, since it favors anabolism in general and can thus aggravate the disease. It is indicated only for the most refractory conditions, never for acute or subacute conditions.

This may explain the remarkable efficacy of the thermal springs at Bad Gastein, Austria. The combination of radioactivity and warmth brings about the needed catabolism as well as the needed dissolution.

---

6. See volume 2, p. 417.
7. A. Selawry, *BEH* (1972):125 and (1973):74.

The state of organic resignation characteristic of chronic diseases makes it possible for unusual stresses not only to worsen the disease but also to cause a physiological oversensitivity. This is what happens in the case of a focus. Here the organism sloughs off or at least isolates a more or less dead area of tissue, as in a granuloma. The focus, which may lie in a dead tooth, a tonsil, or some other tissue, can "spread" when resistance is lowered. It represents an additional burden on an organism that, because of its chronic disease, is already ill-equipped to handle it. Even minor stresses can initiate this process, which explains the oversensitivity frequently observed in focus-prone patients. The removal of a focus, like the removal of metabolic stresses by means of appropriate diet, is therefore a sensible measure; although it does not strike at the root of the disease, it does free the organism's forces for a battle with the disease proper.

A practically specific remedy for organic deposits is birch leaves. The birch is peculiar among plants for the way it separates the production of proteinaceous substances from that of mineral salts. Proteins are produced primarily in the leaves, whereas salts are produced in the bark.[8] The effect of birch leaves can be intensified by pharmaceutical applications of warmth. Betula, Folium (birch leaves processed as a remedy) encourages dissolution and excretion. It can be administered as injection, liquid, or as an elixir or tea. It is also a constituent of Rheumadoron 102A.

Rheumadoron 102A also contains aconite, arnica, and mandrake. The mandrake is a typical nightshade, exhibiting a strong astral impulse, particularly in its root. In addition to the spasmolytic effect common to all members of its family (the Solanaceae), it is also a sedative and analgesic. Mandrake root is a specific for the mineralization process typical of gout.

8. R. Steiner, *SM,* lecture 15.

Degenerative Joint Disease

Degenerative joint disease is a gradual, noninflammatory process. The case history usually reveals a major stress or injury that need not be recent. Repeated minor traumas can also lastingly damage cartilaginous tissue, which becomes less elastic, atrophies, and ossifies. Degenerative joint disease is thus a sclerotic disease. Although cartilage can usually degenerate only if it is somehow constitutionally deficient, even healthy cartilage can be damaged by unusual stress or traumas. In any case, the goal of therapy should be to eliminate stresses and progressive sclerotization and, as long as no irreversible damage has occurred, to stimulate new cartilage formation.

Cartilage formation is a typical result of the tin process, which acts primarily on gelatinous materials and also regulates the organization of fluids. Cartilage is gelatinous and is a highly organized form of "moisture." The basic remedy for the treatment of degenerative joint disease is therefore Stannum. Application can alternate between the 5% triturate taken internally, the 0.4% ointment, and injections of D6.

The therapy of degenerative joint disease will also include the remedies Equisetum and Formica. Equisetum is a highly siliceous plant and possesses silica's formative power, but is also rich in sulfur salts. By virtue of this combination, it exerts both a forming and a dissolving influence. Formica is derived from ants, whose role in nature is to incorporate decaying organic matter back into the cycle of life. A particularly useful form of both these remedies is the combination ampule Equisetum D10/Formica D15, injected subcutaneously twice a week near the affected joints. Stannum 5% triturate should be taken internally in conjunction with this.

Degenerative joint disease, like all chronic disease processes, runs its course independently of the guidance of the ego. One means of engaging the ego in metabolism and thus awakening its interest in restructuring is phosphorus, the most effective form being phosphorus oil capsules in the morning. Antisclerotic therapy is also effective, especially after the therapy already described has been carried out for about two months. The most important antisclerotic remedy is sulfur, the substance in nature that has internalized the most warmth. Sulfur may be administered in baths, compresses, and thermal springs. Compounds of sulfur, such as argentite (natural silver sulfide), are also indicated. Silver has the virtue of leading substances into the realm of life, and in argentite, it directs the effects of sulfur into just that realm.

Quite apart from drug therapy, external warmth and protection against cold are also indispensable. Furthermore, although tin is a specific for joint diseases, it should be withheld until the organism has been prepared by the other remedies to respond to it properly. If it is applied too soon, the effectiveness of later therapy may be restricted. Therefore, in addition to warmth, sulfur, phosphorus, Equisetum, and Formica, tin should be used only in salve form at the beginning. Later it may be administered internally, at which point it may be complemented by external applications of Arnica comp./Formica ointment or oil or of Arnica/Symphytum comp. ointment. Another basic remedy is Absinthium/Resina Laricis liquid, which is indicated for indurations and deposits. Like the other treatments, it should be administered for a few weeks at a time and then be replaced with another therapy.

Therapy of Spinal Diseases

The therapy of diseases of the spine must take into account all the formative tendencies and influences, both physical and spiritual, that act upon the spine. Actual physical changes in the spine, which may be apparent to radiological examination, are usually only the end result of a long process that began as a functional disorder. For this reason, radiological findings and subjective symptoms often bear little relation to one another. Organic changes that cause no symptoms, such as pronounced senile exostoses, roughness of the edges of the vertebrae, and even subluxations, are often discovered only accidentally, while serious symptoms and substantial functional impairments frequently occur in the absence of any specific radiological findings.

As has been mentioned, what damages the spine is not activity or stress in general, but rather the one-sidedness of an activity, the unhealthy prolongation of an unphysiological posture or stress. The stress, although frequently occupational, can also be due to such factors as improper footwear or bedding. The repeated wearing of high heels, for example, causes postural anomalies. Mattresses that consist of several sections have "gaps" that fail to provide support to crucial portions of the spine. Strains such as these provoke undue muscular tension, which creates further postural anomalies, which leads to more unhealthy tension, and so on in a vicious circle. One the other hand, postural anomalies are usually due to deficient muscle tone, which, however, can be accompanied by abnormal tension in other muscle groups.

The choice of therapy depends upon the specific condition and on the organs affected. Spondylarthrosis, for example, can be treated like degenerative joint disease, but the therapeutic effect can be directed specifically at the spine with preparations from the intervertebral disk. Such preparations not only guide other remedies to the spine but also activate the ego organization, the formative impulse underlying the embryonic chorda dorsalis and its residue in the mature spine, the nucleus pulposus. The intervertebral disk may be combined with bamboo, as in the Disci preparations produced by Wala,[9] or with Solutio siliceae, a preparation modeled after the horsetail and contained in the disk preparations produced by Weleda.[10]

These combined preparations have been used for decades with beneficial results. The general guidelines for their use are as follows. When inflammatory processes predominate or a condition is worsening acutely, especially in the region of the neck (for example, cervical migraine), the indicated remedy is Disci comp. cum Argento (Wala), especially in patients who are neurasthenic or oversensitive. In conditions that are predominantly chronic and degenerative, the indicated remedy is Disci cum Stanno, which may also be employed after treatment with silver. Deformities can be counteracted with remedies containing Nicotiana. For other combined preparations, consult the remedy lists of Wala and Weleda.

Injections given two to three time weekly are usually more effective than oral administration of the same medication. However, the oral form may be given as a follow-up to the injections. Injections made in an area of the skin that has been cupped and thus made hyperemic are more effective. This form of administration is similar to the injection of the patient's own blood combined with the remedy (see volume II, p. 33)

Disk preparations can be complemented with belladonna, which helps relieve muscle tension. Daily injections of D20 or D6 are advisable,

9. See "List of Indications" for address.
10. See "List of Indications" for address.

particularly at the beginning of treatment or during acute phases. Aconite D6 or D30 may be used instead of belladonna to influence accompanying neuralgias or to counteract exposure to cold. Rhus toxicodendron D30 may be added for edema, sciatica, torticollis, or rheumatic symptoms, especially when these worsen during rest but improve during movement, an indication in keeping with this remedy's homeopathic proving. Nerve compressions can be treated with Arnica Radix D6 or D20 in combination with the organ preparation corresponding to the affected nerve, for example, Nervus ischiaticus or Plexus brachialis D4.

A frequent symptom of a functional disorder of the cervical spine is so-called "housewife's arm," brachialgia paresthetica nocturna. As its common name indicates, it affects women more often than men. Contributing factors include nerve compression and insufficient blood supply. A specific for this condition is injections of Crotalus terrificus D30. All snake poisons are blood and nerve poisons, and to a certain extent they regulate the relationship between those two systems. The primary symptom of housewife's arm is an arm "falling asleep." This alone indicates an impaired awakening process, which is precisely the sort of disorder influenced by snake poisons. A single injection of Crotalus usually suffices to alleviate the condition; if it fails to do so, this is a sign that the condition has become organic and is no longer merely functional, so that repetition of the treatment is useless. In such cases the therapy described above should be applied, after which Crotalus may achieve the desired effect.

The variety of diseases of the spine permits a corresponding variety of therapeutic approaches. Antispasmodic therapy with belladonna, warm baths with copper sulfate, chestnut, or lavender, and careful massage can all help the organism break out of its vicious circle and open the way for therapies that address the underlying causes. Physical therapy, including movement therapy and posture exercises, can do much to relieve the stresses and postural anomalies that almost always precede diseases of the spine. Even chiropractic treatment, when practiced competently, can effect a marked improvement, although it seldom prevents relapses.

As justified and effective as these measures can be, it should also be remembered that unhealthy emotional and mental stress almost always precedes physical disease of the spine. Curative eurythmy helps the ego regulate the influence of emotional and mental forces in a very specific way. For example, vowels such as *I* (pronounced ee as in "bee"), which "reveals the inner self," help strengthen the inner forces of uprightness. Although exercises that focus solely on physical posture can be effective, they are concerned only with the end result of an inner process. Curative eurythmy effects more lasting improvements because it activates the ego.

The universal increase of complaints and diseases of the spine is due to our way of life. Everything, from education and nutrition to physical posture, plays a role in the ultimate development of organic disease. Hence the therapy and prophylaxis of diseases of the spine must seek to comprehend and modify all these influences, not just their end result.

Osteoporosis is a frequently made diagnosis today, customarily based on radiological determinations of bone density. The related issues would require a more thorough discussion. (See Vol.2 pp 137, 174; also in *Merkurstab* 1993, pp 440-447 and *Erfahrungsheilkunde*, 9/1995, pp 563-567).

Since the decline of bone calcium content during menopause has been verified and can be measured, it is believed today that the administration of calcium preparations can replenish bone calcium. This view, however, contradicts the familiar observation that the administration of a "lacking" substance cannot necessarily replenish an obvious deficiency (e.g. rickets). In such cases it was discovered that the calcium uptake was under the control of Vitamin D. For this reason it is customary today to prescribe not only calcium but also Vitamin D or calcitonin (in earlier days, for several decades, flourine was prescribed in addition to calcium).

In treating the presumed calcium deficiency it must be clearly realized, however, that though the organism can definitely be constrained to take up calcium, especially with the addition of Vitamin D, such treatment can potentially bring about a general sclerotization. The reason being that the organism can direct the calcium not only to the bones but also to the arteries.

While the above measures may well increase calcium in bone, it is generally completely forgotten, that the hardening of the bone may also make it more brittle. The proclivity to bone fractures is not just a matter of the calcium content but also of the organic bone matrix (organic silica content). For that reason silicea is indicated in every case, e.g. as highly dispersed SiO_2 (water glass), or as Equisetum silicea cultum D2. A further helpful preparation is Agaricus comp./Phosphorus, originally recommended by Rudolf Steiner for tuberculosis of the bones.

VIII

Psychiatry

RUDOLF TREICHLER

A GOOD WAY TO UNDERSTAND something is to ask how it has come into being and how it has developed. Our descriptions of the psychiatric syndromes will therefore start with their genesis within the framework of psychological development. First, however, a rough outline of that development must be sketched.

Psychological Development and Pathology

The psyche, like the physical body, is an organism, and as such has its own laws of development. These laws must be dealt with by the human being's spiritual individuality, the ego. They also decisively shape developmental crises and pathology. The most important law of psychological development is the seven-year rhythm described by Rudolf Steiner, upon which the discussion of childhood and youth in the first volume was based.[1] This rhythm, which is gaining recognition among researchers in psychology, will also form the basis of the following discussion.[2]

One aspect of this rhythm is of fundamental importance: The transitions from one developmental period to another are separated by phases of crisis, points at which "the wave of an individual's life ... crests."[3] From these "nodal points" emerge the new features of the next seven-year period. Rudolf Steiner described these transitions as "births," thereby complementing the biological approach to development with a spiritual-

---

1. R. Steiner, *Education of the Child and Early Lectures on Education* (Hudson, NY: Anthroposophic Press, 1996). See also R. Steiner, *Metamorphoses of the Soul: Path of Experience*, vols. 1 and 2 (London: Rudolf Steiner Press, 1983).
2. H. Hessenbruch, *Die Bedeutung des Siebenjahr-Rhythmus beim heranwachsenden Menschen* (Unterlengenhardt: 1938).
3. H. Thomae, "Psychologische Probleme des Erwachsenenalters," *Universitas* (1957):688.

scientific one. As with physical birth, in each of the later ones a new constituent of the human being separates out of the supersensible world to commence an individual existence, after having been previously active on an unconscious level in the formation of the person. The human being thus incarnates in seven-year stages.

A. Psychological Development

The development of the psychological organism must be distinguished from that of the living and ensouled physical body. As was illustrated in the first volume, bodily development proceeds in three stages. The physical body's essential structures are formed during the first seven years after birth. This stage ends with the change of teeth around the age of seven. Creative forming forces are then partially freed, especially in the head. The life or etheric body is then "born" and begins to lead a more independent existence. Although it remains connected with the physical body, sustaining it and causing further growth, at the same time it nourishes the child's embryonic inner life. Growth forces that are "freed up" are now metamorphosed into the ability to think. The child's temperament also begins to emerge, influenced by the forces of individual organs. In short, the child's basic mood and character are shaped now for the first time.

The psychological organism proper is born with sexual maturity around the fourteenth year. Psychological forces, like the life-forces seven years previously, are at that time partially liberated from their formative activity within the body. The psyche continues to be dominated by physiology, particularly by sexual processes, a fact reflected in the name that Rudolf Steiner gave to the psychological organism of this stage, namely the sentient (or astral) body. Now aware of itself as a separate, personal entity, the soul must come to terms with physiology before it can begin its own development, as the many crises of puberty and post-puberty attest. Personal development proper begins around the early twenties, when physical development comes to a close. By that point growth in height has stopped, and the face has taken on its mature form.

The fact that in former times people were declared "of age" when they turned 21 is therefore not without foundation. The self or ego is born around that time, after years of having shaped the physical body and the rest of the organism. It is now freed from these tasks and enters the world of social and personal responsibility.

Personal development thus begins with the birth of the self. Individuals act to acquire new capacities and to develop latent ones, enhancing rather than simply "unpacking" what they have brought with them into earthly life. The goal of the ego, the highest constituent of the human being, is to become more and more the focus of inner life. Personal development is thus really self-realization according to the laws of metamorphosis.[4]

Young people of around 20 want to experience the world directly rather than through the medium of school and apprenticeship. They want to test themselves and grow in personal strength. Formal education now gives way to self-education. Between the ages of 21 and 28, the ego is engrossed in the outer world. Rather than being the nucleus of inner life, it lives in the periphery, absorbing the world in perception and approaching it in desire. These two elements give rise to *impressions*, which allow perception and desire to mature into more personalized forms.[5] By immersing itself in both realism, the ego is able to achieve an initial balancing between self and world. It is quite healthy during this turbulent period for impressions to completely determine thought and volition. Rudolf Steiner named the aspect of the soul born at this time through the activity of the ego the sentient soul.[6] Its central question is, "How do I experience the world and myself through it?"

Around the age of 28, people begin to want to organize their experiences. Career choices are now reaffirmed or changed in the light of an overall plan for life in the world. Personal relationships and attitudes about them also undergo many changes. The central question now

4. Cf. F. W. Zeylmans van Emmichoven, *The Anthroposophical Understanding of the Soul* (Hudson, N.Y.: Anthroposophic Press, 1982), chapter 4.

5. R. Steiner, *A Psychology of Body, Soul, and Spirit: Anthroposophy, Psychosophy, Pneumatosophy* (Hudson, NY: Anthroposophic Press, 1999; previously published as *The Wisdom of Man, of the Soul, and of the Spirit* and as *Anthroposophy, Psychosophy, Pneumatosophy*).

6. For a further characterization of the dimensions of the soul, of which the sentient soul represents the first, see R. Steiner, *Theosophy*, repr. (Hudson, N.Y.: Anthroposophic Press, 1994) and *An Outlind of Esoteric Science* (Hudson, N.Y.: Anthroposophic Press, 1998). The development of these dimensions over the course of a lifetime is described by Steiner in *Metamorphoses of the Soul: Paths of Experience* (see note 1). This is elaborated in R. Treichler, *Die Entwicklung der Seele im Lebenslauf: Stufen, Stoerungen, und Erkrankungen des Seelenlebens*, 2nd ed. (Stuttgart: 1982) and pbk. (Frankfurt: 1984).

becomes, "How is the world structured, and how shall I structure my own life within it?" One person in whose life this question became particularly decisive was Goethe, who at the age of 28 forsook his creative period of "storm and stress," turning to affairs of state and to the study of the natural sciences. Judgments based on acquired opinions yield at this point to thoughtful reflection, and the next aspect of inner life, which is guided more by thinking, is born. People begin to internalize their experiences more; for most, this is the first time that they can really begin to think and judge for themselves. At the same time, feelings, deepened and clarified by repeated reflection, break free of the troublesome passions and drives of the earlier period.

This second aspect of inner life Rudolf Steiner called the intellectual or mind soul. In it the ego begins to awaken to itself; a process of internalization has begun that draws the ego from the boundary of the soul toward the center. Living between boundary and center, the ego of the mind soul strives toward a balanced, rhythmic exchange with the world. As with the sentient soul, however, development must be prepared for in earlier periods. The striving to think for oneself, to deepen feeling through reflection, should be initiated already before puberty, with an eye toward what ought to take place at the end of the twenties. The same can be said of the third epoch of adult inner development, which we shall now describe.

In the middle of life (based on a life span of seventy years), the ego should reach the center of the soul, where it can rise above the merely personal and achieve a new spiritual connection to life and to the world. As the focus and culmination of the soul's development, the fully conscious ego looks back in judgment upon its past and makes resolutions for the future. Up to this point, individuals reflect on the phenomena of the world and on themselves; now, in moments of true knowledge, they experience the fusion of their thoughts and the phenomena into an organic whole. The question about the structure of the world and of their own existence now becomes: "How do I find the world's true nature and realize my own being within it?"

"Hindsight," or reflection on the past, now develops into "foresight," a faculty toward which the mind soul already strives. This faculty attempts to comprehend the forces that have created the world and that continually recreate it.[7] It can do this in artistic or scientific form:

Goethe, for example, after studying the ordering principles of the plant kingdom, discovered the "archetypal plant" (*Urpflanze*), the primal creative essence of all plants, in his thirty-eighth year. All of us, however, who desire to become "artists at life" can practice this by finding our own special purpose, the unique idea hidden in the material of our lives. Whenever the connection of a physical with a spiritual reality is experienced in true presence of mind and manifested in individual life, the third dimension of inner life, the consciousness soul, is at work. In the consciousness soul, the ego awakens completely and becomes conscious of the nature of the world, ultimately even of the spiritual world. This unification of self-knowledge and world-knowledge is exemplified by the discoveries that Goethe made during his travels in Italy: the statement, "In Rome I first found myself,"[8] is complemented by, "Here is necessity, here is God." Both are united in a third: "I would like...to achieve spiritual eternity."[9]

In the ego of the consciousness soul, the eternal, the spirit shines forth, the spirit that incarnates in the human being through the ego and subordinates psychological forces to itself. Just as independent thinking emerged from the life of sense impressions to produce the mind soul, so now does a creative will emerge from the mind soul, borne by latter's expanding life of feeling. This can lead both to what we have called foresight and to the realization of consciously grasped spiritual aims.

With this step, the human being becomes truly adult, for "inner maturity is achieved only by those who live consciously."[10] Many things in the soul that were previously only germinal now reach fruition. People who before were primarily receptive can now become creative for the world.

The period of the consciousness soul lasts roughly from the ages of 35 to 42. After that, psychological development in a strict sense comes

7. H. Hessenbruch, *Die Bedeutung des Siebenjahr-Rhythmus beim heranwachsenden Menschen* (Unterlengenhardt: 1938).

8. C, Bühler, *Der menschliche Lebenslauf* (Leipzig: 1933), p. 301. (New ed. Göttingen, 1959).

9. Quote taken from R. Steiner, *Goethe's World -View* (Spring Valley, NY: Mercury Press, 1984). Concerning the seven-year rhythm in Goethe's life, see also F. Hiebel, *Goethe* (Bern: 1961), p. 47f. and R. Treichler, *Metamorphosen im Lebenslauf: Krankheit und Entwicklung in Goethes Leben* (Dornach: 1984).

10. A. L. Vischer, *Seelische Wandlungen beim alternden Menschen* (Basel: 1944), p. 215.

to an end, and the members of the germinal spiritual organism first begin to stir.[11]

An analogy from the plant kingdom may help summarize. The sentient soul can be compared to the leaves of a plant. Like the plant through its leaves, the psychological organism through the sentient soul encounters the surroundings and builds itself up out of elements from those surroundings. The "interiorizing" mind soul, on the other hand, corresponds to the calyx. The consciousness soul, which reflects spirit back into the world, is comparable to the blossom, which in the second half of life begins to bear fruit for the world.

This analogy also makes it clear that when new dimensions of the soul emerge, the previously developed ones continue to exist. The plant does not lose its leaves when it blossoms; it needs its leaves to continue growing. In a similar way, the sentient soul can be a source of renewal throughout life, but in order to do so its forces (or those of the other aspects of the soul) must be continually re-enlivened. Naturally they must also be metamorphosed into the form appropriate to the particular stage of life. Goethe had this in mind when he referred to his "repeated puberties." Every human being who strives to change in this way will continue to learn and grow throughout life.

At the end of this survey, it must be emphasized that the developmental pattern we have described is not a rigid schema, but a basic rhythm of human life. Like every rhythm, it is subject to modification, in this case by individual nature and destiny. It is therefore not surprising that, more so than minors, adults occasionally take longer or, less frequently, less time than normal to go through a particular developmental phase. Such irregularities are not in themselves pathological; they become so only in the context of verifiable disorders of psychological development. It is to

---

11. A thorough presentation of psychological development and its disorders is found in B. Lievegoed, *Phases: The Spiritual Rhythms of Adult Life* (London: Rudolf Steiner Press, 1997): in R. Treichler, *Die Entwicklung der Seele im Lebenslauf* (see note 6); in H. E. Lauer, *Vom richtigen Altwerden* (Freiburg: 1972); in N. Glas, *Jugendzeit und mittleres Lebensalter* (Stuttgart: 1960); and in D. Lauenstein, *Der Lebenslauf und seine Gesetze* (Stuttgart: 1974). See also H. Hahn, *Der Lebenslauf als Kunstwerk* (Stuttgart: 1966) and R. Treichler, "Lebensstufen und Seelenentwicklung," *Anthroposophisch-Medizinisches Jahrbuch*, vol. 2 (Dornach, 1951). A number of relevant observations are collected in C. Bühler, *Der menschliche Lebenslauf*, and M. Moers, *Die Entwicklungsphasen des menschlichen Lebens* (Ratingen: 1953).

these that we shall now turn, referring where appropriate to the connections of psychological development with adult human physiology.

B. Disorders of Psychological Development

Since the source of all impulses for psychological development is the ego, everything that hinders the ego's development leads to disorders of inner life. The ego first awakens to itself in the formation of opinions based on personal impressions. This activity should be schooled from puberty on as a preparation for later independent thinking. Relevant sentiments and feelings should be elicited and thoughts clarified. Any opportunities of this sort that are missed at this time ultimately weaken the ego. What is appropriate after puberty, however, can be hazardous before: the premature encouragement of independent judgment also weakens the ego. Contemporary civilization tends especially toward this latter error, with the result that young people tend to borrow their opinions from others and ultimately to accept common prejudices. In the first case, the adolescent is inwardly understimulated; in the latter, the preadolescent is prevented from drawing his or her judgments out of the depths of a thoroughly individualized psychological organism.

Both conditions tend to be found together today. Adolescents develop a superficial, one-sidedly intellectual kind of judgment while their ego fails to unfold itself fully in the realm of the feelings and the will. Soul and ego fail from the beginning to fully penetrate the body, remaining trapped in the head, which in healthy development is merely their point of entry. This can complicate all of later development, since the soul, if it has not properly integrated itself into the body in the first place, cannot properly disengage from the body later as it should. This point is addressed in greater detail below in the section on schizophrenia.

1. Developmental Disorders of the Sentient Soul

Young people who are not protected from some of the influences of modern civilization will have a relatively difficult time. After all, very few of the sensory stimuli afforded by our artificial environment evoke rich or active inner responses. Nevertheless, it is only when young people lack interest, even for valuable impressions, that their inner life begins to atrophy. This lack of interest is frequently due to faulty education and results in an inability to "digest" perceptions properly. The encounter between perceptions and desires, which should stimulate interest and thus open inner life to the world, fails to occur, and emotional development suffers accordingly.

Many young people today are succumbing to an inner emptiness they call "boredom." The innocuous designation, of course, belies the fact that boredom can literally be deadly, since in extreme cases it can lead to suicide. Those who do not attempt to kill themselves may resort instead to drugs or violence. No matter how empty the soul might be, the elemental desire of the sentient soul or sentient body makes itself felt. Since young people cannot be satisfied with undigested impressions, they seek sensational or ecstatic experiences instead that require no inner elaboration. Although such experiences bring rapid fulfillment and movement to an empty, paralyzed soul, they do not provide the lasting impressions that young people so deeply desire. Instead, they merely evoke emotions, which—in contrast to differentiated impressions—go as quickly as they come. The soul feels its emptiness all the more keenly after the intoxication passes.

Extensive investigations of such phenomena prompted Viktor Frankl to speak of a new, collective type of neurosis that can develop out of boredom and climaxes in the experience of an "existential vacuum." Sufferers become convinced that life is meaningless and gradually lose all initiative. The depression that results defies every traditional treatment. Frankl, quoting Boss, who spoke of boredom as "the neurosis of the future," added that the future has already arrived.[12] From our point of view, both Boss and Frankl were describing the stunted development of the sentient soul, that is, the failure to master the first crisis of inner development, which occurs in the early twenties.

2. *Developmental Disorders of the Intellectual or Mind Soul*

After the crisis just described, the modern person's sentient soul still usually develops to a certain degree. The second crisis, the one most common in our time, involves the transition from emotional judgments

12. V. E. Frankl, "Die Heimholung der Psychotherapie," in *Medizin. Acta psychotherap* (1962):99–110 and *Anthropologische Grundlagen der Psychotherapie* (Bern: 1975), p. 13f.

and borrowed opinions to an individual search for truth, from fluctuating emotions and sensations to greater internalization and maturity (*Gemüt*). It is at this point that the development of the soul nowadays tends to come to a standstill. The preceding discussion, as well as a large body of experience, suggests that this transition occurs around 28, when the intellectual or mind soul is born.

Toward the end of the twenties, the curve of physical vitality levels off: up through the mid-thirties, the body receives one final reinforcement and consolidation. Initially, a parallel tendency can be observed in psychological development, which, as before, bases itself on the life of the body. The sentient soul's instinctive liveliness gradually fades; orientation in the world must now occur more with the help of thinking than of feeling. If, however, independent thinking fails to develop or develops only imperfectly, the attitude that was appropriate for the sentient soul will be retained and henceforth merely reinforced and consolidated. For example, other people's thoughts will continue to be borrowed; however, since these thoughts no longer inspire, they become mere prescriptions and dogmas. On the emotional level, drives that cannot be sublimated and internalized are instead anesthetized in order to avoid the inner conflicts to which they give rise. The chief means of the anesthetization in our time is the mass media, the so-called "entertainment industry."

If the forces of the sentient soul are preserved rather than metamorphosed, a rudimentary, ghostly mind soul is born, one that fails to liberate itself sufficiently from the body, which is now merely consolidating itself. In such cases the oft-heard complaint that people today are less cultured, have less character, and are ultimately less wise than those of earlier times is certainly correct. In fact, it is arguable that many modern adults not only do not know "more" than the young but also do not know "better," that is, that they lack any knowledge of a deeper, more mature sort than that possessed by the young. The "generation gap" so widely discussed in the 1960s was no doubt due to young people's perception that their elders were in many cases not really wiser and had not developed emotionally any further than the young themselves.

A person who does not take advantage of the possibilities of the mind soul's birth will also not be able to produce anything new for the world. At best he or she will be able to consolidate and perfect earlier achievements, or to realize an as yet unfulfilled youthful ideal.[13] This is connected with the fact that native talents frequently peter out as the twenties come to an end.[14] "What you have inherited from your fathers, earn it, that you may possess it." This maxim of Goethe's, in extended form, now becomes critical for psychological development. The inherited and the acquired must now be made one's own. This task begins in the mind soul but can be completed only later, within the consciousness soul. If, however, the mind soul fails to develop at all, then the "inner space" necessary for the later completion of this task is not created.

Many people at this stage of their lives are not satisfied with the mere preservation of previous achievements. For them, emptiness and boredom once again rear their heads. Consequently, such people begin to feel an urge to reawaken their lost youthfulness, to restimulate their languishing sentient souls. Some try merely to look and act young (many with the aid of hormones designed for that purpose), while others resort to alcohol, drugs, television, or enthusiasm for sports to fill the inner void. Rather than furthering the development of the sentient soul's neglected forces, however, these actions merely agitate them. Illusory gratification leads to the need for stronger and stronger doses of intoxicants. The impoverishment of the sentient soul accelerates and eventually causes regression into the period of the sentient body, meaning that experiences and desires become increasingly physical and eventually can be gratified only in that way. The purest expression of this is drug addiction, in which the physical body can literally no longer survive without the drug.

3. Developmental Disorders of the Consciousness Soul

In the early to mid-thirties, psychological development should begin to detach itself from bodily life; the consciousness soul should emerge from the accelerating process of physical decay and condense the body's formative forces into inner powers. In this way it can gain a new, wakeful consciousness, a consciousness that may even encompass the spiritual world. The consciousness soul's task is to make the peak in the biological

13. See R. Steiner, *Aspects of Human Evolution* (Hudson, N.Y.: Anthroposophic Press, 1987), lecture 1.

14. Cf. A. Steffen, *Die Krisis im Leben des Künstlers* (Zurich: 1925).

curve, which is valid for everyone, into a turning point in inner development, a point from which the soul gradually ascends into the world of living spirit. If the consciousness soul cannot or can only partially achieve this, then it remains chained to the decaying physical body, thereby creating the basis for the hypochondriac, depressive, and delusional illnesses of the aging. Physical deterioration dominates and depresses the person's inner life whether or not he or she is aware of it. Normal physical deterioration is here accompanied by a psychological regression into the bodily realm. The resulting subconscious experience of physical diminishment can, when projected outward, lead to delusions of poverty or even of being robbed.

The so-called midlife crisis, the third in the soul's development, is a crisis of the consciousness soul. Often it has its roots in the second crisis and is then all the more difficult to overcome. Independent thought and the inwardness of the mind soul are vital preconditions for the development of the consciousness soul; without them, the consciousness soul merely rigidifies into a cold, intellectualistic awareness. On the other hand, a person may have developed a mind soul but be unable to move beyond it. In either case the midlife crisis is insurmountable. A more or less imperfect, ghostly consciousness soul arises that clings to the body and is drawn into its deterioration.

A consciousness soul that does not achieve awareness of the living spirit is filled instead with the inner consequences of its arrested development. Connected with this is the fact that at midlife, previously latent conflicts originating in earlier periods can now make themselves felt for the first time, for example, the suppressed crisis of the 28th year. The same is true for emotional illnesses rooted in still earlier seven-year periods of the patient's life. From midlife on, all are experienced more consciously and become more well-defined.

The crisis of the consciousness soul is thus ultimately a spiritual crisis. Through it, the materialistic world view can become painful experience and practice. Around the age of 28, the ego begins to pull in from the periphery of the soul toward the center; this process occurs in everyone, whether or not it is affirmed or the center is ultimately found. If it is not, if the consciousness soul does not find the spiritual content of the world, then the soul loses its former intuitive, emotional relationship with the outside world. Inner life shrivels rather than condenses; instead of inwardness, isolation is achieved. People who fail to grasp the inwardness of the world at this stage are instead captivated by its material, outer surface, which from then on appears to them as the only reality. They feel themselves to be intellectual observers, outsiders who are "thrown into the world" (Heidegger). The spiritual "all" that suffuses the world becomes for them a "nothing."

The consciousness soul is called upon "to find the all" in this "nothing" (Goethe). However, it never accomplishes this once and for all. Every human being struggling for the consciousness soul must repeatedly confront the prospect of meaninglessness; indeed, this is the precondition for continuous spiritual renewal.

In order to be completely understood, the developmental disorders of the individual soul must be seen against the background of humanity's spiritual evolution as a whole. According to Rudolf Steiner, the modern European's inner development proceeds of its own accord only up through the age of 27, the last phase of the sentient soul. After that, only individual effort can produce further progress.

This has not always been the case. In ancient times, human beings developed and acquired knowledge well into advanced age. During the first half of life, the soul developed naturally along with the body. The body's gradual decay in the second half of life led, with the help of the gods, to a flowering of the spirit, which freed the soul from the body. Older people developed a natural, god-given wisdom that today must be achieved through individual effort.

As history progressed, the age at which psychological development stopped of its own accord became ever lower. In other words, the soul's healthy dependency on the body has ended sooner and sooner, and the ego has been called upon and enabled that much earlier to take charge of the soul's further development. If it fails to assume this responsibility, then the soul, rather than being inspired through the physical body as it was in former times, is instead "overwhelmed" by it.[15] The result is a pathological dependency on the body such as was described above.

Since the dawn of the natural scientific era, humankind as a whole has had the capacity to develop the consciousness soul within itself; our

15. See R. Steiner, *Aspects of Human Evolution* (Hudson, N.Y.: Anthroposophic Press, 1987), lecture 1.

greater awareness of details in the outer world can be extended to encompass the spiritual world as well. The light of the consciousness soul has since illuminated all preceding stages of inner development. Individual development is enhanced if every stage up to and beyond the birth of the consciousness soul is shaped and guided by enlightened consciousness.

C. Neurosis

1.Psychosomatic Connections

Many adult neuroses, although prepared for by earlier developmental disorders, are ultimately caused by the halt in psychological development just described. The consequences of this half can extend throughout life. This is not to deny that neuroses are also conditioned by individual circumstances or by specific emotional traumas; however, the latter, in order to produce neurosis, must act upon a properly disposed medium. Included in this disposition are not only the psychophysical organism of childhood and youth, but also the way in which this organism has developed further. (The unfortunate designation "neurosis" is retained here to avoid confusion.)

People in their twenties have a tendency to become trapped in the experiences and feelings, the drives and affects of the developing sentient soul. Thereafter they may, as was mentioned, seek to dull or to "ration" these drives in order to continue to be a "normal," functioning member of society. Some people at first succeed so well in this that they have only minor symptoms if any at all. However, repression is becoming more and more difficult, and even those who succeed at it experience periods when the repressed psychological forces begin to rumble again ominously. At such times neurosis may develop. It is significant that repression for the sake of social conformity is no longer a given, whereas neurotic disorders are unquestionably on the rise.

A tendency toward neurosis is present in all emotionally labile persons who have retained a certain youthfulness. Such people even tend to look younger than they actually are.[16] Their sentient souls tend to be

16. A. L. Vischer, *Seelische Wandlungen* (see note 10), p. 202.

stronger, causing many to be artistically gifted or to retain their artistic talents longer than usual. The development of the mind soul is relatively difficult for these people, and the danger is especially great that the unmetamorphosed inner forces of youth may lead to a psychic disorder. On the other hand, neurotics of this type are also more capable of growing through and beyond their illness than those in whom the sentient soul is underdeveloped and the ego is not fully born.

For both, however, the following holds true: Every soul that is not mastered by the ego is subject to its own inherent law. That law is determined by the universal polarity of pleasure and aversion, of sympathy and antipathy.[17] Either the sentient body and soul are given over to the world in pleasure, or they experience themselves set against it in aversion. All sensations and emotions can be seen in terms of this polarity, which determines the soul of ... neurotic to an excessive degree. Extreme devotion and love coexist in him with extreme self-assertion and hate, fanatic striving for power with the profoundest feelings of inferiority, all without a psychological middle ground. The ego cannot exercise its usual function of balancing extremes; like a rudderless ship, it is driven hither and thither on the waves of the emotional sea, being first flung high into ecstasy and then plunged into the deepest despair. Here the physiological situation of puberty is repeated in individualized and pathologically intensified form.

In reaction to such externally caused, rapid mood swings, the ego may attempt to anticipate and forestall unpleasantly intense emotions, leading to what is known in psychiatry as "overcompensation." From what has been said, however, it should be clear that such attempts cannot succeed, since they remain on the emotional level and thus only cause further inner instability. Even if the ego should succeed in neutralizing an emotion, it has not thereby come to grips with it. Only when passion is transformed rather than controlled can feeling and then character arise. For example, anger, once mastered, can turn into love, whereas if merely suppressed, it can become fear.[18] Both types of transformation will be discussed later. We touch here upon the vast subject of

17. R. Steiner, *GG*, lecture 6. See also Steiner, *Theosophy*, and F. W. Zeylmans van Emmichoven, *The Anthroposophical Understanding of the Soul.*

18. R. Steiner, *Metamorphoses of the Soul*, p. 28ff.

emotional repression, a phenomenon that arises through forces of antipathy acting from consciousness into the depths of the psyche.

The human ego is an extension of the spiritual world. If it remains trapped within the confines of the soul, however, it follows a vicious circle. Every feeling calls forth another; all the ego can do is surrender, or at best give the feeling an individual coloring. The feeling of humiliation, for example, can engender a wish to humiliate others, which increases the fear of requital, which in turn increases sensitivity to possible humiliation by others: so the vicious circle progresses.[19]

Psychoanalysis follows such labyrinthine paths into the subconscious, investigating the forms that neuroses take. As a first step, this is indispensable: however, to find the true causes and an eventual cure, it is necessary to take psychological development into account as it was sketched above. Insight into that development reveals that psychiatry must be extended in two directions: the spiritual and the physical.

The spiritual direction recognizes that the ego is the core of the personality and the ultimate goal of psychological development. The physical direction attempts to discover the role of the physical body in mental illness. Psychopathological processes do not spring full-fledged out of nothing; like the soul itself, they gradually emerge from physical development and are closely connected with physiology. Furthermore, their connection with the *entire* physical body must be considered, not just their connection with the brain. To regard the brain as the only organ of the psyche, as is done today, is to ignore other and equally vital relations between mind and body. From an anthroposophical point of view, the brain is merely the point where these relations enter conscious awareness. From there they can be modified by the ego throughout the entire organism.

The addition of a physical emphasis to psychiatry will aid in understanding healthy inner life as well. For one thing, it will increase awareness that the soul remains closely tied to the physical body even as it emerges from it. In childhood, the higher constituents of the human being are active primarily in the physical body; later they gradually learn how to use the body as an instrument for conscious aims. No physical structure can arise in the absence of inner and spiritual activity, any

19. K. Horney, *Der neurotische Mensch unserer Zeit* (Stuttgart: 1951), p. 175.

more than a musical instrument can be built without thought. Furthermore, just as music cannot be made without an instrument, so too is life impossible without the instrument of the physical body. Life, however, is much more closely connected to its instrument than is music, since it creates and sustains that instrument itself.[20]

As was shown earlier, the soul, like the physical body, is an organism. The living physical body is constituted by distinct activities and forces. Is it not likely that body and soul are connected in such a way that each psychological force is tied to a specific organ of the body? That, having developed out of that organ, it continues to use it as an instrument of its activity? Such correspondences, described in detail by Rudolf Steiner, are of inestimable value in the investigation and treatment of psychological illnesses.[21]

2. *Organ Neurosis and Psychoneurosis*

Developmental disorders and the psychological illnesses that can result from them lead us to consider where psychological forces go if they cannot be transformed. It seems logical that they would sink back into the physical organs form which they first arose. When development is reversed in this way, an originally healthy situation is pathologically repeated. Psychological forces that in childhood were unconsciously active in building up the body become active in the body again, but, since they are now accompanied by consciousness, their effects are disruptive and catabolic rather than constructive.

This burdening of an organ with forces of the psyche and ego results in what is called an "organ neurosis," which in turn affects experience in

20. W. Bühler, *Living With Your Body* (London: Rudolf Steiner Press, 1979).
21. More recent researchers who have pointed to the possibility of such connections include H. Schultz-Hencke; see his work, *Der gehemmte Mensch* (Stuttgart: 1947), p. 197. Another school, represented by M. Boss (*Einführung in die psychosomatische Medizin,* Bern 1954) and B. Staehelin (*Die funktionellen kardio-vaskularen Störungen als psychosomatische Syndrome,* Bern 1965), views the basic mood as dependent upon a particular organ system, which in turn is connected with a particular relationship with the world. Should the latter be frustrated in some way, the disturbance is carried back into the organ system, producing organ neurosis. This interesting view can be expanded to include the developmental aspect presented here. The relationship to the schools of psychiatric thought is presented in R. Treichler, *Erweiterung der Psychiatrie durch Anthroposophie* (Dornach: 1984) and by M. Treichler in an afterword to R. Steiner, *Spirituelle Psychologie* (Stuttgart: 1984).

a way characteristic of that particular organ, that is, in a way characteristic of that organ's relationship to inner life. Every abnormality in the life of the soul is based on abnormal bodily function.[22] When an organ has been "put out of tune" by psychological forces, the soul will sometimes focus its entire energy on that organ. The organ's impairments will then enter consciousness as physical symptoms. On the other hand, the source of the disruption need not enter consciousness at all. In that case, experience as a whole will be colored by fear, confusion, excitement, or depression—all "dissonances" arising from the "mistuned instrument," the organ. The first situation corresponds to organ neurosis and is characterized by psychosomatic complaints; the second represents psychoneurosis proper, a pathological mode of experiencing that always has an organic foundation. Both forms of neurosis can be combined, although at any given time one will tend to be more conspicuous than the other.

The first symptom of a reactive effect of an organ on mental life is generally a feeling of anxiety that differs according to the organ involved. This is the "basic anxiety" that accompanies every neurosis.[23] "Anxiety" is derived from a Latin word connoting narrowness.[24] Sinking back into the confines of the physical organism, the soul is stricken with fear of physical influences that affect or threaten to affect it, including external influences mediated by the physical body. This is the physical aspect of neurotic anxiety, which we shall treat later in more detail. The spiritual aspect arises when neurotic anxiety expands into the primal fear experienced when the human being first abandoned the transcendent, paradisiacal connection with the gods for the dark confines of earthly, physical existence. This narrowing later gave rise to fear of the unknown, the void, nothingness.

Modern civilization is structured in such a way that the burdening of physical organs with psychological forces can begin as early as childhood. Child absorb psychological influences from the environment that, if the child's etheric body can assimilate them, partly shape the organs. If, on the other hand, these influences are foreign to the child's nature, as is

22. R. Steiner, *Health Care as a Social Issue* (Spring Valley, N.Y.: Mercury Press, 1984).
23. K. Horney, *Der neurotische Mensch unserer Zeit*, p. 175.
24. "Anxiety" derives from the Latin *angere*, meaning "to choke or oppress"; it is also related to "anguish," which derives from *angustia*, a Latin word meaning "narrowness" (see Hoad, *The Concise Oxford Dictionary of English Etymology*, 1986).

often the case today, they remain unassimilated in the organic sphere, disrupting both organ function and the soul. Because of this, psychological forces cannot dissociate the way they should from physical organs. They remain pathologically fixated upon the intruding external influences, vainly attempting to overcome and assimilate them.[25] Thus even in childhood, neuroses can arise or the seed of later neuroses be sown.

As we have mentioned, between the physical and the mental realms lies the realm of the etheric or life-body, where metamorphoses between the physical and mental take place. It therefore stands to reason that whenever the soul initiates a pathological organ process, the process must first be transferred to the etheric body. In the fourth (as yet unpublished) volume of this book, the human water organism is described as the characteristic vehicle of the etheric body. Incipient functional disorders indicate a disturbance in the etheric body and hence make themselves felt primarily within the fluid organism. The first sign is disruptions in blood circulation, known to be a highly sensitive indicator of psychological processes. Disruptions of normal secretory processes then follow. When congestion and its corollary, spasm, move yet a stage deeper, movement disturbances of the organs arise, which in turn can change gradually into inflammatory or degenerative disorders and thus ultimately destroy the organ's physical structure. Functional-neurotic disorders can thus lead to actual organic deformations and disease.

The same is true of psychoneuroses, which are based on functional disorders. Here as well, the etheric boy mediates between the circulatory, secretory, and movement disorders of particular organs and the soul, whose experiences are accordingly modified.

For some time a discipline known as psychosomatic medicine has endeavored to link organic disease with psychological phenomena and processes. The goal of anthropomorphically-oriented medicine is even more concrete and comprehensive than this: it adopts the existing approaches of psychosomatic medicine and attempts to extend them in the two directions discussed above, the physical and the spiritual. This includes determining the connection of a specific organ and its genesis with psychological processes. It also includes recognizing and treating organic and corresponding emotional illnesses as disorders of personal

25. Cf. R. Steiner, *SM,* lecture 16.

and spiritual development. This, however, is possible only when the physician recognizes and makes therapeutic use of the connection of the organs and of personal development with the entire cosmos.

D. Psychosis

Psychosis—like psychoneurosis—results from the influence of organic disorders upon the mind. This was one of Rudolf Steiner's most basic insights in the realm of psychiatry. While many physical illnesses are rooted in the psyche, in the case of psychoses the reverse is true. "The primary factor in so-called 'mental illnesses' lies in the organs." It is through these and with appropriate medications that psychosis should be treated. The spirit itself cannot fall ill; the ego, through which spirit lives in the human being, is always healthy.[26]

But, according to Steiner, neither can the soul fall ill. "Illnesses of the mind or soul are essentially impossible."[27] So-called "mental illnesses" are rooted neither in emotional nor in spiritual life. On the other hand, the migration of physical disorders into the soul, which will be discussed more thoroughly below, is a pathogenic process. The soul does not become ill of itself, but it can be made ill by the body. Even then it is not essentially ill, but rather only in its perceptible functioning, that is, in its thinking, feeling, and willing, its three basic forces, each of which is closely linked to specific processes in the body ("the threefold nature of the human organism"). It is in this sense that Steiner spoke of "a pathological inner life,"[28] of "defects" of the will and of thought, and of "deformed thoughts,"[29] all of which are rooted in the body. The expression "mental illness" is used in this chapter only in this sense. Even when the illness is ultimately due to emotional factors (e.g. trauma), the latter never produce the illness directly; they always first leave their mark on the body in the form of an organic disorder, and by that means indirectly produce a psychological illness.

---

26. R. Steiner, *SM,* lecture 13.
27. R. Steiner, *Die Ergänzung heutiger Wissenschaften durch Anthroposophie* (GA 73), p. 290f. Not translated; typescripts of translations of individual lectures available.
28. R. Steiner, "Sickness and Healing," in *Metamorphoses of the Soul,* vol. 2.
29. R. Steiner, *CE,* lecture 1.

The purest expression of this concept may be found in endogenous psychoses, which for that reason will form the basis of our discussion of psychosis in general. In contrast to neuroses, endogenous psychoses are based on deeper, often hereditary organic disorders, which cannot be understood—at least not solely—as manifestations of emotional disorders. The idea of reincarnation allows the organic bases of psychosis to be seen as the physical result of a disordered inner development in a previous life on earth. Incarnating individuals use the hereditary material of their physical ancestors as a means of expressing the spiritual result of a previous life, in order to come to terms with their individual destiny and thus further their spiritual development.[30]

The disposition toward a particular form of psychosis is embodied in the physical constitution. Kretschmer's classic studies have shown that ectomorphs are more disposed toward schizophrenia, whereas endomorphs (pyknics) tend toward manic-depressive insanity.[31] The constitution, which includes both physical build and temperament, indicates how spiritual and physical existence are connected. From this it can be gathered that the etheric body, the substrate of both physical and spiritual development, shapes the constitution. The constitution, moreover, can change over time. Kretschmer, for example, postulated "reforming" processes of the "highly plastic hereditary disposition in the first stages of life," and described actual cases of constitutional change. From this it follows that the course of psychological development may contribute to the emergence of psychoses that might otherwise remain latent within the constitution. Psychological forces that fail to develop "congest" within organs that are already weakened and deformed in their finer structure. There they intensify the existing disorders and deformations and can thus initiate the psychotic process, which carries the congested forces out of the organ, but in a pathologically excessive way.

In the psychotic process, physically active forces of the soul that have been hindered in their development by a defective organ take hold of conscious inner life.[32] Just as psychological forces that have become conscious should remain in the soul, so should forces that have

---

30. See note 6.

31. E. Kretschmer, *Körperbau und Charakter* (Berlin: 1944), p. 297f.

32. R. Steiner, *Physiology and Therapeutics* (Spring Valley, N.Y.: Mercury Press, 1986), lecture 2. See also R. Steiner, *GG*, lecture 6.

remained subconscious remain and act within the body. Whereas in organ neurosis (and many organ diseases) the boundary between body and soul is overstepped in the direction of the body, in psychosis and psychoneurosis it is overstepped in the other direction. Disturbed forces of the soul and ego rise up out of the body and affect inner life. In psychosis, however, these forces are disturbed in a more profound, organic way than in psychoneurosis; furthermore, unlike psychoneurosis, psychosis also involves the partial liberation of the structuring and growth-producing forces of the defective organ protein.[33] These forces impress their structure upon the soul and cause the formation there of more of less "malignant neoplasms."

The formative tendencies of a particular organ can often be recognized in psychotic patients' modeling or painting. The "neoplasms" with which the soul is affected are primarily hallucinations and delusions. Most hallucinations, particularly acoustic ones, manifest something of what inwardly moves the patients. An anxiety, a wish, a sudden idea, a memory or fragment of a memory becomes to them a voice that appears to come from without. Prior to actual auditory hallucination, however, the patients may merely experience their own thoughts becoming audible. These phenomena all express the excarnation typical of psychosis, which involves an "extrusion" of internal formative forces, so that previously inner corporeality now appears to become "outer." This is why the environment of psychotic patients seems to them to be so "full."

In the growth of delusions, organic formative forces magnify and distort a complex of mental pictures in complete defiance of the laws of logic. The patients' critical faculties are completely overwhelmed by the foreign process invading inner life, a process that at the beginning of the patients themselves may experience as sinister. For example, an isolated, thoroughly normal emotional hurt that has crystallized into a complex of memory pictures can grow into an unbounded, totally irrational persecution complex. In the end the victims perceive the world solely in terms of this complex: they feel they are being persecuted by every imaginable type of person. In reality, however, it is the forces of their own organism that pursue them. Every persecution complex is at bottom the expression of a primal persecution by the psychotic process itself.

33. R. Steiner, *GG*.

Rudolf Steiner distinguished between forces originating in metabolism and growth on the one hand and latent "force-extracts" on the other that have a formative action only in the next earthly life. Within the present framework we can do no more than indicate this distinction.[34]

1. Metabolic Disorders in Psychosis

The organic weaknesses and defects associated with psychosis are also accompanied by metabolic disorders. These in turn exercise a negative influence upon inner life. Our understanding of these disorders has been greatly enhanced by the results of pathophysiological research during the last few decades. Specific results will be discussed below in conjunction with each organ. In general, however, it can be said that in no case do the organic findings correspond to the severity of the psychopathology. Especially in schizophrenic psychoses, it was found that the metabolic disorders diminished or eluded detection entirely precisely when the psychological symptoms became most pronounced. Researchers therefore concluded that the metabolic disorders had no causal significance. Due to this and other objections, initial optimism in this field yielded to widespread skepticism. Only recently have grounds for renewed hope been found. The outlines of a "biological psychiatry" are being worked out, albeit largely within a reductionist framework. The tendency, in fact, is to locate the causes of psychopathology exclusively in the brain.[35]

The disproportion between metabolic disorders and the severity of psychopathology becomes less puzzling in the light of the following observation: severe physical illness usually causes the psychological symptoms of a psychosis to diminish or even to disappear. Symmetry suggests that the

34. R. Steiner, *Therapeutic Insights: Earthly and Cosmic Laws* (Spring Valley, N.Y.: Mercury Press, 1984), lectures 3 & 4.

35. The results of earlier research are collected in O. Bumke, *Lehrbuch für Geisteskrankheiten* (Munich: 1942). Research results of more recent decades appear in surveys in C. Riebling et al., *Fortschritte der Neurologie und Psychiatrie.* Regarding depression and mania, see also Menninger-Lerchenthal, *Periodizität in der Psychopathologie* (Vienna: 1960). Recent biological research and theories are summarized by J. R. Smythies in *The Neurological Foundations of Psychiatry* (Oxford: Blackwell Scientific Publications, 1966) and by H. Beckmann in *Biologische Psychiatrie* (Stuttgart: 1982).

reverse should also be true, that organic disorders should become less noticeable when the disease process shifts back from the physical into the psychic domain. In contemporary psychiatry, the concept of "change of field" has been coined for this dynamic.[36] During this shift, the metabolic disorders could recede to such an extent that they might no longer be detectable by customary methods.[37] However, this would not necessarily negate their ultimate responsibility for the psychosis.

The subtlety of metabolic disorders is thus no reason to deny their causal significance. As research on hormones and trace elements has shown, even the minutest quantities of certain substances can have marked effects upon experience; who is to say that small amounts of pathological metabolic products may not have equally potent effects? Future research into the genesis of psychiatric disorders will have to take "the effectiveness of highly diluted substances" (Kolisko) into account. When such substances are produced, or when the function of a particular organ is subtly disturbed, the cause may be a mild, chronic metabolic disorder that the soul and ego have attempted to overcome but failed.[38] As a result, they sometimes withdraw from the process. However, this does not allow them to escape the problem, since the deformed organ's neglected forces also eventually withdraw from the body, carrying the unresolved disorder into the soul by way of the etheric body, which also partially withdraws. This leads to pathological distortions and exaggerations of the temperament, which in turn set the stage for the psychotic process. In severe psychosis, the tendency toward partial and temporary withdrawals of the soul and ego from the body can lead to complete obliviousness to earthly concerns.

Minor organic disorders are thus the most likely to cause psychiatric disorders. An increase in organic symptoms indicates that the soul and ego have renewed their efforts to overcome the pathological process in the body. Because of this, their own pathological symptoms diminish, in some cases yielding to the mostly nonspecific mental disorders that accompany physical disease ("exogenous reaction type"). Rudolf

36. H. Bürger-Prinz and F. I. M. Winzenried in *Probleme der phasischen Psychosen* (Stuttgart: 1961), p. 8 and p. 27f.
37. This promises to be a fruitful area of application for the blood crystallization and capillary dynamic blood tests described in vol. 1, which can detect even subtle disorders.
38. R. Steiner, *SM*, lecture 20.

Steiner frequently used the word "subtle" to describe the organic disorders connected with mental illness. For example, certain falterings of the will he attributed to a "subtle liver defect."[39] Infiltration of the lung by a substance "in subtle distribution" could be important in the genesis of epilepsy.[40]

The discussion of individual psychoses will show that the crucial factor in their genesis—besides organic disorders—is an enhanced emotional receptivity to physical influences. This factor is just as important as the environment. As we shall show, it can be inferred from a premorbid character. It can also result from a particular life situation, such as a congestion of psychological forces resulting from a developmental disorder, a general sensitivity at or around the nodal points of psychological development, or other special experiences that render a person oversensitive to physical influences.

Such factors enable us to explain why certain metabolic disorders and pathological metabolic products provoke mental illness in some people and not in others. This fact has understandably contributed to the skepticism regarding the role of metabolic disorders in psychosis. Such skepticism can be overcome only if the whole human being, whose uniqueness is expressed in a particular disposition, is also taken into account.

In summary, physical and emotional illnesses arise when metamorphoses that should occur at particular points in inner development remain incomplete. The healthy transformation of forces of growth into forces of thought is so thorough that the forces of growth wholly subordinate themselves to the laws of logic in constructing a sequence of thoughts. In a pathological transformation, the growth forces, although they have left the realm of the "cosmic logic" that maintains the form of the physical organs, do not completely enter the realm of human logic.[41] This failure explains the logically incomprehensible, burgeoning growth of representational complexes that was mentioned above, which can penetrate and fill inner life like a malignant tumor.

As we have seen, the first incomplete metamorphosis contributing to disorders of inner life occurs when forces that retain the character of

39. R. Steiner, *CE*, lecture 1.

40. R. Steiner, *CE*, lecture 2.

41. R. Steiner, "Der Mensch als Gedankenwesen" (1921), in *Menschenwerden, Weltenseele und Weltengeist*, erster Teil (GA205).

consciousness to an excessive degree disturb the function and ultimately the structure of a physical organ (organ neurosis to organ disease). In the second incomplete metamorphosis, the reverse takes place: forces of the etheric body, astral body, and ego that should remain active in the diseased physical body rise into inner life and imprint organic disorders upon it. To the extent that these forces retain their physical-organic character, the soul is confronted with a foreign process. The result, if the soul is susceptible enough and unable to overcome the invading process, is a deformation, in some cases even a dissolution of psychological structure, whereby the astral body may take on a "physical-etheric structure."[42] The soul and ego, which by this time will have begun to withdraw from the organism anyway, now do so even more strongly. Self-destructive impulses originating from the physical body are now given free rein.

In what follows it will become clear that all psychological disorders involve an increased tendency of the soul and ego (as well, in some cases, of the etheric body) to excarnate. It can even happen that these constituents are simply dislodged from the physical body by the organic processes just described; this will prove to be the case in schizophrenia and mania.[43] In other experiential disorders, such as depression and epilepsy, the partially excarnated higher constituents, while remaining in the body, are unable to fully master it. When Rudolf Steiner describes mental illness as the result of an overly intense connection of the astral body and the ego with the physical body, by "physical body" he means the physical *functions* that have risen up into inner life, not the physical body itself.[44] Thus the "overly intense connection" of the higher constituents with the physical body is an indirect rather than a direct one; this explains in what sense the higher constituents become "trapped" in the physical body even though they are essentially excarnated. The excarnation is always primary. In my view this accords with Lievegoed's descriptions of the "inward" and "outward" paths in mental illness—an important differentiation, indicated above, of what can happen *after* the initial excarnation.[45]

---

42. R. Steiner, *Course for Young Doctors* (GA 316), lecture 5. (Spring Valley, NY: Mercury Press, 1996)
43. R. Steiner, *Health Care as a Social Issue.*
44. See R. Steiner, *Philosophy, Cosmology and Religion* (Hudson, N.Y.: Anthroposophic Press, 1984), p. 125f.
45. B. Lievegoed, *Man on the Threshold: The Challenge of Inner Development* (Stroud, U.K.: Hawthorn Press, 1985).

2. Psychosis and Supersensible Worlds

As has been shown elsewhere in this book, through our etheric body we belong to an etheric world, through our soul to an astral world, and through our ego to a spiritual world. Throughout our lives, these higher constituents remain bound up with their respective worlds. This connection is more immediate in childhood than later in life; in childhood, our higher constituents are active exclusively within the physical body, whereas later they serve consciousness. To regain a closer relationship to supersensible worlds, healthy adults must exert themselves. In psychosis, on the other hand, something of the early immediacy is restored. Forces of the higher constituents that are active in the organs convey an awareness of the soul's original connection to supersensible worlds. The forces that shaped the child now rise up into the light of adult consciousness, but chaotically because the soul is ill.

Psychotic hallucinations and delusions may thus have more than a purely organic dimension. Beings and events of higher worlds can express themselves through organic forces. Schizophrenics are able, because of their closer connection to the etheric world, to experience the processes of nature more immediately than healthy people can. Because the formative forces and egos of schizophrenics have expanded into the surrounding world, schizophrenics may experience themselves as the cause of the blossoming and withering in their surroundings. In a state of trance, such people can even perceive something of the reality of demonic or divine beings, particularly in hallucinations.[46]

Thus, as the English psychiatrist Ronald Laing has pointed out, psychosis is one way for the human being to cross the threshold into the supersensible world.[47] "Certain transcendental experiences seem to me to be the original wellspring of all religions. Some psychotic people have transcendental experiences." The "madman ... may be irradiated by light from other worlds. It may burn him out." According to Laing, it should be recognized that the patient's "voyage" into other worlds is "a natural way of healing our own appalling state of alienation called nor-

46. R. Steiner, "Wie kommt man zum Schauen der geistigen Welt?" in *Rhythmen im Kosmos und im Menschenwesen: Wie kommt man zum Schauen der geistigen Welt?* (GA 350). Not translated; translations of individual lectures are available in typescript.

47. R. D. Laing, *The Politics of Experience* (New York: Pantheon Books, 1967), chapter 6: "Transcendental Experience."

mality." The patient, "even through his profound wretchedness and disintegration," can be "the hierophant of the sacred."

Laing points out that we have become increasingly alienated from our everyday world, and that the surface of that world has begun to "crack," allowing supersensible worlds to stream in, worlds that we are no longer content merely to believe in. In Laing's view, the psychotic patient can convey the kind of direct experience of the supersensible that we are all beginning to want. This is of course possible, but is in the long run unlikely to help either the psychiatrist or the patient. Patients can make their psychiatrists aware of the existence of the supersensible and, if they notice that the psychiatrist has a positive attitude toward it, may feel that they are really being understood for the first time. However, the mentally ill also want to be healed, preferably in a way that does not simply cut them off from the supersensible world and force them into an alienating state of "normality." Because the psychotropic drugs in use today can have such an alienating effect, Laing demands a different approach, in particular one that respects the patients' inner development and supports them during the stormier passages of their voyage into the supersensible world. However, such an approach is possible only if psychiatrists have themselves crossed the threshold in a healthy way.

Rudolf Steiner crossed the threshold in a healthy way and indicated to others how it might be done. The path of inner discipline that he inaugurated involves an enhancement of mental health, an increase in consciousness and discriminative capacity, and the crossing of the threshold to which it leads is fundamentally different from the crossing that occurs in psychosis. Unlike the healthy crossing, which tends to bear fruit both for the individual and society, the psychotic crossing frequently disrupts the patients' lives and surroundings, sometimes severely enough to isolate them from all adult society. It can lead to a pathological, chaotic repetition of the conditions of childhood and youth. Distorted supersensible experiences overwhelm the mental patient's largely passive mind, eluding the ego's oversight and judgment. Every psychotic crossing of the threshold is connected with a backward step in inner development, and only in exceptional cases can this backward step be transformed into an advance.

Even healthy inner development is characterized by the gradual liberation of the soul from the body. This process culminates in the path of spiritual discipline, through which consciousness ascends to the spiritual world. The metamorphosis of bodily forces, of which the genesis of thought is a basic example, is intensified, leading ultimately to the formation of spiritual organs. In psychosis, on the other hand, the soul, rather than leaving the body of its own accord, is drawn up out of it by an illness, and even though it has disengaged from the body, it is still pursued and permeated by the body's forces. For this reason, psychosis may be viewed as the pathological counterpart of healthy inner development; in severe cases it can even be seen as the opposite of the path of spiritual discipline. It follows that whoever succeeds in following that path also takes a significant step toward avoiding psychosis. Treatment, on the other hand, must proceed differently.

The Relation of Physical Organs to Psychological Disorders

In this section, the general principles we have already established for neurosis and psychosis will be elaborated for each of the four basic organ systems: kidney, liver, lung, and heart. All the other organs can be assigned to one of these four systems; for example, the spleen to the hepatobiliary system: "hepatolienal system"; the reproductive organs to the kidney system: "urogenital system." This classification derives from Rudolf Steiner, who drew attention to the significance of the four organ systems for a new psychiatry and also discussed their connections with the four elements.[48] The physiology of the organs, which has been explained in detail elsewhere, will be mentioned only to the extent necessary to establish a psychology of the organs. Such a psychology, proposed by Steiner, is the basis of the physical diagnosis of psychological disorders and of their treatment with remedies and other physical measures.[49]

In the course of our discussion, it will become clear that each of the four organ systems corresponds to a basic personality type. Each of these types is dominated by the corresponding organ process and by one of the four essential constituents of the human being. Since each of the

48. See R. Steiner, *SM*, lecture 13.
49. R. Treichler, "Von einer Psychologie der Organe zur organischen Behandlung psychischer Störungen," in *Anthrop.-Medizin. Jahrbuch*, vol. 3 (Dornach: 1952).

four elements has internalized itself in a particular organ system, a set of correspondences will also become apparent between inner life and the elements. Thus, each major psychiatric syndrome is characterized not only by a particular essential constituent and organ process, but also by one of the four elements, whose dynamic has become exaggerated by the illness.

In what follows, the major psychiatric syndromes are discussed under the heading of the most closely related organ system, although no syndrome can be so rigidly defined. The organs and the psychological disorders associated with them are much better conceived of as foci from which psychopathological processes can originate and interact with each other. However, in order to recognize and treat the various components of a particular case, it is necessary to possess the pure concept of all the major syndromes. The same may be said of the four organ types, which also seldom occur in pure form.

When dealing with mental illnesses, one must always keep in mind that the ego transcends all that is typical. Ultimately, it is the ego itself that has allowed the disease to arise in the first place, that determines its character, and that comes to terms with it in an individual way. On the other hand, part of the nature of mental disorders is that they also more or less overwhelm the ego. Knowledge of the typical disease processes of the soul will therefore help us assist the ego in its confrontation with them.

A. The Renal System

The kidney is generally thought of only in terms of its role in excretion, particularly of protein. However, the kidney's catabolic, excretory activity is just the end of a process that begins in the prerenal activity of the tissue fluids surrounding all cells. Furthermore, it is only one aspect of the kidney's function. According to Rudolf Steiner, the kidneys also "radiate" forces that influence the diverse anabolic processes of "incretion" via the liver (see vol. II, p. 269f.). Starting with nutrients that have been absorbed from the intestine, this inner renal activity permeates material processes with psychological forces and carries them toward formative forces proceeding from the nervous system. The latter limit the expansion of the outward-radiating material processes, rounding them off spherically. The secretions of the adrenal gland are a hormonal expression of this activity. Rudolf Steiner described the adrenal gland as the kidney-based "regulator oriented toward the middle human being";[50] it helps the forces radiating from the kidney to enter the blood, which in turn, in conjunction with the forces of the upper human being, integrates material processes into the forms of the body and its organs. Protein is the chief actor in this blood-based anabolic process.

"Excretion" and "incretion" can be seen as metamorphoses of exhalation and inhalation, which are themselves physical expressions of antipathy and sympathy.[51] With this we have entered the realm of the astral body, the soul active in the organs. The astral body's excretory, "antipathetic" activity enters from above and ends in the kidney, while its "incretory" activity, entering from below, radiates into the organism through the kidney in a kind of "organic sympathy." "Kidney radiation" is an expression of the activity that impels all involuntary movements in the physical organism.

The unconscious desires of the astral body active in the organism, namely, hunger for oxygen and for nutrients, influence the circulation of blood in the "middle human being."[52] The vehicle of these desires in the physical body is the air organism, which is centered in the renal system. "Air hunger" causes the inner exchange of gases. However, the concentration and dilution of substances in urine by the renal system is also related to the element of air, inasmuch as air is also characterized by constantly alternating compressions and rarefactions.

The experiences associated with the renal system acquire their character from subconscious processes of sympathy and antipathy, which appear inwardly as emotions.[53] In these elemental affections, the human being reacts more or less involuntarily to external influences, whereas more conscious feelings of sympathy and antipathy entail a greater degree of reflection or control. Everything that agitates us, either pleasantly or unpleasantly, is bound up physically with the kidneys. (The con-

50. R. Steiner in *Krankheitsfälle*, A.G. Degenaar ed., manuscript ed. for physicians, p. 80. See also R. Treichler, "Nierenstrahlung und Konstitutionstherapie," *BEH* 4 (1951).

51. R. Steiner, *GG*, lecture 6. See also Steiner, *Theosophy*, and F. W. Zeylmans van Emmichoven, *The Anthroposophical Understanding of the Soul*.

52. R. Steiner, *Rhythmen im Kosmos und im Menschenwesen* (GA 350), lecture of June 6, 1923. Translation available in typescript only.

53. See R. Steiner, *Therapeutic Insights: Earthly and Cosmic Laws*, lectures 3 & 4.

nection between emotional excitation and the adrenal medulla has been known for some time.) Accordingly, all nervous conditions of the excitable neurotic are to be understood and approached through the kidney. Even such psychotic symptoms as hallucinations, however, insofar as they are accompanied by agitation, also point toward the kidney.[54] Both pleasant and unpleasant agitation can lead to aggression, whose volitional character points to an involvement of the bile system.

The aspect of the soul that bases itself upon the renal system is the sentient soul, which is characterized by elemental emotionality, affects, and drives.[55] Sensations experienced within the sentient soul also extend via the blood into the feeling life of the lung. Once the sentient body frees itself from the urogenital system in puberty, the resulting sentient soul must learn to use that system as its instrument and to transform its forces. In this process—through the ego of the sentient soul—the hepatobiliary system also becomes involved. This becomes apparent in the anger typical of this stage, which is merely emotional and connected not only with the kidney, but also—more so than aggressivity—with the bile. In anger, willfully but chaotically directed at an external goal, the spiritual will is involved more than the astral body. However, it cannot achieve its goal of change, no matter how clearly conceived it might be.[56]

As we have seen, every manifestation of the soul has its opposite. Each organ, too, is characterized by a definite psychological duality; the opposite of the kidney's enhanced excitability is impassiveness that can reach the point of total apathy. In this state, the dull, barely conscious nature of experiences based on the kidney becomes particularly clear. The excitable "renal type" occasionally sinks into semiconsciousness. Phases of mild excitability can be grounded in a sanguine temperament, which is basic to the kidney type and is also connected with the air organism. Sanguine types are quite often and correctly described as "flighty."

The neurotic's basic emotion, fear, is strongly connected with the physical body. It is physical anxiety, and patients often describe it as an

54. See previous footnote.
55. See R. Steiner, "Anthroposophische Grundlagen für die Arzneikunst," in *Physiologisch-Therapeutisches* (GA 314). Not translated; typescripts of translations of individual lectures are available.
56. K. König, *The Human Soul* (Hudson, N.Y.: Anthroposophic Press, 1987).

indefinite feeling rising out of the upper abdomen, often connected with the experience of being "trapped" in the body. Fear is essentially an obstructed emotion that can turn into or discharge itself in aggression, a fact that becomes particularly apparent in physical anxiety.[57]

The emotional opposite of physical anxiety is physical addiction. By this we mean a consuming urge to enjoy the body and through it the world: from exaggerated sexual drives to drug addiction, which like every addiction can be a reaction not only to inner emptiness, but also to fear. The sentient soul, and even more so the sentient body, can seek through such cravings to dissolve physical anxiety and flee bodily confines, only to feel confinement and anxiety all the more keenly when intoxication has passed.

Renal neurotics are particularly likely to be agitated by external influences that they cannot assimilate. They become filled with physical anxiety and excitement, while in the background, an inner isolation from the world, the insensibility of an animal existence threatens. It is possible that the sensations of inner vibration reported by excited or addicted renal neurotics are nothing more than processes of their own air organisms rising into consciousness, while neurotics with physical anxiety are really only experiencing the solidity of their own bodies. Both sensations may occur simultaneously.

1. Schizophrenia

The polarity "excitable-inexcitable" is reminiscent of Kretschmer's description of the schizoid psychopath.[58] Such psychopaths may indeed be found among renal types. They tend to have a leptosomic or, less often, a dysplastic physical build. They tend to react to the world with either excitement or apathy; their sensitivity is frequently balanced by a tendency toward dispassionate, abstract reflection. Their inner split may sometimes be accompanied by autism, which represents a complete break with the outer world. A character of this kind may eventually predispose a person toward schizophrenia.

On the level of the organs we have here the polarity "renal system-brain"; on that of the elements the polarity "air-earth." The renal system's

57. K. König, *The Human Soul*, chapter 4.

58. See E. Kretschmer, *Körperbau und Charakter* (Berlin: 1944), p. 297f.

main feature is its relationship to the air organism, with which the astral body, the seat of emotion, is directly connected. The physical opposite of the renal system is the brain, which tends toward rest and rigidification and is closely linked with the solid element, as evidenced by the skull. The brain, as we shall see, is the one organ that during the schizoids' childhoods receives the most stimulation. Their postpubertal excitability is essentially a revolt against the rational pole of their own being.

In the schizophrenic process, which in typical cases develops out of a character with some schizoid traits, excitement can intensify into madness and dullness into stupor. These processes correspond, respectively, to storms and stillnesses in the external atmosphere. While motionless, both air and the soul are under the spell of the solid element. The motionless, passively absorbing, stuporous patients remain connected to the world only through the brain, through perception and ideation. In madness, on the other hand, an emotional "thunderstorm" bursts destructively forth from the renal system into the world. The astral body's forces of movement, which even in ordinary emotions influence the body through the air organism, are magnified and distorted and rise violently into consciousness. In this process, the patients' lower organizations cause them to be literally "beside themselves," whereas in stupor, they are *outside* themselves, being present almost solely in the head. Increased excitability may also be thought of as a pathological exaggeration of the sanguine temperament. The connection of madness with forces of the heart and of the ego is discussed below in the section on the heart.

Particularly at the beginning of a schizophrenic psychosis, excitability and stupor intermingle and partially neutralize each other, causing experience to become chaotic. Anxiety-filled, increasingly wild thoughts show that forces from the emotional pole have invaded the head, whereas hesitation and jerky movements show that paralyzing forces from the head have invaded the metabolic-limb system. Further polarizations occur as the disease progresses, as, for example, when patients do the opposite of what they think. The ego's activity in the soul is being split; because the ego is essentially indivisible, it has been driven out, and the soul makes use of its forces. Figuratively: the sun, reflected off a choppy sea, seems to split, yet—like the ego—is in its actual being indivisible. The inner split sometimes goes so far that patients experience themselves as more than one person.

Chaos and division intensify when formative forces from the organs invade the mind, producing hallucinations and delusions. Voices of inner origin are experienced by patients as coming from without—commanding or accompanying them, conversing with one another—and referred to actual people in the environment, a sign that the ego's divided activity is being even further split off and personified. Inner life fuses chaotically with the outside world. (The difference between the representing and the willing ego and their respective involvement in the schizophrenic process is discussed in the author's work, *Der schizophrene Prozess.*[59])

In contrast to such paranoid-hallucinatory forms, which mainly involve thought and perception, other forms, centered in the emotions, are characterized by silliness or by simple emotional atrophy: dementia simplex or hebephrenia. Catatonic schizophrenia, as evidenced by its motor symptoms, chiefly affects the will. Stupor and frenzy are most severe in acute catatonia; physical symptoms are especially pronounced and generally eclipse psychological ones. A particularly prominent physical symptom is the impairment of protein breakdown in the kidney.[60]

As can be seen from the asthenic constitution or asthenic reactions of many preschizophrenics, the dominant metabolic process in such people is catabolism. In schizophrenia proper, it has been assumed that not only stored protein but also the protein structure of the organs themselves is attached. Here we may recall our earlier discussion of the organ deformations that arise in the course of life through various influences, sometimes favored by an innate disposition. In acute catatonic schizophrenia, the body ceases to excrete the products of protein catabolism, causing severe illness and a high fever. Circulation begins to stagnate; blood extravasates, giving rise to superficial hematomas. These symptoms have also been connected with an insufficiency of the adrenal cortex.

In the acute stage of psychosis, the ego and astral body partially dissociate themselves from the moribund physical body. Fever is a sign of an attempt by the ego to reintegrate itself into the physical body, which of course causes further catabolism. The combination of impaired excretion

59. R. Treichler, *Der schizophrene Prozess*, 2nd ed. (Stuttgart: 1981). See also B. Peipers, *Vom Wesen der Schizophrenie* (Bonn: 1982).
60. Cf. D. Richter, *Schizophrenie: Somatische Gesichtspunkte* (Stuttgart: 1957).

and enhanced incretion causes kidney radiation to transcend its normal, anabolic activity in the physical body and to invade conscious inner life, where it contributes to the proliferation of psychotic delusions.

Based on the foregoing, we may suppose that in most forms of schizophrenia that are not explicitly catatonic, these pathophysiological processes occur only marginally and make themselves felt mainly in consciousness. They can, however, also express themselves physically in so-called "febrile episodes." The schizophrenic process results when catabolism and the dynamic of subtly toxic breakdown products are carried by organic forces into a soul predisposed to division.

The sentient body and sentient soul react with particular sensitivity to these processes. Personal impressions, which up to now have served a mediating function, split off from the outer world or flow out into it, become distorted, drown in overwhelming affects, or rigidify and atrophy. A lack of emotional responsiveness is a recognized early symptom of schizophrenia. Even in older schizophrenic patients, the unifying, integrating ego evidently withdraws earliest from the sentient soul, where by nature it is most weakly anchored. Organic forces assert themselves in its place, forces that originate in disorders of the renal process, with which the sentient body and sentient soul have a special connection. (Regarding the role played by the intellectual and consciousness souls in schizophrenia and in psychosis generally, see note.[61] When schizophrenia first emerges, these aspects of the soul are usually not yet born, which means that they are still very closely boundup with the physical and etheric bodies. In this "embryonic" stage they are thus much more likely to succumb to the psychotic process.)

A disturbance of the renal protein process, which affects the entire organism, can initiate pathological changes in other organ systems as well. The psychological symptoms characteristic of these systems then combine with the schizophrenic ones. Mixed psychoses can eventually form, in which, for example, schizophrenic and cyclothymic traits, which are connected with the liver, are combined.

One significant cause of schizophrenia is developmental disorders occurring in childhood. If education during the first and second seven-year periods of life is not based sufficiently on the principles of imitation

61. See R. Steiner, "Error and Mental Disorder," in *Metamorphoses of the Soul,* vol. 2.

and authority, then the development of schizophrenia later in life is favored.[62] The one-sidedly intellectual education characteristic of modern civilization, by neglecting to influence the child's will and feelings through imitation and authority, prevents the ego and soul from integrating themselves properly into the lower and middle organizations. Instead, ego and soul remain too strongly centered in the head, stimulating an excessive metamorphosis of organic forces into forces of thought. Intellectual precocity is bought at the price of poor organ maturation, and a disposition toward defective protein structure is created. Existing organic defects are aggravated, and a pathologically asthenic constitution can develop, through which stressful experiences can easily invade the organ structure, unleashing organic forces and thus causing psychosis.

After puberty, an organism into which the soul and ego have not sufficiently incarnated reacts with an excarnating psychosis. Forces of emotion revolt against the overdeveloped intellect. The mistreated organism withdraws its forces from intellectual development, and the metamorphosis that was previously exaggerated now becomes incomplete. Liberated organic forces are free to wreak havoc in the soul, which, having been freed from the body at puberty, can no longer be protected by it. The previously overemphasized or overtaxed intellect is thereby transformed and partially dissolved. Schizophrenia can thus be seen as the organism's inevitable reaction to modern intellectualization, as a physiological as well as an emotional revolt.

The schizophrenic process usually begins between puberty and the 25th (in women, the 30th) year of life—in other words, almost entirely within the periods of the sentient body and the sentient soul. In addition to a schizoid character formed before puberty, one factor predisposing the mind to invasion by the schizophrenic process is an inner emptiness, an emotional life that is underdeveloped and only weakly individualized. (The now archaic designation "dementia praecox" pointed to the connection of this syndrome with youth.)

In light of the developmental aspect, the significance of education for the prophylaxis of schizophrenia can well be appreciated. Although an unfavorable family situation is sufficient to undermine imitation and authority as pedagogical principles, the intellectualizing influences of

62. R. Steiner, *SM,* lecture 16.

school and a technological environment only aggravate the problem. Furthermore, while much research has been devoted to family conditions in the development of schizophrenia, the significance of formal schooling has as yet been little recognized. A number of authors do, however, report an increase of schizophrenic syndromes in primitive peoples who have been exposed to Western civilization.[63]

2. *Vegetative Neuroses as Disorders of Kidney Radiation*

The renal system's psychological polarity manifests itself in nonpsychotic kidney types as well, some of whom tend toward excessively weak, others toward excessively strong kidney radiation. In deficient kidney radiation, the astral body fails to intervene strongly enough into the physical organism from below. Persons so disposed have few or feeble emotions, which flare up quickly and then fade; they tend toward slackness and exhaustion due to deficient mental intensity, and are dominated by the apathetic pole, the solid element. This situation is mirrored physically by poor circulation, which can even entail hemostasis in the lower extremities, leading in some cases to hemorrhoids, varices, and excessive menses. Since the astral body does not sufficiently permeate the material processes of the blood or carry them far enough toward the forces of the upper organization, blood sugar levels drop. Blood pressure, for which the astral body is always responsible, also falls, giving a measurable indication of the weakness of kidney radiation. Staehelin remarks of this type of hypotensive; "The basic mood...is faint-heartedness, the attitude one of resignation."[64] These symptoms can intensify to the point of adrenal insufficiency syndrome. Overall, incretion recedes and excretion dominates, albeit more in the sense of a "running out" into the periphery of the organism and into the environment.

The type with excessive kidney radiation, on the other hand, has intense emotional reactions that are repeatedly suppressed. The astral body acts too strongly from below to be contained within the lower organization. Forces of the metabolism "boil over" into the upper organization, invading thinking with emotion and flooding the brain with superfluous metabolic and circulatory forces. One result of this can be

63. *Fortschritte* 27 (1962).
64. Staehelin (see note 21), p. 37.

migraine, a condition in which exudative processes and toxic effects from the intestines are believed to play a role.[65] Free astral forces that can no longer harmoniously penetrate the physical body appear now in the lower organization as well. One direct manifestation of this is flatulence, whose relation to a dominant air organism is clear. Muscular coordination is impaired when the astral body grasps convulsively "from above" into the physical body; the etheric body, active in the fluid element, can no longer mediate, so that cramps may develop as well.[66] In the vascular system, the accumulation of astral forces from the head leads to increased turgor. High blood pressure and various vasomotor sensations (vibrating, shivers, tingling, throbbing, etc.) are in part due to this. The heightened material processes of the lover pole express themselves in a rise in blood sugar, among other symptoms. Overall, excretory processes falter, while incretion is enhanced. In Staehelin's words, the "basic misattunement" of the essential hypertensive is characterized by "checked aggression," by a "struggle to overcome obstacles," and by an "unhealthy drive for achievement" (the "overachiever").[67]

Most people with excessive kidney radiation are corpulent endomorphs, although a dysplastic body type is also possible. The metabolic pole appears overemphasized. By contrast, in people with deficient kidney radiation, the upper pole dominates over the lower pole, making for a more ectomorphic build (unless here again a dysplastic form develops).

Even more that with the constitutional types described by Kretschmer, which only partially correspond to the more dynamic types outlined here, it is important in disorders of kidney radiation to be aware of variations and combined forms. The relatively inactive astral body of people with deficient kidney radiation may occasionally seek to intervene more intensely in the physical body, causing uncharacteristic cramps or excitability. Such symptoms, however, result from a lack rather than a superabundance. Their difference from the cramps and excitability of excessive kidney radiation is clear, for example, from their location: they tend to occur more in the internal or external periphery (in the skin or mucosae), and can be linked to a convulsive withdrawal from the world

65. *Handbuch der Inneren Medizin,* vol. V (Nervensystem) (Berlin: 1939), pp. 1506–1507.
66. Steiner/Wegman, *FT,* chapter 19.
67. Staehelin (see note 21), p. 31.

out of inner weakness. By contrast, the spasmodic processes of excessive kidney radiation occur more in the center (in the organs and large vessels) and indicate an accumulation of excess forces on the inside. Hence in evaluating and treating such syndromes as migraine, it is important to ask whether the metabolic and circulatory processes in the head stem primarily from a lower organization that is "boiling over" or from an upper sphere that is too much at the mercy of the outer world and is thus "hollowed out." In the latter case, which nowadays is more frequent, the intensified metabolic activity in the head is merely secondary, a reaction to the weakness of forces from above.

The distinction of excessive from deficient kidney radiation can help the physician to deal properly with the whole spectrum of vasomotor-vegetative complaints, all of which must be seen against the background of the disharmonious activity of the astral body. For very many people in their twenties, including those who are not renal types, such complaints can be the first symptom of a developmental disorder of the soul. This disorder can then extend to whichever organ is dominant and become chronic there.

The person with deficient kidney radiation tends to have poor circulation and to be overly timid, traits that a developmental disorder of the soul only tends to intensify. This is especially true in the case of an underdeveloped sentient soul, whose emptiness can lead to hypotensive vasoneurosis. After desperate attempts to incorporate the normal measure of forces of the soul into the body, the astral body can gradually falter and circulatory disorders can become more pronounced. In effect, the astral body surrenders to the physical body, and the resulting stagnation causes mental life to languish even more. The opposite occurs in people with excessive kidney radiation. In them, excessive emotional forces are suppressed, which intensifies excitability and the tendency to outbursts.

These considerations can help the physician transcend merely symptomatic therapy. Instead of repeatedly deadening pains, relieving spasms, suppressing agitation, or stimulating the nervous system, he or she can attempt through appropriate medication and psychotherapy to harmonize the relationship between the soul and the body by way of the kidney, so that eventually the symptoms disappear.

At the end of each organ chapter, the key concepts will be summarized in a table, which will of course be incomplete and open to elaboration and modification. In any event, the reader should keep in mind that the relationships depicted in the table are not static, but rather the expression of living processes.

Table 9.

	Kidney		
constituents:	astral body	⟷	physical body
elements:	air	⟷	earth
temperament	sanguine		
character:	emotional		
relationship to body and world:	physical addiction	⟷	physical anxiety
physical polarity:	incretion	⟷	excretion
emotional polarity	excitability, agitation	⟷	dullness, stupor

diseases: schizophrenia, epilepsy (see next section), vegetative neurosis

B. The Hepatobiliary System

The liver is the central organ of metabolism and embraces the inner world of substances. It is also the central organ of the water organism. With five different fluids streaming through it, the liver embodies in incomparable fashion the anabolic processes of the etheric body, which, in the process of assimilation, molds solid substances out of the fluid element, and in dissimilation, releases them back into fluid circulation. In contrast to the renal process, which mediates between the outside and the inside, the liver exercises its functions entirely *within* the organism. "Hepatic" or "liver types" have high turgor and are usually of pyknic body type. Their inner life is based upon their ceaselessly moving water organism, which leads to the formation of a phlegmatic temperament. This temperament combines external sluggishness with deliberate and steady inner activity.

Within the liver and in contrast to its mainly anabolic activity, bile is produced through a catabolic process. Bile flows into the intestine, creating the conditions necessary there for the breakdown of fats. The primary result of this is warmth, the element in which the ego's forces of will are most at home. Bile formation is a sign that the ego's will forces have entered the liver's etheric realm; they carry the fiery element into the fluid element and thus create the metabolic foundation for the choleric temperament. Through bile, the ego as a being of purpose and will enters the realm of earthly activity.

It is in the contents of the intestine that the ego first encounters something foreign to itself.[68] After this "preliminary exercise," bile (mainly in the form of bile acids) is absorbed into the blood. There, according to Rudolf Steiner, it provides the foundation for the power to act: out of the warmth of the blood, the ego reaches out to the surrounding world. A person whose liver secretes only small amounts of bile tends to be inwardly lethargic; one whose liver secretes large amounts of bile absorbs a correspondingly large amount from the intestines and thus tends to be "fiery." An excess of bile makes a person hot-tempered.[69] A person who has been "galled," i.e. provoked to anger, becomes red in the face: bile has flowed from the liver and gall bladder into the intestine and from there into the blood, which in turn rises to the head. This must be distinguished from "turning livid with rage," which can point to a direct absorption of congested bile from the liver.[70] A rage of this sort can develop from pent-up anger and vent itself in aggression.

Bile acids absorbed from the intestine may be thought of as working together with iron to enkindle the will. Iron is released into the blood as a by-product of the breakdown of hemoglobin into bilirubin, a bile pigment. The cycle comes to a close when bile acids in the blood are used to produce new bile. The liver's bile process is thus an organ for the development of forces of the will. At the starting point of this cycle, guiding it via the bile system, stands the ego. At the end of the cycle the ego reaches out into the world through the bile acids in the blood.

---

68. R. Steiner, *Occult Physiology* (London: Rudolf Steiner Press, 1983); lecture 8.
69. R. Steiner, *Mensch und Welt: Das Wirken des Geistes in der Natur* (GA351), lecture 2.
70. Kleinsorge-Klumbies, "Psychotherapie," in *Klinik und Praxis* (Munich: 1959), pp. 108ff.

Forces of will and of the ego are at work in the phlegmatic temperament, but are circumscribed there by the liver's calm inner activity. They exercise an even greater influence when this unconscious inner activity is transformed into the capacity for reflection. The ego, the source of willing and thinking, is more active when experiences are elaborated more consciously. When this happens, the liver and the bile process that radiates into it cooperate harmoniously. The hepatobiliary system then becomes the organic foundation for the *intellectual or mind soul.* Independent thinking and a more mature experience of the world come into being through the activity of the ego in the etheric body, which is supported by the liver.

A stronger will and the internalization of feelings and thoughts distinguish the intellectual or mind soul from the emotionally reacting sentient soul. Because it is more thoroughly permeated by the ego, the mind soul is less subject to inner divisions; it remains intact even in mental illness.

1. Depression

The psychological polarity that characterizes mental disorders of the hepatic type results from disturbances of the water organism's innately balanced temperament in one of two directions. One direction is toward the pole of fire, which has already been mentioned and will be treated further below. A hint of the other pole, that of the solid element, may be found in phlegmatic liver types who, in addition to being calm, are also serious and overly conscientious. In such people, the tendency to mull things over becomes an inability to let go of the memory of troubling or, less often, of pleasantly stimulating experiences; although they remain outwardly calm, they cannot come to terms with their experiences. This sets the stage for an internally conditioned, endogenous depression, where the decisive factor is not some specific experience, but rather the manner of experiencing prior to the illness.[71]

In this psychosis of the hepatobiliary system, which for practical and didactic reasons we shall treat in some detail, the metamorphoses between the mental and physical realms are particularly clear-cut.

71. H. Tellenbach, *Melancholie* (Berlin: 1961).

Endogenous depressions are conditioned by physical factors; in them, one can observe how normal sadness intensifies into the so-called depressive reaction. In severe cases, sometimes clearly subsequent to upsetting experiences, symptoms of a hepatobiliary disorder will frequently occur, including sensations of pressure and fullness around the liver, bitter tastes in the mouth, nausea, intolerance of fatty foods, and (less often) increased thirst or biliary colics. Sometimes the disorders underlying these symptoms can develop into actual liver disease, such as hepatitis (with or without jaundice) or, less frequently, gallstones. This development is usually accompanied by the partial or even complete regression of emotional and mental symptoms.

The physical basis for endogenous depression is created when hepatobiliary disorders short of actual hepatitis or subsequent to hepatitis enter a hidden, chronic stage. The liver "gets used to the chaotic influences of the astral body. This need only continue long enough, and the process will be reflected into the soul; what the liver ought to integrate into the physical, it pushes off onto the soul, and we have depression."[72]

Accordingly, endogenous depression can be indirectly linked to unresolved conflicts that have settled into the physical realm. To the discussion of the preceding section we might now add that the resolution of painful and joyful experiences should contribute to development toward spirituality; significant truths should be recognized and creative faculties gained. If this fails to occur, untransformed psychological forces accumulate and eventually carry experiences down into the constitutionally predominant organ, which in the overserious hepatic type is the liver. The ultimate result of such a "chaotic influence of the astral body" is that latent disorders of the liver now manifest, or that liver disorders already present are intensified.

A. DISORDERS OF THE HEPATOBILIARY SYSTEM The first expression of these disorders is congestion in the circulation of both blood and lymph, which, as already mentioned, can eventually cause hepatitis or jaundice, the direct absorption of bile from the liver into the blood. The chronic state of congestion out of which depression develops manifests itself subjectively in the digestive complaints already mentioned.

72. R. Steiner, *SM,* lecture 20. Regarding bile, cf. lecture 1. Regarding mental symptoms, cf. lecture 13.

Studies done many years ago show that depressive or depression-prone individuals with pyknic metabolism have higher levels of serum sugar and cholesterol; cholesterol is of course manufactured primarily by the liver. In addition, the results of these studies suggested that glycogen storage in the liver was also higher than normal.[73] In recent years these findings have been partially confirmed and the locus of pathology has been further isolated. "The lowered glucose tolerance of depressive patients, in the sense of a latent diabetes with normalization after clinical recovery, is held to be the most firmly established metabolic abnormality of endogenous psychoses."[74] Furthermore, a higher concentration of serum cholesterol and triglycerides has been found here than in other diseases.[75] An indication of severe impairments of mineral metabolism was found in the fact that cellular sodium "rises by around 50% during depression, but returns to normal again after clinical recovery." A tendency toward fluid retention has also been demonstrated.[76]

The congestive tendency of the liver may be assumed to culminate in the retention of bile, which directly affects the will. The ancient designation "melan-cholia" (illness from black bile) points to this, and physicians as early as Hippocrates conceived of bile as thickening in a very real, material sense.[77] Unfortunately, no tests of this hypothesis have yet been performed. Despite this, some researchers assume that anxiety and other emotions can inhibit bile secretion and flow.[78] Physically, this would lead to a thickening of the bile, to hepatitis, biliary colics, and ultimately to gallstones; inwardly, it would inhibit the will, as we will see in the description of the psychological symptoms of endogenous depression. The ego, which stimulates and activates the will, cannot penetrate a congested biliary system.

From our point of view, the metabolic findings in endogenous depression indicate that the hepatobiliary process has in part detached itself from the watery element and subjected itself to the solid principle, caus-

---

73. See footnote 35.

74. N. Petrilowitsch, R. Baer, "Zyklothymie (1964–1969)," in *Fortschritte der Neurologie und Psychiatrie* 12 (1970):647.

75. O. Schrappe, in *Die chronisch endogenen Psychosen* (Stuttgart: 1967), p. 137.

76. *Biologische Psychiatrie* (see note 35), pp. 61–62.

77. R. Steiner, *SM,* lecture 20. Regarding bile, cf. lecture 1. Regarding mental symptoms, cf. lecture 13.

78. Kleinsorge-Klumbies, "Psychotherapie," in *Klinik und Praxis* (Munich: 1959), pp. 108ff.

ing congestion and hardening. The functional disturbance of the fluid organism settles into the physical body. In contrast to schizophrenia, however, in which an acute phase can cause permanent damage, both physical and mental, here the structure of organs and of the soul is less permanently affected. Typical of the liver are reversible disturbances of rhythmic carbohydrate and fat metabolism. This is undoubtedly connected with the reversible, rhythmic phases that characterize depression on the experiential level and can be compared to waves.

During endogenous depressions, hereditary or acquired liver disorders of a mild sort have their greatest psychological impact. However, inasmuch as many people suffer from mild liver disorders and only a relatively small number of them (around one percent of the total population) succumb to endogenous depression, it is helpful to consider the previously mentioned factor of temperamental disposition, which is what allows physical congestion to develop into depression in the first place. Such a disposition is found in a brooding, compulsively orderly character, which tends toward inner rigidification even before mental illness sets in. Of course, to call such a character a "disposition" requires that we broaden the concept designated by that word; brooding, in this sense, can result not only from outer experiences, but also from the subconscious experience of solidification in one's liver or of congestion in one's metabolism. The soul, in other words, becomes susceptible to organic processes and is eventually overwhelmed by them.

When a brooding disposition is absent, other disposing conditions must be considered, including the widespread modern trait of superficiality. Disturbing experiences that are not confronted can oppress the liver, the organ of mature emotional life, and thus contribute to depression. Furthermore, the superficial person's passive, irresolute inner life is more susceptible to mild hepatic disorders than is that of a person devoted to a search for meaning.

B. PSYCHOLOGICAL SYMPTOMS Through the organic process, a brooding attitude intensifies into melancholy, a tendency toward hardening culminates in inner rigidity, and endogenous depression develops. The solidification that affected the liver now affects the mind, which accordingly is threatened by stagnation. This is evidenced by sluggishness, both physical and mental, a dazed or apathetic expression, and emotional flatness.

The depressive inhibition consists mainly in a paralysis of the will, which is centered in the hepatobiliary system. Some endogenous-depressive patients cannot carry out even the smallest actions or trains of thought. Despite the best of intentions, they cannot fulfill their duties. It is this experience of inner paralysis that first gives rise to a depressed mood.[79]

An excessive emphasis on the dynamic of the head in the metabolism and in the will becomes especially clear in the depressive patient's experience of time. In our will we turn toward the future. If it is paralyzed, we can no longer deal with anything but the past. This is why depressives bury themselves so hopelessly in the past—hopelessly, since hope can arise only through the experience of a future. Depressives thus feel that every mistake they have made is final and irreparable. Further, since all human action is imperfect, if only the imperfections are experienced in memory, then every memory is at the same time a self-reproach. Depressive patients, tormented by this, can feel nothing for the future but fear. In place of the renal syndrome's physical anxiety, a self-imposed *fear of life* develops, and the person recoils from the world. Depressives fear everything that life will bring them; everything that comes will be either an impossible demand or a looming punishment.[80]

These symptoms are most pronounced in the early morning, after the higher constituents, the ego and astral body, have left the body-free state of sleep and reintegrated themselves into the physical and etheric bodies. In preparation for this, the dissimilation phase in the organism begins around 3 a.m.; bile secretion and the conversion of glycogen into blood sugar begin to increase. The depressive patient's organism apparently remains caught in the assimilatory, anabolic phase of sleep; good evidence for this would be the finding that depressives secretes less bile and other fluids and that they store more glycogen. What was anabolism at night becomes congestion during the day, and the existing psychophysical processes of stagnation and hardening are reinforced. In this sense, depressives are quite literally "benighted."

---

79. W. Schulte, in *Almanach für Neurologie und Psychiatrie* (Munich: 1961), p. 200f.

80. Cf. also V. von Gebsattel, "Die Störungen des Werdens und des Zeiterlebens im Rahmen psychiatrischer Erkrankungen," in *Gegenwartsprobleme der psychiatrisch-neurologischen Forschung* (1939).

According to Guenther Wachsmuth's summary and interpretation of the researches of Forsgren, et al. on the hepatic rhythm, we are awakened by our bodies in the morning and turn actively toward the world.[81] In the evening, we draw back into ourselves, finally dissociating entirely from the world and regenerating our bodies in sleep. As the depressive patient's ego and astral body reenter the body at around three or four in the morning, they encounter an obstruction in the hepatobiliary system, causing an emotionally painful awakening. If the obstruction is severe enough, it can also be physically painful. The ego and astral body remain partially caught in the congested liver, resulting in a tormenting half-sleep or a paralyzed wakefulness lasting well into the day. The higher constituents succeed only imperfectly in penetrating the physical and etheric bodies, specifically the hepatobiliary system, leaving the patient unable to enter into a fully wakeful and volitional relationship with the world. In severer cases, it is only toward evening that the patient is able to become somewhat active, which of course then interferes with normal sleep patterns. The morning's extension of night into day is complemented by an extension of the day's wakeful activity into the night. Both shifts have been noted by researchers of biological rhythms.[82]

In light of this, it is understandable why sleep deprivation with some form of activity during the night can have a therapeutic effect on endogenous-depressive patients. The ego is encouraged to become active in the more favorable situation of the evening, and the liver's impaired metabolism is thus stimulated.

C. FORMS OF DEPRESSION In depression, the soul does not leave the body with the ego as it does in schizophrenia. Instead, it experiences itself as enclosed within the body, which explains the somatic sensations that are the chief symptoms of *masked depression.* The most characteristic sensations are tension and constriction combined with physical restlessness. When these sensations intensify into physical anxiety, the kidney is clearly also involved. Hypochondria develops when the soul's confinement leads to fixation on particular physical symptoms. Not infrequently this is accompanied by delusional elaborations of genuine symptoms.

81. G. Wachsmuth, *Erde und Mensch* (Konstanz: 1952), chapter 8, and R. Treichler, *Schlafen und Wachen: Vom rhythmischen Leben des Ich* (Stuttgart: 1985).
82. M. Papousek, in *Rhythmusprobleme in der Psychiatrie* (Stuttgart/New York: 1978), p. 78.

Life in a body that is impervious to the higher constituents becomes for the depressive a life of imprisonment in earthly existence. The suicidal urges that endogenous depressives repeatedly experience reveal that they are becoming desperate, that their sense of duty toward earthly life is being overwhelmed by an urge toward liberation. Such cases call for extreme vigilance on the physician's part, so that the patient can be admitted to a closed psychiatric ward if a suicide attempt seems imminent.

All forms of depression have a certain endogenous component. Since the liver is the instrument of mature emotional life, it is reasonable to assume that every disturbing experience that is not properly mastered weighs a little upon the liver, leading to a minor hepatic disorder and to depression, the so-called *depressive reaction.* The frequent depressive mood swings that neurotics experience, also called *neurotic depressions,* and the neurotic's basic fear (to the extent that it is fear of life) arise through a complication of this process. In mild form this process may be classed among the psychoneuroses of hepatic origin. Endogenous depression proper arises when an emotional trauma encounters a liver already defective in its constitution. The same situation can produce the endogenous component of a reactive depression, leading to a mixed or *endoreactive* depression.

It is in depression associated with exhaustion that the endogenous component is most obvious. Physical or emotional exhaustion naturally affects the liver most strongly, since the liver is the chief organ of the etheric body. Congestion combines here with a weakening of vital forces. Given the appropriate disposition, exhaustion can produce a depression characterized by physical and emotional fatigue and by an attitude of resignation. Patients suffering from such a depression may experience lows in the evening as well as in the morning.

Despite the existence of hybrid forms, it is important to maintain the distinction between endogenous depression and depressive reaction. In the latter, the liver responds to conscious experiences, while in endogenous depression these experiences are shaped by the liver's own impaired activity. That the liver is involved in depressive reactions means that even severe cases of reactive depression may be treated physically as well as psychologically, leading to a faster and more thorough recovery. There are grounds for hope that anthroposophic drug therapy of the liver can also help prevent later and more serious disorders of the liver and the soul. Here, the family practitioner can find new opportunities for psychiatric prophylaxis.

The liver responds not only to the mind, however, but also to the activities of other physical organs. For example, events in the female reproductive system can lead to *postpartum* or *menopausal depression*. The brain and the spleen contribute to the widespread *involutional depression*, to which cerebral sclerosis and sclerosis of the portal vein should always be considered as possible contributing factors. All depressions, however, are rooted at least in part in an impairment of the liver process, especially when there is a disposition to hepatic depression proper. In the latter case, it is possible for another organ simply to initiate the development of a chiefly endogenous depression.

The involvement of the liver in depression means that the treatment of the liver should be a part of every therapy of depression.[83] The importance of this is underscored by the rising incidence of depression of all kinds. Depressives currently make up ten percent of the inpatient hospital population, and it is estimated that every year, over one hundred million to one hundred fifty million people around the world are affected by a clinically significant depression.[84]

2. *Mania*

The other pole of the liver dynamic, which appears less frequently than depression, is mania. The painful congestion accompanying depression can be followed by a pleasurable manic discharge.[85] All the emotional symptoms of the depressive patient yield to their opposite in mania: fear of life becomes an uncontrolled lust for life leading to a renewed, intense involvement in the world. Patients becomes joyful and lively; their thoughts and their movements become more animated, accelerated; their wills become excessively active, driving them from one ill-considered action to the next. Whereas in depression they were at the mercy of their past, patients are now wholly given over to a future that continually invades the present, making all past experiences seem irrelevant. Every wish the patients have they must fulfill at once.

---

83. A more detailed account with case histories is presented in R. Treichler, "Leber-Gallensystem und Depression," in *BEH* (1974)/6 and (1975)/1.

84. Kielholz. Lucern Symposium of Nov. 2, 1976, and *Ärztliche Praxis* (1976)/Dec. 28.

85. R. Steiner, *CE*, lecture 4.

A sudden outburst of anger on the part of an otherwise phlegmatic liver type can be the first symptom of an isolated mania, a relatively uncommon condition that in many respects represents a degeneration of the choleric temperament. Very often, however, it is merely the sign of a hypomanic component, which can either discharge itself in the outburst or be mixed with the consolidating tendency of a depression-prone constitution. In the latter case, such liver symptoms as stubbornness and self-righteousness may appear, in whose development once again the solid element is involved, together with an intensified, but rigidified will activity.[86]

The manic's more or less pronounced sanguinity, like the depressive's restlessness, stems from an involvement of the kidney. The increase in hydrocortisone secretion by the adrenal glands observed in certain forms of depression makes sense in light of this.[87] In mania, however, the human being not only becomes too "airy," but primarily too "fiery." The element that determines inner life in depression is stagnating fluidity, whereas in mania it is inflamed air. From this alone, an excessive secretion of bile and a correspondingly excessive absorption of cholic acids from the intestine might be inferred. Such a bile process, we may assume, is no longer under the ego's control; the ego's organic forces are liberated, rising up as impulses of will into the soul. Admittedly, no such disturbance in the bile process in mania has yet been demonstrated; however, this does not preclude its presence to a mild degree or its possible later discovery. Furthermore, the impairments of hepatic metabolism that have been verified for depressives have also been found in manics, along with a number of opposite physical symptoms.[88] This could be a physical indication that the forces that discharge themselves in mania fail to harmoniously penetrate the congested liver process.

In fact, according to Steiner, mania represents an excarnation of the most extreme sort.[89] However, in the actions of the manic patient who has gone "out of himself," the formative forces, desires, and forces of will that have been liberated from the body change their direction. They turn once again with excessive vehemence toward the body and the

86. R. Steiner, *SM*, lecture 13.
87. H. Beckmann, *Biologische Psychiatrie* (Stuttgart: 1982), p. 148f.
88. See footnote 35.
89. See Steiner, *Physiologisch-Therapeutisches* (see R. Steiner, "Anthroposophische Grundlagen für die Arzneikunst," in *Physiologisch-Therapeutisches*).

world, whereby they evidently do not properly penetrate the physical organ system, but merely "flood" it. The body that the depressive felt to be a prison from which he had to flee now becomes a plaything of inner life; in neither case is it an instrument through which a healthy relationship with the world might be established.

This "flooding" appears to be connected with a partial permeation of the body by forces of the astral body and ego, a permeation mediated by the escaping etheric body. This might explain the partial reversal of the metabolic conditions of depression, as well as observable increases in peripheral circulation, in saliva and tear secretion, and in intestinal motility; all of these functions represent the prevalence of dissimilation over assimilation in the external or internal pheriphery. The surmised increase in bile secretion, which aims at the inner periphery, the increase in the basal metabolic rate, and other factors lead one to deduce a more profound activation of the metabolism. This, however, does not extend to the impaired carbohydrate and mineral metabolism.[90]

3. Cyclothymia

Depression and mania, which can be combined in hybrid conditions, are primarily an affliction of the intellectual or mind soul. The emotions that petrify into melancholy or dissipate in the exuberance of mania belong to this realm, as does the intellect that rigidifies in depressive brooding on the past or dissolves in the fire of manic resolves for the future. Such wide swings in mood are indicated by the term "cyclothymia," which is often used today instead of "manic-depressive psychosis." The mood swings of the sensitive liver type, as described by Kretschmer, constitute the typical inner disposition for cyclothymia.[91] The hardening tendency of the brooding soul may be seen as a first metamorphosis of this character in the direction of pathology, particularly toward endogenous depression.

Cyclothymia most typically develops between the ages of 21 and 28, the intellectual or mind soul's "embryonic period." It can also develop in the seven-year period following this, when the intellectual soul is matur-

---

90. For the phenomenology and nature of mania, cf. W. Blankenburg, "Die Manie," in *Almanach für Neurologie und Psychiatrie* (Munich: 1967).

91. E. Kretschmer, Körperbau und Charakter (Berlin: 1944), p. 297f.

ing.[92] An emotional disorder may result in either of these periods if the mind soul fails to develop properly, or depression may develop later in life, even in people who are not liver types. The ego simply cannot cope with the oscillations of an underdeveloped or defective mind soul. Even depressions in which the liver is only secondarily involved can be partly rooted in an underdeveloped mind soul. Finally, the increased incidence of depression in our time is doubtlessly related to the intensifying and universal developmental problems of the twenties discussed above in the context of humanity's overall spiritual evolution.

Although the typical diseases of the hepatobiliary system are depression and mania, the liver can also play a role in other disorders of the soul. For example, a participation of the liver may be inferred when the hallucinations and delusions of schizophrenia are calmly conceived and carefully elaborated. The systematization and centralization of these pathological constructs indicates the structuring activity of formative forces that have dissociated from the liver and that are permeated by the ego. The hallucinations and delusions of depression and mania (e.g., delusions of sinfulness and of grandeur) are also based on such a dissociation; however, as the disturbance of organ protein is less severe in depression and mania; the "mental neoplasms" discussed earlier in connection with kidney-related psychological disorders are not as much in the foreground.

In both depression and mania, the etheric body plays an important role as a mediator. The formative forces of the organs carry the solidifying process of depression, with which they have imbued themselves, into conscious mental life. Several researchers have indicated an awareness of this mediation process in their writings on depression.[93]

92. See O. Bumke, *Lehrbuch für Geisteskrankheiten* (Munich: 1942).
93. See, for example, V. von Gebsattel, "Die depressive Fehlhaltung," in *Handbuch der Neurosenlehre,* second installment (Munich: 1962), p. 149; or H. Tellenbach, *Melancholie* (Berlin: 1961).

4. Epilepsy

In the disease process of epilepsy, stagnation and consolidation have more of a physical than a psychological effect, though they stop short of producing actual organic disease. According to Rudolf Steiner, epilepsy arises when the astral body and ego achieve consciousness in the physical body but are unable to penetrate it fully.[94] The particular organ in which the astral body and ego "congest" thus becomes as obstacle to conscious existence rather than an instrument of it. The cause of the deficient penetration, according to Steiner, is either that the organs are too densely structured or that they are subject to a slight infiltration.

Metabolically, this denseness manifests itself in congestions within the water organism of the liver. Much like depression, genuine epilepsy involves an accumulation of substances such as sugar, cholesterol, nitrogen, and carbonic acid in body fluids or tissues, combined with sluggish circulation and elimination. In the brain, the chief obstacle to the ego and astral body is scar tissue ("residual epilepsy"), but as with the other so-called symptomatic epilepsies, an epileptic constitution, typified by metabolic congestion, also plays a role.

In depression, the effects of impaired metabolism and insufficient penetration are primarily psychological; in epilepsy, they are primarily physical. Thoughts and reactions slow down in epilepsy, and the mood is disturbed, but in a way more suggestive of a physical disorder than of a well-defined depression. This is because adult epilepsy has its roots essentially in the years before puberty, during which the astral body, as such not yet born, was active primarily in the physical body.

In fact, the majority of epilepsies manifest before puberty.[95] A particularly crucial time appears to be around the age of nine, when the ego enters the metabolism. The sadness and "dull apathy" that afflict some children during the second seven-year period (especially around the age of nine) can develop into an epileptic constitution.[96] Adult depression can also be rooted in that period. Typical epileptics retain certain character traits of the second seven-year period throughout life; they

94. See R. Steiner, "Der Mensch als Gedankenwesen" (1921), in *Menschenwerden, Weltenseele und Weltengeist.*

95. H.J. Weitbrecht, *Psychiatrie im Grundriss* (Berlin: 1973), p. 181.

96. W. Holtzapfel, *Krankheitsepochen der Kindheit,* 4th ed. (Stuttgart: 1984), p. 44.

can even have the "structure of a grown-up child" (Tellenbach). As witnessed by their awkward, sluggish movements, such patients have not completed the move from metabolism into the limbs, a move that in healthy youths takes place in the years preceding puberty. A frequent urge to stretch themselves, a transitory phase in the development of the healthy prepubescent, can affect epileptics for their whole life. This stretching can even take the place of a seizure, and, when it does, is always an attempt to overcome metabolic congestion, as are the seizures.

The excitability of epileptics indicates that the renal process and their water organism, which is based in the liver, are both impaired. In addition to metabolic congestion, we find the deficient "aeration" and elimination mentioned earlier in connection with the kidney. In fact, during seizures, the renal system actually predominates. The brain also participates in seizures, as epileptics' brain waves indicate; the brain gives all spasmodic phenomena their specific form.

Seizures represent a violent, chaotic, "convulsive" attempt by the astral body to overcome obstacles to its penetration into the physical body, and in fact, they can improve elimination of retained substances. A state of agitated rage sometimes arises in place of a convulsive fit and has more or less the same effect. In the semiconscious state of absence, the astral body finally surrenders to a physical body that it cannot penetrate harmoniously. This can become the foundation for an epileptic psychosis.

The underlying disorder in epilepsy is thus distinct from the seizures. Seizures are at first merely symptoms of this disorder, and can be seen as attempts by the organism to heal itself, attempts that nevertheless remain largely unsuccessful.[97] A rational therapy will thus not merely try to eliminate seizures, but rather to make them gradually superfluous by means of organ and metabolic therapy.

On the other hand, seizures do involve psychological and spiritual forces in the organic process to a certain degree. The attacks impair conscious mental life as well as the instrument of that life, the brain. To that extent they constitute a disease in their own right. A portion of epileptics' mental problems are due to the affects of seizures on the brain, effects that can lead to dementia. For this reason, the seizures must be

97. J. Lutz, *Kinderpsychiatrie* (Zurich: 1972), p. 262.

treated. As long as they cannot be controlled otherwise, the usual antiepileptics must be given in addition to the medications to be described below. It must be kept in mind, however, that antiepileptics, though they prevent seizures, also promote the character changes typical of epilepsy, i.e., slowing and dulling of the mind, and even psychosis. Dosages should therefore be kept as low as possible, though not to the point where they become ineffective. Simultaneous treatment with the medications to be described in the section on therapy below increases the effectiveness of antiepileptics, so that lower doses can be given

Table 10

	Bile		**Liver**		
constituents:	ego	→	etheric body	←	physical body
elements:	fire	→	water	←	earth
temperament			phlegmatic		
character:			mature, reflective		
relationship to body and world:	lust for life	↔			fear of life
physical polarity:	dissimilation	↔			assimilation
emotional polarity	exuberance, willfulness	↔			sadness, paralysis of will

diseases: cyclothymia, epilepsy

Infrequent attacks may be less harmful to the patient than high doses of antiepileptics. According to Schulte, "some patients ... seem actually to need a certain number of attacks in order to lead a symptom-free existence that is tolerable to themselves and others."[98] With more frequent attacks, however, the damage will always outweigh these benefits.

The pathology of epilepsy can extend to organs other than the liver and kidney. The psychological symptoms vary accordingly, and the additional organic disorders will have to be treated. (For a more detailed

98. W. Schulte, "Epilepsie und ihre Randgebiete," in *Klinik und Praxis* (Munich: 1964), p. 5.

account of these relationships, see Rudolf Treichler, *Vom Wesen der Epilepsie.* Further literature is indicated there.)[99]

In contrast to the kidney chart, which was characterized by simple polarities, in the liver chart the polarities are mediated.

C. The Lung

Through the lung, more immediately than through the other three organ systems, the physical body opens itself to the external world, which enters directly in the form of air. Inhalation is to the lung what incretion is to the kidney, while exhalation corresponds to excretion. This alone establishes a special relationship between the lung and the kidney, a relationship that also holds for inner life. Both lung and kidney are intimately bound up with the astral body, the kidney in the metabolism, the lung in the rhythmic organization. "With each breath, we breathe our astral body more deeply in, incarnate ourselves a little more; and with each exhalation we undergo, in a small way, the beginning of an excarnation."[100] We can experience the airy element, which carries the astral body, in every inhalation. In each exhalation, if we attend to it, we can sense the weight, the solidity of the physical body as the air leaves it, especially if we are "lung types."

Such experiences no doubt always play an important role in the subconscious inner life of the lung type. The sensation of weight that accompanies exhalation is the key to the deeper nature of the lung: specifically, the lung is the central organ of the solid element and of the physical body that is built up out of it.

The astral body's lability in the lungs indicates a greater freedom of astral activity there. This activity oscillates between the encounter with the world on the one hand and with the physical body on the other. Sympathy and antipathy, expressed physically by inhalation and exhalation, do not submerge themselves as deeply in material processes in the lung as they do in the kidney.

The astral and physical bodies are more susceptible to external influences in the lung than in any other organ. Conversely, joy and pain in

99. R. Treichler, *Vom Wesen der Epilepsie,* 2nd ed. (Stuttgart: 1979).

100. F.Husemann, *Das Bild des Menschen als Grundlage der Heilkunst,* I. Band (Stuttgart: 1951), p. 93 (not translated). See also *The Anthroposophical Approach to Medicine,* vol. 1, pp. 324–327.

the astral body directly influences respiration, while respiration provides the foundation for the emergence of feelings. Every feeling involves "a modification of the respiratory rhythm ... through which a feeling comes inwardly to life."[101] The lung is a highly sensitive instrument of the soul, one in which—more explicitly than in the kidney or the liver—physical and psychological phenomena interact. Naturally it will be possible here as in the other organs to observe how the accent shifts from one plane to the other.

Experience is related to the world in a much more differentiated way through the lung than through the kidney. In comparison to the kidney's emotional reactions, which bear little resemblance to the experiences that evoke them, the feelings of the pulmonary type are a much more accurate reflection of outer impressions. They encompass all the nuances of feeling and sensation that can color emotional responses and mental images. That we are able "to make inner pictures of the outer world," images whose development is influenced by feelings, is one of the experiential effects of respiration. Part of the physical basis of this connection is, according to Steiner, the movement of cerebrospinal fluid, through which the respiratory rhythm extends into the brain.[102]

It is evident that a higher level of consciousness is achieved in the lung than in the kidney. The final and highest level of consciousness is found in the sense impressions of the upper organization, in which the organism has completely opened itself to the environment. Because of this openness, the sensory process may be thought of as a refined respiration process. Conversely, of all the organs of the lower and middle organization, the lung has the greatest affinity to the head, being related to it through the element of solidity.

"Lung types" have a highly differentiated inner life. They react with marked sensitivity, but can also balance their reactions better because of their inner life's rhythmic component. Their sensitivity reflects the physical sensitivity of the bronchial mucosae, which can also become oversensitive, resulting in either a mental or physical "allergy." Mental oversensitivity usually precedes physical, but both can appear simultaneously.

---

101. R. Steiner, *Riddles of the Soul* (Spring Valley, NY: Mercury Press, 1996; quote translated here from the German edition); see pp. 131ff.

102. R. Steiner, *Die Gestaltung des Menschen als Ergebnis kosmischer Wirkungen* (GA 208), lecture of Oct. 29, 1921 (individual lectures available in typescript translations).

As with everything else about lungs type, their characteristic psychological polarity results to a large extent from their relationship with the surrounding world. Their primary tendency is to succumb to external influences and to experience the body as foreign to themselves, as part of the environment. External influences dominate their inner life; in response, they may become excessively orderly and conscientious. Against this background, the lung type's frequent depressive mood swings become comprehensible; they may even derive from a melancholic temperament.

The melancholic brooder who continually withdraws from the world is always more or less bound to the solid element of the body. However, the melancholic temperament must be distinguished from melancholic illness, i.e., from endogenous depression, to which lung as well as liver types can succumb. The preliminary stage of endogenous depression can be provoked not only by the element of weight in the brooding, overly disciplined disposition of hepatic types, an element that coincidentally derives from the pulmonary sphere, but also by the lung type's melancholic temperament. When the latter occurs, the melancholic temperament, becoming unhealthy, sinks out of the lung into the hepatobiliary sphere. The solid element now begins to act too intensely in the liver, causing an affective disorder. Of course, even under normal conditions the lung type's melancholic temperament has certain repercussions in the liver by its very nature, as the name (Latin *melancholia* = "black bile") indicates. It is only in the illness of "melancholia," however, that the liver system actually dominates.

Lung types' impressions of the external world are more sharply defined than those of any other organ types. Through brooding and reflection, they struggle to come to terms with their own solidity and with their overpowering, "inflexible" experiences, a process that can paralyze their feelings and their will. Thus arises the anxiety characteristic of the pulmonary type, *fear of the world*, which causes the soul to withdraw into the body.

In response to this fear, the lung type may retreat into a fantasy-filled inner world. The experience of being overwhelmed by the world is then converted by the opposite pole of the pulmonary dynamic, the one determined by the element of air, into something quite different. Brooding and reflection suddenly give way to enthusiasm and daydreaming, both of which are borne by an airy, sanguine attitude. The emergence of the latter may indicate an involvement of the kidney. However, this sanguine attitude lacks the purity of the sanguine temperament based in the kidney and has the characteristically pulmonary quality of oversensitivity.

In the sensitive schizoids described by Kretschmer, the physiological emphasis is on the head as well as on the lung: their emotional oversensitivity is combined with a tendency toward abstraction.[103] The former leads them to withdraw from the world in a form of autism. An incipient psychosis must be suspected when the schizoid lung type loses interest in outer life, sinks into brooding and finally succumbs to delusions. Such delusions may be abstract or tinged with religious fanaticism. In any event, the mental formations created by the pulmonary formative forces are either very definitely contoured or else ephemeral. According to Steiner, such mental symptoms are based on disturbances of the pulmonary metabolism.[104] Although very little is yet known of pulmonary metabolism in psychoses, Steiner's indications concerning the mucous process in the lung, which tends toward either solidification or dissolution and plays an essential role in the physical syndromes outlined below, may yet prove to be significant.[105] Schizophrenia in lung types involves a combination of metabolic disorders in both the lung and the kidney.

Even more so than with the previous types, the pulmonary types' neurotic symptoms represent intensifications of their underlying psychological polarity. Their oversensitivity allows even insignificant experiences to traumatize them. Such traumas also affect their respiration, leading in some cases to actual physical disorders, such as bronchial asthma. The spasms of bronchial asthma indicate a disharmonious, convulsive penetration on the part of an astral body that has previously withdrawn due to an upsetting experience. During exhalation, the astral body cannot relax its grip on the respiratory passages and thus hinders the expulsion of oppressive air.[106] This explains the asthma patients' intense fear of their surroundings. The antipathy pole of respiration, which dominates at the beginning of exhalation, intensifies in their strained efforts to exhale.

103. E. Kretschmer, *Körperbau und Charakter* (Berlin: 1944), p. 297f.
104. See R. Steiner, *SM,* lecture 13.
105. R. Steiner, *Mensch und Welt: Das Wirken des Geistes in der Natur* (GA351), lecture 2.
106. R. Steiner, *Physiologisch-Therapeutisches* (see note 55), lecture of Jan. 2, 1924.

1. Obsessive-Compulsive Illness

Asthmatics can "outgrow" their illness; on the other hand, it may never fully surface, in which case there may be some wheezing or shortness of breath in reaction to upsetting experiences, but not to the extent that the patient would complain. On the basis of the close connections between physical and emotional processes in the lung, one might imagine the following further development: the spasms of respiration shift, perhaps by way of an irregular "respiration" of the cerebrospinal fluid, into the soul, where the astral body now seeks vainly to free itself of the invasive outer world. Sense impressions and mental pictures deriving from the external world dominate the respiratory system's emotionally-tinged pictorial experience. This calls forth defensive reactions and new fear of the surroundings, which is frequently accompanied by minor constrictions of the bronchioles. The critical factor in the development of obsessions is that liberated pulmonary formative forces, including "extract forces" from the lung parenchyma, force mental pictures upon the mind.[107] The "extract forces," in fact, have the greatest solidifying effect of any bodily forces and produce the most resistant formations known to psychiatry.

This situation in the lung can be complicated by an asthenic constitution in which the metabolic-limb system is too weak and the protein of the organs contains too little sulfur. The sensory experiences accompanying this constitution generally impress themselves too weakly upon the metabolic system; that is, they cannot be completely forgotten, and rise up again and again out of organic metabolism, defying all efforts at control.[108] These experiences are then permeated in the pulmonary sphere by solidifying forces, and the astral body becomes fixated upon them. They enter consciousness as obsessions, which repeatedly surge out of the semiconscious emotional life of the lung and into the head.

This describes the development of the so-called obsessive-compulsive neurosis. This neurosis need not be accompanied by any impairments of respiration, though it is frequently accompanied by asthma. Emotional hypersensitivity and anxiety figure prominently as predisposing factors, as they do for asthma.[109]

---

107. R. Steiner, *Therapeutic Insights: Earthly and Cosmic Laws,* lectures 3 & 4.
108. R. Steiner, *CE,* lecture 5.
109. J. Rattner, *Psychosomatische Medizin heute* (Zurich: 1964), p. 122.

The first psychological symptoms are usually obsessions, which in turn can lead to the avoidance of certain actions out of fear (phobias), and finally to compulsive acts. For example, the obsessive idea that touching anything causes one to become soiled can produce a fear of contact, *haptephobia.* This can lead in turn to a compulsion to wash one's hands, which can eventually dominate the patient's entire life. Considered from the point of view of the etheric body, obsessive-compulsive neurosis is actually a psychotic process, since it involves the liberation of organic formative forces. The designation "obsessive-compulsive illness" is therefore preferable.

Whereas hepatic depression typically entails omissions in the train of thought, here—in the sphere of the rhythmic system—a tendency toward *repetition* can be observed.[110] In contrast to delusions, the pulmonary formative forces create nothing new, but rather only constantly repeat external impressions within the soul.

The most characteristic feature of obsessions and compulsions is the fact that patients occasionally recognize their irrationality; rather than losing themselves in them, they are able to maintain a certain critical, albeit impotent distance. The patient's antipathy pole dominates, but as with asthma on the physical level, it fails to produce any relief for the astral body in the form of "exhalation."

"The beginning often falls in childhood."[111] In any event, obsessive-compulsive illnesses are rooted in the first seven years of life, during which children's sensory organisms, both physical and emotional, develops out of their perceptions and mental images. If, however, a child is not completely comfortable with these experiences, they tend to settle as foreign bodies into the subconscious. A restrictive, overly rigid upbringing can favor this and thus prepare the ground for obsessive-compulsive illness. The formation of alien structures in the soul leads in this case to obsessions, but also to disruptions of anabolism in the organs, which can produce the constitution described above as the foundation for obsessive-compulsive pathology.

Actual obsessive-compulsive neuroses, however, are seldom observed before the age of ten.[112] In the second seven-year period, the astral body,

110. R. Steiner, *SM,* lecture 13.
111. E. Bleuler, *Lehrbuch der Psychiatrie* (Berlin: 1983), p. 531.

together with the ego, is active in the lower organization. Through the rhythmic system, it seeks a differentiated, affective relationship with the world.[113] Children who in their ninth year do not submerge themselves in their metabolism and also do not develop the heart as a counterweight to the lung can become emotionally oversensitive. However, a compulsive disorder arises only when ideation becomes pathological as described above and combines with the lung's enhanced sensitivity. At this early stage, a critical distancing from obsessive ideas such as was mentioned above is scarcely possible.

Another precondition is the release of formative forces from the lung that harden mental pictures into obsessions. This release is enhanced by a brain-oriented education, which withdraws too many formative forces from the organism, especially during the child's second seven-year phase, and is part of the reason why these "often highly intelligent children"[114] develop a compulsive illness of the lung rather than a later schizophrenia.

So much for the organic aspect underlying obsessive-compulsive phenomena. The ego is involved differently in phobias than it is in obsessions, notwithstanding the fact that the latter tend to play a part in the development of the former. This aspect was elaborated by Steiner.[115]

The sympathetic role of respiration culminates physically in inhalation. In the disordered soul it encourages the elaboration of daydreams, which are an attempt to inwardly shape the world of actual experience according to one's desires. Daydreams can then lead to delusions, which are also usually based on actual experience. Delusions can be aggravated by distorted perception, that is, by psychiatric delusions proper; for example, the wishful misapprehension of a real situation can cause a romantic delusion, whose emotional relation to the environment points to the lung, but whose forcefulness points to the reproductive organs.

The displaced pulmonary formative forces active in such illusionary representations imitate the airy rather than the solid element: the

112. G. Nissen, in *Lehrbuch der speziellen KinderundJugendpsychiatrie* (Berlin: 1971), p. 72. H. Müller-Wiedemann, *Mitte der Kindheit* (Stuttgart: 1973), p. 21. The latter is particularly helpful on the subject of the ninth year.

113. W. Holtzapfel, *Childrens' Illnesses* (Spring Valley, NY: Mercury Press,1989), p. 32.

114. G. Nissen, in *Lehrbuch der speziellen KinderundJugendpsychiatrie*, p. 72. H. Müller-Wiedemann, *Mitte der Kindheit*, p. 21.

115. R. Steiner, *The Boundaries of Natural Science* (Hudson, N.Y.: Anthroposophic Press, 1984), lectures 6 & 7.

deluded person "builds castles in the air." Rudolf Steiner indicated that solidifying pulmonary "extract forces" are also involved in this, a fact that should be considered when illusions take on the form of *idees* fixes, or when the "cloud castles" have unusually sharp contours.[116]

Delusional patients will occasionally develop an outright lust for experience, with the tendency to use the world to mirror themselves in or to "inhale themselves from." This affective syndrome is related on the physical level to catarrhs of the bronchi and lungs. Whereas the asthmatic process tends toward hardening and ultimately toward the calcifications of tuberculosis, in catarrh the tendency is toward dissolution. Experiences and situations in which individuals "lose themselves in the world" and becomes inwardly "feverish" can lead to catarrhal inflammations, which are specific to the respiratory tract. Again, whereas asthma tends to be preceded by a sudden excarnation due to emotional trauma, in catarrhal ailments the excarnation is more diffuse and gradual, although it too can be initiated by a trauma. Even in this preliminary stage, however, individuals can react strongly and "feverishly" to their passive absorption by the world.[117] Inflammation and fever represent the "breathing in" of the soul back into the body, whereby the dominating influences of the outside world are kept at a distance, unlike in asthma. The metabolic blood-process intensifies, destroying foreign bodies and processes, whereas in asthma, external influences can invade the organism directly through the lung, in which the astral body has become "caught" in its attempt to reintegrate itself. Asthma places a strain on exhalation and intensifies consciousness, whereas catarrhal inflammations emphasize inhalation and diminish consciousness with fever.

The inflammatory process, when diverted from the body to the soul, produces delusions and fantasies; the emotion-and desire-filled metabolic pose asserts itself in the lung, counterbalancing both physically and mentally the soul's absorption by the world.

Both the hardening and the inflammatory poles are at work in tuberculosis. Chronic, indurative forms of tuberculosis, which are frequently connected with asthma, can be preceded or accompanied by obsessions, whereas inflammatory, exudative forms are characterized more by delu-

116. R. Steiner, *Therapeutic Insights: Earthly and Cosmic Laws*, lectures 3 & 4.
117. R. Steiner, *Krankheitsfälle* (footnote 50), p. 75.

sional wishes and fantasies. The latter forms also tend to be accompanied by a euphoria that is also typical of slightly febrile pulmonary patients, a euphoria distinguishable from the manic patient's driven exuberance by its diffuse, "floating" quality.

2. *Hysteria*

In hysteria, the lung type's emotional lability and sensitivity are modified in a special way. In contrast to the epileptic, the hysteric's organs are too *permeable* to the astral body.[118] The permeability that is normal for the lung spreads to the other organs, enhancing the overall dominance of the pulmonary system. The astral body, rather than thoroughly penetrating the organs as it should, merely "suffuses" them as air does the lung during respiration. Hysterics surrenders their astral body too much to the surroundings even as children, reacting prematurely and exaggeratedly to outside influences. Their emotional pole is strongly emphasized, and their relationship with the world is delusional. Out of the hysterics' constitutional discarnation arises an increased urge to find themselves reflected in the world, to "inhale themselves" from it. The lust for experience can be a transition to hysteria; hysteria, however, draws upon other sources as well.

Obsessive-compulsive conditions result, as we have seen, when pulmonary psychopathology combines with an unhealthy representational process in the head. Obsessive-compulsive conditions thus have their roots in the first seven-year period. Juvenile and adult hysteria, by contrast, are anchored most fundamentally in the second seven-year period, which is characterized by pulmonary hypersensitivity, "emotional irritability."[119] At puberty, which in hysterics is frequently premature (at least on the emotional level), this hypersensitivity combines with metabolic forces. The latter subsequently dominate and become overly independent, leading sometimes to an adipose, amorphous (i.e. dysplastic) constitution accompanied by digestive disorders and "sexual symptoms." This contrasts with the predominantly delicate build of the prepubertal hysteric child. "Hysteria proper," "mental hysteria," can develop out of this constitution.[120]

118. R. Steiner, *CE*, lecture 4.
119. Ibid.
120. R. Steiner, *SM*, lecture 2.

Puberty releases the astral forces of the hysteric patient's urogenital system to an excessive degree. Intensified desires and emotions lead to an effort to realize previously harbored pulmonary delusions. The sexual forces occupied in this way are withheld from the genitalia, leading to either anatomic or functional underdevelopment. On the psychological level these forces produce the hysteric patient's characteristic preoccupation with sex or act as creative forces within the etheric body and soul, leading among other things to an artistic bent.[121] However, in hysteria, these creative forces always elude individual control and instead lend reality to the dominant astral body's wishes and fears.

For example, the unrealistic desire to avoid an unpleasant confrontation can produce a "hysterical" paralysis in which the legs can in fact no longer be moved (in distinction to feigned paralysis). The wish to be paralyzed acts directly upon the etheric body, even to the extent of producing hemostasis in the affected limb. In contrast to actual organic paralysis, however, the solid substance of the nerves is not damaged. The astral body's excarnation favors an abnormal influence of consciousness upon the limbs.

Functional disorders of this kind express an organ-neurotic process of hysterical type. They can manifest even before puberty, since the hysteric constitution begins drawing emotional forces from the sexual organs even before those organs mature. Conversely, should a "hysteric character" emerge after puberty, "remnants of the prepubertal stage" may persist throughout life. Just as the hysteric child of the second seven-year period shows signs of sexual precocity, so can the adult hysteric appear more or less a naive preadolescent for the rest of his or her life.[122]

The hysteric's affected, theatrically demonstrative behavior likewise points to a connection of deep psychological forces with the lust for experience and with the delusional tendency of pulmonary psychopathology. Patients can even subconsciously stage "dramas" that in the long run create an illusionary external world corresponding to the world within.

The word "hysteria," derived from the Greek word *hystera* ("womb"), indicates a special connection of hysteria with the female reproductive

121. R. Steiner, *Physiology and Therapeutics.*

122. E. Kretschmer, *Hysterie, Reflex, und Instinkt* (Stuttgart: 1958), p.34f.

system. This is borne out by the fact that hysteria is predominately an illness of the female sex, and that hysterical men display feminine character traits.

Many hysteric symptoms, especially fear, can manifest themselves physically at the opposite pole form hysteria. For example, hysterics may experience asthma attacks. In this way the hysteric enters physically into the condition that the compulsive patient lives in psychologically. Alexander finds that "some asthmatics are compulsives, while others are of a more hysterical nature."[123] This fact is mentioned to show that mixed forms exist not only between two disease poles on a given plane, such as a compulsive reaction in a hysteric or a hysterical reaction in a compulsive; the mixture can also involve elements form both the psychological and the physical planes.[124]

The lung schema, like that of the kidney, is characterized by polarities.

Lung

constituents:	physical body	⟷	astral body
elements:	earth	⟷	air
temperament	melancholic		
character:	sensitive		
relationship to body and world:	fear of surroundings	⟷	addiction to surroundings
physical polarity:	exhalation	⟷	inhalation
emotional polarity	antipathy, compulsions	⟷	sympathy, illusions

Diseases: Obsessive-compulsive disorder, hysteria

Table 11

123. F. Alexander, *Psychosomatische Medizin* (Berlin: 1951), p. 104.

124. R. Treichler, *Vom Wesen der Hysterie* (Stuttgart: 1964). See also *The Anthroposophical Approach to Medicine,* vol. I, chapter 8.

D. The Heart

As the central organ of the rhythmic organization, the heart displays many appropriately modified characteristics of the central organ of the metabolism, the liver. The material processes set in motion by the kidney are centered around the water organism of the liver; similarly, the products of metabolism that rise up through the blood are centered around the heart, flowing from there into the lungs and head, where they enter into a more highly differentiated relationship with the world. The heart thus mediates between above and below as well as between inside and outside, supporting an inner life that emphasizes the center and is sensitive to the surrounding world.

The entire activity of the lower human being is perceived and transformed in the heart. The physical basis of this is the passage of blood, through which the heart receives the warmth produced by the ego in the metabolism. The heart is the organ of warmth par excellence. Through it the ego perceives the relative warmth of the various streams of blood and strives to balance them. Through the heart, the ego also directs the transformation of physical into emotional warmth. Emotional warmth then streams into thinking, which otherwise would remain abstract and lifeless. In addition, the heart harbors the processes that ultimately liberate formative forces in the head, making realistic, living thinking possible ("etherization of the blood").[125] Furthermore, the heart mediates the realization of insight in action. Only after an intention has been "weighed in the heart" and the heart has "warmed" to it can a person perform deeds that fit meaningful into society. Emotional and spiritual warmth is thereby transformed back into physical warmth in the processes of will and movement.[126]

The ego lives primarily in the blood, or more specifically, in the blood's nearly constant warmth. It radiates out into the world but must also assert its independence from the world. The center of this independence is the heart, which is the organ of the ego in the middle organization, just as the hepatobiliary system is that organ in the metabolism. The heart is the "center of the center" and thus the ego's most character-

125. R. Steiner, *Wonders of the World* (London: Rudolf Steiner Press, 1983), lecture 9.

126. See R. Steiner, *The Bridge Between Universal Spirituality and the Physical Constitution of Man* (Spring Valley, N.Y.: Anthroposophic Press, 1979).

istic organ. From it the ego radiates into the blood and the fluid organism; the bile process described in the section on the liver is only a special case of this. In fact, the example of bile makes it clear that from its center in the heart, the ego unites with the etheric body and its forces of warmth more than with any other aspect of the organism.

The rhythmic system establishes our emotional relationship to the world, upon which our sense of self is based. The heart is responsible for our consciousness of earthly life, which Rudolf Steiner characterized as a "consciousness of the center."[127] The ego uses the heart to establish a personal relationship with the future, the present, and the past. The emotional life of the heart tends toward a more stable equilibrium between sympathy and antipathy than is possible in the lung. Sympathy and antipathy, positive and negative feelings, can thus be put to greater practical use. For example, sympathy can be transformed from mere resonance into creative activity, while antipathy, by providing distance from its objects, can help develop insight.

The emotional life of the healthy "heart type," whose physical build approximates the pyknic type, is based upon inner warmth that is permeated by the ego and constantly transforming itself, and that in the process affects all the other elements of the body. Heart types' warm-heartedness warms the hearts of others as well. In their courage we see a sublimation of the volitional bile forces; similarly, their choleric temperament, which feeds upon the bile forces and issues from the heart, is distinguished from the choleric eruptions of the hepatobiliary type by its more disciplined manifestation. "Righteous anger" is an anger of the heart.

The heart type is governed more than any other organ type by conscience and by a sense of responsibility. Through conscience, each one of us can bring our actions into harmony with the world. True courage involves responsibility and conscience, as does love, the heart's supreme force. Love unites all the polar forces and tendencies of the soul. It can transform fruitless rage about the state of the world into constructive action, provided desire and will are purified and permeated with knowledge and perception. Then devotion can be balanced with independence and action with respect for the objects being acted upon.

---

127. R. Steiner, *True and False Paths in Spiritual Investigation* (London: Rudolf Steiner Press, 1985), lecture 3.

Striving in this way toward harmony with the world, mediating between the world and the soul, the intellectual or mind soul, out of which the power of love arises, issues from the heart and lung while remaining rooted in the hepatobiliary system. The mind soul's emotional aspect is connected more with the heart, its intellectual aspect more with the lung.

Exhalation and inhalation in the lungs are matched in the heart by systole and diastole, which together represent a concentration of the "above-below" polarity encountered in the lung. In the systole (contraction), the head-pole strives toward form, while in the diastole (relaxation), the pole of the metabolic-limb system favors dissolution. Another polarity expressed in the heart is that of "inside-outside," which is the most decisive determinant of the life of the lung. In the systole, blood flows outward from the center, thus exhibiting a kind of diastole, whereas in the diastole, the blood returns from the periphery to the center, exhibiting a kind of systole. Through pulmonary circulation, individualized emotion encounters the surrounding world; here, however, in contrast to respiration, the emphasis is on the center of the organism and of the soul.

The two poles of the heart's activity alternate with each other in a stronger and more centralized way than do those of the lung. Each pole responds to and compensates for the effects of the other almost immediately; ultimately it is the ego that intervenes in the pauses between systole and diastole and initiates the contrary movement.[128] The heart can thus be seen as the center of all striving toward equilibrium, the center in which the ego constantly struggles to balance extremes. As it struggles, however, it creates a larger "inner space" for itself, which it can then fill with greater intensity. Each polarity is thus an opportunity for the ego to enhance its activity, upon which all personal development is based.

1. The Heart and Psychosis

The pathology that results form a loss of equilibrium in the heart is, as with the lung, distinguished by the individual's relationship with the world, but here with a greater emphasis upon the ego. Either the diastolic or the systolic tendency can be intensified to the point where a balance can no longer be struck.

128. R. Steiner, *Rhythmen im Kosmos und im Menschenwesen* (GA 350), lecture of June 6, 1923.

Anger originating from the heart can intensify into fits of rage, sometimes associated with outright destructiveness. This can be preceded or accompanied by delusions of grandeur. In this process, a boundlessly growing sense of self is suffused with unbridled will forces and unleashes itself upon the world, utterly insensitive to the world's own needs and demands. Here the diastolic tendency toward dissolution wins out. The purity of such rage distinguishes it from the liver-gall type's choleric eruptions and from the renal type's aggressive outbursts. However, as mentioned in the discussion of schizophrenic raving, agitation flowing from the kidney can also take hold of the heart, converting the storm of the air element into a raging fire storm.

Such outbursts are always connected with the heart's forces of warmth, which in this case can no longer be contained within the organ.[129] In short, the heart's creative warmth becomes a consuming fire. This is observed in various psychoses, especially in catatonic schizophrenia, which, as described, can be fatal if left untreated. Fits of rage are here accompanied by an extremely accelerated heartbeat, indicating the source of the disturbance.

Attacks of rage can also occur after episodes of heart disease, when the forces that enhanced cardiac activity on the physical level begin to affect the soul as well. Here it may be mentioned in passing that palpitations, like all other cardiac symptoms, can represent the effects of physical or emotional processes occurring in other organs, since everything that happens in the organism ultimately makes itself felt in the heart, the center of the rhythmic organization.

The raging person's urge to destroy can be accompanied by feelings of pleasure, especially in mania. To a mind expanding in inner diastole, even the prospect of one's own death can bring pleasure. In some cases, an outright death wish can drive the patients to suicide, whereby they may feel that they are flying or freeing themselves from the body. Like Goethe's Faust on the eve of Easter, suicidal patients can be filled with hope of entering a new and more beautiful world.

The psychological phenomena related to the systole, on the other hand, are determined by the solid element, by a tendency toward hardening. In terms of warmth, the systole is the "cold" pole. People who

129. R. Steiner, *Therapeutic Insights: Earthly and Cosmic Laws*, lectures 3 & 4.

feel threatened by the world in their innermost being and for that reason retreat into themselves manifest the emotional dynamic of the systole. Indeed, the systole is the physiological basis of fear, an emotion that has been repeatedly associated with the heart.[130] Confined within an earthly body in the earthly world, many people feel their individuality slipping away; their fear of annihilation can become fear of nothingness, which materialistic consciousness equates with the time after death.

Cardiac fear is always at bottom a fear of death, based on an experience of our death-like confinement in the body and the world. Though we may seek liberation from this fear by becoming destructive (a tendency of the diastolic pole), the true emotional opposite of the fear of death is the manic death wish.

Even when cardiac fear is not overtly a fear of death, it still involved consciousness of an existential threat. It may, for example, be fear of a disgrace that could destroy one's career, or of a debilitating disease. Guilt feelings, self-reproaches, and notions of sinfulness are added when depression is present. All of these emotions are predisposed in the liver but arise only through the involvement of the heart, inasmuch as the heart is the organ of conscience. They are the polar opposites of the experiences of grandeur arising out of the unhealthy diastole. In contrast to the manics, who are boundlessly confident about the future and expect all kinds of honors, depressives are sure that everything they have ever done is wrong and that they have burdened themselves with immeasurable guilt. Profound despair of this sort can deepen into a depressive stupor; feelings of sinfulness and tormenting self-reproaches can literally immobilize the patient. Such a stupor, which always indicates the involvement of the heart, can be called a "stupor of conscience." This is the opposite of madness, in whose general process of dissolution all conscious ideas and feelings can be totally submerged.

Pathological self-reproaches, toward which the overconscientious cardiac type is disposed even before depression, correspond to the pulmonary type's pathological obsessions. However, they indicate a pathological contraction of the ego, not, as with the pulmonary type, a pathological

130. Schultz-Hencke (see note 21), p. 297; here, sadness is assigned to the liver, and vexation (anger) to the bile.

contraction of the soul. Combining with the destructive urge of madness, they can produce an elemental, self-destructive urge, which, as a motive for suicide in endogenous depressions, indicates the involvement of the heart in more than one way.

The physical basis of cardiac fear is spasms of the coronary vessels. Just as fear can cause the blood vessels of the fact to constrict and make us "go white," so can the heart constrict as the ego pulls back into it through the blood. The resulting feelings of oppression or constriction can escalate into a sense of impending death, especially during an attack of angina pectoris. Here the connection between physical and emotional processes, between organic and psychoneurotic symptoms, is particularly close. Even guilt feelings tend to be accompanied by sensations of pressure around the heart. When these sensations appear by themselves, the presence of suppressed guilt feelings or of cardiac fear can often be inferred. It is likely from our point of view that every guilt feeling, no matter how small, incites a contraction of the coronary vessels and thus ultimately favors angina pectoris. Here, in contrast to raving madness, which springs from the heart's interior, we are dealing with the surface of the heart, in which memories become "pangs of conscience."[131]

Summarizing, we may say that every psychosis can affect the heart. Manic-depressive phases rising from the liver tend to do so particularly, resulting either in a heightening of manic willfulness to the point of maniacal rage or in the emergence of overwhelming depressive guilt feelings and notions of sinfulness. Any involvement of the heart signifies a decisive and frequently final inner struggle. The heightened danger often seems to rouse the ego's will to live; its retreat into the body in cardiac fear is at the same time a gathering of its forces. The catatonic forms of schizophrenia that take hold of the heart in rage have the best prognosis of all forms of schizophrenia. Cardiac psychotics may also count on more sympathy from their surroundings due to the dramatic, moving nature of their symptoms, for example, their notions of sinfulness, or their suicidal despondency. These they may express spontaneously or, failing that, should be elicited from them by sympathetic questioning.

131. R. Steiner, *Therapeutic Insights: Earthly and Cosmic Laws*, lectures 3 & 4.

2. Cardiac Neurosis

Cardiac or heart neurosis, which is present in 30% to 40% of all cases of heart disease, encompasses all psychosomatic disorders of the heart.[132] The cardiac neurotic complains initially of a pounding, rapid, or irregular heartbeat. Other complaints include piercing or burning pains and tightness in the chest, sometimes accompanied by respiratory distress. Tightness and an accelerated heartbeat are frequently connected with the cardiac fear discussed in the last section (fear of death, disgrace, or annihilation). The physical symptoms produced by cardiac neurosis cause this fear to be focused on the heart, leading to organically unfounded fears of death by heart attack (cardiophobia).

The absence of organic causes for cardiac symptoms should prompt investigation of the patient's mental history. Frequently the patient has a history of stressful experiences, especially of separation. A heart-rending separation, the death of a loved one, or even the mere witnessing of a cardiac death or of a fatal accident can be the initiating experience, as can merely hearing about someone else's death due to heart disease. The distinguishing feature is that the experience is "taken to heart" and perceived as a threat to one's own existence. An additional factor can be occupational stress, which affects the coronary arteries and leads to pains and sensations of tightness that can radiate out from the heart into the left arm.[133]

The mental history holds the key to why some patients become cardiac neurotics in response to stressful situations and others do not. Many cardiac neurotics have always defined themselves in terms of others. Their neurosis can be triggered, for example, by having to cut the apron strings to a domineering mother or having to separate from a lover. The predominant symptoms are cardiophobia with episodes of rapid heartbeat and fear of death, or simply the paralyzing or agitating fear of such episodes.[134]

Cardiac neurotics who experience tightness in the chest or organically-based angina pectoris often tend toward the personality type that

132. Cf. H. Richter and D. Beckmann, *Herzneurose* (Stuttgart: 1969), p. 19f.
133. Kleinsorge and Klumbies, *Psychotherapie in Klinik und Praxis* (Munich: 1959), p. 10f.
134. W. Bräutigam and P. Christians, *Psychosomatische Medizin* (Stuttgart: 1975), p. 105f., p. 138f.

has been associated with coronary artery disease. In contrast to the emotionally dependent neurotics just discussed, neurotics of this type usually have had a strict upbringing. Overly self-controlled, they distance themselves from life intellectually and seek refuge in incessant "achievement and activity."[135] In contrast to the first type of cardiac neurotic, they tend to suppress or belittle their symptoms. The spasms of their coronary arteries, however, may indicate the beginning of organic heart disease, which can culminate in a heart attack.

Both of these symptom groups, which can overlap, indicate an unhealthy predominance of either the diastole or the systole, of expansion or of contraction. In the first group, characterized by increased cardiac activity and emotionality, the diastole or lower pole of the organism predominates. In the second group, characterized by spasms of the coronary arteries and angina pectoris, the systole or upper pole predominates. Patients in the latter group submerge themselves in work and intellectualize their emotional problems, whereas those in the former group give in to their emotions and try to rid themselves of them through aggression. Both groups experience the fear of death, the fear of losing their individuality. Inasmuch as their egos are prevented from exercising a balancing influence of their hearts, this fear has a rational basis. The functional disorders associated with each syndrome can further contribute to this fear.

All forms of cardiac neurosis are favored by the increasing lack of rhythm in our hectic lives, a loss that strikes particularly at the rhythmic organ par excellence, the heart. The coronary arteries become involved when in addition to loss of rhythm there is an overburdening with responsibility. The cardiac type, when they lose their inner balance, are especially endangered by cardiac neurosis; furthermore, the psychoses that afflict them involve the heart more deeply than in other people. This may be seen as the price they pay for the natural privileges that, when healthy, cardiac types enjoys over other organ types.

All experiences that impede the development of the ego in the heart also prevent the mind soul from freeing itself from the heart. An incomplete detachment from one's mother or from other figures in childhood can prefigure such disorders. "Symbiotic" relationships hinder the ego's

135. Ibid.

development and cause it to remain in its childhood state, when it is more or less contained within the heart. Later experiences of separation cause the ego's powers of love to withdraw into the heart. The escape into work cannot transform this burden into healthy activity.

These and other existential problems can tax the heart as early in life as the twenties. In many cases, however, they do not produce a cardiac neurosis until the end of that decade. Statistics show that most cases develop between the late twenties and forty, that is, during the middle of life. This is the period when the mind soul should be developing; hence the forces that first afflict the heart with instability and constriction are those of the mind soul striving unsuccessfully to free itself from the heart. In my experience, many cardiac neurotics are better able to deal with their symptoms when they learn that their heart ailments are caused not just by external factors, but also by an inner developmental crisis, by a struggle of the forces within their souls.

Table 12:

		Heart			
constituents:	etheric body (warmth ether)	⟵	ego	⟶	physical body
elements:	fire	⟵	warmth (median)	⟶	earth (cold)
temperament			choleric		
character:			courageous		
relationship to body and world:	lust for death	⟵		⟶	fear of death
physical polarity:	diastole	⟵		⟶	systole
emotional polarity	delusions of grandeur, raving madness	⟵		⟶	guilt, "stupor of conscience"

Diseases: all psychoses and neuroses involving the heart; cardiac neurosis

This crisis, however, is more than just individual. The continuing rise in cardioneurotic illness (currently estimated at two to five percent of the population[136]) is a symptom of the growing developmental crisis of humanity as a whole as described by Rudolf Steiner. The spiritual organ "heart" perceives the threatening standstill in inner development that occurs in the twenties; this perception is what ultimately underlies the cardioneurotic's fear of heart failure. On the other hand, when healed of their neurosis, cardioneurotics can feel inspired to devote themselves more courageously and lovingly to their lives and to their inner development; in a word, their illness proves to have been meaningful.

The heart is also centrally important to the development of the consciousness soul. Our "higher selves" act through the heart into earthly life, uniting with our "lower selves."[137] The dawning of the spirit in the consciousness soul is at the same time a spiritual event in the heart, namely, the uniting of the light of knowledge with the expansive forces of love. Through the voice of conscience that resounds from the heart—the same voice that the depressive patient hears in an unhealthily magnified and distorted form—our higher selves can speak to us. Thus, on the deepest level, the cardiac distress of our time is quite simply the birth pangs of the consciousness soul. The more the consciousness soul can raise itself to the spirit out of the body's gradual deterioration, the more energetically will it issue from the heart, bringing spiritual life to thinking and spiritual aims to the will.The heart schema, like that of the liver, is once again characterized by mediated polarities. The ego's position between the physical and etheric bodies in the heart indicates its function as mediator between physical and spiritual activity, which are connected in the heart by the processes of warmth-transformation described above.

---

136. Cf. H. Richter and D. Beckmann, *Herzneurose* (Stuttgart: 1969), p. 19f.
137. R. Steiner, *How to Know Higher Worlds* (Hudson, N.Y.: Anthroposophic Press, 1994). See "Changes in the Dream Life of the Esoteric Student."

The Treatment of Psychological Disorders

In anthroposophically oriented medicine, pathology holds the key to therapy. The nature of an illness itself gives clues on how to treat it.

A. Therapy of the Spirit

The addition of a spiritual dimension to psychiatry changes the nature of psychotherapy. In keeping with the nature of the mind, the treatment of mental disorders must be oriented toward spiritual goals. Therapies that restrict themselves to the confines of the individual soul can help resolve a neurosis, but if they do not call on the patient's ego and thereby help initiate a period of personal development, they can have no lasting effect, nor can they truly heal. Viktor Frankl, following Carl Jung, renewed attention to this fact with his demand for a "spiritual psychotherapy," a "logotherapy."[138]

Not all the details of a proper therapy of the spirit can be discussed here.[139] The most fundamental principle, however, is that no techniques should be employed for which the patient is not ready or has no profound need. A beginning can often be made by appealing to spiritual interests that patients once had but have since forgotten. For example, they can be encouraged to return to literature that once was personally meaningful or to a subject of previous part-time study. Their conversations with the therapist can also stimulate them to seek out new reading material or objects of study. In any event, therapy of the spirit should help patients realize the meaning not only of their life, but also of their illness, so that they can emerge from its strengthened and full of resolve for the future. The therapist can ease the way into that future by advising and conferring with the patient's family and friends.

The most powerful method of spiritual therapy is meditation, specifically as developed for western humanity by Rudolf Steiner. Steiner emphasized the significance of meditation in connection with the question whether missed opportunities in psychological development could

---

138. V.E. Frankl, *Ärztliche Seelsorge* (Vienna: 1947); *Theorie und Therapie der Neurosen* (Munich: 1956).

139. Cf. in this regard: Paul von der Heide, "Wie fügt sich Psychotherapie in die Erweiterung der Heilkunst?" *BEH* (1957)/3–4; F. W. Zeylmans van Emmichoven, *Gespräche über die Hygiene der Seele* (Arlesheim: 1957); P. von der Heide, H. Lauer, and W. Priever, *Das therapeutische Gespräch* (Stuttgart: 1980); and R. Treichler, *Die Entwicklung der Seele* (see footnote 6).

be made up for later.[140] Meditation unites all the forces of the soul—the cognitive, emotive, and volitional—in regular concentration upon a single thought or image. It is the best means of strengthening and stimulating the ego and the consciousness soul, although other aspects of the soul are similarly enhanced.

Not all patients will be mature enough for conscious meditative practice. However, all therapeutic measures employed should have a meditative character. That is, they should be regular exercises that the patients enjoy and completely immerse themselves in. In this manner the patients re-enact on a conscious level the unconditional, instinctive devotion they had as children, and thereby reestablish the connection they once had with the spiritual world by virtue of their bodily development.

All therapy of the spirit must be evaluated before it is applied, lest it do the patient more harm than good. This is particularly true of the reading of anthroposophical or other spiritual literature, which psychotic or borderline-psychotic individuals can use as material for delusions and hallucinations. The ego of these patients is inaccessible, and their etheric body in part discarnated, so that even the best spiritual reading material can contribute to the emergence or aggravation of psychosis. The same applies to meditations the patient cannot perform properly. Severely ill patients do not need the concepts and exercises of anthroposophy; in many cases they must even be protected from them. What they do need are the medications of healing techniques of an anthroposophically oriented medicine.[141]

No such cautions are necessary regarding the so-called preliminary exercises of the meditative path, which train thinking, feeling, and willing and can be useful in the healing of many neuroses and chronic psychoses.[142] Similarly, Goethean-style studies of nature have a healing effect on neurotic and psychotic patients who are able to participate in them.[143]

---

140. See R. Steiner, *Metamorphoses of the Soul.*

141. *Fortschritte* 27 (1962).

142. R. Steiner, *An Outline of Esoteric Science* (Hudson, N.Y.: Anthroposophic Press, 1998). chapter 5: "Cognition of the Higher Worlds."

143. R. Steiner, "Practical Training in Thought" (in *Anthroposophy in Everyday Life,* Hudson, N.Y.: Anthroposophic Press, 1995).

Another useful exercise, which should be performed each night before falling asleep, is a silent *review* in reverse order of the day's event. During this exercise, the events of the day should be viewed as if they had happened to someone else. Although this exercise is difficult and can only be mastered gradually, it provides distance from the day's events and makes for better sleep.[144] Similarly, a morning *preview* of the day ahead, in which resolves to accomplish necessary tasks are renewed, helps patients to take charge of their lives and to start the day on a better foot. Patients with severe apathy and boredom or with mild cases of depression may wish to practice a modified form of each of these exercises. In the evening review, they should first focus on events that made an impression on them before they attempt the more comprehensive, impersonal review already described; similarly, in their morning preview, they should concern themselves more with the events or activities of the coming day that they most look forward to.[145]

In some cases, religious sensibilities can be appealed to; if they are latent, the therapist can sometimes encourage them. Here it is desirable to have the collaboration of a cleric, who ought to assume direction in such matters. Clerical advice is important in deciding whether the patient is ready for religious discussion or rituals, or whether the same temporary reserve is called for here as with spiritual concepts. Conversely, it should be emphasized that images and sacraments, especially those of the Christian Community, can have a healing effect.

The therapy of the spirit is important even in cases where patients' egos—their healthy faculties of cognition and judgment—are inaccessible. Delusive patients, for example, cannot be swayed from their delusions by logical argument; however, they can be periodically confronted with reality, which can shock them into an awareness of the senselessness of their delusions.[146] Similarly, endogenous depressives cannot be talked out of their depressed state; on the contrary, admonitions and unfulfillable demands by the therapist can even cause them emotional harm. Instead, regular, heartfelt encouragement is much likelier to be of help. Recovered depressives frequently report that although during

144. See R. Steiner, *An Outline of Esoteric Science.*

145. Further discussion in *Soziale Hygiene* (Stuttgart: 1973), esp. p. 179ff. See also O. Koob, *Erkennen und Heilen* (Stuttgart: 1984).

146. R. Steiner, *Manifestations of Karma*, lecture 8.

their illness they could not believe encouraging remarks made by their doctors and nurses, the sympathetic attention they received was a genuine comfort to them. Their egos responded to the warmth in other people's hearts.

In cases such as these, the technique of *therapeutic imaging* is especially effective and should completely replace arguments based on logic. Depressives have been helped by imagining the following scene: sun and sky are obscured by vapors rising from a swamp. This is analogous to depression, where the ego is engulfed by the effects of physiological disorders. However, just as the sun continues to shine above the clouds, so does the ego continue to exist even in the most severe depression; it is only temporarily prevented from "shining its light" upon the patient's life. When the "swamp," the dysfunctional body, no longer obscures inner life in "vapors" (a goal that is to be achieved as quickly as possible through therapy), the ego can shine forth once more.

Such techniques must be used with any patient who has regressed to a preadult developmental stage and is thus incapable of independent, mature judgment. Patients who have regressed into the situation of the *second* seven years of life require a loving authority figure whom in their innermost being they wish to emulate, someone to whom they can confide all their troubles and from whom they can receive guidance in the form of stories and pictures. Patients who have regressed even further, to the condition of the *first* seven years of life, are severely ill and require a healthy atmosphere that invites imitation. At this level all learning is instinctive and occurs only through immediate reaction to the perceived environment. Hence the way the people around such a regressed person think, feel, and act is of extreme importance to the way the regressed person's ego gradually reawakens. Especially decisive in the recovery of mentally regressed patients is their therapist's view of the nature of mental illness. The conviction that the ego can never fall ill, that it can only be prevented from manifesting itself in the body and in life, is a great source of therapeutic strength, enabling the therapist occasionally to connect with the ego of even the most severely ill patient, to see the ego light up in the patient's eyes. Such experiences, however, are usually only possible at the end of a long road. In fact, with some patients, particularly schizophrencis, it is advisable at first entirely to avoid direct eye contact and verbal address, so that their fragile ego will not retreat even further. Instead one should look or speak into the patients' surroundings, where their ego and feelings primarily reside.

It is always possible that no attempt to help patients regain control of their lives will succeed. The therapy of the spirit must reckon with these so-called "incurable cases" and alleviate suffering as best it can. Even here, however, unpredictable improvements, even cures, are always possible; the patient's ego can suddenly break through. Therapists convinced that the ego reincarnates in successive earthly lives can see meaning in every therapeutic measure, no matter how seemingly hopeless the case. Every therapeutic measure, every manifestation of the will to heal is taken up by the patient's ego and eventually helps it achieve a new state of health—if not in this life, then in a future one.

B. Psychological Therapy

1. Art Therapy[147]

In ancient Greek, *psyche* meant soul. In the anthroposophic view of the human being, the soul is distinct from the spirit. Whereas spirit is the faculty of knowledge, through which we grasp timeless truths, soul encompasses everything constituting our individual existence, thoughts, memories, feelings, desires, and acts of will. In the last section, "psychotherapy" as usually understood was equated with therapy of the spirit; by contrast, the treatment of the *soul* in the strict sense, i.e. "psychotherapy," consists for the anthroposophically oriented psychiatrist in the application of artistic exercises to specific ends. Such exercises speak most immediately to the emotions, and, as in the case of the therapy of the spirit, one can frequently build here on earlier inclinations. Artistic activity blends form and substance, thought and will into ever new experiences of harmony, allowing us to reconcile our emotional extremes and to find our center. The poet and philosopher Friedrich Schiller called the wellspring of this highly conscious process the *Spieltrieb*, the playfulness innate in all of us. Art therapy appeals to that playfulness, helping patients to recapture and develop their original potential.

147. See vol. 2, pp. 80–85. Also: M. Hauschka, *Zur künstlerischen Therapie* (Stuttgart: 1971) and P. von der Heide, *Zur künstlerischen Therapie* (Boll: 1978).

Art therapy, or even just the enjoyment of works of art, stimulates the ego to activity by way of the soul. Television, radio, and film on the other hand, do just the opposite. The more people become addicted to these media, the more they try to fill an inner void with a flood of images and sounds or to distract themselves from illness-induced fears with prepackaged "entertainment" and "excitement," the more passive they become. This is particularly true of the mentally disturbed. It should be evident that in such people the electronic media only increase an existing weakness of the ego by overwhelming the ego with a flood of impressions. Exposure to mass media also lessens sensitivity to artistic impressions. Radio and television are also known to have socially isolating effects; in particular, they aggravate the mentally disturbed person's inability to relate.

Apart from the frequently unsavory content of programs, the physically detrimental effects of watching television should also be considered. For example, the psychiatric patient's subtle organic disorders could be aggravated by the decreased circulation that results from prolonged television watching. As much as possible, therefore, patients undergoing psychiatric treatment should avoid exposure to the mass media or, if necessary, be prevented from receiving such exposure by the therapist.[148]

2. *Forms of Art Therapy*

Every form of art therapy is related to a specific aspect of the human soul and constitution. In this section we will follow the guidelines for art therapy set forth by Rudolf Steiner and others.[149] These have proven useful for the indication and evaluation of artistic exercises.

CLAY MODELING is directly related to the etheric body, which is both the "sculptor" of our physical body and the foundation of inner life. Stimulation of the etheric body through modeling is important for all types of organ pathology, from the schizophrenic's subtle defects in protein structure to the cyclothymic's or epileptic's congested hepatic metabolism, in short, for all organic disorders that demand an impulse

148. See *Soziale Hygiene, op.cit.*; and O. Koob, *Erkennen und Heilen.*

149. R. Steiner, *The Influence of Spiritual Beings on Man* (Hudson, N.Y.: Anthroposophic Press, 1982). For its relevance to art therapy, see Treichler (note 6), chapter 6.

toward restructuring. The formative effect of modeling also works upward from the etheric body into the patient's disharmonious or disintegrating psyche. A useful beginning exercise is the modeling of platonic solids (cube, tetrahedron, octahedron, pentadodecahedron, icosahedron), which brings an architectural element into the modeling experience. Many other forms can be developed out of these, including forms of the human body, such as the ear and hand. Equally important is the modeling of some kind of vessel, since this stimulates the consolidation of the organs as vessels for inner life. The plastic experience can be further enhanced through the firing of the pots and vases.

WOOD CARVING conveys an experience of the plastic processes occurring in bone. The carving tool acts in a way similar to osteoclasts, bone cells that complete the structuring of bone by removing substance from its outer surface. *Weaving*, by contrast, calls to mind the network of the nervous system, which gives rise to bodily forms in much the same way that the network of threads on the loom allows a pattern to arise in the cloth. With outlines, *drawing* emphasizes the boundary between self and world and is thus especially suitable for patients who have trouble fixing that boundary.

PAINTING stimulates the sentient soul, in which the experience of color primarily resides. Every time we remember something, we unconsciously "paint ourselves a picture" of it, adding colors from our current perceptions to the essentially colorless memory. To the extent that we remember, then, we are all "painters." A varied experience of color helps heal the dismal, atrophying, or distorted sentient life of the severely bored, of schizophrenics, obsessive-compulsives, and sclerotics.

"An education in the experience of color awakens a lively interest in the surrounding world" that the ailing sentient soul has more or less lost.[150] Wet-on-wet watercolors are the best way to start; from pure colors one may progress to forms such as landscapes or human figures. At first only one color should be used; others may then be added gradually as the patient's condition permits or demands. Blue, for example, calms, whereas red stimulates. The enlivening of the sentient soul through color renews the imagination, enriching the inner life of some and enhancing the creativity of others.

150. M. Hauschka, *Zur künstlerischen Therapie*, p. 60.

MUSIC speaks primarily to the intellectual or mind soul and aids in healing its disorders. It leads away from the sensuous, visual experience of outer works of art and into the soul, where it evokes emotions. We are all "inner musicians" to the extent that we experience harmonies and dissonances among our emotions. Music helps to purify and objectify these experiences, partly by virtue of its mathematical structure. The mere fact of rhythm, of the division of music into beats and measures, helps bring order into inner life.

Mood swings toward sadness or overexuberance can be tempered with music. With depressives, one should start with the more sympathetic minor mode and work toward the major. With manics, the opposite applies. Schizophrenics can also benefit from the objectification of emotional dissonances through music. The use of certain older scales, such as the pentatonic, has proven useful in cases of psychotic regression into more juvenile mental states. One instrument that has been used for several decades in this connection is a new form of lyre developed by Gaertner and Pracht. Of all instruments, this one, with its subtle, reflective sound, has the most profound inner therapeutic effect.[151]

RECITATION AND POETRY appeal directly to the consciousness soul. In this realm, the soul transcends its merely personal existence; the ego reaches out into a larger world that includes other selves. Speech in its most natural form is conversation, but it is also self-expression; in the quality of speech, we can experience the level of personal development, which recitation exercises are designed to further.

Lyric poetry appeals to autistic schizophrenics, objectifying and enlivening their autism and thereby helping them to overcome it. The exaggerated emotions of depressive and manic patients can also be objectified with the help of the appropriate lyric works. *Hymnic poetry* frees obsessive-compulsives from their inner constriction and fear. The same applies to hymnic music in the realm of music therapy. The images of *epic poetry* encourage all patients to emerge from their inner isolation. In *drama,* patients can either read a part aloud or participate in an actual performance, encountering other human selves in a way that involves them emotionally but at the same time leaves them free.

151. E. Pracht, *Einführung in das Leierspiel* (Dornach: 1955).

Recitation and drama thus have therapeutic applications in addition to artistic ones.[152]

SINGING, which combines the emotional effect of music with the social tendency of speech, has proven useful as a transition from music therapy to recitation. It helps emotionally reserved patients share their feelings with the world and intensifies the music's inwardly liberating effect.

In EURYTHMY, the body becomes an instrument of the soul to a degree unmatched by any other art form. In eurythmy's flowing gestures, which transform speech and music into movement, all the other art forms are combined: modeling reappears in the shaping of gestures in space, painting in the colors of the costumes and the lighting as well as in the inward experiences of color that accompany the movements. Through gesture, patients engaging in eurythmy reach into the cosmic sphere from which all art forms flow and out of which we descend into earthly life; they experience as a whole something that every other art form gives them only from a particular point of view.[153] The etheric body receives that whole and communicates it as new forces to the body and to the soul.

Using special exercises, *curative eurythmy* applies eurythmy's beneficial effects to specific illnesses and organs. Impairments of an organic process are visible in the way a patient performs particular eurythmic movements. By correcting those movements, the therapist can positively influence the corresponding organic process. However, because of its organ-specificity, curative eurythmy is comparable to drug therapy and thus transcends the realm of art therapy proper.[154]

Starting from the concept of the four organ systems and their associated elements, one can begin to recognize connections between the various vocal sounds made visible in eurythmy and the organic disorders underlying psychological disorders. For example, the rolling, aspirant sound of *R* has a regulating effect upon the renal system's fluctuations in vitality. Similarly, the enclosing gesture of *B* is archetypally related to the interior of the kidney and to the renal process. This sound figures prominently in the treatment of schizophrenics, who are literally "beside them-

152. R. Steiner, *Speech and Drama,* (Hudson, N.Y.: Anthroposophic Press, 1986).

153. R. Steiner, *The Influence of Spiritual Beings on Man.*

154. R. Steiner, *Curative Eurythmy* (London: Rudolf Steiner Press, 1983). See also Kirchner-Bockholt, *Grundelemente der Heileurythmie* (Dornach: 1962).

selves" and in need of inner protection. The *B*-gesture stimulates both excretion and incretion in the kidney, and helps reintegrate renal forces that are escaping into the soul. The very shape of the kidney is that of a crystallized eurythmic *B*. The vowel *A* (pronounced *ah* as in "father") stimulates the astral body to unite more strongly with the physical body through the renal system. For schizophrenics and epileptics, the outstretching of the limbs in the *A* expresses the self's reawakening to an experience previously lost in the organic obscurity of the renal system. Sensory impressions above all are given a new impulse by this gesture.

The fluid *L*-gesture, which can be likened to the growth of a tree, primarily stimulates the dissolution and consolidation of substances in the water organism of the liver. It re-enlivens the depressive's stagnating etheric activity and directs it back into the body. The resulting emotional relief is especially noticeable. A physical analogy to the *L* may be seen in the liver's rise and fall with the diaphragm in respiration. The liver is also the center of the fluid organism and in that sense further related to the L

The crossing gesture of the vowel *E* (pronounced *ay* as in "day") incarnates the ego into the etheric body. It is thus closely related to the bile system and to iron. Once the flow of bile has been reactivated by *L*, the depressed ego can be helped to regain control of it with *E*. This gesture also noticeably increases the patients' level of activity and dispels their anxiety. In manic patients, it has been found to exercise a restraining influence on the bile process. In epileptics, it helps transform a convulsive movement toward incarnation into a healthy one. In some cases the *E*, when performed with both the arms and the legs, can actually prevent an approaching seizure.

Psychological disorders that issue from the lung are best treated with the pushing gesture of the sound *G* (as in "get"), which reflects the behavior of solid matter. This gesture supports patients in their efforts to keep tormenting obsessions or seductive delusions "at arm's length," and to reintegrate the forces underlying them into the structure of the lung. The *E*-gesture should also be mentioned here as the vowel most closely associated with iron and hence also with the formation of the lung. It can help overcome both fear of and addiction to the surroundings.

In addition to the fire-sound *S*, one particular exercise involving *E*, the so-called "love-*E*" exercise, is useful in the treatment of emotional disorders of the heart (see vol. II, p. 107). In it the arms are alternately outspread and then crossed over the chest, paralleling and harmonizing the systole and diastole. The blood is thereby suffused with warmth from the heart, which affects inner life as well.

These examples must suffice to provide an impression of the many curative eurythmic exercises that have proven useful in the treatment of psychiatric illnesses over the last several decades.[155]

Unlike eurythmy, which acts primarily on and through the plasticizing etheric body, *gymnastics* starts with the physical body, thereby connecting with the architectonic experience of space and as such exercising an art-therapeutic effect. Gymnastics concentrates on the spatial element, which in eurythmy is subordinated to the flow of time. The educational gymnastics devised by Count Fritz von Bothmer at the first Waldorf school is perhaps the most effective.[156] It helps emotionally disturbed patients reunite with their physical body as a spatial form and with physical space in general.

The contrast between modeling and painting should make it clear that the various artistic therapies act in very different ways. Accordingly, no therapy should be applied without the consultation of a physician who can determine the patient's special needs. Distracted patients should first model, emotionally flat or inflexible patients should first paint. Acutely excarnated psychotics, before they can achieve a healthy relation to the world through speech, must first have the groundwork for a new incarnation laid for them by other means. Similarly, gymnastics should only be used to consolidate an incarnation process that has already been stimulated through curative eurythmy. Singing, for the reasons already mentioned, should usually be prescribed before recitation or drama.

Artistic therapy, like drug therapy, must sometimes be supplemented with more drastic measures. Furthermore, psychiatric patients who are more seriously ill need *occupational therapy* to prepare them for a new connection with their own body. Helping out in the garden, the house, or the kitchen can make a patient much more receptive to artistic and other forms of therapy.

---

155. R. Treichler, "Heileurythmie in der Psychiatrie," in *Arzt und Heileurythmie*, (Dornach: 1984).
156. Fritz Graf von Bothmer, *Gymnastische Erziehung*, (Stuttgart: 1981).

C. Therapy of the Physical Body

The recognition that the physical body contributes to mental disorders suggests the need for treatment by way of the physical body. Since this is the most novel as well as the most important mode for the practitioner to know, it will be dealt with here at greater length. In addition, a number of concrete therapeutic suggestions will be made. These suggestions are based on the clinical experience of Friedrich Husemann, of doctors at the psychiatric hospital founded by him, of the author of this chapter, and of several other neurologists and practicing physicians.[157]

In many cases, the psychological and spiritual therapies outlined above can be fully effective only when a physical treatment is carried out simultaneously. In neuroses, for example, psychological forces are frequently so deeply bound up with a particular organ that they cannot respond to artistic or spiritual stimuli. This may help explain the length of many conventional psychotherapeutic treatments. On the other hand, if psychological and spiritual forces are freed from their organic confinement by means of the appropriate medications, art therapy and therapy of the spirit can stimulate their development much more readily and lastingly.

Neuroses fluctuate between the soul and the physical body. By contrast, psychoses are determined almost entirely by organic factors. Their treatment must accordingly start with the organs. In addition to liberating the soul from organic influences, the treatment of psychoses has the additional task of reintegrating the weakened and excarnating higher constituents and their organic forces into the physical body. In protracted or prophylactic treatments, the therapist must also attempt to affect the organic disposition, as for example in depression (see below).

All psychiatric treatment is aimed at regulating the "breathing" of the higher constituents into and out of the physical body. Its chief tools are the metals, which help re-establish harmony between the body and the soul. The exact connections prevailing here will become clear to anyone who studies the spiritual metamorphoses that the human ego undergoes before birth. According to Steiner, our spiritual essence "contracts" out of the expanses of the cosmos prior to physical birth, and in the process passes through the several spheres of the planets, in each of which a par-

157. These observations were gathered mainly at the annual psychiatric conference and symposium at the Goetheanum in Dornach, Switzerland, 1955–1980.

ticular physical organ is spiritually preformed.[158] Against this background, the traditional assignment of metals to specific planets and organs can be understood anew. Each metal represents the physical condensation of a planetary process that can be liberated through potentization of the metal into a remedy. Administering a metallic remedy to patients suffering from a disorder of the corresponding organ thus reconnects them with their own spiritual genesis out of the cosmos. It also gives them the chance to "start over," to establish a new relationship between the organ and their higher constituents.

Each metal also regulates in its own way the balance between gravity and levity, between the forces of the physical body and those of the etheric, in which the ego primarily resides.[159] It also helps establish harmony among the organs, either by reducing the emphasis on a constitutionally predominant organ or by helping weaker organs to assert themselves. Whether one treats by way of the kidney with copper, of the liver with tin, of the bile system with iron, of the lung with iron and mercury, or of the heart with gold, inner life is stimulated to connect in a more healthy way with the organs. In other words, the functional and organic disorders that give rise to psychiatric syndromes can begin to be healed.

The organic disorders responsible for mental illnesses are always subtle and often chronic. Only substances potentized in the manner of homeopathy can achieve specific therapeutic aims with such subtle disorders or with the corresponding psychological symptoms. However, less subtle medications and treatments will also occasionally be necessary to properly sensitize a patient to the potentized remedies, as will become clear in the more detailed discussions of therapy below. Clearly, however, no drug therapy can ever replace the patient's own efforts toward spiritual development. Remedies are meant only to free the ego from its entanglement in disturbed organic or psychological processes and to help it realize its true spiritual nature.

---

158. R. Steiner, "Adam Kadmon," in *Das Geheimnis der Trinität* (GA 214); not translated. See also B. C. Lievegoed, "Über den doppelten Planetenprozess," in *Anthrop. Medizin. Jahrbuch,* Band I (Dornach: 1950). H. Walter, *Die sieben Hauptmetalle* (Dornach: 1966).

159. R. Steiner, *Physiology and Therapeutics* (Spring Valley, NY: Mercury Press, 1986), lecture 4.

The principle of polarity upon which the discussion of psychiatric syndromes was based will also be used to describe remedies. These remedies are primarily preparations from metals, which act to balance the polarity of particular organ processes. Organ processes will be discussed mainly in psychological terms; physical aspects will enter in only to the extent necessary to explain mental phenomena. On the other hand, the discussion of the psychological effects of the metals will also shed light on their physical dynamic and on that of the corresponding organs. In addition, selected nonmetallic remedies that have proven effective in conjunction with the metals will be discussed.

Unlike the psychotropic drugs so widely used today, the medicines to be described here attempt to eliminate the underlying causes of mental illness. Although the effect of psychotropic drugs is unquestionably strong, it is also, in the judgment of most authors, purely symptomatic. These drugs eliminate or take the edge off such symptoms as hallucinations and delusions, yet remain powerless over the psychotic process as such, which may persist "beneath the surface," only to flare up when the drugs are discontinued. Or, in cases where the drugs are administered over a long period of time, the psychosis may take on a tolerable but chronic form.

This is not to deny that psychotropic drugs can occasionally bring about a cure. In such cases, the self-healing tendency is evidently so strong that, once the symptoms have eliminated by the drugs, the disease process can actually be overcome. More commonly, however, prolonged treatment with psychotropic drugs, by changing the personality, makes true healing either more difficult or simply impossible. The patient may be calmer, more relaxed, more easily managed, but will also be less productive, more apathetic, more lacking in initiative. Such changes need not be drastic in order to significantly hinder emotional and spiritual development. This is especially true in milder cases where psychotropics have been administered regularly for a long time. Such patients will sometimes volunteer that they feel inwardly "walled in." These symptoms are doubtless based on impairments of organic function, particularly that of the liver, where cholestasis may occur.[160]

In light of this, the administration of psychotropic drugs should be restricted wherever possible to acute phases, during which their effect can

160. H.L. Haase, *Therapie mit Psychopharmaka* (Stuttgart, New York: 1972), p. 113.

be mostly positive, comparable perhaps to that of a crutch or a body cast in an external injury—indispensable for a time, but only subsidiary to the actual healing process. Dosages can sometimes be kept lower and the duration of administration can sometimes be decreased when potentized remedies are applied at the same time. However, severe chronic schizophrenia will almost always require regular administration of psychotropic drugs in order to achieve and maintain improvements in the patient's condition.

An effect more favorable than that of psychotropic drugs is produced by the naturally occurring salts of lithium, which have been used successfully to treat mania and to prevent manic-depressive mood swings. One way of understanding this is to consider that lithium lowers the elevated intracellular sodium levels found in both manic and depressive phases.[161] Cyclothymia, as was described above, is connected through the liver and gall bladder with an impairment of mineral metabolism, which would also include sodium. After extended use, however, even lithium has been found to exert a negative influence on psychological development: patients have complained of a dulling and automatization of their inner life.[162]

As a rule, anthroposophical psychiatric remedies do not produce effects as immediate or strong as those of psychotropic drugs. However, a distinction must be made between effects and effectiveness (Kienle[163]). Psychotropic drugs achieve symptomatic *effects* of limited therapeutic significance. Anthroposophical remedies are directed at the underlying disease process and are thus therapeutically *effective*. They do better justice to the patient's long-term emotional and spiritual development. The improvements they bring about are also more permanent, since they stimulate the self-healing forces of the whole human being and of the ego in particular. Therapy based on these remedies is admittedly still in an early stage of development, but we may draw confidence and patience from the fact that they aim to treat the entire human being.

161. See *Biologische Psychiatrie*, pp. 61–62.
162. E. Bleuler, *Lehrbuch der Psychiatrie*, p. 492.
163. G. Kienle, *Arzneimittelsicherheit und Gesellschaft* (Stuttgart: 1974), esp. p. 108.

1. Metallic and Other Remedies[164]

SILVER[165] In the sphere of the moon, the cosmic origin of silver, incarnating human beings conclude their passage through the various planetary spheres and form their anabolic organism, the etheric body, through which spiritual impulses toward formation become realized in physical structures. During the embryonic period, there formative forces are concentrated in the mother's reproductive organs. The reproductive organs are the part of the body through which the silver process radiates at all times into the rest of the physical organism. Silver provides the most direct means of leading the organism out of material rigidification and back into cosmic structuring by way of these organs. It reopens the organism to cosmic influences, making a partial rebirth out of the cosmos possible, a rebirth that can be built upon in subsequent metal therapy.

Silver is particularly important after a death process, such as severe emotional trauma or the spiritual disruption caused by psychotropic drugs. Since such events are now common in the history of most psychiatric patients, silver should always be considered as the remedy of first resort. Silver may be supplemented with abdominal application of oxalis ointment (30%), which acts directly upon the center of the autonomic nervous system, the solar plexus (also known a the "abdominal brain"), which is particularly sensitive to traumas. According to Rudolf Steiner, the chief result of emotional shocks is to disturb the labile connection of the astral body to the reproductive organs. Dislodged from there, the astral body grasps immediately onto a neighboring part of the organism, usually the gastrointestinal tract. The application of oxalis noticeably relieves spasms proceeding form that region.[166]

A vegetabilized form of silver, Bryophyllum Argento cultum (inj. or liq., 1% or 0.1%) may be used as a first silver treatment or as a supplement to the mineral form of silver. Silver is potentized in this remedy

164. For the following section, cf. vol. II, pp.-145–182 ("The Seven Metals") and W. Pelikan, *The Secrets of Metals* (Hudson, N.Y.: Anthroposophic Press, 1998) and *Heilpflanzenkunde I und II* (Dornach: 1958, 1962).

165. For a more detailed account of the psychological aspect, see A. Selawry, *Silber und Silbertherapie* (Ulm/Donau: 1966) and R. Treichler, *Silberprozess und Silbertherapie* (Stuttgart: 1954).

166. R. Steiner, *Physiology and Therapeutics,* lecture 2.

through the robust, succulent kalanchoe, a plant that is almost all leaf and that reproduces through the leaf. Bryophyllum Argento cultum is particularly recommended for neuroses accompanied by restlessness and sleep disorders, both of which are signs of an overactive astral body. It is also recommended for cases with a hysteric component, inasmuch as kalanchoe by itself is an effective remedy against hysteria; it reins in overactive psychological forces and reintegrates them into the etheric body, the constituent most emphasized in the kalanchoe. Since hysteria is also based upon an inharmonious penetration of the lower organization, in particular of the reproductive organs, silver is also indicated for it.

As injection, Bryophyllum 5% can help control more intense states of restlessness with a hysteric component. (Up to 10 ml i.m.) In patients with "pasty" complexion, the combination Bryophyllum/Conchae should be administered s.c. or i.v. Internally, Bryophyllum may be administered as 10%, 20 drops t.i.d, or 50%, a pinch t.i.d. By contrast, psychotic restlessness should be treated with Hyoscyamus 5%/Valeriana D3 (up to 10 ml i.m.). Use of these medications makes it easier to discontinue or lower the dosages of psychotropics and soporifics, but in most cases cannot immediately replace them.

The organic polarity affected by silver may be characterized by the words "anabolism" and "elimination." All silver preparations act to balance this polarity in some way, either by reducing overactive anabolism and encouraging congested elimination or vice versa. The emphasis is upon a healthy anabolism in the fluid element of the body, balanced by proper elimination. Through anabolism, silver stimulates development "from below," development that is subsequently modified by the forces of the upper organization.

Silver's polarity on the psychological level may be characterized by the words "somnambulism" and "desiccation." In somnambulistic and similar states, anabolism has gained the upper hand over elimination, and the effects are felt in consciousness. Patients have visionary or even hallucinatory experiences; furthermore, since their connection with the world is now dominated by the unconscious lower realm, they may experience extrasensory perceptions of their surroundings. Rudolf Steiner called this "abdominal clairvoyance," and deemed it out of keeping with the spirit of the modern age.[167] Thus, when it occurs, it is usually the symptom of a pathological state such as hysteria or schizophrenic psychosis. More frequently, however, the pole of "desiccation" dominates. Here anabolism is weak and elimination begins to tend toward catabolism, with the result that the patient "dries up" both outwardly and inwardly. Inner life is dominated by passive, emotionless perception and by the abstract thinking characteristic of the head, and it slowly begins to waste away. The first stage in this process may be boredom, whereas the culmination is the death of all creative forces.

The medium between somnambulism and desiccation is a healthy imagination, the psychological process to which silver is most closely related. Imagination is fueled by transformed forces of the reproductive organs; it creates new formations in the soul in the same way that the silver process creates them in the body. Imagination combines silver's anabolic processes with the formative forces of the upper organization. Thus one of the most common effects of a successful silver therapy is an enlivening of the imagination, which makes thinking more pictorial.

Anabolism is particularly stimulated by the sulfur compound of silver, argentite. The sulfur component rekindles metabolism and reactivates impaired elimination. Most importantly, however, it stimulates protein synthesis. Hence it is used in cases of constitutionally deficient anabolism (asthenia), cachexia, genital hypoplasia, and as a basic remedy for anorexia. Psychologically it stimulates creativity and imagination. It is appropriate for intellectually precocious, small-headed children, and as an intermediate treatment for the psychological effects of arteriosclerosis, where it is usually applied in low potency, e.g., D6 or D10 as injection, D3–D6 as triturate. For fair-haired, sulfuric types, Argentum praep. is more appropriate.

The most universally applicable silver remedy is Argentum praep. When given alternately with phosphorus, it helps alleviate somnambulism and related conditions. (Argentum praep. D6 while the moon is waxing, Phosphorus D6 while it is waning.) Phosphorus helps the ego reintegrate itself into regions of the body that have been readied for that purpose by silver.

---

167. R. Steiner, "Gehirndenken und Denkkraft," in *Weltwesen und Ichheit* (GA 169). Individual lectures available in English as typescripts.

In silver's antimony compound, dyscrasite, greater emphasis is placed upon the structural pole of the silver dynamic. Dyscrasite is called for when physical and emotional boundaries are ill-defined, as in somnambulism and hysteria. In these cases it is given as injection, D6, combined with Bryophyllum or Gencydo 1-7%. Even more than Argentum praep., dyscrasite stimulates a renewal of the forces of thought and strengthens a failing memory, effects that derive from its antimony component. High potencies (e.g., D20) are usually required to achieve this. The same level of potency is effective against the inflammatory and degenerative processes of multiple sclerosis.

MERCURY This metal, like the following ones, can be characterized more briefly, since its description is based upon organ processes that have already been described.

Mercury, the metal of the lung, oscillates between inhalation and exhalation, mediating at the same time between the gaseous and the fluid states. In the form of Mercurius viv. nat. (D1–D15, inj.), it helps alleviate obsessive-compulsive illness, smoothing out disturbances in the rhythmic exchange between the soul and the world. The vegetabilized form Bryophyllum Mercurio cultum (inj. or liq., 1%) reduces restlessness in obsessive-compulsives and in depressives tormented by self-reproaches. An effect on the opposite pole, that is, on the tendency toward delusions, has also been observed. In general, mercury seems to act upon emotional imbalances, on abnormal fluctuations between sympathy and antipathy. This is apparent from its homeopathic proving symptoms, namely, oversensitivity, hesitation, emotional imbalance, a "tendency to become upset, to laugh and cry without reason."[168] In higher potencies (D15, inj.), mercury can help bring stagnating psychopathological processes back into motion (e.g., protracted depressions).

COPPER Physically, copper, the metal of the kidney, mediates between incretion and excretion. The emphasis is on incretion, or more specifically, on anabolism occurring through the movement of blood and lymph. Psychologically, copper helps strike a balance between excitability and apathy. Its main psychological effect is to enliven, but it can also calm, as in the treatment of thyreotoxicosis.

168. A. Stiegele, *Homoopathische Arzneimittellehre* (Stuttgart: 1949), p. 389.

In Melissa Cupro culta (D2 or D3 as inj. or liq.), copper's enlivening effect stands in the foreground. This preparation is most effective in cases of exhaustion, where stagnating circulation produces nervousness and shivering. Copper's sulfur compound, chalcocite, directs metabolism into the formation of new protein (incretion). It should be the first remedy used in cases of thyrotoxicosis, where catabolism and excretion dominate; the recommended form is injections of D6 combined with Bryophyllum D3, although this treatment may need to be prepared for by an initial silver therapy.

In the further course of any disease process involving the kidney, it is advisable to turn more toward copper's structuring pole. Cuprum praep. moves in this direction, while Cupro-Stibium (antimony copper) is its most perfect expression. The silicate of copper, dioptase, establishes a direct connection between copper and the surfaces of the body and of the internal organs, leading out of the interior of the organ and toward consciousness. Dioptase is therefore the main medication in the copper treatment of epilepsy (D20, inj.).

In recent years, a new organic copper preparation for the treatment of schizophrenia has been developed at the Friedrich Husemann Clinic by Otto Wolff and others. Called Cuprum-Ren (D4 or D6, inj.), it is made from a nitrogenous copper compound processed with animal kidney protein. It has been observed to have positive effects on apathetic, inwardly exhausted, and stuporous patients whose sensory activity needs stimulation.[169] During an acute phase or when relapse threatens, Cuprum-Ren should be injected alternately with antimony (see next section).

Cramps or spasms caused by an overactive astral body can be treated with copper vegetabilized through chamomile, Chamomilla Cupro culta (inj. or liq., 1% or 0.1%). This remedy has a relaxing effect, influencing even the relatively severe spasms of bronchial asthma.

Drug Therapy of Epilepsy: Chamomilla Cupro culta can also reduce both the number and severity of epileptic seizures. Epilepsy, however, can be rooted in other organs in addition to the kidney, and must also be approached through those organs. This is done chiefly through the silicates of the appropriate metals: Dioptase D20 for the kidney, Arandisite

169. Cf. M. Uhlenhoff, "Krankengeschichte einer schizophrenen Patientin," in *BEH* (1974)/4.

D15 for the liver, Nontronite (iron silicate) D15 for the lung, all as injection. Aurum praep. is recommended for the heart. The kidney and liver must always be treated, no matter what other organs may also be involved.

Another copper-related plant that influences the disease process of epilepsy is belladonna. In potentized form, it helps epileptics complete their impaired process of awakening and thereby acts prophylactically against further seizures. (Inj. D10 and D20, internally D6 and higher.) Belladonna is best used in combination with the metal of the organ most affected by the epileptic process. For example, the liver can be treated with injections of Arandisite D15 + Belladonna D10. Belladonna can also be injected alternately with Chamomilla Cupro culta or supported by oral administration of that medication. In cases of diminished catabolic and excretory activity between attacks, which can manifest itself in increased drowsiness, absence, apathy, and a puffy, swollen appearance, Arum maculatum/Pteridium aquilinum D3 as injection and per os is recommended instead of Chamomilla Cupro culta. In cardiac epilepsy with irregularities of heartbeat, combined injections of Aurum and Mucilago Levistici D6 should be given, while belladonna should be injected alone.

While these other treatments are going on, the kidney and liver should also be treated internally with such preparations as Equisetum, Renodoron, Choleodoron, and Hepatodoron. In addition to such peroral therapy, insufficient or excessive kidney radiation will require series of injections of the appropriate medications (see further below) combined with belladonna.

Residual epilepsy and brain damage caused by seizures are treated with Arnica, Radix D10–D20; cerebral scars in particular respond to injections of Nicotiana tabacum D10–D20 or to internal application of Agaricus muscarius D3–D6. Helleborus niger is the vegetable remedy most recommended for a combined involvement of the brain and kidney, a combination frequently observed. As injection (D3–D10) it is given during the pauses in belladonna treatment along with whatever metal is being used; when belladonna injections are resumed, Helleborus is given orally (D2 or D3).

The treatment of epilepsy must frequently be continued for a long time before any improvements are observed. The simultaneous use of anti-epileptics has already been discussed earlier in this chapter.

ANTIMONY[170] Antimony combines the healing effects of silver, copper, and mercury. It is thus a comprehensive medication for organic anabolism. Not only does it promote blood coagulation, as is known, but also stimulates the buildup of organs out of the blood, a kind of "higher coagulation process." Antimony makes all anabolic processes receptive to the upper pole's formative forces and to structuring forces streaming in from the cosmos. Significantly, it mediates the internal rather than the external structuring of the organs, maintaining that structure against the liquefying forces of the metabolism. Rudolf Steiner referred to this fact when he spoke of "the internal organizing forces of the organs," of their "inner structure," as that upon which antimony acts.[171] The outer forms of the organs, by contrast, are determined by structural forces from the upper organization.

Antimony (Stibium) has only an indirect but nevertheless highly significant relationship to consciousness. Specifically, it supports the forces that structure our subconscious mental activities and that make it possible, for instance, to retrieve several memory fragments and consolidate them into a single picture (once again the analogy of "coagulation"). Thus psychologically as well as on the physical plane, antimony takes incipient formations and lifts them toward the structuring activity of the ego and astral body. This lays the foundation for a consciousness in which all subconscious and organic influences have been transformed and mastered by the ego.

For this reason, antimony is an important remedy in all illnesses accompanied by impaired consciousness. It effects a "strengthening of memory, an elevation of the creative forces of the soul, an inner coherence of the emotional disposition,"[172] particularly in neurological diseases like multiple sclerosis and in related neurasthenic disorders. Injections of Stibium praep. D6 have proven useful as a supporting remedy in the treatment of mania, where they counteract the overflowing, liquefying will forces of the bile system.

---

170. The following is an abridged version of the chapter on antimony found in R. Treichler, *Der schizophrene Prozess* (Stuttgart: 1981). References to other literature on antimony may also be found there. For more on the use of antimony in psychiatry, see also R. Treichler, "Vom inneren Weg des Arztes," *BEH* (1983) 1.

171. R. Steiner, *SM,* lecture 19.

172. Steiner/Wegman, *FT,* chapter 20.

Antimony is the chief mineral remedy for schizophrenia. It acts upon the defective organs of the asthenic constitution, the disintegrative tendencies within these organs, and the soul that has begun to divide and come apart. The "coherence of the emotional disposition" cited by Steiner as one of the effects of antimony is precisely what schizophrenics need. They can also be helped by the "elevation of the creative forces of the soul," since in them those forces have been displaced by organic forces, and by the "strengthening of the memory," since their chaotic drive to remember things needs to be replaced by a memory strengthened by the ego.

If silver represents the "childhood" phase of metal therapy, antimony represents its "youth." A markedly "youthful" substance, antimony checks the aging and dying processes of schizophrenia and encourages a healthy new beginning rather than a chaotic lapse into immaturity.

Some favorable outcomes of schizophrenia treated with antimony have been described in papers written by Bertram von Zabern.[173] Von Zabern observed that antimony, used either together with or in alternation with other metals, had a healing effect on schizophrenic patients. In some cases the effect was almost immediate. Shortly after receiving intravenous injections of Stibium praep. D10, two patients reported that they could think more clearly: their concentration had improved and the feeling of having "foreign" thoughts in their heads had diminished. Such effects are, however, the exception rather than the rule. Usually one may expect a healing effect only after repeated administration.

Drug Therapy of Schizophrenia: The standard treatment for schizophrenia consists of seven-week or three-month series of injections of either Stibium praep. or antimonite, first in low, then in higher potencies (D6–D20). In acute cases, up to 10 ml D6 may be given intravenously together with 1 ml of Ren D6. Stibium is preferred for cases of pronounced organic and mental disintegration, antimonite for anabolic deficiencies or in cases with a depressive component. Extensive experience has shown that several ml act more strongly than 1 ml, perhaps because of increased stimulation of the fluid organism. In cases where there is a pronounced loss or confusion of identity, subcutaneous injections of Gencydo should also be given.

173. B. von Zabern, "Zur Metalltherapie der Schizophrenie," *BEH* (1966)/4.

Milder, chronic cases call for oral administration rather than injections (Stibium praep. or Antimonite, D6 or D3, a pinch t.i.d.). The same applies for follow-up treatments. The external applications described in the section on antimony (vol. 2, p. 133) are not necessary in schizophrenia, since the schizophrenic's weakness of will is secondary, deriving from the kidney, rather than a fundamental symptom.

The Christmas rose (*Helleborus niger*), known since ancient times for its healing effect on mental and brain disorders, is suitable in most cases as a supportive medication. This hardy plant blooms in the winter, demonstrating that the organic forces of metabolism, represented by the blossom, have been displaced into the cold realm of the head and consciousness. Helleborus also has a special relationship to the kidney: it reintegrates the discarnating astral body into the kidney and thereby stimulates diuresis. It is effective against both agitation and apathy, the emotional polarity proper to the kidney (inj., D3–D10, together with Stibium or Cuprum; per os, D2 or D3).

A second vegetable remedy for schizophrenia is Anhalonium, a potentized extract of the Mexican peyote cactus. It contains mescaline, a narcotic that in pure form can produce hallucinatory-psychotic states similar to those of schizophrenia.[174] The peyote cactus's outer form suggests an affinity to the inner life of many schizophrenics: it closes itself off against the desolate, hostile surroundings, and occasionally "explodes" into blossom. Anhalonium is therefore recommended for markedly autistic, emotionally unstable patients, particularly during hallucinatory episodes, as well as for any mental disorder involving powerful hallucinations. Injections of Anhalonium D6 + Stibium praep. D6 may be given instead of Helleborus.

Combinations of antimony with other substances, such as dyscrasite or Cupro/Stimium, may be used where indicated, either alone or as an oral supplement. Intravenous injections of Stibium in alternation with Argentum + Lachesis D20 are effective in cases of febrile catatonia. Renal excretion may be stimulated in catatonic patients with Equisetum c. sulf. tost. D4, a pinch t.i.d. In some cases, the daily alternation of low-

174. W. Priever, report during the Psychiatric Conference at the Goetheanum in 1962 and at a physician's conference at the Friedrich Husemann Klinik in 1965. See also Pelikan, *Healing Plants I (Spring Valley, NY: Mercury Press).*

potency with high-potency Stibium injections seems to have a favorable effect. For chronic enervation, such injections should be accompanied by injections of Cuprum/Ren D4 or D6. In cases of restlessness, they should be combined with Hyoscyamus 10%, 20 drops t.i.d., or D3, inj.

For patients debilitated to the point of stupor, instead of copper (or alternately with it) one may try injections of Apis D2 c. Levistico. Apis, like Cuprum, acts through the kidney, stimulating sensory function and the warmth organism, where it acts more strongly than copper in promoting the incarnation of the ego. Hence moderate temperature rises are desirable after injection of several ml of the Apis preparation, provided the patient's initial temperature was normal or subnormal. "Renal iron" (Solutio Ferri comp., described below) should be used in cases of deficient kidney radiation with hypotension, either together or in alternation with Stibium. Carbo Betulae c. Methane D6 should be applied internally in all cases. Furthermore, treatment should always extend to the liver, which the kidney draws into the schizophrenic process.

Mistletoe has been introduced by Boie as another vegetable remedy for the therapy of schizophrenia.[175] Taking the polarity of cancer and psychiatric syndromes as his starting point, Boie reasoned that in cancer, formative forces that should be transformed into mental forces remain within the organism, whereas in schizophrenia, formative forces that should remain active within the physical body are drawn up into the mind. The result is uncontrolled growth of foreign structures in either the body or the soul. According to Boie, mistletoe is effective against both processes. In schizophrenia, it stimulates the reintegration of escaped formative forces and a new incarnation of the ego and of the astral body. Female adolescent schizophrenics treated by Boie with injections of Iscador M St 6 responded favorably and sometimes immediately. For males, Boie recommends Iscador Qu St. 6.

In addition to drug therapy, cases of schizophrenia that are more severe require the use of the drastic physical measures described below. These include phlebotomy, baths, enemas, mustard compresses over the kidneys, fever cures, and, most importantly, low to medium doses of insulin.[176]

175. D. Boie, "Zur Behandlung der Schizophrenie Jugendlicher," *BEH* (1968) 2–3 and *Mistel und Krebs* (Stuttgart: 1970).

GOLD[177] Gold is the metal of the sun and of the heart. It harmoniously unites contraction and expansion, heaviness and light into the polarity of systole and diastole.

The connection of this polarity with our innermost essence, our inner sun, the ego, which always strives for balance, was discussed above in relation to the heart. The final, greatest balance that can be struck by the heart and the gold process is that between the poles of "spirit" and "matter," or, in terms of human development, between our tendency toward incarnation and toward spiritualization.

Our existence, split as it is between the life process and the death process, between the lower and the upper organization, is based upon the existence of the heart. Since the goal of the heart is balance, it is only natural that the gold process, which supports and acts through the heart, influences both the upper and the lower poles of our organization equally. This is in contrast to the other metals, which are associated either more with the lower pole, as with silver, copper, and mercury, or more with the upper, as with tin, lead, and iron. Gold as a remedy acts in both directions, always favoring the pole that needs the most assistance.

Accordingly, gold is suitable for stenocardic, "systolic" conditions as well as for tachycardic, "diastolic" ones, for anxiety as well as for the tendency toward outbursts of rage. It is effective in depression as well as in mania and in all varieties of cardioneurosis. However, which pole gold influences depends above all on its potency. In lower potencies, which in all medications tend to affect the metabolism more, gold checks the overreaching, liquefying lower pole and reinforces the systolic tendency. Aurum D6, in combination with Stibium D6, is a key remedy for mania and for violent outbursts of temper, as well as for psychogenic tachycardia. By contrast, in higher potencies, which affect the upper pole more, gold counteracts rigidity and stimulates the diastolic tendency. Aurum D12–D30 tends to dispel depression, an effect first noticed many years ago by Husemann. The forms of depression most responsive to this are those associated with self-reproaches, fear of death, and stenocardia. With gold, the choice of potency is particularly important, since it

176. See *Fortschritte* 27 (1962) and the section on physical applications later in this chapter.

177. A more detailed account of the psychological aspect is given in R. Treichler, *Goldprozess und Goldtherapie* (Stuttgart: 1959).

addresses the patient's ego more directly than any other metal and therefore demands the most individualized application.

Gold encompasses the physical and supersensible dimensions of the human being. It is therefore always indicated when physical symptoms seem to be rooted in mental history. It is also indicated for cardiac complaints, whether primary or secondary. Cardiac neurosis, partly because of its psychological origin, is one of the key fields of gold therapy. However, organic heart diseases can also call for gold, for example, when emotional distress threatens to exacerbate an existing organic condition. Just as silver is the metal of preference for the initiation of therapy, so is gold for its conclusion, since it helps to actualize the new balance between physical and spiritual dimensions that has been prepared for by the preceding treatments.

The chief gold preparation is Aurum praep., which leads from processes of life into those of consciousness. In gold's mercury amalgam, Mercurius auratus, gold is combined with the psychologically stabilizing and relaxing effect of mercury, which also carries the gold process into the pulmonary and glandular systems. Mercurius auratus can therefore be prescribed for obsessive-compulsives who experience fear of death and guilt feelings. It can also be prescribed for lingering hepatic depressions and manias whenever it seems that gold by itself is not reaching the liver. Severe cases of either of these disorders can be treated with Aurum praep. D15 or Mercurius auratus D15, 5 ml i.v.

Among the vegetabilized remedies, the vitalizing Primula Auro culta is best for stenocardia and nervous exhaustion, while the energizing Hypericum Auro cultum, which also leads from life to consciousness, intensifies the gold therapy of anergic depression accompanied by confusion and disorientation. Cardiodoron is recommended as an internal supplement to all metallic gold therapy. Its primary indications are cardiac irregularities: tachycardia, arrhythmia, and emotional agitation, but it also has a generally harmonizing effect.

Drug Therapy of Cardiac Neurosis: For disturbed heart function and tachycardia, including paroxysms: Aurum/Hyoscyamus comp. (Aurum D10/Stibium D6/Hyoscyamus D5), 2–3 amp. For stenocardia: injections of Aurum praep. D12 or D15 with Magnesium phosphoricum D8 or Nicotiana tabacum D10. Concurrently Cactus grandiflorus D3, internally, and Aurum-Lavendulae-Rosae ointment. In every case of cardiac neurosis: Cardiodoron, 20 drops t.i.d. For accompanying exhaustion: Primula Auro culta 0.1%; for accompanying depression and listlessness: Hypericum Auro cultum 0.1%; both as injection or per os. All Aurum injections should be administered in the upper left arm.

IRON Iron, the metal of the bile, is special inasmuch as it influences all the other metal processes and polarities. Just as the entire organism is permeated with bile, so it is permeated with the influence of iron, from the inside out to the skin, from the head down into the limbs, with an intensity unmatched by any other process. Iron establishes an active relationship between the interior of the organism and the outside world; like gold, it integrates our individual existence into the world as a whole, enabling us to act out of a state of inner balance. The iron process paves the way for the gold process; however unlike gold, which always seeks a balance and thus holds itself more "aloof," iron plunges actively into the physiological realms of the other metals.

The iron-bile process stimulates our ability to act. For thinking to become active, this ability must rise up out of the lower organization into the head. In the heart, iron's energy metamorphoses into courage, which releases the will from the bonds of fear and permits constructive action. Iron's activity in the kidney is dealt with in the section on the therapy of vegetative neuroses.

The significance of the iron process for the bile system, and hence for the liver, has already been discussed. All the processes of congestion and release, both physical and mental, that were described in connection with the liver culminate in the behavior of bile. Iron is thus an important medication in the treatment of depression. Even in ointment form (Ferrum praep. 5%, applied over the gallbladder), it stimulates the flow of bile. Even more effective in this regard is a new preparation developed in collaboration with Otto Wolff, Ferrum/Acidum cholalicum D4 or D6, in ampules and per os.[178] The cholic acids in this remedy guide iron to the gallbladder, where iron stimulates the formation and flow of bile. As mentioned before, one may assume an interaction between iron and bile acids in the blood, so that this preparation would be a model of that interac-

178. See R. Treichler, "Leber-Gallensystem und Depression," in *BEH* (1974)/6 and (1975)/1.

tion. This remedy is most appropriate for hesitating, chronic patients of pyknic constitution, and is best injected together with Oxalis D3 or D6.

In the form of scorodite (iron arsenate), iron dissipates fear and liberates the feelings via the blood. It cuts through the pyknic depressive's congestion and, much as Ferrum/Acidum cholalicum in the bile system, both makes room for and stimulates new volitional processes. Scorodite's arsenic component energizes on the plane of the astral body, while the iron component activates the ego (potency D6–D10, as injection and per os). In some cases (for example, in depressive anorexia), the combination ampule Ferrum sidereum D10/Pancreas D6 has proven effective. Internally, Levico water tends to have the same effect. The vegetabilized iron of this stage is Chelidonium Ferro cultum. Celandine carries the iron impulse into the bile system.

In the lung, the organ of the earth, iron energizes the mercurial movement of respiration and, combined with oxygen, allows it to permeate the rest of the organism. Respiration is metamorphosed in the larynx into speech, and can be strengthened by iron there as well (see vol. I, pp. 78–9).

Iron's psychologically liberating effect may be observed in pure form in obsessive-compulsive illness. In the treatment of obsessive-compulsive illness, whose main symptom is fear of the surroundings, iron is even more important than mercury, since it stimulates the reincorporation of escaping formative forces into the lung and also restrains tendencies to delusional dreaming. These tendencies also appear in hysteria and in some forms of anemia, and are caused by the excessive activity of metabolic forces in the blood. Finally, attention should be called here to nontronite (iron silicate), which plays a role in the treatment of epilepsy involving the lung.

Drug Therapy of Obsessive-Compulsive Illness: The chief remedy for this disorder is Cinis Urticae Ferro cultae, injection D6, since plant ashes have an especially close relationship to the lung. This remedy should be administered together with Pulmo D6 (per os D3). A mineral iron preparation that can be used here is pyrite, injected in alternation with Cinis Urticae. Pyrite D8 can also be injected with Vaucheria D6, an alga that transmits the sulfur process to the lungs (D3 for oral administration). Bryophyllum Mercurio cultum may also be given internally. Ferrum sidereum, meteoric iron, reopens the organism to cosmic influences. It is indicated in all cases where disorders calling for iron (compulsive and anxious conditions) are associated with exhaustion, that is, with a predominance of the nervous system and of catabolism. A strengthening of the cosmic iron forces in the blood is essential in such cases. In addition to silver at the beginning (preferably argentite, then dyscrasite), in compulsive disorders iron may be followed by injections of Mercurius viv. nat. D10–D15 + Pulmo D6.

MAGNESIUM[179] Many depressive patients with a neurasthenic disposition or tendencies, and in some cases patients of asthenic build, tend not to react, or to react unfavorably, to iron treatment. Such patients become restless and edgy when treated with iron, and their depression can assume an agitated form. This is because their weakened and discarnating etheric bodies cannot sufficiently assimilate the iron impulse, which penetrates to the physical body, producing spasms or spasmodic sensations. The astral body reacts to this inharmonious incarnation with agitation and restlessness. Such cases are a first indication for magnesium, the "iron of the plant realm," which plays the same role in chlorophyll that iron does in hemoglobin.

In the human organism, magnesium is an indispensable component of many metabolic processes and bears a special relation to the fluid element. It can therefore reactivate impaired metabolic processes, an affect that in particularly important for the liver, the central organ of the fluid organism. Magnesium relieves the liver not only by virtue of its laxative quality, it also stimulates the flow of bile and helps prevent gallstone formation. Finally, it has a healing effect upon the liver parenchyma.

Magnesium's most essential quality, however, is its intimate relationship with light. This relationship is highlighted in the synthesis of chlorophyll, which occurs only in the sunlight. With magnesium, the light-process primarily serves life, not consciousness as it does with iron. Rising from below by way of the liver, the "radiant force of magnesium"[180] suffuses the entire organism even into the periphery, where if flows into such formations as muscles and tooth dentin. Through the etheric body, it joins forces with astral kidney radiation, which also exercises an ana-

179. K. H. Simon, *Das Magnesium* (Stuttgart: 1967), p. 68.

180. R. Steiner, *GG*, lecture 5.

bolic influence on the organism through the liver. In this process, magnesium also unites with "original light," which is based in the kidney process.[181] From the point of view of consciousness, magnesium acts between the etheric and astral bodies, the region where mood arises. The depressive's bleak mood can thus be dispelled with magnesium therapy. The ego, awakened to activity by a new light from within, can now unite with the renewed flow of the hepatobiliary metabolism and develop new processes of will.

The chief indications for magnesium in depression, aside from an asthenic constitution, are exhaustion, restlessness, and spasmodic sensations or states, a frequent combination in modern times. The condition of depressive patients who are susceptible to exhaustion tends to worsen toward evening; this is in addition to the usual morning slump. The preparation recommended for this condition is Hepar/Magnesium D4, a combination of magnesium hydroxide and liver protein developed in collaboration with Otto Wolff (ampules and orally). The administration of one to two ampules of Hepar/Magnesium with one of Oxalis D3 strengthens the etheric body's releasing and energizing effect and counteracts spasms. In combination with one ampule of Prunus spinosa D3 it specifically counters exhaustion. Application with one ampule of Taraxacum D3 is recommended for aging and sclerotic or prematurely aging patients.

Particularly sensitive patients may react to Hepar/Magnesium D4 with restlessness, sleep disorders, or migraine. In these cases, it is advisable to raise the potency to D6, which can also be appropriate for protracted treatments (always combined with Oxalis D6). In severe cases, intravenous administration of 5–10 ml of Hepar/Magnesium D10 has yielded results not obtainable by subcutaneous injections.[182]

TIN[183] Tin, the metal of the liver, mediates on the physical plane between the consolidation (assimilation) of material processes and their renewed dissolution (dissimilation) into the fluid state in the liver, thereby supporting

181. R. Steiner, *SM*, lecture 11.

182. See R. Treichler, "Leber-Gallensystem und Depression," in *BEH* (1974)/6 and (1975)/1.

183. The psychological and other aspects are presented comprehensively in G. Husemann, *Erdengebärde und Menschengestalt* (Stuttgart: 1962) as well as in A. Selawry, *Zinn und Zinntherapie* (Ulm/Donau: 1963).

the organism's vital plasticity. Psychologically, it aids in finding the balance between the will's stagnation in depression and its overflowing in mania.

The tin process tends toward order and structuring. Hence it plays in important role in the upper organization, where it helps form thoughts out of perceptions and mental images. In depression, where the soul is passively fixated on memory pictures and the stagnating liver threatens to "solidify," tin counteracts stagnation, both physical and mental, and begins a restructuring process. Tin exercises its releasing effect best through the remedy Taraxacum Stanno cultum, a vegetabilized metal (inj. or liq., D3). Also to be recommended is a new tin preparation, Hepar/Stannum D4 (in ampules) and for older patients Stannum mellitum D8 + Hepar D6 (also in ampules). Arandisite, tin silicate, primarily transmits the structuring impulse of tin; in epilepsy, it is combined with belladonna. Otherwise, injections of D15 + Hepar bovis D6; internally: D6 to D20.

Drug Therapy of Mania: Especially appropriate for mania is Arandisite (D6). The vegetabilized tin recommended for mania is Cichorium Stanno cultum, Radix D2 (+ Hepar bovis D6). In contrast to Taraxacum, the dandelion, which accents dissolution by dispersing its seeds, the siliceous Cichorium (chicory) tends much more strongly toward form. Chicory root was recommended by Rudolf Steiner for excessive bile secretion, a condition that, as previously suggested, may underlie mania.[184] Roots, after all, are the part of the plant that transmits the most formative forces. Taraxacum Stanno cultum + Hepar can be prescribed for milder depressions, while Cichorium Stanno cultum, Radix + Hepar is best for milder cases of manic mood instability with a tendency to choleric outbursts (inj. or orally), where it supplements the usual renal treatment. Even when administered per os, Cichorium Stanno cultum effectively calms children who are restless and tend to tantrums. In all cases of mania, a concurrent gall bladder therapy should be carried out with Cichorium, Radix 10% (after meals). In more severe manic disturbances, Cichorium Stanno cultum will be used only in support of other treatments. Here, the best results are achieved with the previously mentioned injections of Aurum D6 + Stibium D6.

184. See R. Steiner, *Mensch und Welt: Das Wirken des Geistes in der Natur* (GA351), lecture 2.

Drug Therapy of Depression The therapy of depression can be summarized as follows: in protracted cases, silver should be used first (thrice weekly, injections of Argentite D6 or Argentum praep. D6 + Hepar D6 + Bryophyllum D3). If necessary, even in this initial phase gold may be brought in on the intervening days as Aurum praep. D15 or D20, or as Mercurius auratus D15 (inj.; i.v. as needed); in older or more strongly degenerated patients, together with Solutio alkalina 0.005%. In severe cases, gold is injected in the morning, silver in the evening.

After two to four weeks of silver therapy or immediately: usually magnesium—Hepar/Magnesium D4 plus either Taraxacum D3, Prunus D3, or Oxalis D3 (or all D6)—or iron (Ferrum/Acid. chol. D4 or D6 together with Oxalis D3). In cases of pronounced anxiety, Scorodite D6 or D10 + Oxalis D3 instead of Ferrum/Acidum cholalicum, injected daily if necessary or, as with silver, in alternation with Aurum. In more severe cases: gold in the morning, magnesium toward evening; or iron and gold in the morning. In patients oversensitive to iron but still needing it, it is advisable to try iron after magnesium. In patients needing magnesium, Hepar/Magnesium can be combined with silver from the beginning in injections in daily alternation, or daily: magnesium in the morning, silver in the evening. All courses of treatment should be continued for four to seven weeks. Injections are subcutaneous and made over the gall bladder. In severe cases, 5–10 ml of Hepar/Magnesium D10 is administered intravenously.

Milder depressions are best treated with tin. Tin is also recommended for prolonged depressions, and should be administered between the other metal treatments. It is also useful for the basic treatment of the hepatic system in the intervals between depressive or manic phases (usually as Arandisite D6 and Taraxacum Stanno cultum or Cichorium Stanno cultum, inj. or per os).

In all cases of depression, the liver should be treated internally as well as with injections. When injections of either Hepar/Magnesium D4 or Ferrum/Acidum cholalicum D4 are being given, the same medications should also be given orally. In milder cases these medications may be prescribed exclusively p.o., 10 drops or 1 pinch t.i.d. This should be accompanied by Choleodoron, 20 drops after the morning and midday meals, that is, in the dissimilatory phase, and Hepatodoron, 3 tablets at suppertime, in the assimilatory phase. The appropriate vegetabilized metals are injected alone in milder cases, in more severe ones alternately with the mineral metal preparations, or given internally to support the mineral injections. Besides Choleodoron, Amara drops are also often indicated—before meals for lack of appetite, after meals for feelings of fullness. Phosphorus D6, 10 drops in the morning, and Phosphorus D25/Malva, Flos 5%, 20 drops at bedtime, support the iron and magnesium treatments and are fundamental in the treatment of sleep disorders.[185]

Fever cures can sometimes be decisive in stubborn cases and are best brought about by hot baths. As mentioned previously, sleep deprivation can also initiate improvement. In severe cases, a number of supportive measures are indispensable: intravenous Laevosan or honey injections (M2 Woelm), baths with oxalis oil (carefully controlled hyperthermic, if desired), liver compresses with yarrow, enemas, and, in the appropriate cases, phlebotomy. This applies especially to involutional depression, against which the medications described above are often insufficient. Here, a supplementary treatment of the degenerative processes of age and sclerosis is required (Solutio alkalina). Furthermore, any other organs besides the liver that are involved in depression must also be treated. For example, the restlessness of an agitated depressive responds to a treatment of the kidney with copper (Chalcocite D6 + Hyoscyamus D3, inj.).

Long experience has shown that the therapeutic measures just described can make the course of endogenous and other depressions more tolerable and sometimes also shorten the course. In some cases, a prophylactic action against new phases could be inferred. During treatment, less severely ill patients have been able to continue working without the benefit of psychotropic drugs, which before had not been possible.[186]

Unfortunately, since the remedies described here usually act only gradually and since there is no point in increasing a seriously ill patient's suffering, particularly in view of the danger of suicide, at first psychotropic drugs may also be necessary. The doses, however, when used in conjunction with anthroposophical remedies, can usually be kept relatively low. In addition to the doubts already voiced, one reason for hesitating to use large doses of psychotropics is that by masking depression they deprive

185. See G. Wachsmuth, *Erde und Mensch* (Konstanz: 1952), chapter 8, and R. Treichler, *Schlafen und Wachen: Vom rhythmischen Leben des Ich* (Stuttgart: 1985).

186. See R. Treichler, "Leber-Gallensystem und Depression," in *BEH* (1974)/6 and (1975)/1.

patients of all opportunity to grow through their illness. Many patients who recover report that they experience life more deeply and inwardly after their depression than before. In other words, an excessively deep settling-in of unconfronted experiences can eventually transform itself into an overall emotional deepening. Thus, provided patients are allowed to experience and to confront it, depression, which rises from the body into the soul, can further the development of inwardness. This is especially true in cases with a background of superficiality.[187]

LEAD Lead, the metal of the spleen and last of the seven metals, concludes the spectrum begun with silver. In the Saturn sphere, where the lead process originates, human beings experience the last expansion of their planetary being after death. In the moon sphere, the home of silver, the emphasis was upon etheric forces that assemble themselves into an etheric body and lead us into earthly incarnation. In the Saturn sphere, by contrast, we come to know the archetypal forms of the life of the soul. Through the Saturn forces we gain the capacity for overview and self-knowledge.

If with silver the accent lay upon life and anabolism, with lead it lies upon consciousness and catabolism. It is only through the breakdown of the physical body that the human spirit achieves self-awareness. With silver, a second emphasis was found on elimination, subordinate to the primary silver dynamic, anabolism. With lead, this second emphasis is on rigidification, which promotes the effects of the primary dynamic, catabolism.

On the psychological and spiritual levels, the pathological polarity that responds to lead expresses itself in two series of symptoms. Each is a metamorphosis of the symptoms of silver's psychological polarity. One side of that polarity, "inner desiccation," culminates when consciousness comes to be dominated by excessive catabolism. The nervous system's tendency toward decomposition can lead to a one-sidedly analytic, atomistics way of thinking that breaks the world down into a myriad of details to which no living connection can be found. In other words, the normal transformation of living perceptions into conscious but devitalized mem-

187. For the spiritual and psychological treatment of depression, see the preceding sections. A more detailed account may be found in R. Treichler, *Die Entwicklung der Seele* (see note 6), in the chapter entitled "Depression und Manie."

ory-pictures, a process aided by lead, goes beyond the healthy medium. However, every form of intellectuality that is divorced from life in this way runs the danger of its own extinction. It can organize its perceptions of the outer and inner worlds only with the most superficial of concepts. Hardly worthy of being called thought, it merely registers perceptions that are themselves only passively and fragmentarily absorbed. The tendency to analyze that is characteristic of modern society can thus lead to the primitive, merely reactive kind of thinking that is envisioned by electronic theories of intelligence and that is also typical of the terminal stages of certain degenerative brain diseases. Atomism in thought thus eventually leads to the automatization of inner life and manifests the second, rigidifying pole of the lead process.

Just as the anabolic, lower pole defends itself by means of the blood against physical morbidity originating in the upper organization (e.g., in strokes brought on by cerebral sclerosis), so too does it seek to counteract the psychological morbidity just described. The astral body reacts from below in uncontrollable emotions and in heightened, animal-like impulsivity and restlessness. Mental and emotional life are gradually dulled and overpowered by the dark, purely organic consciousness of the lower pole. Degenerative diseases of the brain and brain damage in children, which entails a premature loss of cerebral plasticity, also have this effect. In such cases, the brain is powerless against even the normal amount of confusion and restlessness rising up from the lower organization.

It is also possible, however, for anabolism to assert itself too strongly and for catabolism to be too weak. Whereas in the cases described above, lead in higher potencies will restrain excessive catabolism, in lower potencies it can be applied to counter excessive anabolism. The latter occurs, for example, in dreamy, large-headed children, in infantile, overfed adults, and in menopausal women whose failing lower processes rise to the head. In these cases, the catabolic pole can be strengthened with low potencies of lead (D6).

When catabolic disorders are concentrated in the liver in the manner described earlier, lead can be important for the treatment of depression as well. It is especially appropriate when a psychological disease process shows signs of rigidification. Mostly these are geriatric depressions or schizophrenias, in which arteriosclerosis may play a role, arteriosclerosis being an indication for lead even when it occurs by itself. Another factor to consider in depression is the interaction, both physical and psychological, of the liver and the spleen. Specifically, the spleen cooperates with the liver to generate impulses of will, and, as the organ of lead, helps direct the will toward spiritual aims. According to Steiner, the spleen also generates the forces of enthusiasm, which is probably connected with the fact that red corpuscles are broken down in it. Spleen disorders can cause a kind of "inner paralysis" observable in some psychologically inflexible depressive patients; in such cases, both liver and spleen can be treated with high potencies of lead and with Lien D6.[188]

In summary, on the physical level, lead therapy emphasizes the spirituality of the human form between the poles of catabolism and rigidification; on the psychological level, it should be used wherever the ego's formative influences need support. Higher potencies of lead are indicated for cases of excessive catabolism with devitalized thinking; lower potencies for excessive anabolism with exaggerated instinctual impulses and clouded awareness.

Lead therapy is for the most part mineral therapy. But, a vegetabilized form of lead, Cichorium Plumbo cultum, may be used as a supplement. In addition to Plumbum praep., Plumbum mellitum, the chief remedy for arteriosclerosis, may be used. Its honey component connects the mineral lead process with the organism's formative forces, reversing decay and rigidification and initiating constructive activity. Plumbum mellitum D12 is a component of the internal medication Scleron; Plumbum mellitum D20 may be injected by itself. In depression or in tendencies toward depression, D20 only; in cerebral sclerosis D12 at first, then later D20. In this connection, the combination ampule Arnica/Betula comp. can be highly recommended; it contains Plumbum mellitum D20 as a third ingredient. The remedy with the closest relation to the lead patient's restlessness and agitation is Plumbum chloratum (D3 and D6), which can also help in epilepsy or hysteria with corresponding "lead symptoms." Lead silicate, Plumbum silicium, is recommended for confusion due to an influx of forces from below (as inj. and trit. in higher potencies). Plumbum silicium D20, injected together with Belladonna D10 or D20, is a specific for senile hypertension.

188. R. Steiner, *Spiritual Relations in the Human Organism* (GA 218), (Spring Valley, NY: Mercury Press, 1984)

Drug Therapy of Vegetative Neuroses: (Disorders of Kidney Radiation) It will be evident from the above that the basic remedy for disorders of kidney radiation is the renal metal, copper. With copper and its compounds, the sensory-supersensible organism can be stimulated to correct kidney-based imbalances. Melissa Cupro culta is prescribed for weak, Chamomilla Cupro culta for excessive kidney radiation. These remedies, however, are used mainly as a preparatory treatment and between phases of the therapy to be described below.

The kidney is the organ furthest removed from the pole of consciousness and is the site of the most immediate, subconscious interactions between body and soul. It is therefore understandable that for the initial treatment of disorders of this realm, Rudolf Steiner proposed plant remedies.[189]

For the therapy of deficient kidney radiation, Steiner recommended the stinging nettle, Urtica dioica, a plant that embodies the iron process to a remarkable degree (see vol. I, p.84). As discussed elsewhere, the iron process stimulates arterial circulation. Its incarnating effect on the lower organization is intensified in Urtica by sulfur, which reactivates stagnating metabolism and permits psychological and spiritual forces to intervene in the physical body. The sulfur in stinging nettle thus paves the way for iron. Finally, the stinging nettle also contains alkaline salts that specifically stimulate the etheric body and thus also the water organism to assimilate the astral body's renewed activity.

The effect of introducing the iron process in this way into the lower organization is not simply to stimulate the underactive astral body, which one might at first expect to be the goal of treatment. Such an effect could also be achieved, for example, with potentized arsenic, but would only be of limited duration. Many modern symptomatic remedies have a similar temporary effect, but act even more crudely than arsenic, combining temporary increases in circulation and blood pressure with mood elevation. They frequently cause agitation as a side effect, and exercise other purely astral influences upon the emotions and drives. With the kidney as with any other organ, however, the physician's most important task is to further the patient's spiritual development, not merely to stimulate emotion. Iron, unlike symptomatic remedies, strengthens the

189. R. Steiner, *Physiology and Therapeutics,* lecture 4.

astral body only secondarily, by way of the ego or spirit, and hence has a more permanent effect.

Such permanence of effect, in the sense of a constitutional therapy, can be considerably enhanced with remedies that are composed after the model of healing plants (see vol. I, p. 312). The composite preparation corresponding to Urtica is Solutio Ferri comp. Circulation can be strengthened by combining Solutio Ferri comp. D6 with Glandula suprarenalis D3 (comb. ampule or liq.). This combination has proven particularly effective against the hypotension associated with insufficient kidney radiation. Combined injections with Tabacum D6 are given for migraines.

In contrast to deficient kidney radiation, in excessive kidney radiation activities that should be confined to the lower pole invade the upper pole. Accordingly, the therapy is the opposite of the preceding one; the upper rather than the lower organization must be strengthened. Here again one might think that the best way to counter excessive kidney radiation would be to weaken it directly. In the human organism, however, as numerous examples demonstrate, the direct way is not always the best. Thus, although it is certainly possible to relieve the upper organization by mitigating the invasion of astral forces from below, the effect will be only temporary. Effects of this sort could be achieved, for example, by stimulating excretion with Equisetum or with external application of warmth over the kidneys. In this way, incretion is reduced and the action of the astral body is turned away from the upper pole toward the lower. However, from the point of view of anthroposophically oriented medicine such a simple subduing of astral overexcitability is insufficient. Like the direct stimulation of the astral body discussed above, mere suppression also has long-term negative consequences. By prescribing drugs that merely tranquilize the patient or induce sleep, one again circumvents the ego, which should learn to control inner life without such aids. Besides, once such a treatment wears off, the original agitation and restlessness return with greater force, in much the same way that the anergy following a temporary stimulation is greater than the one preceding it.

To activate the ego of the upper organization and balance out the astral body's intrusion from below, Steiner recommended the chamomile root, Chamomilla, Radix, which, as described elsewhere, has a special affinity to the nervous system. Even more important than this affinity is the silica process embodied in the chamomile root, which is the basic material process of the nerve-sense system. Silica makes matter accessible to the structuring forces of light (the most beautiful example being the transparent rock crystal). Similarly, it opens nerve substance, and through it the rest of the organism, to the physically and mentally structuring forces of the ego. Silica clears and illuminates both the head flooded with metabolic processes from below and the consciousness clouded by a migraine attack.

We saw above that to do more than merely temporarily mitigate deficiencies in kidney radiation, the iron process had to be helped by sulfur to permeate the lower organization. Both iron and sulfur are present in the stinging nettle, Urtica dioica. Analogously, silica's healing effect must be intensified in order to counteract the astral body's excessive involvement in the material processes of the lower organization. To this end silica is combined with sugar, another important constituent of the chamomile root. Blood-borne sugar mediates between the structuring ego and the material to be structured; it helps "to orient subhuman (vegetative-animal) corporeality toward humanness."[190] Thus, together with the alkaline salts present in the chamomile root, it relieves the nervous system of animalizing astral influences.

Chamomilla, Radix has proven effective for the acute symptoms of excessive kidney radiation, such as cramps, flatulence, and some types of migraine (as liq., D1–D30; as inj., D3–D30). If a lasting effect is desired, the appropriate inorganic composite preparation is Solutio Sacchari comp. (liq. D3–D30, inj. D6–D30). This preparation, injected in D15 or D20, has proven effective for essential hypertension. In arteriosclerotic hypertension, it can be applied to support lead therapy.

Finally, we should mention Bidor. This remedy combines sulfur and iron with silica, so that it can be administered as a supplemental medication in migraines associated with both deficient and excessive kidney radiation. It is also a basic remedy for nervous exhaustion, a condition that nowadays threatens everyone.

190. Steiner/Wegman, *FT*, chapter 8.

2. Shock Therapy and Other External Applications

Several mental illnesses frequently either do not respond at all or respond only poorly to the medications discussed here. The therapist may feel the desire to "shake patients out of their lethargy" so that they will become more receptive to therapy. In all such cases, more direct physical measures are in order, measures that have both a physically and mentally bracing effect. Through them the metabolism and circulation are made more responsive, as a result of which the etheric body can better transmit the desired therapeutic effects. Similar effects on the mind and ego may also be observed. All of these treatments help conquer the hopelessness that in one form or another tends to accompany mental illnesses. In addition, each treatment encourages the excarnated higher constituents to reintegrate themselves in a very specific way.

For example, purging and phlebotomy challenge the organism with a sudden unburdening, thus enabling the higher constituents to integrate themselves better into the physical body. Phlebotomy in particular stimulates the reintegration of the ego. Enemas, on the other hand, flush out the intestine and the kidneys, thereby stimulating the water organism to renewed activity. The symptoms of each case indicate the most appropriate physical treatment; for example, constipation suggests an enema, whereas congestion and elevated blood pressure indicate phlebotomy.

A fever cure carried out with hyperthermic baths stimulates the ego by way of the warmth organism, involving it more deeply in the metabolism. Fever encourages thorough reintegration and new anabolism through the increased breakdown of proteins. Fever cures are primarily useful for dispelling metabolic congestion in severe depression. In other cases they can help dislodge chronic psychic disease processes, such as schizophrenia. In acute cases of schizophrenia, however, they should be used only sparingly or not at all, since the intensified protein breakdown associated with fever can aggravate the condition. When all other methods have failed, such cases are best handled with insulin shock. In contrast to fever, insulin shock, by lowering the blood sugar level, at first causes the ego to excarnate more severely. However, this exaggeration of the usual psychotic excarnation challenges the ego, which always strives for balance, to compensate by incarnating more strongly. Insulin treatment is more physiological than the now only rarely used electroshock therapy. The shock produced by insulin need not go as far as a complete coma; a stuporous subcoma suffices to achieve the desired effect. Emaciated and asthenic patients in particular benefit from the weight gain that usually follows such a shock.

The higher constituents' activity in the physical body may be further stimulated by a number of means: intravenous injections of dextrose or of specially diluted honey, baths accompanied by cold showers, oil baths, organ massages according to the Hauschka method with the appropriate metal ointment, or warm compresses. Yarrow compresses applied over the liver are helpful for depression, while ground mustard compresses over the kidney help in schizophrenia. For details of these treatments the reader is referred to "Aspects of Therapy" in volume II, from which the treatments relevant to psychiatry have been selected.

In summary, the physical measures described here sensitize the organism to the more subtle effects of medicinal, artistic, and spiritual therapies, for which reason at least one and possibly several of these measures will be necessary in every severe mental illness. Although every treatment contributes to an eventual cure, it is significant that the physical world, in the form of these drastic therapeutic measures, should play such an important role in therapy, since the problem of many psychiatric patients is their alienation from earthly existence.

3. Nutrition

The basis of every therapy, drug or otherwise, is wholesome nutrition. The diet can be varied according to each syndrome's characteristic organ disorders: for example, many depressive patients should receive a diet that is easy on the liver. Schizophrenics who have an elevated temperature and faulty protein metabolism will occasionally require a low-protein diet, while epileptics should receive only small amounts of salt and fluids. Many patients can benefit if their interest in food is reawakened by good-tasking meals. Biodynamically grown agricultural products should be used whenever possible because of their higher quality.

D. The Three Dimensions of Therapy

The division of the treatments described above led naturally to a threefold outline, corresponding to the three dimensions of the human being—body, soul, and spirit. The holistic treatment of mental illnesses in particular must address all of these dimensions, since mental illnesses, as we have shown, are rooted in the body, grow in the soul, and obscure the light of the spirit.

This threefold division certainly does not mean that any of these therapeutic modes can or should be separated from the others in practice. Like the constituents of the human organization at which they are directed, they must act in harmony, physical therapy influencing the spirit and spiritual therapy influencing the body (both by way of the soul), while psychological or art therapy helps heal both the body and the spirit by speaking directly to the soul.

LIST OF INDICATIONS

Preface

The following suggestions for therapy are intended to facilitate the practical application of the ideas expressed in this book. They should be understood as suggestions only, never as mandatory courses of treatment. For this reason, diseases or disorders of the same organ system or function (e.g. kidney, intestine, pregnancy) have been grouped together rather than divided according to the specific diagnosis. An attempt has been made to list only medications that have been found effective by a majority of anthroposophical physicians and that can be assigned to a traditional patho-anatomical diagnosis.

This list is the result of the cooperation of several experienced anthroposophical physicians. It is not meant to exclude other medications or therapeutic measures; healing can be achieved in many ways that are not mutually exclusive. In many places in this book, it was not always possible to justify the choice of a particular medication for a disease, but in most cases the reader will be able to do this independently with the help of the examples given in the text.

Many of the medications listed here have been long known and used by homeopaths. However, the suggestion for their use is usually not based on the homeopathic proving, but rather on insight into the deeper connections between the remedy and the corresponding disease. Homeopathic and anthroposophical remedies therefore do not always coincide, although frequently the use of a homeopathic remedy, which is based on experimentation alone, may be understood in anthroposophical terms. Anthroposophical medicine can have no objection to such remedies, since its goal is to extend medicine, not to refound it; however, it will apply such remedies in view of the totality of the human being, that is, toward the effects on the essential constituents and on the entire course of life.

All medications, unless otherwise indicated, can be obtained from Weleda (Arlesheim, Switzerland; Schwäbisch Gmünd, Germany; Congers, New York). The names of vegetabilized metal remedies may vary from country to country, and therefore a list of equivalent names is included (see below). Products of the Wala Company (Eckwälden/Bad Boll, Germany), which are also based on Rudolf Steiner's anthroposophy, are followed by the designation "(Wala)." Products of other manufacturers are indicated as such. Information concerning ingredients and methods of preparation may be obtained from the respective manufacturers; the reader may also wish to review chapter 10 of volume 1 (p. 302f.).

Vegetabilized Metals: Equivalent Names

The following list shows new names adopted in Germany and the United States. The earlier names, which may still be used in some other countries and occur in older literature, are in parentheses following the newer designations.

Aconitum Plumbo cultum	(Plumbum per Aconitum)
Bryophyllum Argento cultum	(Argentum per Bryophyllum)
Bryophyllum Mercurio cultum	(Mercurius per Bryophyllum)
Chamomilla Cupro culta, Radix	(Cuprum per Chamomillam)
Chelidonium Ferro cultum	(Ferrum per Chelidonium)
Cichorium Plumbo cultum	(Plumbum per Cichorium)
Cichorium Stanno cultum	(Stannum per Cichorium)
Cichorium Stanno cultum, Radix	(Stannum per Cichorium, Radix)
Equisetum Silicea cultum	(Silicea per Equisetum)
Hypericum Auro cultum	(Aurum per Hypericum)
Melissa Cupro culta	(Cuprum per Melissam)
Nasturtium Mercurio cultum	(Mercurius per Nasturtium)
Primula Auro culta	(Aurum per Primulam)
Tabacum Cupro cultum	(Cuprum per Nicotianam)
Taraxacum Stanno cultum	(Stannum per Taraxacum)
Thuja Argento culta	(Argentum per Thujam)
Urtica Ferro culta	(Ferrum per Urticam)
Urtica Ferro culta, Radix	(Ferrum per Urticam, Radix)

The following name changes were also deemed necessary:

Ferrum hydroxydatum	(Ferrum cum aceto praep.)
Kalium aceticum comp.	(Kalium aceticum cum Stibio)

Translator's Note

Many of the remedy names in the following list of indications have been anglicized, primarily those of mineral remedies ending in "-ite." This is worth noting for the reason that the American Weleda, located in Congers, New York, usually uses the German names for these remedies, despite the fact that good English cognates exist (e.g. "nontronite" for "Nontronit"). Only in a single instance is this likely to cause confusion, namely, with "scorodite." The American Weleda remedy list has a reference to this under the German name "Skorodit" and refers the user to Ferrum arsenicosum. However, the German Weleda's remedy list contains both "Skorodit" *and* "Ferrum arsenicosum," and although the substance from which they are derived may be identical, the former medication is available in a much greater variety of potencies than is the latter, potencies that are explicitly referred to at many points in the following list. For that reason, "Skorodit" (appropriately anglicized to Scorodite) has been retained here in favor of "Ferrum arsenicosum."

In keeping with the style of the American Weleda Remedy List, the abbreviation "met." has been eliminated from the names of all medications in which it occurs in the German. "Met." simply refers to the pure metal as opposed to an ore or chemical compound; hence in what follows, wherever the Latin name of a metal (e.g. "Argentum") appears unmodified (except, of course, by a potency, or by the abbreviation "praep."), it may be assumed that the basis substance is the pure metal.

Many vegetable remedy names consist of two parts separated by a comma (e.g. "Betula, Cortex"). The first refers to the plant ("Betula"), the second to the part of the plant from which the remedy is derived ("Cortex"). It is important to realize that such names refer only to a single remedy, not to two. To forestall confusion, it may perhaps be desirable to list here the other frequently used Latin names for plant parts, which are: Flos, Folium, Radix, and Summitates (referring to the flowers, leaves, root, and buds, respectively).

Eigenblut, literally "own blood," refers to injections with the patient's own blood. This is done by taking one to ten cc of venous blood and injecting it intramuscularly either immediately or after exposing it to ultraviolet radiation. The blood then releases its etheric forces and thus stimulates the etheric body. In principle, every remedy used to influence the etheric body can be combined with the patient's blood. For further details see *The Anthroposophical Approach to Medicine,* vol. 2, p. 33.

The standard Latin abbreviations for the frequency of administration have been used (q.d. = once a day, b.i.d. = twice daily, t.i.d. = three times daily, and q.i.d. = four times daily). Ranges of frequencies (for example, "three to five times daily") or frequencies higher than four times daily have been written out rather than abbreviated.

In this translation, the German word *Messerspitze*, indicating a very small dose of a powder, has been translated as "a pinch." Other translations of this term currently in use include "knife-tip" and "pea-sized portion."

The abbreviations used for the form in which the remedies are administered are: "amp." for ampule (usually injected); "glob." for globules (taken orally); "liq." for a liquid (taken orally); "supp." for suppositories; "tab. or tb." for tablets (taken orally); "trit." for a triturate (powder, taken orally or sometimes through the nose); and "vag." for vaginal tablets and suppositories.

Indications

(All medications are products of Weleda unless otherwise specified)

Abscesses and Suppurations
Low protein, initially protein-free diet

Furuncles, Paronychia, Abscesses:
Mercurialis perennis 10% oint.; Mercurialis / Mel oint.; Stannum 5% oint.
Compresses with a paste of Bolus alba moistened with either calendula essence, Mercurialis perennis 20% ext. (one tsp. to one cup water), or with calendula oil 10%
At night: Mercurialis 10% oint.
Erysidoron 1 and 2
Arnica, Planta tota, D4, D6 amp., s.c. locally
Bismuth / Graphite / Stibium oint. (esp. for chronic paronychia)
Argentum comp. amp.
Sulfur iod. D3, D6 liq.
Eigenblut 1 ml or radiated Eigenblut with all injections

For weak suppurative reaction:
Hepar Sulfuris D3, D4 trit., 2 to at most 5 pinches daily
Myristica seb. D4 liq. ("homeopathic scalpel")
Prunus spinosa, Fructus ø, 15 drops frequently; blackthorn elixir
Prunus spinosa, Fructus D3 amp.

For spreading of disease process (incl. sepsis):
Argentum D30 / Echinacea D6 aa amp. or Echinacea / Argentum amp. (Wala)
Lachesis comp. amp. (Wala)

Phlegmons:
Therapy as above, with addition of:
Apis D3 / Belladonna D3 aa amp., poss. w. Arnica D3 amp., all s.c. around the abscess
Injections of irradiated Eigenblut, poss. w. ampules just mentioned
Echinacea ang. ø, liq.
Argentum D30 / Echinacea D6 aa amp.
Lachesis D12, D20 liq. or amp.

Pyoderma, Impetigo:
Mercurius viv. 0.1% oint.

Compresses w. calendula essence
Erysidoron 1 and 2
Thuja D3-D10 liq. or D3, D6 amp.; as bath additive, 20%
Quartz D12 trit., D20 amp.

Acne
Diet, strictness depending on severity: initially raw foods only, then vegetarian and low protein if poss.; intensive cure with and millet. Forbidden: pork, cured meats, chocolate, pungent spices, alcohol.
Wash affected areas with previously boiled water; water should be as hot as possible, and definitely not cold.
Sulfur selenosum D6 amp. and D3-D6 trit. or Sulfur iod. D6 liq.
Sulfur D12 trit. for four to seven days (initial worsening possible), then Digestodoron
Hepar Sulf. D12
Thuja D6 liq. and Quartz D12 liq.
Vaucheria D6 liq.
Urtica dioica D3-D6 liq.
Lac Taraxaci D10 / Parmelia D10 as amp. or liq. (if liver is involved)
Constitutional therapy:
for dark-haired women: Sepia D6 liq.
for fair-haired women: Phosphorus D6 liq., Pulsatilla D6 liq.
for women in general: Tormentilla D30 amp., once weekly
for men: Chamomilla, Planta tota D30 liq.
liver treatment: relieve constipation; Digestodoron
Eigenblut, poss. irradiated, poss. w. Quartz D20 amp. or Argentum praep. D20 amp.

Acne rosacea
Congested, hardened constitution which is addressed through:
Lac Taraxaci D10 / Parmelia D10 (2 x week, ampule sc), works especially upon the liver
Diet: no salt or meat
Carbo animalis e sanguine D3-D6 trit.
Antimonite D6 trit.
Vaucheria D3-D20 liq.
Aesculus, Cortex/Alumen amp., liq.
Irradiated *Eigenblut*, 1-2 ml, poss. w. Quartz D6 amp.

Adenoids
Spongia D3 liq.
Barium iodatum D4 liq.

Encourage nasal breathing and singing
(See also Lymphatic Constitution)

Adnexitis—see under Gynecological Disorders

Ageusia
Topaz D8 trit. over several months

AIDS
Sugar and alcohol free nutrition
Iscador St. 7 (0.0001) 1-2 x weekly sc as long term treatment + Mercurius viv. nat. D8 once weekly sc, alternating monthly with Ferrum sid. D6 2 x weekly
Medulla ossis D4 or D5 with Sol. sil comp. with Medulla aplasia
Carduus marianus capsule tid for hepatopathy
Ferrum per Chelidonium D2 dil. 10 dr. tid or amp. 2 x week for bilirubinemia
Viscum Pini 10% gel applied to Kaposi sarcoma bid

Allergy
Temporary protein-free diet; reinstate protein gradually, starting with vegetable protein only
Gencydo 1%, 3% amp.
Echinacea ø, D3 liq. for several months
Irradiated Eigenblut, 1–2 cc with indicated remedy, particularly
Ferrum sidereum D6, D20
Light- or sun-allergy: Hypericum D4 liq.
Cold-allergy: Dulcamara D6
See also Hay Fever; Allergic Eczema (under Skin Diseases)

Alopecia areata
Quartz D20, D30 trit. and amp.
Fluorite D10 trit., Quartz D10 trit., Malachite D6 trit., either alternately or together in equal portions
Species Urticae dioicae
Thallium aceticum D6 liq.
Pel Talpae D3, D6 trit.
Topically: Oleum aeth. Rosmarini 10% spiritus, poss. with arnica essence (undiluted)
Hairwater: Spiritus Rosmarini comp. (Leukichthol 1.0 + Menthol 0.25 + Thymol 0.1 + Ol. Eucalypti 3.0 + Tnct. Arnicae 40.0 + Spiritus Rosmarini ad. 100)

Oleum Aconiti comp. (Wala) Brief ultraviolet light therapy

Alzheimer's
Rubellite D20 dil. 10 dr. tid
Formica biweekly sc D3, D6, D15, D20, D30, and back D20 etc. to D3, each potency for 2 weeks

Amenorrhea—see under **Gynecological Disorders**

Anabolism, deficiency of *(Aufbauschwaeche)*
Bryophyllum Argento cultum D2 liq. (esp. for children)
Cuprum sulfuricum D4 liq.
Calcon 1 and 2
Organum quadruplex (Wala)
Prunus Iron D6 amp., D3 glob. (Wala)
Iris Bovis D4 amp., liq., poss. + Argentum praep. D6 amp. trit.
Eigenblut, poss. + Argentum praep. D6, D20 amp.
Prunus spinosa, Summitates D1 liq.
Nutritive baths (see volume II, p. 39) twice weekly
For inadequate intake and digestion of food: Argentum praep./ Cuprum praep./ Mercurius, each D15, aa liq., trit.

Anal Fissures
Achillea comp. liq.
Millefolium / Hypericum oint.
Bismuth / Graphites / Stibium oint.
Sitz baths with chamomile or calendula essence
Intermittently: Sulfur D6 trit. or liq.
Relaxation exercises to widen sphincter

Anemia
See also vol. 1, p. 79f.

Hypochromic Anemia:
Gentian Amadoron, 10–20 drops t.i.d.
Levico-water treatment (cf. vol. I, p. 85)
Urtica dioica Ferro culta D2 amp., liq.
Ferrum ustum comp. trit.
Siderite D1 trit.
Ferrum carbonicum D1 trit.
Stimulation of light-metabolism:
Adequate sunlight exposure (poss. sunbathe)

For fair complexions: Cerite D4 trit., D6 amp.
For dark complexions: Cuprum D4, D6 trit. or Malachite D4-D6 trit.
Bitters; gall therapy (e.g. Chelidonium Ferro cultum D2 amp., liq.)

Pernicious Anemia:
Carbo Betulae cum Methano D4 trit., D6 amp.
Sassafras D3 / Spinacia D3 aa amp. and liq. (also externally as a rinse)
Cuprum D4, D6 trit.
Ferrum 0.4% oint. over the liver
Cobaltum D6 amp., D3 trit.
Treat the liver; HCl substitution
Spleen massage with Cuprum praep. 0.4% oint.

Anosmia
(e.g. following the flu):
Jaspis D10 + Bulbis olfact. D4 amp. 2-3 times weekly

Anxiety, Panic, Agitation
Hyoscyamus/Valeriana amp. (2-5 cc i.m., poss. several times daily, or D1 liq.)
Cuprum aceticum D5 / Zincum val. D5 aa amp.; Cuprum acet. D4 / Zincum val. D4 liq.
Long baths with Papaver rhoeas 20% ext.
Bryophyllum ø liq.
Agaricus musc. D6 amp., poss. + Zincum val. D4 amp.
Bryophyllum D5 / Conchae D7 aa amp.
Mustard foot baths (one handful mustard powder to 2-3 gallons water); length of bath no more than 10 minutes
For stage fright: Aurum praep. D6, D8, D10 amp.; Crataegus D3 / Ferrum sidereum D20 / Saccharum tostum D3 amp.

Aortic aneurysm
Aorta abdominalis D5 amp. + Tabacum D6 sc 2 x week
With arterial hypertension in addition Belladonna Rd D3

Appendicitis
(Conservative therapy for cases where surgery is not possible)
Fasting
Antimonite D4 trit., D6 amp., together with Apis D3 / Belladonna D3 as amp. locally
Carbo Betulae D4 trit.
Cichorium D3 (in alternation with Carbo and Antimonite)

Topically: Mercurialis perennis 10% oint.
Mustard paste over the tonsils

Arterial stenosis
Corresponding artery (e.g. renal artery) D5 amp + Tabacum D6 amp sc 2 x week

Arteriosclerosis
Diet: limit fats and meats
Scleron, 1 tablet b.i.d. (esp. prophylactically, in early stages, and in the presence of hypotension)
Principal remedy: Betula, Folium, esp. D2 amp.
For metabolic types add Betula, Cortex D2, D3 amp.
Birch elixir, birch leaf tea
Arnica, Planta tota in higher potencies (e.g. as Arnica / Betula comp. amp.)
Belladonna D5, D6 liq.
Helleborus niger, Planta tota D2-D5 liq., D3, D6 amp.
Aurum praep. D30 amp.
Chamomilla Cupro culta, Radix, esp. for hypertensives
Ferrum hydroxydatum 2% trit. (esp. for dizziness)
Iodine, e.g. as Kalium iodatum D5-10%, 3 x 10-15 drops

Arteriosclerosis, Cerebral sclerosis
1/4 mg Strophantin 1 ml (poss. Ouabain) + Levulose or Glucose 5-10% 9 ml iv 2 x week
Belladonna Rd D30 10 dr am and D6 10 dr pm
with aggressiveness: Convallaria, Flos D1 20dr tid
Kalium jodatum 10% 10.0 + Aqua dist. ad 100.0, 20dr tid
preapoplectic states: Ferrum cum aceto praep. 1/4 tsp tid

Arteritis temporalis
Arteria temporalis D30 amp + Arnica, Pl. tota D20 sc 2 x week, for 4 weeks, then instead of Arnica use Stannum met. praep. D8
Diet- no sugar, no meat, low protein
Acute:
Rheumadoron I and II each 2 x day alternating
Cortisone may be necessary

Arthritis, Rheumatoid
Chronic:
Diet: low salt, low protein, to begin for 4 weeks without animal protein;

birch-leaf tea, birch elixir
Draw the process to the skin w. hot compresses of Arnica essence 20% (one tbsp. to one pint water)
Rheumodoron 1 and 2 in hourly or half-hourly alternation, 5-10 drops (components also individually)
Heart treatment (esp. with Cardiodoron)
Stannum praep. D8, D10 amp. or trit. or Stannum comp. trit. (Stannum only as a follow-up, not in acute cases)

Acute:
Absinthium D1 / Resina Laricis D3 as liq., 5-10 drops every three hours
Apis D3 / Bryonia D3 as amp.
Cepa D3-D10 liq., poss. with Bryonia and Arnica
Symphytum comp. liq.; Symphytum 10% oint.
Mercurius (viv., dulcis or solute.) D3, D4 trit. (short-term only)
For fever: Argentum D30 / Carbo Betulae D30 aa amp. daily, Plumbum sil. D20
Vit E, 3 x day 400 U

Effusions:
Bryonia D3, D6 amp., liq.
Carduus benedictus D1 / Paeonia off. D1 aa liq.
Short-term Mercurius (see above)

To stimulate inflammatory reaction:
Sulfur compresses

Chronic:
The basis of the effectiveness of the following treatment is the general alleviation of metabolic problems through appropriate diet, drawing the process off to the intestine or the skin, sweating, hydrotherapy, and physical therapy
Basic metabolic remedy: Absinthium D1 / Resina Laricis D3 as liq., 15 drops t.i.d.
Iron therapy: Iron in various forms and potencies, always twice weekly, e.g.: Levico D3, Ferrum sidereum D10, Pyrite Do, D15, Hematite D6, all amp.
Betula, Folium 3%, D2 amp., poss. several ampules at a time
Solum oliginosum (moor lavender; esp. for pains; poss. even 10ml i.v.)
Oleum Solum oliginosum comp. (Wala)
Rheumodoron 102A (components also individually and in other potencies)
Antimonite D6 amp., D4 trit. (directed at protein metabolism)

Spiraea D2 liq.
Formica liq., amp. (increasing and decreasing in potency)
Primula farinosa D6 liq., D3 amp.
Arnica D3 / Formica D3 amp.
Equisetum arvense D15 / Formica D10 as amp.
Arnica comp. / Formica oint.
Argentite D6-D10 amp. (to stimulate reaction while moon is waxing)
Plumbum silicicum D20 amp. (esp. while moon is waning)
Bitters
Stannum praep. D8 trit., D10 amp. (only for deformations)

Arthrosis—see **Degenerative Joint Disease**

Articular rheumatism
Acute: Quark compresses, total body soaping (alkalinization)

Irritate skin in joint region e.g. Nettles, Ungt. irritans, dry brushing, Cantheride plasters
Low salt diet, raw food diet, no animal protein,no sugar, no alcohol
Natrium mur. D20 dil.
Nettle leaf extract
Moor baths, Fango
Subacute: Betula comp. amp. s.c.

Ascites—see under **Liver Diseases**

Asthma
Basic treatment:
Quercus D1 liq., 10 drops in a.m.
Prunus spinosa, Summitates 5% or D2 liq., 10 drops in afternoon
Veronica off. D1 or D2 liq. (and/or Melissa Cupro culta D2 liq. or Chamomilla Cupro culta D2 liq.), 10 drops in evening
Acute asthma:
Phlebotomy of 250-300 ml
Ipecacuanha D3 1 tsp (emetic)
Chamomilla cupro culta D2 amp. sc between shoulder blades
Also weekly injections of:
Prunus spinosa, Fructus D3 in the nape of the neck
Gencydo 1%–3% between the shoulder blades
Tabacum D6, D10 over the kidneys (Dry, thin types should receive Argentum praep. D6, D8 or Argentite D6, D10 in place of Gencydo)
Cinis Tabaci D3–D6 trit.

Plumbum praep. D8 amp. (esp. in allergic asthma)
Formica D6, D8, D30 amp.
Cuprum-Ren D4, later D6 amp. (one inj. twice weekly)
Cuprum aceticum D3, D4 liq. (antispasmodic, esp. for pertussis or spastic bronchitis)
Conchae D10 + Tabacum D10 amp.
Quebracho D30 amp.
Cinis Arnicae D3, D6 trit.
Camphora comp. (Wala)
Lobelia comp. amp.
Stramonium D6 amp., liq.
Support of specific systems:
For control of water organism: Kalium carbonicum D6, D8, D10 liq.
General structuring of the upper air passages: Kalium bichromicum D6 liq.
Stimulation of the warmth organism: Apis D10, D12, D15 liq.
To enhance light- and air-metabolism: Carbo Betulae D20, Carbo Tabaci D20, or Carbo Equiseti D15 (all amp.)
Acidic baths (vinegar, carbonic or formic acid)
Internal alkalization (e.g. w. Natrium bicarbonicum)
Lemon chest compresses
Mustard chest compresses (for accompanying bronchitis) or mustard foot baths (also during attacks)
For children: Arsenicum album D30 liq., 5 drops q.d. (also when attack threatens)
During attacks: Stibium arsenicosum D10 liq. or D15 amp.
Petasites comp. cum Quercu glob. in alternation with Petasites comp. cum Veronica glob. (Wala)
See also Hay Fever
Curative eurythmy: L A O M

Basedow's Disease—see **Hyperthyroidism**

Bed-Wetting—see **Enuresis Nocturna**

Blepharospasm
Tabacum D20, D30 liq.
Belladonna D20, D25, D30 liq.

Bone Diseases
See also Scheuermann's Disease, Spine (treatment of), Osteomyelitis
Epicondylitis:
Compresses with fresh onion or Cepa 10%, 1% oint.

Rhus tox. D10, D30 amp.
Argentite D6 trit., amp.
Bryonia D3 amp., liq. or Bryonia / Stannum (Wala) amp. or glob.
Apis / Rhus tox. comp. amp.
Antispasmodic measures

Fractures:
see separate entry

Periostitis:
Cepa D3 liq., 1%, 10% oint.
Stannum silicicum D6 trit., amp.

Osgood-Schlatter's Disease:
Stannum praep. D8 or Stannum silicicum D6 amp.
Apatite D6/ Stannum D8 aa trit.
Symphytum 10% oint.

Legg-Calvé-Perthes Disease
Cerussite D8 amp., D4,D6 trit.
Hypophysis D10 liq.
Plumbum 0.1% oint.
Stannum comp. trit.

Breast Diseases

Fibrocystic Breast Disease
Vespa Crabro D3-D6 amp.
Fluorite D12 trit.
Magnesite D4-D12 trit. or liq. starting at D8
Thuja Occ. D12 liq.
Quartz D12-D15 liq., trit.
Mixtura Stanni comp. liq. (for actual cyst formation)
Conium maculatum 5% oint.
Iscador M Series O (or only strength 5)

Mastodynia
Argentum praep. 0.4% oint.
Equisetum tea
Agnus castus D1–D4 liq.
Kalium carbonicum D6 liq. (effect on water organism)

Bone disorders

Luxation (recurring)

Stannum silicium D6 amp

Consolidation of orthopedic or osteopathic therapy

Stannum silicium D6 amp

Non-healing fracture

Arnica planta tota D4 or D6 + Cepa D3 amp + Symphytum D3 amp

Calcon I and II

Brachialgia paresthetica nocturna

Crotalus D30 amp. sc

Bronchitis

Acute:

Inhalations with essential oils, esp. Eucalyptus, Oleum aeth Pini pumilionis, or mixtures of these

Oleum aeth. Eucalypti 10% Oleum

Pneumodoron 1, Pulmonium cough syrup (Wala)

Petasites comp. amp. or glob. (Wala)

Pyrite D3 or Anise-Pyrite D3, tablets

Sytra tea (Weleda)

Plantago lanceolata 10% oint.

Ferrum phos. D8 amp. sc qd

Erysidoron I 10 dr alternating hourly with Mercurius cyanatus D4 10 dr

Bolus Eucalypti comp. trit

Heapr sulfuris D4 tb tid for five days if yellow tenaceous mucus

Mustard chest wraps

for children: warm bath, Plantago oint. 10%, Sytra Tea

Chronic, COPD:

Sugar and alcohol free diet, protein reduction, intestinal cleansing

Kapf's Acid: (Acetic acid 30% 25.0 + Formic acid 25% 275.0) place on cupboard in open vessel to inhale evaporate

Camphora 20% in acute case inject im 1-2ml up to 3 x day (Oil, thus not sc or iv!), otherwise 2 x week 1ml im

Formica amp. 2 x week sc D8, D6, D3, and back D6, etc., every potency for 2 weeks

Etheric oils for sinusitis

Kalium jodatum 10% 10.0 + Aqua dist. ad 100.0 20 dr tid

Mustard or eucalyptus compresses

Camphora comp. amp. i.m. (Wala)

Stimulate perspiration
Baths with pine extracts; salt baths, steam baths
Tabacum D6, D10 amp.
Stibium sulfuratum aurantiacum D4 trit. (for heavy mucus formation)
Ipecacuanha D4 liq. (expectorant)
To stimulate warmth organism: Causticum Hahnemanni D6 liq.
Ferrum rosatum D3/ Graphites D15 amp., liq.
Cinis-preparations in low potencies (e.g. Cinis Arnicae)

Ticklish cough:
Pertudoron 1, 7 drops several times daily
Spiritus contra Tussim
Hyoscyamus D3 liq. (poss. with Bryonia)
Conium maculatum D3 liq.
Rumex crispus D2 liq. ("bifurcation cough")

Bronchiectasis:
Cinis Glechomatis D3 trit.
Graphites D15/ Stannum D10 aa trit.
Tabacum D10 amp.
Camphora comp. amp. (Wala), i.m.
Essential oils internally and as inhalants
Creosote D4 liq.

Burns
Cold compresses of Combudoron essence, one part to ten parts water. Keep compresses moist. Larger areas may be submerged in physiological saline solution containing one tenth Combudoron essence
Arnica, Planta tota D3-D6 liq.
Force fluids
Smaller burns and burns that have begun to heal: Combudoron gel or oint.

Bursitis
Cepa D3 amp., Stannum praep. D10 amp.
Arnica D3 / Cepa D3 / Symphytum D3 as liq.
Cassiterite (Kassiterit) 0.1%, Arnica or Calendula essence, or Symphytum 20% ext., individually or in equal parts, diluted with ten parts water for compresses

Cancer
See Chapter 2

See also Guidelines for the Use of Iscador, available from The Society for Cancer Research, CH-4144 Arlesheim, Switzerland
Basic: Mistletoe therapy. Dosage strictly individual! Don't overdose. Often 0.1 mg 2 x week is sufficient. Patient should improve noticeably (e.g. improved mood, sleep, decreased pain, improved digestion). Patient should not experience a negative reaction, should at no time experience malaise or irritability. A 2 cm erythema at injection site may already be indication of excess dosage and will only be tolerated if tumor is present and there is otherwise no negative reaction. Otherwise a one week rest is indicated and reinitiation of therapy at a lower dosis.

Mild general hyperthermia up to 40°C, local hyperthermia at or over tumor site up to 42°C.
Ozone rectal insufflation 1-2 x week
No Vit B12 or Folic acid (feeds the tumor cells)
For pain: Iscador 0.0001 mg pm, next day Iscador in usual dosis
Cerite D6 amp. 2 x weeks.c., especially if photophobia or light intolerance (stimulates light metabolism)

Carpal tunnel syndrome
Formica D3 amp. sc local injection, D2 still better, but painful, therefore never use at outset of treatment
Vit B6

Celiac disease
Oil dispersion baths (to stimulate warmth organization)
Desensitization with very small quantities of bread, gradually increasing
Amara drops
Digestodoron Tb tid, increase by one tb a day up to 3 tbs tid
Sour milk products
Dental amalgam removal

Cerebrovascular Disease—see Arteriosclerosis; Stroke

Childbirth—see under Pregnancy

Circulatory Diseases
See also Heart Diseases

Hypertension:
Diet: no salt, restricted fluids, vegetarian fare
Rising-temperature arm baths and hot foot baths with one-half tsp. copper

sulfate crystals (except with open wounds)
Minor phlebotomy as indicated
Rauwolfia D1 dil.
Belladonna D4, D6, poss. + Magnesium phosph. acidum D6 liq.
Aorta D6, D4 (Wala) + Belladonna D4 amp.
Arnica / Betula comp. amp., poss. + Cardiodoron 1% amp.
Plumbum mellitum or Plumbum silicicum D20 amp., trit.
Solutio Sacchari comp. D15 amp.
Phosphorochalcite D6 trit., amp. (acts through the kidney)
Birch-leaf tea
Betula, Folium D2 amp.
Ferrum praep. D20 liq. or trit. in a.m., Aurum praep. D8, D10 liq. or trit. in aft., and Cuprum sulfuricum D6 liq. evenings
Aurum D30 / Plumbum D20 as amp.
Cobaltum D30 liq., amp. (for polycythemia)
Formica baths (Formica 5% ext., one tsp. per bath)

Hypotension:
Principal remedy: iron, e.g. as Urtica dioica Ferro culta D2 liq. or amp.
Levico-water treatment (cf. vol. I, p. 85)
Ferrum sidereum D6, D8, D10 trit. and amp.
Glandula suprarenalis D3 / Solutio Ferri comp. D6 aa amp. (to increase "kidney radiation")
Scorodite D6, D8, D10 trit. and amp.
Ferrum hydroxydatum 5% trit. (for tendency to fainting and syncopal episodes)
Pre-treatment and intermittent treatment with copper is occasionally necessary, e.g. as Melissa Cupro culta D2 liq. or Cuprum praep. 0.4% oint.
Prunus spinosa, Summitates 0, D5 liq. or amp.
Spartium scoparium D1-D3 or Sarothamnus comp. amp., glob. (Wala)
Camphora D1, D2 liq.
Carbo Betulae D20 amp.
Rosemary baths, esp. oil dispersion baths with Oleum Beth. Rosmarini 10% Oleum
Dry brushing of skin
To stabilize: Hypericum Auro cultum D2 liq. or Aurum praep. D6 trit.

Circulatory Collapse:
Veratrum album D3-D6 liq., D4 amp., poss. Cardiodoron 1% amp.
Camphora D2 liq., D3 amp. s.c., 20% oleosum amp. i.m.
Carbo Betulae D30 liq., 40 drops in a glass of water, drunk slowly, one swallow at a time

Arsenicum album D20 amp.
Hot arnica compresses over wrists

Peripheral Vascular Disease:
Principal remedy: copper
Hot arm and foot baths with Cuprum sulfuricum, Prunus, or rosemary in alternation with Tabacum
Alternating hot and cold foot baths
Cuprum sulfuricum D6 liq.
Cuprum 0.4%/ Tabacum D6 as oint.
Melissa Cupro culta D2 liq., amp.
Scorodite D10 liq., trit.
Secale / Bleiglanz glob. (Wala)
Bismuth 2%/ Hyoscyamus 5% as oint.
Formica D6 amp. i.v., D4 amp. s.c., liq.
Belladonna D6 + Arnica D6 + Oleum Beth. Rosmarini D3 aa liq.
Tabacum D6 liq., amp.
Aurum praep. D30 amp., once every four weeks
Magnesium phosph. / Tabacum amp.
Curative eurythmy
No nicotine
Additionally, later: Ferrum, e.g. Ferrum 0.4% oint. over the affected arteries

Thrombophlebitis:
Lukewarm compresses with Borago 20% (one tsp. in a glass of water) (poss. + Arnica)
Borago D3 liq. or Borago comp. glob. and amp. (Wala)
Arnica, Planta tota D3-D6 amp.
Kalium aceticum comp. D6 amp.
Formica D4, D6 liq. or amp.
Scorodite D8, D10 liq. or amp.
For women, Pulsatilla D6 liq. is frequently also indicated
Aesculus, Cortex 10% / Borago 10% / Hamamelis, Folium 10% oint.
Lotio Pruni comp cum Cupro
Leeches

Varicosities:
See also Thrombophlebitis, Hemorrhoids
Vigorous walking; avoid standing still.
Technically correct compression bandages or surgical compression stockings. Apply Lotio Pruni comp. cum Cupro (leg gel with copper) to legs

before applying bandages or stockings.
Kalium aceticum comp. D2-D10 trit., D6 amp., 1% oint.
Cuprum 0.4%/ Tabacum D6 as oint.
Solutio Ferri comp. D6-D15 liq.; Glandula suprarenalis D3/ Solutio Ferri comp. D6 aa amp. (to strengthen "kidney radiation")
Carbo D8, D20 amp.
Quartz / Nicotiana glob. and amp. (Wala)
Fluorite D4-D12 trit., D6 amp. (strengthens connective tissue)
Tabacum D4-D6 amp. (counteracts deformities)
Olivenite D6 amp. (for lower leg cramps)
Leg gel with copper
Aesculus / Oleum Beth. Rosmarini oint.
Aesculus, Cortex 5% gel, also 20% ext. for compresses
Liver therapy, esp. with Hepatodoron and yarrow tea
Spartium scoparium D1, D3 liq. (for hypotension)
Silicea D6 amp. s.c.

Leg Ulcers:
Basic treatment: see above under Varicosities and Thrombophlebitis
Initially: bedrest; otherwise use compression stockings
Saline compresses with calendula essence or Hamamelis, Folium 20% ext.
To cleanse wounds: undiluted honey; Carbo Coffeae powder
After cleansing: allow a bit of patient's own blood (drawn from a vein and applied externally) to coagulate on the wound (stimulates healing); dry wound every hour
Kalium acticum comp D6 amp. and Gel
Ozone locally
Chlorophyl 1% oint
Wecesin gel
Arnica, Planta tota D3, D4 amp. locally
Massage at the corresponding vertebrae

Cirrhosis—see under Liver Diseases

Claudication, intermittent
Nicotiana D12 or D15 amp. sc
Ozone therapy
Birchleaf juice 1/2 bottle daily

Colds—see **Influenza**

Colitis—see under **Intestinal Diseases**

Concussion
Quiet surroundings; a minimum of sensory stimulation
Arnica compresses on the head, warm or cold as tolerated
Arnica, Planta tota, Rh D3, D4, D6, initially several times daily as liquid and once a day as amp., poss. with Cerebellum
D5 amp. (Wala) Quartz D30 amp.
Phosphorus 0.1% Oleum, one drop on the temples
Cerebellum comp. glob. (Wala)
Bidor 5% tabl. or Ferrum-Quartz capsules
Conjunctivitis
See also chapter 6
Warm compresses with fennel tea or Species ophthalmicae
Argentum nitricum D4 eyedrops
Euphrasia D3 eyedrops and D4 liq.

Constipation, chronic
Change diet. Laxatives only short-term and as the exception.
Bitters, Karlsbader salt treatment as a cure, with pauses
Weleda laxative tablets or Alpflora laxative tea
Digestodoron 20-30 drops t.i.d.
Opium D30 liq.
Liver/gall bladder therapy, esp. w. Choleodoron (also poss. Chelidonium/ Curcuma comp.), Oxalis 30%, 10% oint. or Cuprum praep. 0.4% oint. (abdominal massage)
Depending on constitution: Nux vomica, Halite, Diaspor, Carbo, Graphites, Bryonia, Sulfur
spastic or atonic: Carpellum Mali comp amp. trit.

Coronary Insufficiency—see "Coronary Artery Disease" under Heart Diseases

Cough—see under Bronchitis

Craniostenosis—see under Growth and Development, Disorders of

Crohn's Disease
Phosphorus D5 liq., 7 drops in mornings and in afternoons.
Iscador Qu or M strength 5, poss. 4 (no stronger), one amp. twice weekly
Dyscrasite D6 amp., trit.
Formica amp. 2 x week sc, D8, D6, D3 and back D6 etc., every potency for 2 weeks
Near the fistulas: Arnica, Planta tota D3, later Quartz D6 amp.

Between exacerbations: Ferrum sidereum D20
Psychotherapy to encourage mental independence
Curative eurythmy and speech-formation therapy

Croup, Laryngotracheobronchitis, Acute Laryngitis
Bryonia / Spongia comp. liq., 3-7 drops every fifteen to thirty minutes with water
Moistened air (wet towels around the bed; vaporizer with essential oils)
Compresses with onions (onions should first be steamed until clear)
For chronic laryngitis, see *Laryngitis, chronic*

Cryptorchidism
Argentum met praep. 0.4% gel or oint. applied over inguinal canal + Olivenite D6 trit. kt tid

Cystitis, Cystopyelitis—see under **Kidney and Bladder Diseases**

Cysts
Multiple or isolated cysts in different organs:
Mixtura Stanni comp. dil. (Weleda), treat for 2 years

Degenerative Joint Disease
For general guidelines see Arthritis and Chapter VII, Diseases of the Spine and Joints in Vol. III
Stannum 5% trit. 1 pinch t.i.d. after meals
Stannum 0.4% or 5% oint.
Phosphorus oil capsules, one daily in a.m.
Equisetum D15 / Formica D10 aa amp., twice weekly (Equisetum may be replaced with Solutio Silicea comp.); Equisetum D15 + Sulfur D10 (for pain relief)
Stannum met. praep. D8, amp. + Mandragora D3 amp., sc 2-3 x a week
Stannum silicicum D6, amp. sc, or trit.
Resina Bryoniae D4 amp. to loosen up a stagnating process
Equisetum D15 + Sulfur D6 amp. (single amp.)
Viscum Mali D3 amp.
Primula farinosa D6 amp.
Mandragora comp. liq. (esp. for soft tissue swelling)
Mandragora 5% Oint.
Between treatments: Argentite D6 trit., Solutio alkaline liq.
Organ preparations, e.g. Cartilago comp. 1 and 2 (Wala), Articulatio genus D3, D4 (Wala), poss. with one of the above preparations
For DJD of knee: Apatite D6 / Stannum D8 aa trit.

For DJD of hip: Formica 5% oint.
Sulfur baths and compresses
Generally: begin with higher potencies; with small joints higher potencies, with larger joints lower ones

Depression (endogenous)
Basic treatment: Aurum praep. in higher potencies; stimulation of light-metabolism
Hypericum, Herba 0 liq., 20-30 drops t.i.d.
Hypericum Auro cultum D2 Aurum praep. D15-D30 amp., liq.
Initially: Argentum praep. D6 amp. and trit. In later phases (to alleviate stagnation): Mercurius auratus D15 amp.
Depression with exhaustion: Hepar-Magnesium D4
To stimulate activity: Ferrum / Acidum chol. aa D4 amp. and trit.

Dermatitis—see under **Skin Diseases**

Diabetes mellitus
Sugar- and alcohol-free diet, vigorous physical activity, e.g. mountain climbing
Poterium spinosum D1 dil. 10 dr tid instead of oral hypoglycemics
Oil-dispersion baths with Oleum Beth. Rosmarini
Phosphorus D5 liq., 8 drops in a.m. and aft.
Quartz D12
Cuprum sulfuricum D4
Resina Abietis D20, D30 amp., liq.
Diabetic retinopathy: Belladonna, Radix D20 amp., Resina Laricis D6 / Retina D4 aa amp., Chrysolith comp. amp.
for abscess formation: Sloe juice 1/2 bottle daily
for gangrene: Kalium aceticum comp. amp. with 1 ml Eigenblut sc, bathe gangrenous area with rosemary and calendula (if gangrene is black and dry) or mercurialis (if pustular)
Ozone locally

Diphtheria—see Throat Inflammations

Dizzy Spells
See also Motion Sickness and Meniere's Disease
Diagnose cause (e.g. hypoglycemia, hypotension)
Nausyn tab.
Belladonna D15 liq.
Arnica, Planta tota D15 + Cerebellum D4-D15 + Ferrum hydroxydatum D6 amp.

Cerebellum D4 liq.
Ferrum hydroxydatum 2% trit.

Dysmenorrhea—see under Gynecological Disorders

Ear Diseases

Basic otitis treatment is Levisticum Rd., however with Aconitum (eg Aconitum comp. ear drops - WALA) rapid pain relief may be achieved.

Acute Otitis Media:

Dry chamomile poultice over ear; hot water bottle or heating pad on top
Induce sweating.
Hot sitz bath with one tbsp. Thuja 20% as indicated
Onion slices behind the ear
Levisticum Rd D2, D3 liq. every fifteen to thirty minutes, poss. alternating with Erysidoron 1
For transition to mastoiditis, Levisticum in hourly alternation with Capsicum ann. D3 liq. and injection of Argentum comp s.c.
Levisticum Rd 10% Oleum or Aconitum comp. eardrops (Wala), warmed and applied with cotton swab in ear (analgesic)
Quartz D12 trit., D20 amp.
Cepa D3 liq.
Chamomilla comp. supp.
Silicea comp. glob., amp. (Wala)
Thuja 0.5% or D3 amp.

For recurrent otitis (during interval):

Belladonna D6 / Levisticum D3 / Thuja D4 aa liq.
Thuja Argento culta D3 liq., amp.

Chronic Otitis Media:

No water in the ear. Wipe or cautiously rinse ear with a mixture of equal parts of hydrogen peroxide, glycerin, and alcohol
Stimulate, resp. protect the warmth organism
Quartz D20 or Onyx D12 trit.; then Fluorite D12 liq. or trit.
Argentum nitricum D20 liq.
Levisticum D10 liq.
Thuja D3 liq., amp. or Thuja Argento culta D3 liq., amp.
Salt baths
Ferrum 0.4% oint. (behind the left ear)
Plumbum 0.1% oint. (behind the right ear)

Middle Ear Effusion:
Warmth, e.g. with infrared
Mercurius solubilis Hahnemanni D4 trit., 1 pinch three to five times daily for three days; thereafter, Mercurius viv. nat. D6, 1 tablet two or three times a day, simultaneously Levisticum D10 liq. (for four weeks)

Mastoiditis:
Arnica, Planta tota D3 amp., locally
Capsicum ann. D3 liq.
Mercurialis perennis 10% oint. behind the ear
Cepa 10% oint. or onion compress (onion chopped fine, steamed until clear, and placed in a muslin sack)
Eucalyptus comp. paste as compress
Echinacea ø, D1 liq.

Otitis externa, Eczema of ear canal:
Argentum praep. 0.4% gel
Quartz D12 trit., amp.
Weeping eczema: dab with Arnica tincture, cover with zinc oil; when dry: apply Kalium aceticum comp. 1%, 0.1% oint. (can relieve itching)
Treat metabolism; in elderly check for diabetes and put on short-term sugar-free diet

Tinnitus:
Lac papaveris somniferi D6 liq.
Plumbum iodatum 5% oint. on the mastoid process
Betula, Folium D6 amp., D1 liq.

Atypical tinnitus:
Arnica / Plumbum comp. glob., amp. (Wala), poss. with Onyx D20 trit., amp.
Cochlea D4 amp. (Wala)
Cerebrum comp. B glob., amp. (Wala)
Belladonna D10-D20 liq. (for pulsating tinnitus)

Nerve deafness:
Onyx D20 trit., amp. (poss. for years)
Organ preparations (Labyrinth, Nervus acust.) with Arnica, Planta tota D20 or Onyx D12, D20
Cerebrum comp. B glob., amp. (Wala)
Otosclerosis:
Betula, Folium D6 amp.

Gnaphalium leont. D2-D6 liq., D6 amp.
Cerebrum comp. B glob., amp. (Wala)
General antisclerotic treatment

Sudden hearing loss:
Rest and relaxation important. Bedrest.
Cochlea D4 amp. (Wala), daily
Labyrinthus D4 amp. (Wala) (for accompanying dizziness)
Poss. vasodilation, e.g. with Tebonin (Schwabe)

Hyperacusis:
Cerebrum comp. B glob., amp. (Wala), s.c. behind the ears

Eczema—see under Skin Diseases

Emotional Shock
Oxalis 20% ext. as warm compresses on abdomen
Bryophyllum Argento cultum D2 liq. or
Argentum praep. D6 trit. or Argentite D6 trit., amp.

Emphysema
Cinis Glechomatis D3 trit.
Stibium sulfuratum aurantiacum D6 / Carbo Betulae D12 aa trit.
Carbo Betulae D20 / Stannum praep. D10 aa trit. or Graphites D20 / Stannum praep. D10 aa trit.
Mercurius viv. nat. D15 trit.
Petasites comp. amp., glob. (Wala)

Encephalitis
See also Meningitis
Draw process off to skin, e.g. with mustard compresses
Argentum praep. D30 or Argentum D30 / Echinacea D6 aa amp., once daily
Agaricus bulb. D6 liq., D30 amp.
Scorodite D30 amp.
Stibium praep. D20 amp.
After resolution of acute symptoms: Arnica, Planta tota D20 amp., twice weekly

Postencephalitic sequelae:
Arnica / Cerebrum D6 amp., twice weekly
Organ preparations as indicated, internally or amp.

Phosphorus 0.1% Oleum, one drop on the temples
Cerebellum comp. liq., amp.
Belladonna, Radix D20, D30 liq., amp.
Occasionally encourage perspiration

Endometritis, Endometriosis—see under Gynecological Disorders

Enuresis Nocturna
See also Incontinence
Protect patient's warmth organism
Hypericum D2, D3 liq., 5-10 drops t.i.d.
Phosphorus 0.1% Oleum, one drop on the dorsum of the feet and on shins in the evening
Argentum praep. 0.4% oint., over the bladder in evening
Berberis D3-D5 liq.; Kalium phosph. D6 liq.
If central nervous system disorder suspected: Agaricus musc. D4 liq.
Causticum Hahnemanni D6-D12 (homeopathy)
Berberis / Hypericum glob. (Wala)
Belladonna D3-D6 liq., or D2 in increasing doses (for extremely deep sleepers)
Hypophysis D6 liq.
Equisetum hiemale D4 liq. (DHU) if worse in winter or due to cold weather
Hypericum, Flos 25% Oleum on the thigh

Epicondylitis—see under Bone Diseases

Epilepsy
Diet: low in protein and salt, reduced fluids.
Ketogenic diet (Fats bring about acidification of the blood which can prevent seizures)
No alcohol. Thorough purging once a month to detoxify.
Hyperthermic baths
Principal remedy: Belladonna
Belladonna D10 / Sulfur D5 aa liq.
Arum mac. D3 / Pteridium aquilin. D3 aa amp. daily, also internally as liq.
Belladonna D6 liq. in a.m., D30 liq. eves
Chamomilla Cupro culta, Radix D2 amp.
Viscum Pini 5% liq. or Viscum Mali D1 liq.
Viscum Pini D3 or D6 amp., Iscador P 0.0001 amp. 1-2 x week sc
Magnesium phosph. D6 liq., poss. + Arnica D10 / Belladonna D10 aa liq.
Quartz D12, D20, D30 trit., amp.

Vaucheria D6, D8, D10 liq.
Quartz 1%, 10% oint. to the feet
Depending on constitution: Kalium carbonicum D6, later D10, D12, D15 liq. (water organism)
Conchae D6-D30 trit. Plumbum chloratum D6, poss. D3 amp., a few amp. and then pause
Later: Plumbum silicicum D10-D20 amp.
Investigate involvement of various organs, and treat accordingly:
Liver: Taraxacum Stanno cultum; Hepar-Magnesium; Hepar- Stannum D4 amp., liq.
Kidney: Chamomilla Cupro culta, Radix D3 (0.1%) / Ren D3 aa amp.; Cuprum-Ren D4, D6 amp.
Heart: Mucilago Levistici D6-D3 liq.; Aurum praep. D10 amp., liq.
Digestive tract: Digestodoron; Absinthium D1 / Resina Laricis D3 aa liq.

Traumatic epilepsy:
Zincum praep. D30 + Arnica, Planta tota D20 amp. and liq.
Compresses with diluted arnica essence on the forearms and shins in the evening, two weeks on, one week off, for years if necessary

Erysipelas
Erysidoron 1 and 2 in hourly alternation
Argentum D30 / Echinacea D6 as amp., poss. + Quartz D30 amp.
Lachesis comp. amp., glob. (Wala)
Compresses with calendula essence (20%)
Purgatives or enemas

Erythema nodosum
Compresses with Equisetum 10% ext. or gel
Aurum praep. D6 oint.
Formica D6 amp.
Kalium aceticum comp. D6 trit.
Urtica dioica Ferro culta D2 liq.
Phosphorus D15 liq

Exhaustion
With nervousness, see also Weakness, general
Argentum, e.g. Argentum praep. D20 or Argentum nitricum D20 amp., twice weekly; also as liq. per os
Prunus spinosa, Summitates D1 / Bryophyllum D1 aa liq., 10–20 drops several times daily

Aqua Maris D3 / Prunus spinosa, Summ. D5 aa amp., poss. + Argentum praep. D6 amp.
Bidor 5% tabl.
Kalium phosph. comp. tabl.
Solutio alkaline liq., 5-7 drops q.d. in a.m.
Eigenblut, poss. + Argentum
Sallow thorn elixir
Blackthorn elixir

Exudative Diathesis—see Lymphatic Constitution

Eye Diseases—see Eye Diseases chapter in this volume

Fibrositis—see Arthritis

Flu—see Influenza

Fractures
To stimulate healing:
Calcon 1 and 2
Cepa D3 / Arnica D3 / Symphytum D3 as liq., 10 drops several times daily
If possible, compresses with arnica essence and locally: Arnica D3, D4, D6 amp.
Plumbum praep. or silicicum D30 amp., once weekly

Fungal Infections—see under Skin Diseases

Furunculosis—see under Abscesses and Suppurations

Gall Bladder Diseases
Basic treatment: dietary. No fried foods. Physical and mental rest.
Ensure adequate bowel movements (e.g. with Karlsbader salts or bitter salts)
Principal remedies: Choleodoron (also poss. Chelidonium/Curcuma comp.), Oxalis, Magnesium, Ferrum
Hepatodoron, 1 tabl. t.i.d. before meals
Choleodoron (also poss. Chelidonium/Curcuma comp.), 5-10 drops t.i.d. after meals (except in cholecystitis)

Bilirubinemia
Chelidonium Ferrum cultum D2 amp. s.c. 2 x week

Cholangitis:
Mercurius viv. nat. D6 tab., amp. (only for a few days)
Apis D3 / Belladonna D3 as amp., locally s.c.
Argentum praep. D30 amp.
Further treatment as with cholecystitis or cholecystopathy, below

Cholecystitis:
No Choleodoron!
Chelidonium, Flos D3 amp., D1, D3 liq.
Apis D3 / Belladonna D3 aa amp.
Mercurialis perennis 10% oint. (on compresses)
Cichorium Stanno cultum D2 amp., liq.

Cholecystopathy:
Choleodoron (also poss. Chelidonium/Curcuma comp.)
Ferrum 0.4% oint. (on compresses)
Hot yarrow compresses over the gall bladder
The following medications may be combined or injected separately:
Oxalis D3 + Ferrum sidereum D8 (or, for long-term use, Oxalis decreasing in potency from D10 to D6)
Oxalis comp. liq., amp.
Cichorium D1, D3 liq.
Cichorium Stanno cultum D2 liq., amp.
Magnesite D3 trit., D10 liq. or Magnesium sulfuricum D6-D3 liq., Magnesium phosph. D6
Chelidonium Ferro cultum D2 liq., amp.
Alkali comp. D3, D6 trit. (later, to stabilize effects of Cichorium)
At the onset of colic (not sufficient for severe colic):
Oxalis D2; Stramonium, Fructus 0.05%; Oxalis comp.; all amp., inj. s.c. near gall bladder, poss. several ampules at once; or Oxalis comp. liq., 15 drops every ten to fifteen minutes
Hot wraps or steam compresses
Oleum aeth. Menthae piperitae, a few drops on confectioner's sugar

Between acute phases:
As with cholecystopathy, esp.
Chelidonium D3-D6 liq.
Oxalis D3 amp. (poss. + Ferrum sidereum D6 amp.), twice weekly
Magnesium phosph. acidum D6 liq., amp.; Magnesium phosph. D6 trit.

Ganglion (e.g. on the wrist)
Apis D3 amp. 2 x week s.c. locally

Aconite 10% oint. compress over night

Gastric Diseases
More important than any diet is to eat slowly and chew well; food should not be too hot
Psychotherapy

Gastritis, acute:
Watch diet. Chamomile tea, one swallow at a time; later Erythraea centauria tea, likewise; finally, Weleda Species stomachicae tea
Chamomile compresses
Nux vomica D5, D6 liq.
Belladonna D4, D5 liq.
Cichorium comp. liq.

Gastritis, chronic:
Species stomachicae tea, two cups a day
Gentiana lutea D1 liq.
Pulvis stomachicus cum Belladonna
Pulvis stomachicus cum Bismuto trit.
Gallbladder treatment
Stibium praep. D6 trit. or Antimonite D6 trit.
Tartarus stibiatus D5 liq.
Cichorium comp. liq.
Iscador Qu (for men) or M (for women) Series O, intermittent series of injections
Malachite D6 trit. (for senile gastritis)
Acid substitution if indicated

Hiatus Hernia:
Digestodoron, Carbo Betulae D6 trit., Tabacum D6 amp., 1% oint.; Vespa Crabro D4 amp., 1% oint.

Gastric Bleeding:
See Hemorrhage

Stomach Cancer:
See chapter 2

Stomach Cramps:
Hot compresses over stomach
Chamomilla Cupro culta, Radix D2, D3 liq., amp.

Anagallis / Malachite comp. amp.
Anagallis 5% trit.
Cuprum praep. 0.4% oint.
Oxalis comp liq., amp.

Pylorospasm:
Belladonna D3-D6 Rh liq.
Cuprum 0.4% / Tabacum D6 aa oint.
Chamomilla Cupro culta, Radix D3 liq., amp.
Cuprum praep. D30 trit.

Gastroptosis:
Cuprum 0.4% / Tabacum D6 aa oint.
Sepia D6 liq. (for women)
Malachite D6 trit;
Argentum praep. D6 + Tabacum D6 amp.
Kalium aceticum comp. D6 amp., D3 trit.
Antimonite / Anisum oint.
Cichorium D3, D1 liq.
Bitters, e.g. Amara drops

Heartburn:
Robinia pseudoacacia D2 liq. or Robinia comp. amp., glob. (Wala)
Pulvis stomachicus cum Belladonna
Gentiana lutea D1 liq.

Gastric Ulcer:
General treatment encompassing emotional problems, specific organs (e.g. liver), and venous congestion
Chamomilla / Malachite comp. amp. (preferably two amp. i.v.), liq.
Anagallis / Malachite comp. amp., liq. (esp. for spastic conditions)
Kalium aceticum comp. D2, D3 trit.
Pulvis stomachicus cum Bismuto praep.
Stibium praep. D6 trit.
Chamomilla D15 liq.
Solutio Sacchari comp. D15, D6 liq., amp.
Iscador Qu (for men) or M (for women) Series O

Duodenal Ulcer:
Treated basically like gastric ulcer, plus:
Stibium praep. D6 trit., amp. five cc i.v.
Chamomilla / Malachite comp. amp. (s.c., i.v.)

Magnesite D3 + Stibium praep. D6 + Bismuth subnitricum D12 aa trit.
Antimonite or Stibium praep. D8, D10 + Quartz D12 aa liq.
Gastritis—see under Gastric Diseases

Goiter
No fresh milk; sour milk, yogurt etc. allowed.
Colchicum / Quercus oint. (available as Chelidonium, Flos ø 0.3 g / Colchicum ø 3 g / Quercus ø 25 g)
Cytisus / Terra rubra D3, D6 trit.
Colchicum D3 amp., D2 liq. in a.m.
Chelidonium, Flos D3 amp., D1 or D2 liq. in evening; amp. in the goiter if poss., if not, s.c. locally
Spongia comp. amp., glob. (Wala)
Iodum D3 liq.

Gonorrhea
Medorrhinum D30 amp. s.c. + Argentit D6 amp. s.c. + Apis/Belladonna amp. s.c.
Hyperthermic sitz baths

Gout
Vegetarian diet
Acute: Colchicine
Principal remedies: Mandragora in descending potency as amp., starting with D8, also as liq. and oint., e.g. Mandragora comp.
Betula, Folium D3, D2 amp., liq.
Acidum uricum D4, D6 trit.
Colchicum D2 liq.
Treat the symptoms not the uric acid values
See also Arthritis

Grave's Disease—see Hyperthyroidism

Growth and Development, Disturbances of
Accelerated development:
Epiphysis D4 liq.
Belladonna D20 liq.; Ferrum praep. D6-D20 trit.
Argentum praep. D~D15 trit., amp.

Hydrocephalus:
See separate entry
Microcephaly and Cranial Stenosis:

Argentum praep. D20 trit.
Hypophysis D4, D6 liq.
Sulfur baths

Retarded growth:
Glandula thymus D4 liq., amp.
Hypophysis D4, D6 liq., amp.
Argentum praep. D6 or Argentite D6 trit., amp.
Nutritive baths (see vol. II, pp. 39- 11)

Gynecological Disorders
Basic remedy: Menodoron

Abortion:
See under Pregnancy, etc.

Adnexitis, Parametritis, Perimetritis, Salpingitis, Oophoritis:
Acutely and subacutely: Argentite D6 amp. or Argentum praep. D20 amp. or Argentite D6 / Tuba uterine D6 aa amp.
Quartz D12–D20 amp.
Lachesis D15, D20 amp.
Arnica, Planta tota D3 / Echinacea D4 aa amp.
Bryonia comp. amp., glob. (Wala)
Pyrogenium D30 amp.
Echinacea D3 or Argentum D30 / Echinacea D6 aa amp.
Erysidoron 1 and 2
Alchemilla vulg. D1 liq.; in transition to subacute stage, D2-D6 liq.
Argentum praep. 0.4% oint. or Argentum / Stibium supp. and oint.
Hot compresses or sitz baths with Species Majoranae / Melissae
Fango mud packs

Amenorrhea:
Argentum praep. D20 amp., twice weekly, poss. + Hypophysis D4 amp.
Ovaria comp. amp. and glob. (Wala)
Melissa D2 liq.
Pulsatilla D3 liq., D6 amp.; frequently ineffective in potencies less than D30
Younger women: Pulsatilla, older women: Sepia D30 liq.
Hot sitz baths with Species Majoranae / Melissae
Foot baths with mustard powder, or mustard packs on calves
Infrared irradiation of ovarian region
For women with high turgor and congestion: minor phlebotomy, esp. prior to expected time of period

Mucilago Levistici D6 / Ovarium D3 aa amp. (or internally: Mucilago D2 liq. and Ovarium D2 trit.)
Tormentilla D30 amp. (esp. for dark-haired, thin types)
Vicia faba D6 liq.
Dab nasal mucosa with Gencydo liq.
Keep feet warm
Avoid or alleviate constipation
Follow-up treatment with Menodoron (between periods)
For genital hypoplasia add:
Inj. of 2-5 ml of Eigenblut with Argentum praep. D6 amp., twice weekly
Argentum praep. 0.4% oint. on lower abdomen
Hypophysis D4-D6 trit.
Majorana / Melissa supp., vaginal tabl., or oint.

Climacteric, Menopause:
Generally: nonspecific measures such as hydrotherapy, Eigenblut, phlebotomy, alternating hot and cold foot baths, etc.
Melissa Cupro culta D2 amp., liq.
Sanguinaria D3 / Belladonna D6 / Lachesis D15 aa liq.
Melissa / Sepia glob. (Wala)
Ovarium comp. trit.
Ovarium comp. amp., glob. (Wala) (for premature menopause)
Baths with Species Majoranae / Melissae
Hot flashes: Flores Sambuci comp. amp. and liq., possibly Bryophyllum/onchae 10ml i.v.
Sanguinaria D3, D6, D15 liq.
Tormentilla D15 liq. (esp. after hysterectomy) Sepia comp. liq. (esp. for mental symptoms)
Berberis / Sepia comp. glob. (Wala)
Ignatia comp. glob. (Wala)
Spongia / Aurum / Pulsatilla comp. glob. (Wala) (esp. with thyroid involvement)

Cystic Hyperplasia:
Treat bleeding (see also Hemorrhage)
In interval between periods: Aranea diadema D6 amp.
Calcium preparations, poss. with Ovarium Uterus D6 amp. (Wala)
Berberis / Sepia comp. glob. (Wala)

Descensus vaginae:
Argentum praep. 0.4% supp. or vaginal tablets (esp. in younger women)
Sepia D4 liq. (esp. in older women)

Senecio comp. amp., glob. (Wala)
Douches with Quercus 20%, poss. with added lemon juice
For edematous tissue and simultaneous liver disturbance: Stannum D6 trit. or Stannum silicicum D10 trit.
For back pains or fluid retention: Kalium carbonicum D3–D6 liq.

Dysfunctional uterine bleeding; Metrorrhagia, Menorrhagia:
Corallium rubrum D6 / Stibium D6 aa amp. and trit. or Marmor D6 / Stibium D6 aa amp. and trit.
In severe cases: Stibium praep. D6, 5-10 cc i.v. (10 cc amp.)
Glacies Mariae D6 amp.
Arsenum naturale D6, D20 amp.
Geranium robertianum tostum 50% trit.
Corallium comp. oint. on lower abdomen
Capsella bursa-pastoris D3 / Tormentilla D4 aa amp. and liq.
Hamamelis D1 liq.
Tormentilla D1 liq., up to 15 drops hourly
Phosphorus D6 liq.
Hydrastis comp. liq., 10–20 drops several times daily
Alchemilla tea
Plumbum praep. D 30 amp., liq., trit. (constitutional therapy)

Dysmenorrhea:
See below under Menstrual Disorders

Endocervical eversion onto anatomic portio ("Erosio portionis"):
Majorana / Melissa vag. tab. in alternation with Argentum / Quercus comp. vag. tab.
Mercurialis comp. supp. or vag. glob.
Mercurialis / Mel oint. on tampons
Stibium praep. 0.4% gel on tampons or as vag. supp.
Dab with Argentum nitricum

Endometriosis:
Iscador M cum Arg. strength 5, once weekly
Berberis, Fructus 5%, D2 amp.
Equisetum arv. Silicea cultum D2 liq.
Stibium praep. D6 amp., liq.

Endometritis:
Argentum / Quercus comp. vag. tabl.
Majorana / Melissa oint., vag. tabl. and supp.

Corallium comp. oint. (affects bleeding)
Metra tea
Pyrargyrite D6 trit.
Argentum / Stibium oint., supp.
Berberis, Fructus D4 amp., daily at first
Application of warmth

Infertility (female):
Alumen / Berberis comp. liq.
Cuprum praep. 0.4% oint. on the calves
Helleborus niger, Planta tota D3 amp.
Baths or compresses with Prunus on lower abdomen
For ovarial dysfunction: Menodoron
Argentum / Ovarium comp. amp. (Wala)
Iscador 0.0001mg amp + Argentum met praep D6 amp
Raw food diet , tsp. honey qd

Kraurosis vulvas:
Argentum praep. D6 amp., trit.
Formica D3-D15 amp., liq.
Iscador M Series O or strength 5 only
Sulfur iod. D4 liq.
Aranea diadems D10 liq.
Bismuth 2% / Hyoscyamus 5% aa oint.
Graphites 0.4% oint.

Leiomyomas of the Uterus:
Berberis, Planta tota / Urtica urens amp. and tab. (poss. alternating between amp. and tab.)
Berberis / Sepia comp. amp., glob. (Wala)
Iscador M Series O
For bleeding: Capsella bursa-pastoris D3 / Tormentilla D4 aa amp.; Hamamelis ø; Corallium rubrum D6 / Stibium D6 aa amp., trit.
Between periods: Menodoron, Metra tea
Postoperatively: Tormentilla D15 liq.; Bidor 5% tabl.

Mastopathia, Mastodynia:
See Breast Diseases

Menstrual disorders:
Basic treatment: Menodoron, 5-15 drops t.i.d. between periods for at least three months

Metra tea
Tormentilla D30 amp. (for headaches due to delayed period)
Tormentilla D15, D30 liq. to shorten interval
Amenorrhea: see above
Dysmenorrhea:
Menodoron (only between periods)
Belladonna / Chamomilla glob. (Wala), 10-15 glob. several times a day (Belladonna more for dark-haired types,
Chamomilla more for blondes)
Chamomilla Cupro culta, Radix D3 amp., liq.
Potentilla anserine D2 liq.
Magnesium sulfuricum D6 liq.
Oxalis D2, D3 amp.
Oxalis 10% oint. (also between periods)
Treat via the nasal mucosa with Gencydo liquid or Berberis, Fructus 20%
Constitutional treatment: Phosphorus, Pulsatilla, etc.
Metrorrhagia, Menorrhagia: see above

Ovarian cysts:
Mixtura Stanni comp. liq., 10 drops t.i.d. over 1-2 months; pause; then repeat
Vespa Crabro D4, D6 amp. and Formica D3-D6 amp.
Ovarium D3-D10 liq., amp.
Sitz baths with Species Majoranae / Melissae

Pelvic Inflammatory Disease:
See above under "Adnexitis"

Pregnancy and Childbirth:
See separate entry

Premenstrual syndrome
Mullein and Borago Oil

Pruritis and Eczema vulvas:
Look for cause (atrophic vaginitis; vaginal discharge; diabetes; moniliasis; precancerosis; psychosomatic, etc.)
Treat accompanying hemorrhoids
Sulfur iod. D4, D6 liq.
Urtica dioica D3 liq.
Graphites D10, D15 trit., D3, D15 amps
Sitz baths with bran or Species Majoranae / Melissae, or sulfur baths

Locally: Argentum praep. 0.4% gel; Wecesin gel; Hamamelis comp. Dint.
Bland diet
Uterine myomas
Berberis fructus D2 (not planta tota)/Urtica urens D3 aa amp. 2 x week

Vaginal Discharge:
Noninflammatory ("physiological"):
Possibilities include Conchae D6, Quartz, Pulsatilla, Sepia, Ignatia, Ferrum phosph. (esp. for younger women)
Aurum (esp. in climacteric and with varices)
Alchemilla vulg. liq., Melissa / Phosphorus comp. liq.
Corallium comp. oint.
Kalium carbonicum D3 liq.
Urtica dioica D3 liq.
Sulfur iod. D4 liq.
Pyrargyrite D6 trit. over long period
Inflammatory (vaginitis, vulvovaginitis):
Mercurius viv. nat. D6 tabl.
For purulent, fetid, burning discharge: Creosotum D3-D6 liq.
For eczematous vulva: Wecesin gel
Intravaginally: Dextrose or lactose preparations or vaginal tablets
Mercurius / Ol. Aeth. Eucalypti or Argentum / Quercus comp.
Douches only as prescribed by doctor, e.g. lemon or sage
Treat accompanying Cystitis see Kidney and Bladder Diseases
Maintain warmth with local applications and sitz baths

Vaginitis:
See "Vaginal Discharge, inflammatory" above

Vulvovaginitis infantum:
Look for cause (oxyuriasis; anemia; foreign body; etc.)
Treat the constitution
Ferrum phosph. D6 tabl.
Mercurius viv. nat. D6 tabl.
Arsenicum album 0.1% oint.
Hot rinses with Species Majoranae / Melissae and/or diluted lemon juice

Hair Loss—see Alopecia

Hay Fever
Diet: low protein; occasional purging of the bowels
Principal remedy: Gencydo, applied before symptoms appear and in

increasing potency; most effective as inhalation of vaporized 3% ampule (fine dispersion is important); also Gencydo eyedrops Plumbum praep. D8, a few injections, or Stannum praep. D8 amp. + Gencydo
Arsenicum album D10 liq. (every half hour for rhinorrhea)
Flores Tritici comp. amp.
Formica D4, D6; Urtica urens D3 liq., amp.
Aurum D30 / Equisetum arv. D20 aa amp. (for accompanying conjunctivitis)
Plumbum D14 / Stannum D15 trit.
For full-blooded types: phlebotomy

Headaches—see Migraine

Heart Diseases
Principal remedies: Cardiodoron and Aurum

Angina pectoris:
Cardiodoron / Magnesium phosph. D3 aa liq.; also separately
Magnesium phosph. D6 amp. or Magnesium phosph. / Tabacum amp.
Cactus grandiflorus D1 liq., up to once every two hours
Cactus comp. II glob. (Wala)
Crataegus drops or tablets, sufficiently dosed
Oleum Strophanthi capsules (poss. Ol. Stroph. forte)
Cerite D6 amp., s.c. in second intercostal region, D4 trit.
Hot chest compresses with arnica essence, one tbsp. to one pint water (also during angina attacks)
Between attacks: Formica chest compresses (Formica 5%, tsp. to one pint water)
Rising-temperature arm baths
Massages with Camphora / Hypericum Oleum (Wala)
Treat spine if necessary (results will often come only after this)

During angina attacks:
Compresses with Orthoclase 0.1%, one tsp. to a glass of warm water
Arnica D30 liq., 40 drops in half a glass of warm water, one swallow at a time
Glonoinum D4 liq.

For metabolic types:
Carbo Betulae D8 / Crataegus D2 aa amp.
Carbo Betulae 5% / Oleum aeth. Carvi 1% trit. (for meteorism)
For hypertensives:

Aurum D30 / Plumbum D20 aa amp.

Atherosclerosis:
See Arteriosclerosis

Arrhythmias and Extrasystoles:
Cardiodoron, 15–20 drops several times a day; 5% i.m.
Aurum / Hyoscyamus comp. amp.
Chinetum arsenicosum D3 trit.
Spartium scoparium D3 amp., liq.
Arnica D10 / Cor D10 aa amp.
Phosphorus D8 amp. i.v.
Aurum praep. D6 trit.

Cardiac Asthma:
Carbo D8 / Crataegus D2 aa amp.
Scilla alba D1, D2 liq.
Arsenicum album D10 liq., D30 amp.
Tabacum D10 liq.
When pulmonary edema threatens: Tartarus stibiatus D3, sublingually every fifteen minutes as trit. or liq.

Cardiac Neurosis:
Aurum praep. D6 trit., D12 amp.
Aurum D10, Ferrum sidereum D10 aa amp.
Cardiodoron
Aconitum D6 amp., D30 liq., 5 drops in the evening
Digitalis purp. D2 liq. (for fear of suffocation)

Congestive Heart Failure:
Diet, rest
Cardiodoron can reduce the need for glycosides but cannot replace them.
Ampelon amp. (not always available), poss. + Aurum praep. D10 or Arnica D15 / Aurum D10 aa amp.
Carbo D8 / Crataegus D2 aa amp.
Prunus spinosa, Summitates ø, 10–20 drops t.i.d.
Crataegus preparations
Lemon compresses
To stimulate diuresis:
Carduus benedictus D1 / Paeonia off. D1 aa liq., 15-20 drops t.i.d.; D2/D2 aa amp.

For congestive bronchitis:
Tartarus stibiatus D6 liq., trit.
Stibium sulfuratum aurantiacum D0D6 trit.
Right-sided failure:
Carbo Betulae D30 + Kalium aceticum comp. D6 + Stannum praep. D10 aa amp.
Kalium aceticum comp. D3 + Stannum met. D6 aa trit.

Coronary Artery Disease:
See Angina pectoris, above, and Arteriosclerosis, separate entry

Developmental cardiac anomalies, valvular insufficiency
Begin asap as young as possible: Cardiodoron 40 dr tid, (children 20 dr tid in some water because of alcohol) + corresponding valvular or cardiac prep. D5 (e.g. Valvula aorta or Cor D5) amp. + Tabacum D6 amp. s.c. 2 x week + Vespa crabro oint. 1% to heart area. Later Vespa crabro D6 as inj. s.c. and Tabacum 5% oint.
For 3 months course of Aurum Hyoscyamus comp. instead of Tabacum or Vespa crabro. Treat for 2 years.

Endocarditis:
Cardiodoron
Chest compresses with Formica 5% or Orthoclase 0.1% in alternation with Diaspore 0.1% (two tsp. to one pint water)
Argentum D30 / Echinacea D6 aa amp. i.v. (poss. several amp. per injection), also Argentum D30 Carbo D30 aa amp.
Aurum D10 / Stibium D8 amp., liq.
Lachesis D12 or Naja trip. D10 liq., amp.
Echinacea ang. ø
Oleum aeth. Eucalypti 1% amp. i.m. (1-3 amp.)
Camphora 20% amp. oleosum i.m.
Arnica D15 / Aurum D10 aa amp., liq.

Heart Block:
Cardiodoron
Arnica D10 / Cor D10 aa amp.
Prunus, Cactus, Aurum
Aurum Hyoscyamus comp. amp.

Myocardial Infarct:
See also Angina pectoris, this entry
Arnica, Planta tota D3 amp., s.c. locally

Carbo Betulae D30 amp. (for collapse)
Oleum Strophanthi forte capsules
During convalescence: Primula Auro culta liq., amp.; Arnica D10/Cor D10 aa amp.

Myocarditis:
See Endocarditis, above

Palpitations ("nervous heart"):
Cardiodoron
Aurum praep. D10 trit.
Aurum D5 / Oleum aeth. Lavandulae 0.3% / Oleum aeth. Rosae 0.3% oint.
Spigelia anth. D4 liq. (piercing pains)
Kalmia lat. D4 liq.
Leonurus cardiaca D1, D4 liq.
Aurum / Hyoscyamus comp. liq., amp.
Compresses with Orthoclase 0.1% (heart pains)

PAT
Mestinon (Pyridostigmine bromide) irreplacable especially at the onset

Pericarditis:
As endocarditis, plus:
Compresses with Formica 5%, one tsp. to one pint water
Stannum praep. D10 amp., trit.
Bryonia D3-D6 liq. (Bryonia / Stannum amp.—Wala)
Equisetum arv. D10-D15 amp.
Kalmia lat. D2 liq. (for dry form; with effusion, Bryonia)

Tachycardia:
Compresses with Orthoclase 0.1%
Aurum / Hyoscyamus comp. amp., liq.
Oleum Strophanthi capsules
Cardiodoron, 10-40 drops every 2-3 hours
Leonurus cardiaca D1, D2 liq.
Levisticum D2, D3 liq.
Phosphorus D20 liq. and amp. (D8 amp. i.v., esp. with hyperthyroidism) or Acidum phosph. D3 liq.
Aconitum D10, D15 liq., D20 amp.
Veratrum album D4 liq. (nocturnal tachycardia)
Lycopus virg. ø liq. (for thyrotoxicosis)

Mucilago Levistici liq., amp. (paroxysmal atrial tachycardia)
For paroxysmal tachycardia: Phosphorus D20 + Cardiodoron amp.
Rule out hiatus hernia
Wolf-Parkinson -White (WPW) Syndrome
Cardiodoron 40 dr bid + Aurum/Hyoscyamus comp amp. + Lavandula/ Rose oint. locally

Hemangioma
Vespa Crabro D3 amp., in increasing potency, twice weekly beneath lesion
Vespa Crabro 1% oint.
Stibium or Antimonite oint., D6 amp., trit.

Hemophilia
Principal remedy: antimony (Stibium)
Long-term medication: Stibium praep. D6, later D20, D30 trit.
For acute bleeding: Marmor D6 / Stibium D6 aa amp., trit., or Corallium rubrum D6 / Stibium D6 aa amp. s.c. or Stibium praep. D6 amp. 10 cc i.v.

Hemorrhage
Principal remedy: Stibium praep. D6 trit. and amp.5-10 cc i.v.
Nosebleeds: Stibium praep. D6 trit., poss. with Corallium rubrum D6 trit. aa (as snuff)
Marmor D6/Stibium D6 aa amp.
Quercus D1 liq.
Capsella bursa-pastoris D2 liq.
Uterine or menstrual bleeding: see under Gynecological Disorders

Hemorrhoids
Suppositories (e.g. Stibium comp.)
Hamamelis comp. oint.
Achillea comp. liq.
Millefolium / Hypericum oint.
Hirudo comp. glob. (Wala)
Kalium acet. comp. 1/2 tsp tid
Treat the liver
Urtica dioica Ferro culta liq. or Solutio Ferri comp. D6 liq. for weak kidney radiation
Hot compresses or sitz baths with Quercus 20%, esp. for strangulated hemorrhoids
Lotio Pruni cum Cupro, local appl.
Quercus 10%/Calendula 10% aa local compresses

Hernia
(For hiatus hernia, see under Gastric Diseases)
Stannum silicicum D6 amp., locally
Stannum met. 0.4% oint. in alternation with Cuprum 0.4% / Tabacum D6 as oint.
Cepa D3 liq.
Fluorite D4 trit. (for weakness of connective tissue)
Tabacum D6 liq., amp.

Herpes labialis
Cantharis D10 liq., at first appearance, 5 drops every half hour
Dab with mouthwash
Between outbreaks: Cantharis D30 liq., 5 drops q.d.
Arsenicum album D30 liq.
Ol. aeth. Melissae 10% (Weleda) local appl.

Herpes zoster
Acute: Arnica Rd. D6 amp.
Ranunculus bulb. D4 liq., amp. (poss. together with Rhus tox. D6, D10, D30 amp.)
Carbo Betulae D20 + Belladonna D4 amp., daily
Arnica D10-D20 liq., amp. (later Arnica, Radix in same potencies)
Apis D10-D20 amp. (poss. with Bryonia)
Hypericum D6-D30 liq.
Mezereum D3-D6 liq., D4 amp.
Argentum nitricum D20 + Quartz D20, D30 amp. (for pain)
Aconitum comp. glob., amp. (Wala)
Aconitum 5%, 10% Oleum (analgesic)
Post-herpetic neuralgia: Arsenicum album D6-D20 liq., Arnica Rd. D20 amp. + Apis D30 amp.
Treat liver
Hot compresses with arnica essence
Wecesin powder

Hiccups
Breathe deeply, hold breath, tilt head back
Hot Pinella tea (Species Stomachicae), one swallow at a time; imagine path that liquid follows with each swallow
Chelidonium D1 liq. sublingually
Belladonna D3 liq.
Hyoscyamus D6 amp., D3 liq.
Nux vomica D3, D5 liq. sublingually

Hodgkin's Disease
Capsicum annuum D10 amp. and Colchicum D5 amp., alternately every day or every other day
Iscador P c. Hg. Series O or strength 5 only; for excessive febrile reaction: Helleborus praep. St. 4, two ampules
Argentum D30 / Carbo D30 as amp.
Ferrum sidereum D20 amp.
Stannum praep. D8, D10 amp. near the glands
Ferrum rosatum D3 / Graphites D15 liq.
Formica baths

Hordeolum
Staphisagria D4 dil
Castor Oil local

Hydrocephalus
Stannum praep. D8 amp., twice weekly, trit.
Stannum 0.4% gel. or oint. on the forehead
Plumbum 0.1% oint. compresses on the back of the head as intermediate treatment
Hypophysis D6 liq.
Shield from light, darken room (unlike rickets)

Hypercholesterolemia
Choleodoron 10 dr tid pc
Stramomium D6 s.c. 2 x week

Hyperemesis—see Nausea or Pregnancy

Hypergammaglobulinemia
Cobaltum D20 amp.
Plumbum praep. D6, D8 trit.

Hypertension—see under Circulatory Diseases

Hyperthyroidism, Thyrotoxicosis
Basic remedy: copper as Cuprite D3 (D2 may be more effective, tsp pc tid) trit., later D6 amp., trit., D8 amp. (for light-haired types); Chalcosite D3 trit., internally (for dark-haired types)
Conchae D6 amp.
Bryophyllum 50% trit., 5%, D3 amp.
Phosphorus D3 (D12) amp. i.v.

Cassiterite (Kassiterit) D3 trit.
Glandula thyreoidea D60 amp., one inj. every one to two weeks
Aurum praep. D10 trit., amp.
For accompanying tachycardia: Lycopus virgin. D1 liq., 20-40 drops, three to five times daily, poss. with Leonurus cardiaca D1 liq. and Cardiodoron
Aurum / Hyoscyamus comp. amp.
Vit A
See also Goiter

Hypotension—see under Circulatory Diseases

Hypothyroidism
Often due to exhaustion
Rest, stress release, ocean
Glandula thyroidea D4 amp. + Spongia tosta D4 amp.
Bryophyllum Argento cultum D2 amp + 1ml Eigenblut s.c. 2 Xweek

Hysteria—see vol. 1, pp. 190–201

Ileus
Smoke enemas: blow cigar smoke into 150-200 cc water until water is yellowish, then insert in rectum with a bulb syringe
Tabacum Cupro cultum amp. and liq.
Nicotiana comp. amp., glob. (Wala)
Oxalis D2, D3 amp.
Colocynthis D4 liq., amp.
Opium D30 liq.: 20 drops in a glass of water, one swallow every ten minutes (paralytic ileus)
Bufo Rana liq. D4, D6
Carcinomatous ileus: shock doses of Iscador strength 2-5% amp.

Impetigo—see Skin Diseases

Immunization, prevention of complications from
Thuja D6 liq., 1-2 weeks before and after immunization, 5 drops t.i.d.; in case of fever: Argentum praep. D20, D30 trit., amp.
Vaucheria D3 liq.
Erysidoron 1 and 2

Incontinence
See also Enuresis, Prostatic Hypertrophy, and Cystitis
Causticum Hahnemanni D12 liq.

Argentum praep. 0.4% oint., supp.
Hypericum, Flos 25% Oleum

Induratio penis plastica
Iscador 0.1 mg amp. + Formica D3 or D4 amp s.c.

Infertility—see under Gynecological Disorders

Influenza
Inludo
Ferrum phosph. comp. glob., esp. when intolerant to phosphorus in Inludo
Gelsemium comp. liq.
Gelsemium D6 amp., initially also D30
Pyrite D3 tab. (tracheitis)
Prophylactically: Phosphorus, Ferrum sidereum, and Prunus as a mixture (liq.) in low potencies; Bidor 5%, 2 tablets t.i.d., or Ferrum-Quartz capsules, one daily in a.m.
Meteoric iron / Phosphorus / Quartz glob., amp. (Wala)
Sallow thorn elixir, Blackthorn elixir, 1 tbsp. t.i.d.

Insect Bites
Dab locally with Combudoron essence

Insomnia
Encourage good life habits; seek for cause (emotional problems, depression, gout, precancerous condition, etc.)
Regulate bodily warmth, e.g. with warm foot bath in evening or alternating warm and cold foot baths
Zincum valerianicum D3 liq.
Conchae D1, 5% trit. (or Calcon 2), one half tsp. in the evening
Conchae D30 amp.
Sulfur D6 liq.
Argentum nitricum D20 amp. (exhausted nervous system)
Phosphorus D25 / Malva liq. (complemented with Phosphorus D5 liq. in a.m.)
Phosphorus D25 / Sulfur D25 aa liq.
Avena sativa comp. liq. or glob.
Species sedativae (Sonio tea)
Bryophyllum D1, ø liq. or Bryophyllum D5 / Conchae D7 aa amp.
Cardiodoron 0.1% / Plumbum D20 aa amp.

With cardiac involvement: Cardiodoron, Aurum D5 / Oleum aeth. Lavandulae 0.3% / Oleum aeth. Rosae 0.3% oint.
Magnesium phosph. acidum D6 liq., amp.
Malva comp. Oleum (Wala) on lower abdomen
Baths with Kalium sulfuratum 10% (Wala), Papaver rhoeas 20% ext., or lavender bath oil

Intermittent Claudication, Raynaud's Disease
Abstain from nicotine
Rising-temperature foot bath every evening with one half tsp. copper sulfate in two and one half gallons of water (except for open ulcers) or with one tsp. of either rosemary bath oil, Prunus bath, or Tabacum 10% ext.
Leg gel with copper
Cuprum 0.4% / Tabacum D6 aa oint.
Secale / Bleiglanz comp. (Wala)
Belladonna D6 amp. and liq.
Later: Cuprum praep. D6 amp., trit.

Intestinal Diseases
Nausea and vomiting:
Nux vomica D6 liq., sublingually
Belladonna D6 liq.
Veratrum album D4 liq.
Absinthium / Caryophylli comp. liq., 5 drops frequently
Weak wormwood tea
Ipecacuanha D4 liq. (esp. for ketotic emesis)
Warm chamomile compresses on abdomen

Anal Fissures:
See separate entry

Constipation:
See separate entry

Diarrhea, acute:
Fasting; fresh grated apple (pectin)
Geum urbanum ø , D1 liq. (esp. for "summer diarrhea")
Carbo Betula comp. capsules
Stibium praep. or Antimonite D4-D6 trit. (affects protein metabolism, putrefactive dyspepsia, bloody stool)
Veratrum album D4 liq. ("herbal arsenic")
Arsenicum album D4-D6 liq. or Stibium arsenicosum D4–D6 trit.

Olivenite D4 trit.
Bolus alba comp. (Wala)
Mercurius sublimatus corrosivus D4-D6 liq. (esp. for strong mucus production)

Diarrhea, chronic:
Argentum praep. D15 / Cuprum praep. D15 / Mercurius viv. nat. D15 aa trit., a pinch 3 to 5 times daily

Diverticulitis, Diverticulosis, Hirschsprung's Disease:
Carpellum Mali comp. trit., amp.
Tabacum D4-D6 liq., amp.
Mercurius viv. nat. D6 or D12
Anagallis 10%
Don't eat small seeds, e.g. berries, liseeds

Duodenal Ulcer:
See under Gastric Diseases

Fermentive Dyspepsia:
Phosphorus D6 liq.
Digestodoron
Carbones / Pancreas / Witherite trit.
Bitters

Incontinence
Because of inadequate consciousness in anal region:
Bufo rana D6dil., amp.

Intestinal Cramps, Infantile Colic:
Chamomilla, Radix D3 liq., amp. or Belladonna / Chamomilla glob. (Wala)
Chamomilla / Nicotiana (Wala)
Anagallis 5% trit.

Megacolon
Carpellum mali comp. amp., trit
Rectal prolapse
Carduus benedictus 100% trit. local
Prunus spinosa/Tabacum supp.

Upset Stomach:
As a digestive aid: Artemisia comp. liq., 10-15 drops in hot water
Poor Digestion:
Artemisia comp. liq. (acutely)
Digestodoron (long-term)

Ulcerative Colitis, Irritable Bowel:
Psychotherapy
Nasturtium Mercurio cultum Rh amp., liq.
Mercurius dulcis D3 trit., two weeks only, then pause
Mercurius viv. comp. tab.
Cuprum praep. 0.4% oint., D6 trit.
Geum urbanum D1 liq. or Gentiana lutea D1 liq.i
Argentum praep. D6 trit.
Arsenicum album D30 liq. for appropriate constitutional types
Carbo Betula comp. capsules or coffee-charcoal
Bismuth praep. D6 trit. or Bismuth subnitricum D3, D4 trit.
Stibium arsenicosum D4 trit.
Oxalis compresses (Oxalis 20% ext.)
Curative eurythmy

Jaundice—see under Gall Bladder Diseases and under Liver Diseases

Keloids
See also Scars, treatment of
Keloid gel (Wala)
Cuprum 0.4% / Tabacum D6 aa oint.
Injections of Vespa Crabro D3, D4 under lesion

Kidney and Bladder Diseases
Glomerulonephritis (acute and disuse), Focal Nephritis:
Diet: fasting and thirsting; no protein or salt
Keep warm, poss. encourage sweating
Bedrest and emotional rest
Hot kidney compresses with Equisetum tea or Equisetum arv. 10% ext. (one tbsp. per quart water), alternating with copper sulfate
Equisetum arv. D3-D6 liq. in alternation with Apis or Erysidoron 1
Equisetum arv. D6, D10, D15 amp.
Carbo Betulae D20 amp. (daily)
Renal insufficiency:
Cuprum-Ren D6 amp. + Equisetum arvense D15 amp. + Carbo Equiseti D15 amp 2 x week s.c.

Hay's diet

Nephritis, chronic:

In addition to or alternating with above medications:
Cuprum praep. 0.4% oint. over the kidneys
Cuprum / Ren liq. D6 amp., twice weekly, poss. + Equisetum D15 + Carbo bet. D20
Pancreas D3 trit. (for albuminuria)
Capsella bursa-pastoris D3, D1 liq. (for hematuria)
Stibium praep. D6 trit., amp.
Hepar Sulfuris D4-D6 trit. (short-term for residual albuminuria)
For transition to nephrotic syndrome: Apis D6 liq.
When renal function is not compromised: Enema with rosehip tea
For oliguria: Olivenite D6 trit., amp.; Argentite D6 trit., amp.
For anuria: Rising-temperature foot baths
Hot kidney compresses with Equisetum arv. 10% ext.
Cuprum praep. 0.4% oint. over kidneys
Equisetum cum Sulfure tostum D6 trit. and amp.
Argentite D6 amp.
Carbo Equiseti D6 amp.
Solidago virgin., Herba 0 liq.

For treatment of transition to renal atrophy add:

Phosphorochalcite D6 trit., amp.
Sulfur compresses over the kidneys in alternation with Cuprum praep. 0.4% oint.
Pteridium aqu. D3 liq., D6 amp. short-term

Hydronephrosis, Renal Cysts:

Mixtura Stanni comp. liq., 10-12 drops t.i.d.
Cuprum praep. 0.4% oint.
Gencydo 1% + Stannum praep. D10 + Ren D6 amp.
Tabacum D10 amp., oint. 1%

Nephrosis:

Watch diet
Principal remedies: ferns, iron, pancreas
Ferns: Aspidium filix-mas D2-D4 liq. or Scolopendrium D3 amp., liq. or Pteridium aqu. D6 amp., D3 liq., esp. during strong anabolism
Ferrum sidereum D3,D6/ Pancreas D1 aa trit.
Ferrum sidereum D10/ Pancreas D6 aa amp.
Levico-water treatment or Scorodite D6 in alternation or together with Olivenite D6

Glandula thyroidea D6 liq., amp.
Carbo Betulae D4 trit., D6, D20 amp.
Phosphorus D5 liq., 5 drops in mornings and afternoons.
Curative eurythmy

Hematuria:
See also Hemorrhage
Capsella bursa-pastoris D3 liq. and amp.
Lachesis D12 liq., amp.
Stibium praep. D6 trit., amp.

Renal Colic:
Initially or prophylactically (not sufficient for severe colic): warm rising-temperature bath (or compress) with 2-3 tbsp. copper sulfate 20%
Hot flaxseed compress around entire torso
Force fluids
Oxalis comp., several ampules, also as liq.,
Tabacum D6,D10 amp.
Belladonna 1% supp.

Kidney Stones:
Potentized preparation of kidney stone from same patient (D15), as liq. together with Renodoron
For phosphate stones: Phosphorus D6 liq.
For oxalate stones: Oxalis D3 amp., liq.
For urate stones: Mandragora D3-D6 liq.; sulfur compresses
Teas: Equisetum, rose hip seeds, Ononis spinosa
Radix Althaeae, macerated
If urine is acid: alkalinize with one tsp. Sodium Bicarbonate bid and sugar and meat free diet
If urine is alkaline: acidify with VitC 1 gm
Wernarzer mineral water

Cystitis, acute:
Bedrest, keep warm
Argentum nitricum D4 liq. in hourly alternation with Hypericum D2 liq.
Cantharis comp. amp., glob. (Wala)
Berberis / Apis comp. glob., amp. (Wala) (for bladder irritation)
Balsamum Copaivae D3 liq., D4 amp.
Argentum praep. 0.4% oint.
If urine is acid: alkalinize with one tsp. Sodium Bicarbonate bid and sugar and meat free diet

If urine is alkaline: acidify with VitC 1 gm
Mandelamine
Apis/Belladonna dil., amp. + Argentit D6
Hyperthermia by sitz bath

Cystopyelitis, Pyelonephritis, Urinary Tract Infections:
Acute:
Irrigation with Equisetum or rose hip rind tea
Force fluids (no mineral water containing calcium)
Lachesis D12, D20 amp., liq. (daily injections)
Equisetum arv. D6, D15 amp.
Argentum D30/ Echinacea D6 aa amp. or Argentum D30/Carbo Betulae D30 aa amp. (for fever)
Kidney compresses with copper sulfate solution or Equisetum arv. 10% ext.
ApisD3/ Belladonna D3 aa amp. or Erysidoron 1 internally

Chronic:
Thuja comp. trit., 1 pinch every three hours for one week only; pause; repeat later
Thuja Argento culta D2 liq.
Equisetum cum Sulfure tostum D3 trit., D6 amp.
Equisetum arv. D6/ Pelvis Renis (et Ureter) D6 aa amp. (for pyelonephritis)
Carbo Betulae D15-D20 amp.
Resina Laricis D3 liq., D5 amp., poss. + Erysidoron 1 or Lachesis (as with acute)
Kalium / Teucrium comp. liq. (for recurrent cystitis)
Hyperthermic baths or hot sitz baths; keep feet warm
Oleum aeth. Eucalypti 1% oleosum amp. i.m. or Eucalyptus comp. amp. (Wala)
Argentum nitricum comp. (Wala)
For calyceal blunting: Mixtura Stanni comp. liq.

Kraurosis vulvae—see under Gynecological Disorders

Laryngitis, chronic
Pyrite D3 tabl. (or Anise-Pyrite D3 tabl.) hourly
Arum triphyllum D3 liq. (poss. + Tussilago farfara D3 aa liq.)
Saccharum tostum D3 amp. poss. + Spongia D3 amp.
Ipecacuanha D4 liq.
Scilla alba D3 liq.
Ferrum sic. D3 trit. 1 pinch every three hours

Locally: Oleum aeth. Lavandulae 10% Oleum or Cuprum praep. 0.4% oint.
Spiritus contra Tussim
Ligamentum vocale D6-D3 glob. (Wala)

Lead Poisoning
Antidote metal: silver
Argentum praep. D6 trit., 1 pinch t.i.d.
Foot baths with 20-40 drops of a 1% silver nitrate solution
Sulfur baths to encourage elimination

Leg Ulcer—see under Circulatory Diseases

Leiomyoma—see under Gynecological Disorders

Leukemia—see Cancer

Liver Diseases
See vol. 2, p. 234f.
Diet
Principal remedies: Stannum, Hepatodoron

Ascites:
Treat as cirrhosis, esp.:
Hepar-Stannum D4 amp., daily s.c.
Betula / Gummi Cerasi liq.
Carduus benedictus D1 / Paeonia off. D1 aa liq., D2/D2 amp.

Hepatitis, acute:
Diet: limit fats, initially no sugar
Yarrow compresses for warmth
Taraxacum Stanno cultum D2 / Hepar Bovis D4 aa amp., D3/D4 aa amp., later Hepar-Stannum D4 amp.
Hepatodoron, poss. + Choleodoron (also Chelidonium/Curcuma comp.) alternating with Carduus marianus 20% liq., 10-15 drops t.i.d., or 1 Carduus marianus capsule b.i.d.
Intermittently Hepar-Magnesium D4, D6 amp.
For intrahepatic cholestasis (icterus): Ferrum sidereum D10 amp.

Cirrhosis:
Magnesite D3 + Quartz D5 aa trit.
Formica D3-D6 amp., D4 liq.

Hepar-Stannum D4 amp.
Taraxacum 0, D1 liq.
Phosphorus D5, D6 liq.
Cautious mistletoe therapy, e.g. Viscum Mali or Pini D6 amp. Or Iscador strength 5, one inj. per week

Lumbago
Hot arnica or hayflower baths
Arnica / Levisticum D3 comp. or D6 comp. amp.
Bryonia / Formica comp. amp.
Arnica comp. / Apis or Arnica comp. / Formica Oleum or oint.
Spinal treatment (see separate entry)
Poss. prophylactic treatment with Iscador Qu or M Series O
Disci comp cum Argento amp. 2 x week s.c. to begin for 2 months then Disci comp cum Stanno amp. for two or three months
Cupping

Lung Diseases—see Asthma, Emphysema, Pleuritis, Pneumonia

Lupus Erythematosus
Aesculus, Cortex 5% gel
Overnight: compresses with Stibium praep. 0.4% oint., or during day: Stibium praep. 0.4% gel
Nontronite D12 trit.
Formica D2 + Antimonite D6 amp., Formica in increasing and decreasing potency
Cuprum sulfuricum D4, D6 liq.
Phosphorus D10, D20 amp.
Quarz D60 as sc inj. every 2 weeks to stimulate the warmth organism

Lymphadenopathy—see Lymphatic Constitution

Lymphatic Constitution, Exudative Diathesis, Lymphadenopathy
Archangelica D1 liq. and 10% oint. or Archangelica comp. Q oint.
Phosphorus D5 liq.
Barium comp. trit. or Barium iodatum D4, D6 liq.
Spongia D3 liq., later Iodum D3 liq.
Juglans regia D1 liq. or Juglans regia comp. glob. (Wala)
Thuja occ. D15 liq. in the morning, Cinnabar D20 tab. in the afternoon, and Quartz D12-D30 in the evening
Urtica dioica Ferro culta D2 liq.
Saltwater baths, Levico-water treatment

Anemia treatment
Berberis, Fructus 10% oint. over the bladder

Malaria, Volhynia Fever, Recurrent & Highly Febrile Infectious Diseases
Oleum aeth. Eucalypti 1% amp., i.m. daily or every other day
Copper (esp. for chronic, "cerebral" forms), e.g. as Cuprum sulfuricum D4-D6 liq., 10 drops every three to four hours
Encourage perspiration
Rosemary oil baths or rinses (esp. prophylactically)

Mania
Aurum praep. D6 amp., poss. + Stibium praep. D6 amp.
Cichorium, Radix D1 liq.
Cichorium Stanno cultum, Radix D2 liq., amp.

Mastitis—see under Pregnancy, etc.

Measles—see Chapter 3

Memory Loss
Bidor 5%, D3 tabl.
Formica D3-D6 liq.
Belladonna D5, D6 liq.
Argentum praep. D20 or Argentum nitricum D20 amp., best between the shoulder blades (for general vitalization and strengthening of nervous system) or Dyscrasite D20 amp.
Ampelon i.v. (not always available)
Thuja occ. D30 liq., 7 drops q.d.
Hypophysis D6 trit. Scleron tabl. (sclerosis prophylaxis)
Treatment of sclerosis (see separate entry)

Menière's Disease
Fasting or fruit diet
Gnaphalium comp. amp., glob. (Wala)
Belladonna, Radix D30 amp.
Nausyn drops or tabl.
Arnica, Planta tota D15 + Cerebellum D4, D6 + Ferrum hydroxydatum D20 aa liq.
Cerebellum D15 amp., poss. + Tabacum D10 amp.
Cerebrum comp. B amp., glob. (Wala)
Betula, Folium D2 amp.
Betula, Folium D6 amp. (best injected with Gnaphalium or Belladonna

over the mastoid process)
Irradiated Eigenblut, 2 cc
Liver treatment

Meningitis
Meningismus: Agaricus musc., Cutis rubra D30 amp. am, Quartz D30 amp. pm
Meningitis (high fever):
antibiotics, no antipyretics
Erysidoron 1
Apis D2-D6 liq.
Arnica Rd. D20
Argentum D30 / Echinacea D6 aa amp.
Colchicum, Radix D15 amp. (poss. only half an amp.)
Later Arnica D20 amp., liq.

Menopause see under Gynecological Disorders

Menstrual Disorders—see under Gynecological Disorders

Meteorism—see vol. 2, p. 225

Migraine
Ferrum-Quartz capsules, one capsule daily for four or (optimally) seven weeks, then pause; acutely up to one capsule every thirty minutes
Bidor tabl. 5%, D3
Secale / Quartz amp., glob. (Wala)
Investigate possible organ involvement (e.g. stomach, liver, ovaries) and treat organs accordingly

Motion Sickness—see Nausea

Mouches volantes
Sanguinaria D15/Spongia D15 amp.
Argentum/Corpus vitreum Eye drops

Mucoviscidosis
Sugar free diet
Kapf's Acid: (Acetic acid 30% 25.0 + Formic acid 25% 275.0) place on cupboard in open vessel to inhale evaporate
Formica amp. 2 x week sc D8, D6, D3, and back D6, etc., every potency for 2 weeks

Ferrum sid. D10/Pancreas D6 amp. 2 x week s.c. right upper leg
Ferrum sid. D3/Pancreas D1 aa trit.

Multiple Sclerosis
Generally: no stress, bedrest, Evers' diet; scrupulous dental hygiene
Two cc of own blood, inj. together with Argentum praep. D6, D20 amp.
Arnica baths
Arnica D20 amp.
Cinis Arnicae D20 amp., liq. D8
Scorodite D30 amp. for paralysis, diplopia
Aurum praep. D30, amp. or Aurum D30 / Equisetum arv. D20 aa amp.
Magnesium phosph. acid. D6 amp., poss. + Chamomilla Cupro culta or Cuprum praep. D30 amp. (antispasmodic)
Plumbum praep. D60 amp. (one inj. every six weeks)
Zincum met. 0.1% oint. on forehead; Cuprum praep. 0.4% oint. on the soles of the feet; also Acidum sulfuricum 5% liq. in increasing doses (5-20 drops, then dropping back down to 5); after these measures, patient should lie down for two hours if poss.
Arnica-Cerebrum D6 amp.
Dyscrasite D30 liq., D20 amp.
Cerebellum D4 liq. (esp. for dizziness)
Dioptase D30 amp. (for myoclonia)
Medulla comp. glob. (Wala)
Apis regina comp. glob., amp. (Wala)
Gratiola D30 amp.
Intermittent liver therapy
Lavender compresses, warm and moist along the spinal column

Mumps
Archangelica D1, D2 liq.; 10% oint. or Archangelica comp. oint.
Barium citricum D6 trit. (or Barium comp.)
Mercurius viv. nat. D8 amp., D6 tabl.
For orchitis: Clematis recta D3 liq., 1% oint.; Erysidoron 1; Argentum praep. D6 trit., amp.

Muscular Rheumatism—see Arthritis

Myocarditis—see under Heart Diseases

Myoma—see under Gynecological Disorders

Nausea, Motion Sickness
Nausyn: 5-10 drops or 1 tab. t.i.d. for two to three weeks before traveling (long term effect); vary dose according to severity
Cerite D4 trit., D6 amp.
Gentiana comp. (Wala)
Nux vomica D6 liq., sublingually
Spiritus Melissae comp.

Neuralgia
Arnica / Levisticum D3 or D6 comp. amp.
Apis D3 / Bryonia D3 aa amp.
Aconitum 1%, 5%, 10% Oleum
Tulipa e red. D6 amp. (Wala)
Draw process off to skin
See also Trigeminal Neuralgia

Neurasthenia—see vol. 1, pp. 206–208

Neuritis
Acute: Arnica/Levisticum D6 comp amp. after decline of symptoms: Arnica/Levisticim D3 comp amp.
Keep patient warm but do not add heat
Aconitum napellus D6 liq., D20 amp.; 1%, 5%, 10% Oleum along the path of the nerve
Apis D10, D20, D30 amp.
Arnica, Radix D10, D15, D20 amp. (poss. + an organ preparation)
Arnica / Apis comp. oint.

Neurodermatitis—see under Skin Diseases

Night Terrors
Bryophyllum Argento cultum liq.
Stramonium D6, D15 liq.
Aconitum nap. D30 liq.

Nosebleeds
Stibium praep. D8 amp. (s.c. in the neck), D6 i.v. (poss. several ampules)
Stibium praep. D6 trit. as snuff
For adolescents: Orthoclase D15 trit.
Phosphorus D6, D8 liq.
Tormentilla comp. amp., glob. (Wala)
Constitutional treatment with Stibium praep. D8 trit.

Obesity
Constitutional therapy
Exercises in self-control, e.g., giving up something every day, are more important than dietary regulations
Hypophysis D3, D4, D6 amp.
Gencydo amp.
Baths with Formica 5% ext., one tsp. per bath, or lemon baths
Fucus D4 liq.
Iodum D3, D4

Obsessive-Compulsive Disorder
See also chapter 8 Mercurius auratus D15 amp., poss. i.v.

Osgood-Schlatter's Disease—see under Bone Diseases

Orchitis-See Mumps

Osteomyelitis
See also Abscesses, etc.
Low protein (initially protein-free), fresh food diet
Conchae comp. glob., amp. (Wala)
Agaricus comp. amp.
Erysidoron 1
Argentum praep. D30 amp. + Lachesis D12 amp.
Solanum lycopersicum D15 liq., amp.
Vespa Crabro D4-D20 amp. (for sequestration)
Later: Cerussite D8, D10 trit. or Plumbum silicicum D20 amp. (stimulates structuring and solidification)
Thuja occ. D3-D12 liq., 0.5%-D6 amp.
Symphytum 10% oint. locally
Acutely: Mercurialis perennis 10% oint.
Arnica D3 / Symphytum D3 / Cepa D3 as liq.
Stibium praep. D6 or Antimonite D6 trit.
Eliminate accompanying venous congestion

Osteoporosis
Agaricus musc. comp. amp.
Agaricus comp.-Phosphorus
Equisetum silicea cult D2 dil., amp.
Fluorite D4 trit. if pain
Cerussite D8 amp.
Plumbum silicicum D20 amp.

Calcon 1 and 2
Watch for overacidity: change diet, no sugar, no meat, no cola or instant drinks and purge intestines when necessary. Gelatin, millet, barley, Equisetum tea (boil 10 min.) can be helpful in the diet.
Avoid Vit D, Calcium, Flouride, calcitonin (favor vascular calcification)
Shark cartilage
Organic or inorganic silica preparations (highly dispersed SiO_2 instead of calcium

Otitis—see Ear Diseases

Ovarian Cysts—see under Gynecological Disorders

Ozena
Nose Balsam (Wala)
Argentite D6 trit. as snuff
Tunica mucosa nasi D6, D4 amp. (Wala) + Argentite D6 amp.
Prunus spinosa, Summitates D3-D6 amp.
Asa foetida e resina glob. (Wala)
Irrigation with diluted Thuja occ. 20% ext.

Pancreas Diseases (incl. Chronic Pancreatitis)
Strict diet, esp. low fat and low meat
Yarrow compresses
Concurrent gall bladder treatment (see under Gall bladder Diseases)
Oxalis 10% oint. (acutely); Stibium praep. 0.1%, 0.4% oint. (chronically)
Siderite D8 + Oxalis D3 amp.
Digestodoron, 20-30 drops t.i.d.

Panic—see Anxiety

Paraproteinemia
AntimonitD6 trit., amp. + Hepar Magnesium D4 amp.

Parkinson's Disease
Equisetum baths; Formica baths
Curative eurythmy
Agaricus bulb. D6 amp., inj. every other day; D3, D4 liq.
Belladonna D6-D30 liq., amp.
Phosphorus 0.1% Oleum on the temples
Organ preparations, e.g. Lamina quadrigemina, Arnica/Cerebrum
Iron preparations, e.g. Ferrum praep. D20 combined with the above

Stannum mellitum D10, D20 amp.
Arnica / Plumbum comp. A or B amp., glob. (Wala)

Parotitis—see Mumps

Pavor nocturnus—see Night Terrors

Periarthritis humero-scapularis
Arnica D20/Equisetum D20 amp.
Stannum D6 trit.
Phosphorus oil 0.1% external, local
Cantheride plaster 1cm^2
Arm movement, physical therapy
Therapeutic eurythmy

Pericarditis—see under Heart Diseases

Pernicious anemia
Carbo Betulae cum Methano D4 trit.

Pertussis—see chapter 3

Phantom Pains
Stibium praep. D20 amp.
Antimonite D20 amp.
Prunus spinosa, Summitates D3-D5
Aconite oil 10 % (Weleda)

Phlegmon—see Abscesses, etc.

Phobias—see Anxiety; Obsessive-Compulsive Disorder

Pleuritis
Dry:
Mustard plaster or compress with fresh horseradish or Cochlearia armor. 20% ext.
Stannum praep. D8, D10 amp.

Exudative:
Plasters of "quark" (curds of soured milk strained through a cheesecloth); Equisetum compresses
Bryonia D3-D6 liq., amp. or even better Pneumodoron 1

Kalium carbonicum D6 liq.
Bryonia / Stannum amp. (Wala), poss. + Equisetum arv. D15 or Tabacum D10 amp.
Carbo Betulae D6 trit. and amp. (esp. for chronic pleural scarring and thickening)
Gencydo 1% amp.

Carcinomatous Pleuritis:
Iscador 2-5% intrapleurally (see Guidelines for the Use of Iscador)

Pneumonia, Bronchopneumonia
Fresh air is important. Encourage deep breathing and ensure adequate bowel movements.
Chest compresses with lemon (esp. for children or for high fever), later mustard compresses (to resolve)
Inhalations of essential oils, e.g. Resina Laricis / Oleum Terebinthinae
Pneumodoron 1 and 2 alternately every hour, 10 drops each
Bryonia D3 amp. (esp. in the beginning)
Equisetum arv. D15 or Quartz D20 liq., amp. (to preserve form)
Ferrum praep. D10 or Ferrum phosph. D8 amp., daily, poss. + Cetraria islandica D3 amp.
Circulation should always be treated simultaneously, e.g. with Cardiodoron and Camphora 20% oleosum amp. i.m. (up to two cc every eight hours)

For poor resolution and persistent fever:
Stibium sulfuratum aurantiacum D10 amp., D3 trit. or Stibium arsenicosum D8 amp., liq. or Sulfur D4-D6 or Hepar Sulfuris D3 trit. (do not exceed three to four doses of any of these medications!)
Also: Bryonia D6 liq. (no lower), Echinacea ang. ø, D1 liq.
Mustard compress; then repeat above therapy

Poliomyelitis—see chapter 3, this volume

Porphyria
Medulla Ossum D4 amp. + Ferrum D20 amp
Hypericum D4 dil.

Pregnancy, Childbirth, Puerperium
Generally:
Small amounts of honey during entire pregnancy
Few potatoes (in the final weeks, none at all)
Calcon 1 and 2 starting in the second month

Iron preparations starting in the sixth month

Habitual abortion:
Berberis, Fructus D3 or Berberis, Fructus D2 / Urtica urens D2 aa amp., twice weekly in the calves
Argentum praep. 0.4% oint. on lower abdomen
Berberis / Nicotiana comp. amp., glob. (Wala)
Metra tea
Pulsatilla D5, D6 liq., 7-10 drops in the evening from onset of pregnancy

Imminent abortion:
Bedrest
Aurum met. praep. D6 trit., amp., daily s.c. inj.
Belladonna comp. suppositories (Wala)
Phosphorus D6, D5 dil.
Sabina D6 dil.

Varicosities, prophylaxis of:
See also under Circulatory Diseases
Leg gel with copper
Cuprum 0.4% / Tabacum D6 aa oint.
Fluorite D4, D6 trit.

Dental Caries, prophylaxis of:
Calcon 1 and 2
Chlorophyllum 1% oint. on the lower abdomen
Fluorite D4, D6 trit.
Magnesium sulfuricum D10-D20 liq. (esp. for toothache or sensitivity)
Aesculus, Cortex D50 liq., 5 drops every other day

Gingival Bleeding, Gingivitis:
Weleda mouthwash (undiluted) or Ratanhia comp.

Labor:
Preparatory treatment:
Cuprum praep. 0.4% oint. on the perineum during the final two months (antispasmodic, esp. for athletic women)
Pulsatilla D6 liq. from the seventh month on; when overdue, D3 liq.
To ease labor:
Belladonna D4 (poss. + Pulsatilla D30 aa) liq., 20 or 40 drops in a glass of water, drink one swallow at a time
Belladonna 1% supp.

In the pauses between contractions: compresses with Prunus spinosa bath oil, esp. when exhausted
To regularize contractions:
Argentum praep. D30 amp.
Caulophyllum D6 liq.
For severe contractions: Belladonna / Chamomilla amp., glob. (Wala)
For weak contractions: Belladonna D6 / Pulsatilla D6 / Vicia faba D6 aa liq., 10-15 drops every fifteen min.

Post-maturity:
Total fast for 1-2 days, herb tea every half hour
Pulsatilla D3 liq.

To aid involution:
Arnica, Planta tota D6 liq.
Berberis, Fructus D2 liq.
Teucrium scorodonia D3 liq.
Argentum praep. D6 or Argentite D6 trit., amp.

Delayed lochia:
Belladonna D4 liq., amp., 1% supp.
Berberis, Fructus D4 amp.
Arnica, Planta tota D4 liq., amp.
Argentite D6 amp.
Secale D2 (DHU) or similar preparations
Compresses with calendula essence

Lactation, stimulation of:
Species lactagogae tea
Oleum lactagogae
Agnus castus D3 liq.

Weaning:
Compresses with solution of boiled oak bark or Quercus 20% ext.
Quercus D1 liq.

Mastitis puerpurialis:
See also Abscesses, etc.
Tight binding of breasts
Draw process off to intestine, gentle pumping of breast
Compresses with skim-milk quark (soured milk curds pressed through cheesecloth)
Mercurialis perennis 10% oint.
Argentum praep. D20 + Arnica, Planta tota D3 amp.
Apis D3 / Belladonna D3 aa amp.

Erysidoron 1 and 2
Quartz D12, D20 amp.
Echinacea D1, ø liq.
Phytolacca D2 liq. in alternation with Bryonia D3 liq.
With high fever: Pyrogenium D30 amp. and Lachesis D12, D20 amp.

Fissures of the Nipples:
(See also Rhagades)
Wecesin gel
Dab with pure lemon juice (esp. prophylactically)
Chamomilla, Flos 10% Oleum

Prostatic Hypertrophy (or Hyperplasia)
Berberis, Planta tota / Urtica urens amp., tab.
Berberis fruct. 5% sc qod
Iscador Qu Series 0 (see Guidelines for the Use of Iscador), once, at most twice weekly (except during prostatitis)
Sabal / Solidago comp. glob. (Wala) or similar preparations based on Sabal serrulata, Populus tremulans, and Solidago
Small flowered willow herb
Nettle root extract
Saw palmetto fruit extract

Prostatitis
Acute:
Erysidoron 1, Apis D3 / Belladonna D3 aa amp.
Argentite D6 amp.
Argentum praep. 0.4% oint.
Prostata D30 amp. (Wala)
Berberis D3 amp., liq.
Medorrhinum D30 amp.

Chronic:
Argentum D30 / Echinacea D6 aa amp.
Echinacea ang. D1, ø liq., Echinacin amp. (Madaus) i.v.
Induce fever; hot sitz baths, hyperthermic baths
Marum verum D1 liq.
Argentite D6 trit., amp.
Argentum / Stibium supp.

Pruritis

Anal Pruritis:
Sulfur iod. D4-D6 liq.
Millefolium / Hypericum oint.
Quercus 1% supp., 5% oint.
Paeonia off. D3 liq. (esp. for hemorrhoids)
Baths with oak bark
Liver treatment

Senile Pruritis:
Bland and salt-restricted diet
Betula, Cortex D2 amp.
Quartz D30 amp.
Magnesium sulfuricum D6 + Conchae D6, D10 amp.
Urtica comp. glob., amp. (Wala)
Between treatments: Sulfur D30 liq., Argentite D6 trit., D20 liq.
Iscador M or Qu strength 5
Formica D30 amp., once every 3-4 weeks
Leg gel
Chamomilla, Flos 10% Oleum
Dry brushings of skin
Birch leaf tea or Birch elixir
Vinegar rinses

Vulvar Pruritis and Eczema:
See under Gynecological Disorders

Psoriasis
Diet: low or no salt, low in fats, no sugar, no alcohol
Antimonite / Anisum oint. or Antimonite 0.4% gel
Stibium praep. 0.1% oint.
Carbo Betulae D10 / Stannum praep. D10 aa trit.
Agaricus musc. D10 liq.
Quartz D30, D60 amp.
Betula, Cortex D2, poss. + Sulfur D6 amp.
Cerite D4 trit., D6 amp. (to stimulate light-metabolism, assuming sunlight improves the condition)
Phototherapy (long-wave ultraviolet)
Graphites D20 amp.
Dermatodoron amp. (at onset of an exacerbation)
Dermatodoron oint., gel
Mercurius viv. nat. D6 + Stannum praep. D8 + Quartz D12 aa trit., one half

tsp. t.i.d.
Liver and kidney treatment, esp. with:
Cynara scolymus ø , Boldo D2, Lycopodium D30 liq.
Hepar Mag. D4 amp.
Vit A
Red currant berry extract
Palmseed oil, laurel oil, Mahonia
Equisetum cum Sulfure Tostum D6 trit., amp.
Hepatodoron
Then: Arsenicum album D10 liq., Pancreas D3 liq.
Lactic acid therapy

Pyelonephritis, Cystopyelitis—see under Kidney and Bladder Diseases

Pylorospasm—see under Gastric Diseases

Pyoderma—see under Abscesses, etc. and under Skin Diseases

Radiation Damage (e.g. from X-ray overexposure)
Acute:
See Burns

Long-term damages:
Stibium praep. D10 trit.
Formica D15 liq., amp.
Oleum aeth. Eucalypti 10% Oleum, or a few drops of Oleum Eucalypti purum on a warm, moist compress
Viscum Pini 5% oint., 10% gel
Quartz D60 amp. (at intervals of several weeks)
Rosemary oil baths
Leg gel with copper, poss. together with Arnica comp. Oleum aa

Raynaud's Disease—see Intermittent Claudication

Rhagades
Mangan aceticum D4 liq.
Stibium praep. 0.4% oint., poss. in alternation with Halite 40% oint.
Millefolium / Hypericum oint.
Unguentum rosarum (Wala)
Rule out anemia

Rheumatism—see Arthritis, Gout

Rheumatoid Arthritis—see under **Arthritis**

Rhinitis

Acute, with watery rhinorrhea:
Cepa D4 liq. sublingually
Arsenicum album D10 liq., 5-7 drops every 20-30 min.

Allergic rhinitis:
Kalium carbonicum D6 liq. (water organism)
Apis D30 amp. (warmth organism)
Gencydo 1%-5%; or Berberis, Fructus D2, D3
Poss. + Arsenicum album D12 amp. (Berberis esp. if pelvic disorders are also present)
Berberis / Prunus oint.

Rickets—see chapter 3

Sarcoidosis

Mercurius viv. nat. D6 tab., D15 trit.
Formica D3-D30 increasing and decreasing in potency, amp. or liq.
Iscador M (for women) or Qu (for men) Series O (see Guidelines for the Use of Iscador)

Sarcoma

see **Cancer** and Chapter 2
Neottia D3 amp.
Cetraria 1mg (St. 4) amp.

Scarlet Fever—see chapter 3

Scars, treatment of

Argentum praep. D8 + Vespa Crabro D4 + Tabacum D6 amp., one half or one ampule of each to be injected under the scar 2-3 times weekly
Keloid gel (Wala)
Cuprum 0.4% / Tabacum D6 aa oint.
Polygonatum off. 5% oint.
Scheuermann's Disease, Kyphosis
Disci comp. cum Nicotiana amp., glob. (Wala)
Plumbum met. 0.4% oint.
Plumbum silicicum D10 amp.
Nontronite D15 amp.
Curative eurythmy

Schizophrenia
See also chapter 8
Stibium praep. D6 or D10 s.c. or 10 cc i.v.; or Antimonite D6 or D10 s.c.or 10 cc i.v.
Anhalonium D6 amp. or Helleborus niger D6 amp.
Cuprum-Ren D6 amp.
For anxiety: Hyoscyamus D1 liq., 10-20 drops as needed, amp. 5%, D3 or Hyoscyamus / Valeriana amp.
For stupor: Apis D2 amp. or Apis D2 c. Levistico amp., 1-2 inj. daily

Sciatica
Keep warm, e.g. with arnica compresses
Arnica / Levisticum D3, D6 comp. amp.
Magnesium phosph. D6 amp. or Magnesium phosph. / Tabacum amp. or Magnesium phosph. comp. (Wala)
Aconitum napellus D6 amp., liq.
Arnica D6 amp., poss. + Nervus ischiadicus D5 amp.
Bryonia / Formica comp. amp.
Arnica comp. / Apis Oleum or oint.
Spinal treatment (see separate entry)

Sepsis—see under Abscesses and Suppurations

Sinusitis
Generally:
Encourage perspiration, keep warm; steam inhalations with chamomile tea (add a few drops of Oleum aeth. Eucalypti purum after a few minutes)

In children:
Sugar and phosphate free diet (no cola or instant beverages, sausage, soft cheese)

Acute:
Berberis, Fructus D2, D3 amp., inj. locally if poss., poss. + Quartz D20 amp.
Mustard plaster over the bladder or the calves
Berberis / Prunus oint.
Gencydo 1%, 3% amp.
Sambucus comp. liq.
Nose balsam (Wala)

Chronic, purulent forms:
Keep patient's feet warm

Argentum / Berberis comp. amp.
Argentum comp. amp. (for suppuration), poss. + Berberis / Quartz (Wala; best injected in the nape of the neck or between the shoulder blades)
Weleda "sneezing cream" (Schnupfencreme)
Irrigation with solution of Calendula 20% / Echinacea D1 ext. in saline
Kalium bichromicum D4, D6 liq., poss. + Alumen D3 aa liq.
Cinnabar D4-D20 trit. or tab.
Absinthium D1 / Resina Laricis D3 aa liq. between other treatments
Resina Bryoniae D4 amp.
Thuja occ. D6 amp.
Silicea comp. glob., amp. (Wala)
Tunica mucosa nasi D4 + Hepar sulfuric comp. amp. (Wala) then Membrana sinuum paranasalium D15 + Myristica comp. amp. (Wala)
Horseradish in compresses and dietetically
Berberis, Fructus 10% oint. over the bladder
Berberis / Mercurialis oint.
Mustard compresses on the calves
Cervical spine treatment as indicated

Skin Diseases
See also Chapter 5
Diet: low salt, fresh foods
Principal remedies: Betula, Cortex; Dermatodoron
Investigate organ involvement and treat accordingly (e.g. liver or kidney)

Acne: See under **Acne**
Acute-Inflammatory:
Argentum D20 / Carbo Betulae D30 aa amp.
Apis D3 / Belladonna D3 aa amp. or Erysidoron 1
Zinc suspension with calendula essence

Weeping Eczemas:
Baths or compresses with calendula or Viola tricolor or Quercus 20% ext.
Gencydo amp.
Aesculus D15 / Alumen D15 amp., liq.
Kidney treatment, e.g. with Equisetum arv. D15 or Solutio Siliceae comp. D15 liq. and amp.; later: Quartz D20, D30 liq., amp.

Dyshydrotic Eczema:
Hypericum D3 liq.
Equisetum arv. D10 amp.
Calendula / Stibium oint.

Quercus D10 amp.

Pyoderma:
See also under Abscesses, etc.
Mercurius viv. 0.1% oint.
Oleum aeth Eucalypti 1% amp. i.m.

Seborrheic Dermatitis:
Thuja occ. D12-D30 liq.
Halite D30 liq.
Quartz D12 trit.
Graphites D6 trit.
Equisetum arv. 10% ext. in bath

Dry, Sclerotic Eczema:
Baths with Kalium sulfuratum 10% (Wala)
Sulfur D6-D12 liq.
Carbo Equiseti arv. D15 amp.
Antimonite D6 trit., amp.
Equisetum arv. 10% oint., gel
Argentite D6 trit., D6, D10 amp.
Arsenicum album D30 liq. (esp. for pruritis)
Quartz D20, D30 amp., liq.
Betula, Cortex D2 / Sulfur D6 aa trit.
Formica D6-D30 amp.
Equisetum cum Sulfure tostum D4-D6 trit., D10 liq.
Lac Taraxaci D10 / Parmelia D10 aa amp.
Calendula / Stibium oint.
Treat liver

Neurodermatitis:
Diet: free from animal protein for a few weeks
Argentite D6 trit.
Argentum nitricum D20 amp.
Manganum aceticum D4, D6 tab., liq. (DHU)
Iscador P or Qu c. Arg. or M c. Arg., strength 5
Magnesium therapy, e.g. with Magnesite D4 trit. or Magnesium sulfuricum D4, D6 trit., later higher potencies; Hepar / Magnesium D4 amp., poss. + Oxalis D10
Plumbum silicicum D20, one ampule in bath, stir vigorously for ten minutes, once weekly
Zincum val. D4 amp., liq.; Dyscrasite D6, D20 amp.
Arsenicum album D30 for the appropriate constitutions

Struma
Spongia D3 amp or D1 dil.

Sweating
Bryophyllum/Conchae trit., amp.
menopausal: Sambucus nigra medulla 5% dil

Thallasemia
Medulla Ossium D4 amp + Saccharum tostum D3 dil. for 6 weeks, then Equisetum silicea cultum D2 Rh di. for 6 weeks, then Cobaltum D6 trit for 6 weeks
Ferrum sid. D6 trit + Eigenblut D30 dil.

Tics
Mygale comp. dil
Cuprum acet. D4/Zincum val. D4 dil., D5/D5 amp.
Vit. B15
Zincum D4 amp. + Arsenicum D12 amp.

Undernutrition
Calcon 1 and 2
Argentum praep. D6 or Argentite D6 trit. and amp., followed by:
Urtica Ferro culta D2 liq., amp.
Cuprum praep. 0.4% oint.
Hypophysis D4, D6 amp., liq.
Organum quadruplex amp., glob. (Wala)
Nutritive baths (see volume II, pp. 3-41)

Urticaria
Urtica comp. amp., glob. (Wala)
Calcium carbon. / Cortex Quercus amp., glob. (Wala)
Plumbum praep. D8 trit., amp. (short-term only)
Treat the intestines

Vaginitis—see under Gynecological Disorders

Varices—see under Circulatory Diseases

Varicocoele
Lotio Pruni comp. cum Cupro
Kalium acet. comp. 1/2 tsp tid

Vitiligo
Dioptase D6 amp. + Cuprum met. praep. D6 trit.

Warts
Bismutum/Stibium oint.
Formica 5% oint. plasters
Thuja D4, D6 liq.
Arsenicum album D6 liq.
Suspect precancerous condition in elderly patients.

Wilson's disease
Cuprum D30 trit + Magnesit D4 trit or Hepar -Magnesium D4 amp.

Worms
Raw carrots, beets, bitters (e.g. absinth, wormwood tea)
Cuprum D3 trit. for a few days
Mercurius viv. 0.1% oint. on and around the anus

Prophylaxis of recurrence:
Cina comp. liq.

Wounds
Calendula essence 20% ext.
Mercurialis comp. oint.
Arnica, Planta tota D4 liq. (except on open wounds!)
Abrasions: Wecesin powder
Dirty wounds: Calendula essence or Mercurialis peren. 20% ext. as compress; calendula oint., Mercurialis peren. 10% oint.
Vulnodoron around the wound

Incisional pain (after trauma or surgery):
Hypericum D6 amp.

INDEX

C

N

O

P